Southern Biography Series
Bertram-Wyatt Brown, Editor

THE CONQUEST OF LABOR

THE
CONQUEST
OF
LABOR

DANIEL PRATT

AND

SOUTHERN

INDUSTRIALIZATION

CURTIS J. EVANS

LOUISIANA STATE UNIVERSITY PRESS

Baton Rouge

00   09   08   07   06   05   04   03   02   01
5   4   3   2   1
Designer: Amanda McDonald Scallan
Typeface: Sabon
Typesetter: Coghill Composition Co., Inc.
Printer and binder: Thomson-Shore, Inc.

Library of Congress Cataloging-in-Publication Data

Evans, Curtis J.
    The conquest of labor : Daniel Pratt and southern
industrialization / Curtis J. Evans.
        p.   cm. — (Southern biography series)
    Includes bibliographical references (p.   ) and index.
    ISBN 0-8071-2695-0 (cloth : alk. paper)
    1. Pratt, Daniel, 1799–1873.   2. Prattville (Ala.)—Biography.
    3. Industrialization—Alabama—Prattville—History—19th
century.   4. Industrialists—Alabama—Prattville—Biography.   I.
Title.   II. Series.
F334.P9 E93   2001
976.1'463—dc21

2001000064

CONTENTS

ILLUSTRATIONS

ACKNOWLEDGMENTS

"A good biography of Daniel Pratt has yet to be written," Eugene Genovese noted thirty-five years ago in his hugely influential book *The Political Economy of Slavery.* The quality of this present work, which revises much of modern Pratt scholarship, I shall leave to the reader to decide, but at least it can now be said that a scholarly biography of Pratt finally has seen the light of day. Without the prior works of Genovese, Randall Miller, and Malcolm McMillan (who generously arranged for his papers to be turned over to the archives of Auburn University at his death), however, I very much doubt that this book ever would have survived the night. In addition, William Cooper determinedly saw the project through its dissertation stage at Louisiana State University. Since then, Professor Cooper has continued to provide valuable advice and support, as has Bertram Wyatt-Brown, current editor of the LSU Southern Biography Series. My thanks additionally go out to Maureen Hewitt, Sylvia Frank, and Jean C. Lee of LSU Press, as well as Larry Nobles, the best and most selfless local historian I have been fortunate enough to encounter, and Tommy Brown of Continental Eagle Corporation, the steadfast caretaker of Daniel Pratt and Company's surviving business records. Lastly, I thank my parents, who are still refraining from saying "I told you so" ten years after I decided to abandon a career in law to become a historian. I hope this book is worth the sacrifices.

Abbreviations

ACHC Autauga County Heritage Center, Prattville
ADAH Alabama Department of Archives and History, Montgomery
CECP Continental Eagle Corporation Papers, Prattville
PMC   Prattville Manufacturing Company

The Conquest of Labor

INTRODUCTION

From the stormy Atlantic their hosts are advancing—
On the Far Rocky Mountains their legions are seen—
Down the wilderness valleys their watchlights are glancing,
And the broad blue Pacific exults in their sheen.

Ever around them rich blessings are springing—
Ever before them the darkness retires—
Peace lends her song to their reveille's ringing
And Plenty reclines by their bivouac fires.

Where round the dark anvil the red forge is gleaming—
Where the swift shuttle flies, where the plow cleaves the sod—
Round the hearth-stones of Toil rise the ramparts of Freemen,
The Altars of Home and the Temples of God.
                    —Francis Orray Ticknor, "The Conquest of Labor"

Francis Orray Ticknor, a Georgia physician and poet and a first cousin of Daniel Pratt's wife, Esther Ticknor, inscribed his poem "The Conquest of Labor" (1854) to Pratt, a New Hampshire native who had become the most prominent manufacturer in the neighboring state of Alabama.

To the extent that Ticknor is remembered at all today, it is for his pro-Confederacy Civil War poems, such as "Little Giffen," not for his paean to a northern-born industrialist. Here we confront a seeming paradox. Many of Ticknor's poems celebrate the South and condemn the North—often in very strident terms. In "The Old Rifleman," for example, Ticknor has his protagonist declare to his rifle, "Old Bess": "If Doodle must be meddling, Why / There's only this to do— / Select the dark spot in his eye / And let the daylight through!" More specifically, one poem, "Slave of the Dismal Scamp" (a reply to Henry Wadsworth Longfellow's anti-slavery "Slave in the Dismal Swamp"), explicitly attacks the northern factory system for cruelly exploiting helpless female workers:

> Under a rattling whirligig,
> Which a Yankee had taught to spin,
> A maiden sat, with bosom flat
> And fingers long and thin;
> And she was the slave of a dismal scamp,
> A man with a soul of tin.

Yet the same man who penned this vitriolic denunciation of northern scamp industrialists with souls of tin had only words of praise for Daniel Pratt, who in addition to being one of the nation's most important cotton-gin manufacturers, employed dozens of women and children in a cotton mill. It would seem that Ticknor, despite his anti-North blustering—provoked, no doubt, by northern challenges over territorial slavery and other matters—actually thought industry a good thing. Where "the swift shuttle" flew, after all, one found "ramparts of Freemen," "Altars of Home," and "Temples of God." This conclusion is bolstered by another, undated Ticknor poem, "Reminiscences—on Visiting the Eagle and Phoenix Mills at Columbus, Ga.," wherein he expressed admiration and amazement at the technological wonder of these cotton factories on the bank of the Chattahoochee River:

> O! Mighty power of human thought, . . .
> That such a wondrous work was wrought!
> In rocks and falling water!
>
> The force to rend the continent,
> Hurled headlong down its bed,
> Halts for this severed filament
> Of weightless, floating thread!

> The demon of a world a-whir
> With rattle, clash and whirl
> Held in a leash of gossamer
> And guided by a girl!

In light of such poems, it comes as no surprise to learn that Ticknor also served as a Columbus sales agent for Pratt cotton gins.[1]

One might dismiss Ticknor as an unrepresentative southerner. After all, not only was Daniel Pratt an in-law, but Ticknor's own father was a Connecticut Yankee who had once run an academy in Clinton, Georgia.[2] But Francis Orray Ticknor's receptivity to southern industry was by no means atypical, as the career of Pratt demonstrates.

Daniel Pratt migrated to Alabama in 1833 after a fourteen-year career in Georgia, first as a carpenter-architect and then as a business partner of pioneer cotton-gin manufacturer Samuel Griswold. In 1839, Pratt established his own gin factory at Prattville, located in central Alabama. Pratt enjoyed great success as a gin manufacturer, and soon his machines could be found on plantations from Georgia to Texas. By 1860, Pratt had become the country's largest cotton-gin maker, manufacturing a quarter of the gins made in the United States. To build his gins, he employed scores of mechanics, a majority of whom were white southerners.

Pratt made a great deal of money from his gin business, but he was a fervent Methodist who wanted to do more in his earthly life than accumulate riches. He hoped to provide employment for poor whites and to build what he called "a village of good morals and good society" that would resemble the New Hampshire towns and villages he had known in his youth, as well as to promote the cause of manufacturing in the South. Toward these ends, he spearheaded the incorporation in 1846 of Prattville Manufacturing Company (PMC), one of the South's most important cotton mills. By 1860, PMC employed more than 140 people, mostly

1. Francis Orray Ticknor, *The Poems of Francis Orray Ticknor,* edited by Michelle Cutliff Ticknor (New York: Neale Publishing, 1911), 62–64, 67–70, 124–26; *American Cotton Planter and Soil of the South* 5 (January 1861): app. For a recent anthology containing several Ticknor war poems, see Paul Negri, ed., *Civil War Poetry: An Anthology* (Mineola, N.Y.: Dover Press, 1997), 33–38.

2. South Carolina politician James Henry Hammond, often treated as a representative southerner, also had a Yankee father who served as an academy principal. See Drew Gilpin Faust, *James Henry Hammond and the Old South: A Design for Mastery* (Baton Rouge: Louisiana State University Press, 1982), 3–4, 7–9.

women and children from poor rural white families. Prattville itself became very much "a village of good morals and good society," possessing strong churches, schools, voluntary associations, and even a lyceum. Nor was Prattville a one-man company town. Rather, merchants and mechanics came to the town and opened their own stores and shops. Frenetic economic boosterism characterized antebellum Prattville as citizens sought to attract railroads and more industry to their town.

During the period when Daniel Pratt built his "Yankee" town in the heart of the Deep South, he also played an important role in Alabama's public life. Beginning in the 1840s, he began writing numerous letters to state newspapers, in which he addressed such economic topics as banking, industrialization, and railroads, as well as slavery and the sectional crisis. Pratt ran three times for the state legislature and served in the Alabama House of Representatives from 1861 to 1863. For most of his tenure in office, he chaired the Manufactures Committee, an especially crucial assignment in the midst of the Civil War.

In the wake of the economic havoc wrought by war and emancipation, many Alabamians concluded that Pratt's way would have to become their way as well. Pratt and the town he created were continually praised by both Democrats and Republicans. In all likelihood, Pratt would have received the Democratic nomination for governor in 1870 had it not been for his age and his deteriorating health.

At Pratt's death in 1873, his reputation in Alabama stood higher than ever. Even in death, he continued to exercise influence in his adopted state. His son-in-law, Henry DeBardeleben, used Pratt's daughter's inheritance to fund the industrial development of Birmingham, a project that Pratt had played a major role in initiating. Moreover, New South boosters in Alabama constantly evoked the name *Prattville* as an example of what one determined manufacturer could accomplish in a southern state.

Daniel Pratt's popularity in both antebellum and postbellum Alabama, his successful use of southerners (black and white) as productive factory workers, and the energy and sobriety of the town he established all belie the assertion of some historians that southerners feared industrialization and urbanization and scorned discipline and piety.[3] That this upright, hardworking Yankee industrialist and the town that reflected

3. For a recent revisionist work that treads some similar ground, see Bess Beatty, *Alamance: The Holt Family and Industrialization in a North Carolina County, 1837–1900* (Baton Rouge: Louisiana State University Press, 1999).

him became revered icons of progressiveness in Alabama as early as the 1840s suggests that at least one southern state was not trapped in the firm and fatal grip of a premodern ideology. In truth, Daniel Pratt found that Alabama held fertile fields for his economic endeavors and his industrial gospel. With Pratt, labor made another conquest.

Thirty-five years ago, Eugene Genovese noted that a biography of Daniel Pratt was needed.[4] Despite his call, no such study has appeared until this one. Pratt's name, which would have been more familiar to the average cotton planter than many a politician's, has fallen mostly into obscurity outside Alabama. One reason for the long absence of a Pratt biography (besides an evident dearth of interest among historians concerning southern industrialists) has been the perception that adequate primary sources did not remain to allow such an effort to be fruitfully conducted. While this belief is mistaken, it is true that the surviving material concerning Pratt has limitations. Although Pratt wrote copiously for newspapers, few of his personal letters survive. None by his wife and daughter do. This biography thus is less a study of Pratt's "personal life" than of the businesses, the town, and the public policies that he devoted his life to advancing. This focus, however, is fitting, for as Shadrack Mims, the man who functioned something like a Boswell to Pratt, wrote, "Work was [Pratt's] element." This study also places great emphasis on what Alabama newspapers wrote about Pratt. Given that most historians who have written about Pratt in the last thirty-five years have asserted that Pratt found himself in a hostile environment, I believe this course is justified. Pratt's story is important because of what it tells us about the South. Properly told, it tells us a considerable amount.

4. Eugene D. Genovese, *The Political Economy of Slavery: Studies in the Economy and Society of the Slave South* (New York: Pantheon, 1965), 323. Only one other historian, Randall M. Miller, has written in any depth on Pratt. See his "Daniel Pratt's Industrial Urbanism: The Cotton Mill Town in Antebellum Alabama," *Alabama Historical Quarterly* 34 (spring 1972): 5–35 and *The Cotton Mill Movement in Antebellum Alabama* (New York: Arno Press, 1978). An underappreciated earlier work with some material on Pratt is Weymouth T. Jordan's *Ante-Bellum Alabama: Town and Country* (1957; reprint, Tuscaloosa: University of Alabama Press, 1987). Most recent works that mention Pratt follow Genovese and Miller. An exception is the discussion of Pratt and, more generally, southern industrialization and urbanization found in William J. Cooper Jr. and Thomas E. Terrell, *The American South: A History,* 2d. ed. (New York: McGraw-Hill, 1996), 1: 304–15.

PROLOGUE: BEFORE ALABAMA

Daniel Pratt was not happy in Georgia when in June 1827 he penned a letter to his father, Edward, back in Temple, New Hampshire. Since migrating from his native state to Georgia in 1819, Pratt had found work as a carpenter, first in Savannah and then in the rich plantation country around the towns of Macon and Milledgeville in central Georgia. By 1827, he dominated the building and contracting business in the area. For his wealthy planter customers, Pratt built not only flatboats that carried cotton down the Ocmulgee River to market in Darien and Savannah, but also fine houses from his own designs. Despite his success, Pratt found only cause for complaint as he wrote his father that evening.[1]

Pratt kept "Batcheldors Hall" in a "little cabin" he had built on the banks of the Ocmulgee below Macon. Along with what he called his "family" of "four negro men" (presumably slaves he had hired), Pratt was at work constructing flatboats. The isolation and the punishing cli-

1. Daniel Pratt to Edward Pratt, 19 June 1827, unnumbered folder, Pratt Papers, ADAH; *Montgomery Daily Mail*, 14 April 1870; S[amuel] H[ardeman] Griswold, "The Cotton Gin—An Interesting History of the Gin and Its Maker" (Gray) *Jones County News*, 2 April 1908, reprinted in *History of Jones County, Georgia: 1807–1907*, Carolyn White Williams (Macon, Ga.: J. W. Burke, 1957).

mate he found unpleasant. "I almost live a hermit's life but could injoy myself tolerably well was it not for the musketoes," Pratt grumbled. "I am now writing by candlelight and if you will believe me they buz about me almost equal to a swarm of beas. I am obliged to have my bed covered over with musketoe netting to keep them from me." His economic situation was no better than his physical one. "Times are verry hard and money verry scarce," Pratt complained. Indeed, having borrowed money at rates of 8 to 16 percent, he now owed six thousand dollars. In his letter, Pratt pleaded with his father to persuade his elder son to arrange an out-of-state loan. "I certainlly work as hard for what little I get as almost annybody in the world," he added plaintively—and defensively.[2]

Pratt maintained his defensive stance as he approached a dangerous subject with his stern Congregationalist father—slavery. Daniel acknowledged to Edward that he owned three slaves, to whom he rented the slightly more than 250 acres he had acquired in lieu of cash for work he had performed over the last couple of years. The embarrassed son admitted to his father that he had not "intended that you should have known anything about that, as I supposed you would think I was ruined eternaly." Daniel then rationalized to Edward that the slaves "which you mentioned are not numerous. I have but three and it is not probal that I shall keep them long." He assured his father that if he knew "my situation and the situation of the country I live in you would think differently." Daniel insisted "that to live in anny country it is necessary to conform to the customs of the country in part." Nevertheless, he hastened to add that he had "brought no man in to bondage" and that he believed he had "rendered no mans situation more disagreeable than it was before." Indeed, Daniel maintained that he may well have improved his slaves' lot in life.[3]

Beyond complaining about Georgia's economy and climate and equivocating about the question of the state's labor system, Pratt had nothing else to say about his adopted home. The rest of his letter he devoted to family matters, eagerly asking his father for news about his sister Abigail's recent marriage. The only Georgia friend Pratt mentioned was his mother's half-brother Samuel Flint (also from New Hampshire), a merchant in Milledgeville.[4]

2. Daniel Pratt to Edward Pratt, 19 June 1827, Pratt Papers, ADAH. For clarity, punctuation has been added to the quoted letters. Spelling has been left uncorrected.

3. Ibid.; Deed Book G, p. 60, Deed Book N, p. 135, Office of the Clerk of the Superior Court, Jones County Courthouse, Gray, Ga.

4. Daniel Pratt to Edward Pratt, 19 June 1827, Pratt Papers, ADAH.

This transplanted New Englander, it seems, had not taken at all to this new "country" in which he had dwelt for nearly a decade. He had no interest, as did many of his contemporaries in the South, in achieving success through agriculture, informing his father that he would sell the land he had if he "could get the value of it," yet he found carpentry an unstable profession.[5] Given his traditional New England upbringing, what might seem most surprising is not that Pratt was unhappy in Georgia, but that he migrated there in the first place. Within six years after writing his disgruntled letter, however, Pratt, having persevered in Georgia, would move to Alabama and launch a career that would make him one of the most successful and admired men in the state, thereby proving that the South could actually be an accommodating region to a determined Yankee artisan.

In many ways, Daniel Pratt was indeed an typical "Yankee." A sixth-generation New Englander, he descended from John Pratt, who had migrated from England to Massachusetts in 1643. Pratt's paternal grandfather, also named Daniel, was a farmer and joiner who died in Reading, Massachusetts, in 1795. The elder Daniel Pratt left half his joiner tools, as well as his Reading house and a religious book by Matthew Henry, to his thirty-year-old son, Edward. Four years after his father's death, Edward migrated with his wife, Asenath, their three small children, and his stepmother to the township of Temple, New Hampshire, nestled in the hills above the Souhegan River some fifty miles northwest of Reading. Less than two miles outside the village of Temple, Edward purchased a house and farm. Over the next ten years, Edward and Asenath had three more children, including Daniel, who was born at the farmhouse on July 20, 1799, a few months after the family completed its move.[6]

Work and religion were the mainstays of young Daniel Pratt's life in Temple. From both his parents and his maternal grandfather, Ebenezer Flint, who settled in nearby Wilton Township with his family in 1802, Pratt learned the intrinsic value of labor. Flint, a farmer and veteran of

5. Ibid. Pratt began selling his land in 1827 and completely divested himself of it by 1832. Deed Book N, pp. 334–35, Deed Book O, pp. 225, 322, Deed Book P, pp. 60–1, 139–40, 167–68, Office of the Clerk of the Superior Court, Jones County Courthouse.

6. On the genealogy of Daniel Pratt, see Eleanor Smith Cooke, *The Genealogy of Daniel Pratt* (Prattville, Ala.: by the author, 1990); Will of Daniel Pratt of Reading, Folder 45, Pratt Papers, ADAH; Henry Ames Blood, *The History of Temple, N.H.* (Boston: G. C. Rand & Avery, 1860), 242–45; Historical Society of Temple, New Hampshire, *A History of Temple, New Hampshire, 1768–1976* (Dublin, N.H.: W. L. Bauhan, 1976), 503.

the Battle of Concord, "had an iron constitution" and was "a man of much decision and very industrious." In his later years, Flint often declared that as a young man, if he could not get more, he would work for one shilling, six pence a day, or for the shilling, or even for the pence. The hardworking Flint accumulated a good-sized estate, sending his two youngest sons, Samuel and Abner, respectively to Middlebury and Dartmouth Colleges and leaving monetary bequests in his 1819 will totaling eleven hundred dollars.[7]

Despite Ebenezer Flint's apparent prosperity, Edward and Asenath Pratt were characterized by their daughter Eliza as "poor but comfortable livers, obliged to use the strictest economy, as their only means of support was the produce of a small farm." Daniel Pratt, one of two sons, was put to work as soon as he grew old enough to help with farming, even though this meant he had to withdraw from the summer term of his district school, attending class only in the winter, when there was no farm work to be done. Daniel's formal education ended completely in 1815, when his father, discerning in him a "mechanical genius," apprenticed Daniel for a term of five years to a house carpenter named Aaron Kimball Putnam, who lived in neighboring Wilton Township. Although Daniel would prove immensely skilled at carpentry, he, according to a friend, would feel the "defect" of a rudimentary education all his life. His spotty schooling having ended at the age of fifteen, Daniel's "knowledge of the common, plain rules of arithmetic was very deficient, and as to English grammar, he knew nothing, except what he learned from reading standard works." Pratt later admitted that his youthful sacrifice of book learning made him all the more committed to educational philanthropy when he became a wealthy man.[8]

Though Pratt's secular education left something to be desired, he did receive a strong religious upbringing that exercised a powerful influence on him for the rest of his life. Despite clearly pinched economic circumstances, Edward and Asenath Pratt spent $33.33 on the purchase of a

7. Abiel Abbot Livermore and Sewall Putnam, *History of the Town of Wilton, Hillsborough County, New Hampshire, with a Genealogical Register* (Lowell, Mass.: Marden & Rowell, 1888), 369–70; Will of Ebenezer Flint of Wilton, Hillsborough County Courthouse, Nashua, N.H.

8. Shadrack Mims, "History of Prattville," in *Hon. Daniel Pratt: A Biography, with Eulogies on His Life and Character,* edited by S. F. H. Tarrant (Richmond, Va.: Whittet & Shepperson 1904), 40–49; Daniel Pratt to Thomas Bugbee, 19 December 1848, Folder 46, Pratt Papers, ADAH.

pew in the Congregationalist meetinghouse upon their arrival in Temple Township. The parents, according to Eliza, were "strict in their duty as church members" and made sure that the Sabbath served not only as "a day of rest, but a day to be devoted to the service of God." Daniel and his brother and sisters attended church and prayer meetings without fail. At home, their parents performed "Sabbath-school duties," either "by catechizing the children or requiring them to read the Bible or some religious book." On the Sabbath, "all vain and trifling conversation was prohibited," and on no day was a novel permitted in the house.[9]

Temple served as a proper spiritual setting for this religiously conservative family. Noah Miles, Temple's Congregationalist minister from 1782 to 1831, stood firm against religious deviation during his long tenure. In 1792, he protested against the playing of a bass viol in the church, calling it "ungodly music." Only after a five-year battle did the church finally vote to allow the instrument back into the building. He also opposed the installation of a stove, fearing that warm worshipers would become drowsy during his sermons, but he eventually relented to the pro-stove faction in 1828. Death spared Miles from having to cope with the ultimate offense, the founding of a Universalist church in Temple in 1832, but he would have been relieved to find that the church remained weak.[10]

When Daniel Pratt left Temple in 1819, he was well-grounded in the traditional New England values of hard work and demanding religion. Pratt's motive for making this move was, it seems, entirely selfless. His master, Putnam, had become financially distressed during the panic of 1819 and was forced to mortgage his home. At the age of twenty, Pratt set out for Savannah, Georgia, intending to make enough money to help Putnam redeem his mortgage. Pratt carried with him twenty-five dollars and a box of tools. Grandfather Flint had given him the money; perhaps the tools included the ones bequeathed in 1795 by his grandfather Pratt. Landing in Savannah in November, Pratt apparently quickly found gainful employment, for he returned to New Hampshire in 1820 and redeemed Putnam's mortgage. Two years later, the grateful Putnam named his newborn son Daniel Pratt, the first of several men to do so over the next five decades.[11]

9. Mims, "History of Prattville," 40–49.

10. Historical Society of Temple, *History of Temple*, 276–306.

11. Livermore and Putnam, *History of the Town of Wilton*, 478; Mims, "History of Prattville," 42–43. Pratt arrived in Savannah in November aboard the brig *Favorite*. *Savannah Advertiser*, 23 November 1819.

Impressed with the opportunities he had seen in Georgia, Pratt returned to Savannah after a few months. Probably after having worked
with a master builder there, he migrated in July 1821 to Milledgeville,
the Georgia capital. Over the next ten years, Pratt plied his trade in the
vicinity of Milledgeville and nearby Macon. His base became Jones
County, which lay between the two towns. The whole area formed part
of the rich plantation belt that stretched across middle Georgia.[12]

Pratt practiced his craft skillfully, becoming one of the two most important carpenter-architects in the area. Today, architectural historians
consider Pratt's work, dubbed "Milledgeville Federal," to be of national
significance. Pratt built fine homes in and around Milledgeville, as well
as boats for the Ocmulgee River trade. He also owned a small store. Yet,
despite his success, Pratt complained of loneliness and debt in June 1827
when he wrote his letter to his father.[13]

Fortunately for Pratt, his personal circumstances and his business
prospects were destined to improve due to encounters with fellow New
Englanders. On September 6, 1827—less than three months after he had
disparaged life in "Batcheldors Hall"—he married Esther Ticknor of
Connecticut, who had come south to visit relatives in Jones County; and
in 1831, he went to work for Samuel Griswold, a Connecticut-born
cotton-gin manufacturer who lived in Clinton, the political seat of Jones
County.[14]

Pratt's marriage to Esther Ticknor linked him with a family that

12. *De Bow's Review* 10 (February 1851): 225; *Montgomery Daily Mail*, 14 April
1870.

13. Daniel Pratt to Edward Pratt, 19 June 1827, Pratt Papers, ADAH. On Pratt's architecture, see John Linley, *Architecture of Middle Georgia: The Oconee Area* (Athens: University of Georgia Press, 1972); John Linley, *The Georgia Catalog, Historical American
Buildings Survey: A Guide to Architecture in the State* (Athens: University of Georgia Press,
1982); Frederick Doveton Nichols, *The Early Architecture of Georgia* (Chapel Hill: University of North Carolina Press, 1957); Richard L. Raley, "Daniel Pratt, Architect and Builder
in Georgia," *Antiques* 95 (September 1972): 425–32. Pratt continued to dabble in architecture after he moved to Alabama. Besides designing and building his own house in Prattville
in 1842 and the Gothic-style Prattville Methodist Church in 1853, while serving as a building commissioner for the Alabama capitol in 1850, he submitted designs for a Gothic-style
structure, which were not accepted. See Robert Gamble, *The Alabama Catalog, Historic
American Buildings Survey: A Guide to the Early Architecture of the State* (Tuscaloosa:
University of Alabama, 1987), 194; Mims, "History of Prattville," 38–39; Donna C. Hole,
"Daniel Pratt and Barachias Holt: Architects of the Alabama State Capitol?" *Alabama Review* 37 (April 1984): 84.

14. *Macon Telegraph*, 24 September 1827; *De Bow's Review* 10 (February 1851): 225.

matched him in dynamism and determination. Esther came from an old and prominent New England family that included such luminaries as George Ticknor, one of Boston's leading Brahmins, and William Ticknor, a partner in the great Boston publishing firm Ticknor and Fields. Two of Esther's uncles, Orray and John, migrated to Georgia, ending up, as did Pratt, in Jones County, where they pursued successful careers, Orray as a physician and teacher and John as a merchant. Esther's aunt Clarissa and Clarissa's Connecticut-born husband, Ebenezer Ormsby, a merchant, also resided in Jones County. While visiting her Georgia relatives in the summer of 1827 (Orray Ticknor had died four years earlier but left a family, including his young son Francis Orray), Esther met and—after what must have been a whirlwind courtship—married Daniel Pratt. The marriage provided Pratt not only an ideal helpmate, but also a trio of brothers-in-law—Samuel, Simon, and John—who would follow Pratt to Alabama and put their money and their considerable talents behind Pratt's nascent gin business.[15]

Samuel Griswold, the South's pioneering gin maker, introduced Pratt to cotton-gin manufacturing in 1831. Griswold needed a superintendent for his Clinton factory, and impressed by Pratt's accomplishments in house and boat carpentry, he chose Pratt for the job. In going to work for Griswold, Pratt was taking several steps up in the world, for Griswold, having started with a small tin shop around 1820, had built the first important gin factory in the South, easily dominating the business in central and eastern Georgia and the Carolinas.[16]

15. James Melville Hunnewell, comp. *The Ticknor Family in America* (Boston, 1919), 1–18, 37–42, 55–56; Ticknor, *Poems of Francis Orray Ticknor*, 9–10; (Milledgeville) *Georgia Journal*, 11 December 1816, 26 October 1819, 4 July 1820, 26 December 1820, 15 July 1823.

16. *De Bow's Review* 10 (February 1851): 222; Griswold, "The Cotton Gin—An Interesting History"; U.S. Census of Manufactures, Georgia, 1820, Jones County; (Milledgeville) *Georgia Journal*, 14 June 1825, 8 July 1825, 26 June 1826, 3 September 1827, 14 July 1828. Historian Malcolm McMillan quite accurately characterized Griswold's factory as "a training school for gin mechanics." Griswold employees besides Pratt who "graduated" from his "school" and started their own gin factories included Joseph Winship of New Salem, Massachusetts, who established a gin factory at Madison, Georgia, and later in Atlanta; the brothers Israel and Dwight Brown of Connecticut, who established a factory at Columbus, Georgia; Orren Webb Massey of Rockingham, North Carolina, who established a factory at Masseyville, near Macon, Georgia; and Turpin G. Atwood of Providence, Rhode Island, who established a factory at Kosciusko, Mississippi. Malcolm McMillan, "The Manufacture of Cotton Gins, a Southern Industry, 1793–1860," typescript (n.d.), p. 11, Box 25, McMillan Collection, Auburn University, Auburn, Ala.; Gris-

Pratt proved so adept at running Griswold's factory that the older man offered to make him a partner in the business after only one year. Pratt assented, and by 1833 the new partners had decided to establish another factory in the fresh cotton lands to the west. Alabama and Mississippi were experiencing their celebrated "flush times," and planters there wanted gins. Because antebellum gins constantly broke down, manufacturers "needed close and constant contact with [them] to keep them running." Gins could be "returned to the factory for repair or repaired by the factory's traveling agents," but transportation and communication difficulties meant that "proximity to the planter [was] very advantageous to the manufacturer." For Griswold and Pratt, then, a factory on, say, the Alabama River in central Alabama would prove a real asset, giving them much greater access to the booming southwestern market.[17]

Despite the bright prospects their plan held, Griswold balked, allegedly because he feared depredations by Alabama's Creek Indians, but more probably because of an innate cautiousness. Pratt, with what would prove characteristic determination, proceeded with the bold endeavor, setting out for Alabama in 1833. He brought with him Esther, two slaves, and material to build fifty gins. The gin material required six horse-teams to carry it.[18]

Before Pratt left for Alabama, he and Esther, a Presbyterian, had converted to Methodism, an action comparable in importance in Pratt's life to his business affiliation with Griswold. He informed his family of this momentous event in 1832, his sister recalled, declaring that "he had been brought to see the sinfulness of his heart, and to trust alone in the atoning blood of the Savior." Edward Pratt would no doubt have found these tidings good indeed, but he had passed away in 1829 at the age of sixty-four, his conflict with his son over slavery apparently unresolved.[19]

Pratt's religious commitment failed to alter his "When in Rome" view

wold, "The Cotton Gin—An Interesting History"; (Milledgeville) *Georgia Journal*, 2 February 1832, 31 May 1832; John Hebron Moore, *The Emergence of the Cotton Kingdom in the Old Southwest: Mississippi, 1770–1860* (Baton Rouge: Louisiana State University Press, 1988), 216–18.

17. Mims, "History of Prattville," 20–21; Griswold, "The Cotton Gin—An Interesting History"; McMillan, "The Manufacture of Cotton Gins," 9, 12.

18. Mims, "History of Prattville," 20–21; Griswold, "The Cotton Gin—An Interesting History"; *Montgomery Daily Mail*, 14 April 1870.

19. Mims, "History of Prattville," 44, 51–52; Shadrack Mims, "History of the M.E. Church in Prattville," typescript (1885?), Box 37, McMillan Collection.

of the South's "peculiar institution." Indeed, his defense of slavery would grow much stronger in the 1850s, when as a prominent Alabamian, he published letters in newspapers defending the institution. Moreover, his own slaveholdings increased greatly over the years. Some historians view Pratt as a minion of the slaveholding elite. After all, he built for planters machines to gin their cotton, boats to carry the staple to market, and fine mansions where they could live in luxury; and he later repeatedly asserted the morality of the institution that made possible their wealth and his. Yet, Pratt, a staunch Yankee, remained his own man in many ways.

Daniel Pratt had told his father in 1827 "that to live in anny country it is necessary to conform to the customs of the country in part." It is crucial to note the caveat "in part" if we are to understand Pratt. As his later conduct abundantly revealed, he had no intention of bowing to the purported will of southern slaveholders. Even in Georgia, Pratt had mostly gone his own way. He sold unwanted farmland he had accumulated from cash-poor customers, brushing aside the southern agrarian ideal in his single-minded determination to find remunerative outlets for his "mechanical genius." Nor did he marry into southern society, though he appears to have had—despite his grumbling to his father—cordial relations with the local planters. Rather, he chose as his bride a twenty-four-year-old Connecticut woman whose temperament was similar to his own and who steadfastly supported his career objectives. Though Pratt must have doubted on more than one occasion that he would achieve success, he refused to lay down his tools.[20]

When Daniel Pratt came to Alabama in 1833, his goal was to establish a factory, not a plantation. This errand into the Alabama wilderness proved a challenging one, for Pratt had to contend with the physical and financial difficulties attendant to setting up a major business enterprise in a frontier region. But he persevered, and by the 1850s, he had become one of the most celebrated industrialists in the South, an accomplishment he could hardly have foreseen on that miserable, mosquito-ridden June night in 1827.

---

20. For evidence of the high personal estimation in which a prominent planter customer held Pratt, see Thomas Maughon to Daniel Pratt, 8 January 1838, CECP.

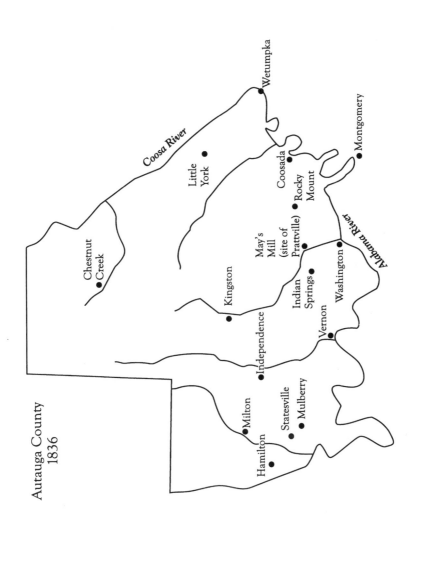

Autauga County
1836

Coosa River

Chestnut Creek

Little York

Coosada

Rocky Mount

Wetumpka

Montgomery

May's Mill (site of Prattville)

Kingston

Independence

Indian Springs

Washington

Vernon

Alabama River

Milton

Hamilton

Statesville

Mulberry

1

MANUFACTURING COTTON GINS: 1833–1850

Daniel Pratt and the small group who accompanied him to Alabama in 1833 traveled via the Federal Road, which ran through Jones County, Georgia. Benjamin Faneuil Porter and his wife had taken the same route in 1829 on the way from South Carolina to their Alabama River plantation in Monroe County. Many years later, this prominent Whig politician and judge recalled his initial disillusionment with Alabama. The Porters found the trip over the Federal Road difficult, with drunken "half-naked savages and beastly negroes," but the most shattering disappointment turned out to be their destination. Porter and his wife had an uncle who had settled early in Monroe County. Now the Porters were "hastening" to their uncle's "mansion," indulging themselves all the while "in golden dreams of his appearance and that of his house." They expected their uncle to be "a portly, well-looking old man" with a "large white house" with "piazzas and green blinds" that would be "the very abode of comfort." Even "amidst the toils and privations" of a trip over the Federal Road, the pair "rioted upon the vapors of benevolence which rose from [their uncle's] face, and the savory smells from his kitchen." Sadly, the grubby reality of the frontier dashed their visions. Instead of finding a jolly, "round-bellied uncle," they found "a small man, with a very lean girdle." His "mansion" was actually "a rail pen, full of squalling mischievous babes, and snapping bull puppies." For supper they had not "fat turkeys and old hams," but "a rasher of bacon with boiled greens."[1]

Although Daniel Pratt never took time to pen reminiscences as did the learned Benjamin Porter, it is nevertheless inferable that Pratt, like Porter, found the primitive agrarian surroundings in Alabama jolting. Pratt clearly could not comprehend planters such as Porter's lean-girdled uncle. Twenty years after his arrival in Alabama, the industrialist published an article in a prominent southern agricultural journal wherein he criticized profit-hungry planters who did nothing to improve their plantations or the communities in which they resided. "For what do we live?" he asked readers of *American Cotton Planter.* "Is it silver and gold? Is it to say that we have a plantation of one or five hundred negroes, or that we make 1000 bales of cotton? Is it to slave ourselves to accumulate property, and not enjoy it? Have no comfortable house to live in ourselves, or for our negroes . . . no roads that we can pass safely over to visit our neighbors?" Conceding that "permanent happiness consists in something more than this world's goods," Pratt nevertheless maintained that people would "take more satisfaction in worshipping God in a good comfortable house, suitable for worship of such a Being," than they would in a drafty, ramshackle cabin. Similarly, Pratt concluded, "When we have finished our day's labor we can see more satisfaction in a good, well ventilated house with good furniture, than we can in a little pent-up log cabin with stools, or chairs but little better, and other furniture corresponding."[2]

Despite laboring under difficulties in frontier Alabama, Daniel Pratt succeeded in greatly improving his surroundings. After a half-dozen years of striving, he established in 1839 an extremely successful cotton-gin factory at the location that would become Prattville, fourteen miles from Montgomery in Autauga County. Seven years later, he started a cotton mill that soon flourished as well. With two large factories and several smaller shops, Prattville became by the 1850s one of the most important manufacturing towns in the South. Pratt was by this time one of the South's most celebrated industrialists, as well as a greatly respected pub-

1. Benjamin J. Porter, *Reminiscences of Men and Things in Alabama,* ed. Sara Walls (Tuscaloosa, Ala.: Portals Press, 1983), 29–30; Henry Deleon Southerland Jr. and Jerry Elijah Brown, *The Federal Road through Georgia, the Creek Nation, and Alabama, 1806–1836* (Tuscaloosa, Ala.: University of Alabama Press, 1989), 105–6.

2. *American Cotton Planter* 1 (January 1853): 27.

lic figure in Alabama. These accomplishments were made possible by the gin factory he started in 1839.

When Pratt arrived in Alabama in 1833, the state's planters definitely stood in need of him. Migrants from older southern states in search of fresh land had poured into Alabama in the 1820s, causing the state's population to more than double between 1820 and 1830. This horde of migrants annexed Alabama to the cotton kingdom. By 1830, slaves constituted 38 percent of the state's population. The slave population was particularly concentrated in the fertile river bottomlands, which had attracted cotton planters. In 1830, five Alabama River counties, including Autauga, had populations that totaled more than 50 percent slave.[3]

Autauga County had fully shared in Alabama's boom. The county's population more than tripled during the 1820s, and the percentage of blacks increased from 43 to 51. But beyond the belt of Alabama River bottomland in the south lay the pine hills, where small yeoman farmers had settled. Here, few owned slaves, and a subsistence economy predominated.[4]

A number of swift creeks coursed from the sparsely settled hills of Autauga County to empty into the Alabama River in the south and the Coosa River in the east. On Autauga Creek, which flowed through the county's center, a sawmill had been erected on the land of Joseph May. Grist mills and a few other sawmills dotted the county, and there were several active gold mines in the north. Beyond these small mills and mines, however, Autauga had little industry.[5]

Autauga's major towns—Coosada, Vernon, Washington, and West Wetumpka—were clustered along rivers. Rocky Mount, a small planter community, lay on higher ground several miles west of Coosada. A number of villages and hamlets—Chestnut Creek, Little York, Indian Springs,

3. Thomas P. Abernethy, *The Formative Period in Alabama, 1815–1828* (1922; reprint, University: University of Alabama Press, 1965), chap. 7.

4. For accounts of the antebellum history and geography of Autauga County, see Willis Brewer, *Alabama: Her History, Resources, War Record, and Public Men. From 1540 to 1872* (Montgomery, Ala.: Barrett & Brown, 1872), 107–12; John Hardy, "History of Autauga County," *Alabama Historical Quarterly* 3 (spring 1941): 96–116, reprinted from (Montgomery) *Alabama State Sentinel*, 10 August 1867; Thomas McAdory Owen, *History of Alabama and Dictionary of Alabama Biography* (Chicago: S. J. Clarke Publishing, 1921), 1: 77–78. Also useful is the series of articles in the (Prattville) *Autauga Citizen* in 1853 and 1859 by Shadrack Mims and Thomas Smith, respectively.

5. Hardy, "History of Autauga County," 97–98. A detailed 1836 map of Autauga County is in Folder 41, Box 4, Bolling Hall Papers, ADAH.

Hamilton, Independence, Kingston, Milton, Mulberry, and Statesville—scattered the county's interior. Washington, the largest of the river towns, served as county seat until 1834, when more centrally located Kingston acquired that status.[6]

Thomas Smith, an early migrant to Autauga who crossed the Alabama River at Washington in January 1818, recalled that by 1820, "more than one hundred and forty white families had settled in the scope of country between [Swift and Mortar Creeks] and within twelve miles of the Alabama River." Among these were "many of the best families of Georgia and South Carolina." Autauga also had its share of rustic folk. The Fielders, who settled in the county's interior, were, according to Smith, "an industrious, frugal people, but *much* given to *backwoods* life. They had no taste for the restraints and formalities of refined society."[7]

Daniel Pratt came to Autauga County with a very different outlook from the Fielders. Looking for an ideal site on which to build a factory village, he planned initially to set up shop in Montgomery, but the building and lumber for which he had contracted were not ready when he arrived. Consequently, he crossed the Alabama River and settled six miles west of Wetumpka, where he leased Elmore's Mill on Mortar Creek. Here, he constructed fifty gins from material he had brought from Georgia. The gins sold rapidly. The next year (1834), he took a five-year lease on McNeil's Mill on Autauga Creek, one mile north of Washington. On this site, he established his first gin shop. At first, Pratt and his wife "lived in a log cabin, with a dirt chimney bending over and propped up by poles." Soon, however, Pratt was able to erect a two-story frame building to house his shop. The Pratts lived on the second floor, and their operatives boarded with them.[8]

Pratt quickly prospered, for his gin shop filled a large void. Eleazer Carver's gin factory in Bridgewater, Massachusetts, delivered gins to Alabama via Mobile, and Carver's Bridgewater rival, Eagle Cotton Gin Company, surely did also.[9] Other gins purchased by Alabama planters were made in small machine shops. Since local producers could not sup-

6. Autauga County Map, 1835, Bolling Hall Papers; Hardy, "History of Autauga County," 103–7; Shadrack Mims, "Reminiscences of Autauga County"; (Prattville) *Autauga Citizen,* 7 July 1853, 4 August 1853, 1 September 1853.

7. Thomas Smith, "The Early History of Autauga County"; (Prattville) *Autauga Citizen,* 7 July 1859.

8. Mims, "History of Prattville," 21; *Montgomery Daily Mail,* 14 April 1870.

9. Abernethy, *Formative Period in Alabama,* 81.

ply the heavy demand for gins and the Massachusetts factories suffered severe logistical problems, Pratt had great advantages over his rivals, and he profited accordingly.

According to his visiting brother, Edward, Pratt in 1835 employed "eleven hands to work in the shop besides five or six blacksmiths." Pratt was manufacturing about two hundred gins annually and marketing them throughout southern Alabama. In 1835, for example, he sent gins down the Alabama River to Charles Tait's plantation in Wilcox County and James Dellett's plantation in Monroe County. Both Tait and Dellett were prominent planters and politicians who certainly could have afforded the best in cotton gins.[10]

Charles Tait's overseer, Joshua Betts Grace, held Pratt's gins in high regard. In March 1835, Grace informed Tait that Pratt's agent, Mr. Davenport, had come "to see me if we wanted a new gin." That agent, Grace noted, had "already sold severl gins in this naborhood and they done well." He added that he "would like to have a better gin than we have at [the plantation]." Tait assented, and in June, Grace informed Tait that he had "got the new gin from Mr. Prats."[11]

At this time, Pratt put together the land deal that would bring Prattville into existence. In March 1835, Joseph May agreed for $21,000 to sell Pratt 2,000 acres of land on Autauga Creek, four miles north of Washington. The property included a small sawmill. This substantial purchase was to be completed in four installments between 1836 and 1838. The first two were payable in cotton gins, while the second two were payable in cash.[12]

Pratt surely had no difficulty with the first two payments because he could meet his obligation with gins he manufactured. But to make the latter two payments, which amounted to nearly two-thirds of the purchase price, he needed cash. For this he turned to two outside sources, an Alabama bank and a New Hampshire in-law. In 1836, he borrowed $9,800 from Elijah and Lydia Chandler of Wilton, New Hampshire, put-

10. Edward Pratt to Dorcas Pratt, 25 September 1835, Box 37, McMillan Collection; Mims, "History of Prattville," 22; Daniel Pratt to Enoch Parsons, 10 June 1835, Enoch Parsons Papers, ADAH.

11. J[oshua] B[etts] Grace to Judge Tait, 24 March 1835, 19 June 1835, Folder 6, Box 2, Charles Tait Papers, ADAH.

12. Deed Book D, p. 381, Probate Office, Autauga County Courthouse, Prattville, Ala. For general accounts of the purchase, see De Bow's Review 4 (September 1847): 136; Mims, "History of Prattville," 22.

ting up much of his newly purchased land as collateral; and in 1837, he borrowed $2,000 from the Montgomery branch of the Bank of Alabama. Four slave mechanics served as collateral for the bank loan.[13]

Pratt's neighbors reputedly thought he had made a foolish investment. He had paid more than $10 per acre for land later characterized as being little more than a "dismal swamp." In the 1850s, an article in an Autauga newspaper drew an evocative picture of this wild area: The "old, dreary and dilapidated" mill stood "in the midst of an almost impenetrable jungle." One could approach the building only by means of "a single road, built over the treacherous earth, with slabs and puncheons." The article deemed the old mill "a speaking evidence of the rude state of the surrounding country, and of the simple wants of its sparsely settled neighborhood." Except when a local farmer's "cart sought a simple load of roughest plank . . . the solitude of the lonely spot was never broken. Silence and solitude held there, undisputed reign."[14]

Despite its primitive condition, May's land had two redeeming virtues in Pratt's eyes: the waterpower provided by Autauga Creek and the abundance of yellow pine on the surrounding hills. The land provided both a power source for a large factory and the raw material for gin stands. Pratt immediately began the arduous process of draining the marshes near the creek. In this endeavor, he used slave labor. By 1839, when his lease with McNeil expired, Pratt had transferred operations to the new site. He originally intended to call the hamlet "Pratt's Mills," but a business associate, Amos Smith, suggested another name, and Pratt acquiesced. Mile-

13. Deed Book O, p. 505, Deed Book DA, p. 266, Probate Office, Autauga County Courthouse. Elijah Chandler returned the property to Pratt on September 13, 1838, in consideration of $8,000. Deed Book DB, p. 281, Probate Office, Autauga County Courthouse. On April 1, 1842, and April 18, 1843, Pratt recorded in his daybook making cash payments of $500 and $550 to Elijah Chandler. Daybook (1839–1846), 38, 103, CECP. Elijah Chandler is identified as a carpenter in the 1838 deed. It seems likely that he was the brother of Joseph Chandler of Wilton, who married, in succession, Pratt's sisters Asenath and Dorcas. In the 1850s, Elijah Chandler moved to Pope County, Arkansas. From a letter that Pratt wrote to Chandler in 1854, it appears that Chandler still held the unpaid balance of the eighteen-year-old loan, $750. "Your money and the intrest on it I will keep just so long as you desire me to do so," Pratt assured Chandler. "Any portion of it will at any time be subject to your order." Pratt added that should he "receive any instructions from you what disposition to make of it in case of your death, they will be complied with if in my power to do so." Daniel Pratt to [Elijah] Chandler, 19 July 1854, Folder 44, Pratt Papers, ADAH; U.S. Census, Arkansas, 1860 Population Schedule, Pope County.

14. Mims, "History of Prattville," 22; (Montgomery) *Alabama State Journal,* 6 October 1853, reprinted from the *Autaugaville Autaugian.*

posts being erected on the road to nearby Washington accordingly were marked "Prattville."[15]

Pratt made impressive progress between 1833 and 1839, but he did not act alone. Just as slaves provided the physical labor necessary to create Prattville, Yankees provided the managerial skill and financial backing necessary to get his new gin factory started. Amos Smith, a co-owner of the Gilford Manufacturing and Mechanic Company of Meredith, New Hampshire, met Pratt in Autauga County in 1837 while demonstrating a shingle machine Smith had invented. In the fall of 1838, he returned to Alabama and accepted the superintendency of Pratt's gin shop at McNeil's Mill. In January 1840, Pratt formed Daniel Pratt and Company in partnership with his brothers-in-law Samuel and Simon Ticknor and with Amos Smith. This partnership, in which the Ticknors invested heavily, remained in force for the rest of the decade.[16]

During the winter of 1839–1840, Pratt erected a blacksmith shop, a sawmill, and houses for his workers. Llewellyn Spigner, a native South Carolinian who had run the sawmill at the McNeil's Mill site, ran the two Prattville shops. In early 1841, Pratt put a gristmill into operation; it proved an immediate success. Amos Smith had installed the best machinery that could be had, capable of grinding wheat, corn, and other grains. On August 28, 1842, for example, Luke Hoffman had two hundred pounds of corn flour, three and one-half bushels of rye, and one and one-half bushels of wheat ground in Pratt's mill. Some farmers brought their wheat to the mill from a distance of up to 150 miles, according to the recollections of a contemporary. As a result of its great popularity, the mill often became so crowded that "eight or ten wagons could be seen at a time, standing waiting for their turn." A native of Galashiels, Scotland, named James Leithhead served as Pratt's first miller.[17]

15. Mims, "History of Prattville," 24–25; Amos Smith, "Reminiscences of Daniel Pratt," in *Hon. Daniel Pratt*, 60–61.

16. Mims, "History of Prattville," 24–25; Amos Smith, "Reminiscences of Daniel Pratt," in *Hon. Daniel Pratt*, 60–61; Daniel Pratt Smith, untitled ms., 4–5, ACHC. After Simon Ticknor's death in Prattville in 1850, his administrators appraised his property at $37,728, most of which represented his assets in Pratt's factories ($12,000 in gin-factory property and $21,228 in the cotton mill). Reports and Wills, Book F, 1850–1853, pp. 97–98, Probate Office, Autauga County Courthouse.

17. Mims, "History of Prattville," 37–38; Amos Smith, "Reminiscences of Daniel Pratt," 60; Daybook, 85, 89; Pauline Jones Gandrud, Autauga County, vol. 75 of *Alabama Records* (Easley, S.C.: Southern Historical Press, 1981), 5. Llewellyn Spigner was a member of Autauga's "Dutch Bend" community, a group of settlers of German derivation who mi-

According to the 1840 census, Pratt's household had thirty-six men engaged in manufacturing. Twelve of these men were white, while the rest were slaves. In addition, one Pratt mechanic, Western Franks, lived adjacent to Pratt in a separate household. The census thus indicates that about two-thirds of Pratt's workforce in 1840 consisted of blacks. Pratt likely had difficulty in finding good white mechanics on the frontier. Over the years, his reliance on slave mechanics would lessen significantly.[18]

Pratt's daybook, which starts in 1839, the year he established the shop at Prattville, allows closer scrutiny of the composition of his workforce in the 1840s. Roughly a dozen white men appear to have been employed by Pratt as mechanics during any given year in this period. Among the mechanics whose nativity is determinable, Yankees predominate, both in quantity and skill. Of Pratt's four highest-paid mechanics (excluding Yankee superintendent Amos Smith), three, John Ticknor, Enoch Robinson, and Ephraim Morgan, came from the North, while one, Western Franks, came from the South. The four lowest-paid mechanics (those earning less than $500 a year) were, with one exception, southerners.[19]

Whatever their nativity, most Pratt mechanics appear to have enjoyed low-cost or free housing as an employment benefit, with Pratt either charging nothing or nominal amounts for lodging. In 1845, for example, Robinson and Franks, two of Pratt's highest-paid workers, paid house rents of $75 and $50, respectively. Workers drawing lesser salaries often paid no rent at all. Marsh Crow, who contracted for only $35 a month in 1843 ($420 a year), received free lodging.[20]

Pratt's other source of labor, slaves, neither received fixed salaries nor paid rent. In the 1830s and 1840s, Pratt expended large sums of money on both the hire and purchase of black mechanics. According to the daybook, from 1841 through 1845, Pratt regularly hired six or more slaves each year at the cost of at least $2,500 annually. Two of the slaves he

grated from Orangeburg District, South Carolina in the 1820s. Hardy, "History of Autauga County," 107; Gandrud, *Autauga County,* 20. James Leithhead died later in 1841 and was buried on the hill behind the cotton-gin factory in an area that later became the private Pratt cemetery. Gandrud, *Autauga County,* 5.

18. U.S. Census, Alabama, 1840, Autauga County.

19. Daybook, 20–21, 67–68, 98, 100–1, 106, 143, 161, 195, 198, 226. Enoch Robinson of New Hampshire was Pratt's highest-paid mechanic, earning slightly more than $1,000 in both 1842 and 1843. Western Franks of Georgia, the highest-paid southern mechanic, earned $855 in 1842, $722 in 1843, and $879 in 1844. The lowest-paid mechanics likely were new employees.

20. Daybook, 230–31.

hired in this period, Andrew and Jake, came from his former business partner, Samuel Griswold. Purchasing slaves likely proved a better investment for Pratt than hiring them, however. The best slave artisans cost him $1,200 each in the 1830s and 1840s, so Pratt could buy two such slaves at roughly the cost of hiring six per year. Not surprisingly then, the prospering Pratt purchased at least twenty-four slaves (eighteen men and six women) from 1834 to 1845, at a cost of $22,775. For the first time in his life, Pratt became a substantial slaveholder.[21]

Clearly wanting artisans for his gin factory, Pratt bought eleven male slaves and only one female slave from 1834 to 1839. Beginning only in 1840, when he and his wife were establishing Prattville as their permanent home, did Pratt begin acquiring more female slaves. Between that year and 1845, he bought another twelve slaves, seven of whom were male and five of whom were female.

Reflecting a shortage in Alabama of black as well as white skilled workers, Pratt purchased some of his slaves from out-of-state owners, especially in the 1830s. William Daniel of Macon, Georgia, sold Pratt the slave Dick in 1834, while T. W. Brevard, also of Macon, sold Pratt two slaves, Robinson and William. Horatio Bowen, a Clinton, Georgia, planter and physician, owned the slave Daniel; Pratt noted on the bill of sale that Daniel was "carried to Alabama in 1835, for me, by Daniel McCloud of Jones County, Georgia." Another seller from Jones County was Samuel Griswold, from whom Pratt purchased a thirteen-year-old "Negro molatto boy named Charles." Charles, who after the Civil War took the surname "Atwood," became one of Pratt's most skilled mechanics.[22]

The high prices Pratt paid for his male slaves (usually from about $1,000 to $1,600) suggest that most of them, like Charles, had valuable mechanical skills, but only in a few cases is there proof. The slave Peter, whom Pratt bought for $1,200 in 1834, was specifically designated on the bill of sale as a blacksmith. In addition, in 1839 Pratt purchased the

21. Ibid., 8, 95, 100–1, 145, 195. The information on Pratt's slave purchases in the 1830s and 1840s comes from the bills of sale preserved in the CECP. In favoring slave purchases over hires, Pratt followed the path of Virginia ironmonger William Weaver, who tried to buy skilled slave forgemen whenever he could. See Charles B. Dew, *Bond of Iron: Master and Slave at Buffalo Forge* (New York: W. W. Norton, 1994), 99–106. Dew notes that fierce competition among ironmongers for the hired services of skilled slaves made hiring "a risky proposition." Dew, *Bond of Iron,* 99.

22. For more on Charles Atwood, see chap. 9.

slave Henry for the very large sum of $1,600 from Durant Nobles, who in 1850 worked as a carpenter in Montgomery. This suggests that Henry was a carpenter also.[23]

Pratt's purchases of at least eighteen male slaves through 1845 and his annual hire of six or more slaves from 1841 through 1845 indicate that he relied heavily on black labor in the 1840s. A notation in the daybook from 1845, however, shows Pratt paying a road tax for only ten "shop negroes."[24] Evidently, not all the male slaves Pratt bought or hired labored in the gin factory. Nevertheless, it does appear that Pratt's hired and purchased slave mechanics outnumbered his white ones even in the mid-1840s.

With hired and purchased slaves alike, Pratt faced the challenge of extracting labor from unfree workers. Like other southern manufacturers, he used "overwork" as a performance incentive for his slave artisans. Under the overwork system, slaves received cash compensation for doing extra work. In January 1844, for example, Pratt paid Samuel Griswold's slave Andrew $58.14, an impressive figure. Part of this amount, $6.37, was for "overwork since Christmas." Griswold's slave Jake netted $8.62 for post-Christmas overwork. Five more hired slaves earned such payments as well: Robertson ($14.94), Benjamin ($6.78), Richard ($5.73), Dick ($5.54), and Henry ($4.47). Pratt also paid overwork to Peter ($12.53) and two other slaves, Jack ($15.13) and Yellow Joe ($19.22). Ironically, sixteen-year-old Thomas Ormsby's name comes at the end of the 1844 overwork list, Ormsby having tallied $21.25 for the year. Thomas Ormsby was a son of Esther Ticknor's aunt Clarissa Ormsby, who by 1839 had migrated with her family from Georgia to Prattville. Pratt evidently viewed overwork as a useful incentive for slaves and relatives alike.[25]

Having a workforce surely numbering more than thirty throughout the 1840s enabled Pratt to become a major cotton-gin manufacturer not

23. U.S. Census, Alabama, 1850 Population Schedule, Montgomery County.

24. Daybook, 228.

25. Ibid., 145. On slave overwork, see Charles B. Dew, "Disciplining Ironworkers in the Antebellum South: Coercion, Conciliation, and Accommodation," *American Historical Review* 79 (April 1974): 405–10; Robert S. Starobin, *Industrial Slavery in the Old South* (New York, 1970), 99–103. The overwork earned by Griswold's slave Andrew compares favorably with that earned by William Weaver's highly skilled slave forgeman Sam Williams, who regularly made more than $50 per year in the late 1840s and early 1850s. Dew, *Bond of Iron*, 179.

only in Alabama but also across much of the South. When he moved to Prattville in 1839, Pratt began employing a network of traveling agents to sell his gins to planters in Alabama, Mississippi, Louisiana, Arkansas, and Texas. In addition to being partners in the gin business, Esther's brothers Simon and Samuel Ticknor acted as gin agents. On June 12, 1840, for instance, Pratt debited the expenses of Samuel on a sales trip to Talladega County, Alabama, and of Simon on a sales trip to Greene County, Alabama. Simon continued up the Tombigbee River into Mississippi, and on June 18, Pratt deducted Simon's expenses to Columbus. The Ticknor brothers only sallied forth on these trips occasionally, but other men acted as full-time agents. These individuals received a fixed monthly salary, plus commissions. In 1843, for example, Pratt hired John Woods and "Mr. Goree" as agents for $40 a month ($480 a year). Commissions could add considerably to salaries. John Gulick, received $338.31 in commissions for the period January 11 to September 4, 1840, while A. W. Gray received $213.04 for the period from September 25 to December 18, 1843.[26]

Normally in the spring and summer of a given year, agents would have their planter customers sign contracts ordering gins of specific makes. The agent warranted that the gin would perform well. When Pratt received the contract, he sent the gin to the planter by boat or, if the planter resided fairly close to Prattville, by wagon. The planter tried the gin during the harvesting season in the fall, and if it did indeed perform well, the contract required the planter to give his note to the agent, which the agent delivered to Prattville. The note would be payable the next spring, after the planter had sold his crop. If the gin did not perform well, Pratt sent the agent or a mechanic to make the necessary repairs (Occasionally, he or Amos Smith would go.). If the gin could not be made to work properly, Pratt provided the planter with another one.

A specific instance of this sales process can be found in the contract a Pratt agent, H. F. Matthews, made with planter N. J. Taliaferro of Lowndes County, Mississippi, on February 26, 1841. Under the contract's terms, a cotton gin would be delivered by Daniel Pratt and Company at Pickensville in Pickens County, Alabama, "on or before the first day of May next." Presumably, Pratt shipped the gin to Pickensville, a

26. Daybook, 5, 7, 25, 69–71, 98–99, 132, 137. John Gulick was born in New Jersey in 1805 and died in 1847. He was interred in the private Pratt cemetery. Gandrud, *Autauga County*, 4.

Tombigbee River port near Lowndes County, and Taliaferro then had it carried to his plantation. The contract warranted that this gin would "perform well." Taliaferro promised that he would "try this gin in the fall of 1841," and if it met expectations, he would give his note to Matthews for $175, "payable the first of march 1842."[27]

At least one planter, Robert Sinclair Gracey, challenged this mode of operation, and Pratt's response to Gracey's complaint is instructive about his general relationship with planters. In the summer of 1839, Gracey contracted with John Gulick to have a gin sent to his plantation in Marengo County, Alabama. Gracey wanted to gin his cotton crop, then return the gin if he considered its performance unsatisfactory. Pratt disabused him of this notion: "I cannot be at the expense to waggon a gin so far let a man gin his crop and then take it back. . . . To let a man use a gin through his whole crop and then take it back is entirely contrary to my manner of doing business." Unfazed by Gracey's presumption, Pratt bluntly informed the planter just what he would accept: "Should you not like [the gin] after using of it two weeks well enough to keep it please set it aside and inform me by mail. . . . I eather go or send and have it fixed. If I cannot make it do well I take it back and send [the customer] another." Since Pratt's innovative marketing techniques made it easier for planters to order good gins and keep them in repair, he had considerable leeway over his customers. In his letter to Gracey, Pratt appears to have been confident that planters would acquiesce to his terms.[28]

Pratt's assessment was correct, for his sales were strong in the 1840s. From 1841 through 1844, he shipped 1,951 gins, almost 500 per year. In the latter year, the firm divided $30,000 among the four partners. In an 1846 article in *De Bow's Review*, Pratt estimated that since he had commenced business in Alabama in 1833, he had manufactured "a little exceeding 5000 gin stands." His market, he declared, extended over

27. N. J. Taliaferro Contract, CECP. Pratt demanded a hefty annual interest rate of 10 percent from planters who could not make their payments on time. See, for example, Andrew R. Hynes Contract, CECP.

28. Daniel Pratt to R[obert] S[inclair] Gracey, 5 August 1839, Box 31, McMillan Collection, Auburn University. For a contrary view of the planter–cotton gin manufacturer relationship, see Jonathan M. Wiener, *Social Origins of the New South: Alabama, 1860–1885* (Baton Rouge: Louisiana State University Press, 1978), 140.

Tennessee, Alabama, Mississippi, Louisiana, Arkansas, Texas, and even Mexico.[29]

Responding to the great demand for his gins, Pratt opened a commission house in New Orleans in 1844. His partner in this venture was H. Kendall Carter, a former New Englander who clerked for Samuel Griswold in the 1830s. Pratt and Carter's firm, H. Kendall Carter and Company, took orders directly from large planters in the Mississippi Valley. The firm kept gins destined for these planters stockpiled in a large warehouse in New Orleans.[30]

In constructing his popular machines, Pratt's mechanics used locally grown timber sawn in Pratt's mill. For the gin saws, which pulled the cotton fibers apart from the seed, Pratt, like Samuel Griswold, turned to Naylor's Steel Works of Sheffield, England. On July 20, 1839, for example, Pratt paid Naylor's $1,462 for steel. Unless a customer specified otherwise, Pratt put ten teeth per inch on each saw and attached the saws to cylinders that stood three-fourths of an inch apart. Screws came from Eagle Screw Company of Providence, Rhode Island. For the iron used in gin castings, Pratt relied on a southern company, Shelby Iron Works, located some fifty miles north of Prattville in Shelby County. The company's owner, Horace Ware, recalled Pratt as his "best customer." Much to Pratt's chagrin, he often found himself forced to rely on northern manufacturers for materials and machinery, even on the eve of the Civil War.[31]

Within only a few years, Prattville began to draw enthusiastic commentary from visitors. In 1842, Elisha Griswold, the eldest son of Samuel, made a two-day visit to Prattville; he spent one day touring the gin

29. Daybook, 3, 22, 47, 79, 95, 145, 195; Daniel Pratt Smith, untitled ms., 11; *De Bow's Review* 3 (September 1846): 151–52. Amos Smith's share of the $30,000 was $5,000, one-sixth. Daniel Pratt Smith, untitled ms., 11. Pratt's share probably was one-half, or $15,000.

30. Daybook, 171; *De Bow's Review* 3 (September 1846): 151. H. Kendall Carter and Company did strong business in the 1840s and 1850s, and credit agents for R. G. Dun and Company consistently gave the firm high ratings. One Dun agent noted in 1854 that some of the "most reliable" banking and exchange houses in New Orleans ranked H. Kendall Carter and Company "No. 1½ to 2. An extra cautious Bank President marks No. 2." Louisiana, 9: 57, R. G. Dun & Co. Collection, Baker Library, Harvard Business School.

31. Daybook, 1, 103, 130, 195; *De Bow's Review* 3 (September 1846): 151–52; Ethel Armes, *The Story of Coal and Iron in Alabama* (Birmingham, Ala.: University Press, 1910), 163; Thomas Avery to Daniel Pratt, 19 March 1849, Folder 44, Pratt Papers, ADAH.

factory and the village. Pratt's factory, he declared, was "better managed for doing work quickly and cheaply than any I have ever seen." He noted that Pratt "had built more than twenty buildings, most of them occupied by his workmen." Prattville, he concluded, "is a monument to industry and perseverance. When [Pratt] moved here in 1833, he was worth $10,000, now he has expended [$100,000?] on improvements." Coming from Samuel Griswold's son, this was high praise indeed.[32]

Writing five years after Griswold, journalist James De Bow also approved of the operations in "the remarkable town of Prattsville [sic]." Pratt's "improvements have been extraordinary," he exclaimed, "and one cannot realize they have been made in so short a period, save by the wand of an enchantress." De Bow saw Pratt as "a remarkable instance of that success which energy, enterprise, and worth of character will everywhere secure." The gin factory, he reported, weekly manufactured from 10 to 12 gins (480 to 576 a year), which generally contained fifty saws, at three to four dollars a saw, depending on the overall quality of the gin.[33]

By the mid-1840s, Prattville had a gin factory, sawmill, foundry, gristmill, and store. Revealing what would be a lifelong determination to foster enterprise in Prattville, Pratt began renting buildings to local entrepreneurs at least as early as 1843, with the result that more businesses began to appear. In November 1845, for example, George Tisdale opened a tin shop in one of Pratt's buildings. Tisdale, a Connecticut native, owned the shop until 1858, when he sold out and moved to nearby Autaugaville.[34]

For several years, Pratt owned a general store in Prattville that supplied the needs of his workers. Pratt's miller, James Leithhead, patronized the store in 1841, purchasing a gallon of molasses on April 19 and twenty-four pounds of coffee on June 3. New Englander Simon Ticknor bought a rocking chair and a box of codfish on February 4, 1843. Later that same year, two brothers from Georgia, Benjamin and Haywood Miles, took over the store as B. F. Miles and Company. Pratt charged the pair store rental of less than $17 per month. He kept recording employees' purchases at the store in this period, however, indicating that he maintained some sort of financial stake in B. F. Miles and Company. Cer-

32. Elisha Case Griswold to Sanford Tippett, 19 October 1842, reprinted in *History of Jones County*, 469–70.

33. *De Bow's Review* 5 (September 1847): 136–37.

34. Daybook, 225; Alabama, 2: 109, R. G. Dun & Co. Collection.

tainly, the store supplied an impressive array of goods for a tiny frontier village, ranging from fancy spices such as nutmeg, cloves, and ginger to expensive musical instruments such as a melodeon and an ophicleide.[35]

Other men established businesses in Prattville by 1850, presumably under similar arrangements with Pratt. Western Franks and N. F. McGraw (both southerners) manufactured horse mills, which millers used to grind corn, and Llewellyn Spigner opened a carriage and wagon shop. Like George Tisdale's tin shop, these concerns were dwarfed by Pratt's factory, all three together employing only thirteen men. Another Pratt employee, Enoch Robinson, launched a more ambitious project. With another New Hampshirite, Thadeus Mather, Robinson started (probably in 1849) a cotton-gin and horse-mill factory in Hayneville, the county seat of Lowndes County, Alabama. Lowndes lay on the southern side of the Alabama River directly opposite Autauga. After this factory burned in 1855, Robinson returned to Prattville to start his own horse-mill shop, McGraw having left Prattville in 1851 and Franks having died. Robinson was a great success with his new shop and became a wealthy man by 1860.[36]

As business in Prattville expanded, Pratt attempted to purchase Washington Landing, located four miles southeast of Prattville on the Alabama River. Washington, the former county seat, had dwindled almost to the vanishing point since the 1830s, the result of transferring the seat to centrally located Kingston and the rise of Prattville as a county business center. Washington now consisted of little more than a dilapidated warehouse and wharf, as well as a ferry. But since Pratt sent his textiles and many of his gins down the Alabama River, the site held great significance for him. The heirs of Wade Cox, who at his death owned much of the land in and around Washington Landing, rejected Pratt's initial purchase offer. In response, Pratt sent Shadrack Mims, the cotton-mill agent, to Kingston to search deeds with the probate judge to determine whether the Cox heirs held proper title to the land. Mims could find nothing that cast doubt on their title. In a letter to Pratt, who was in New York at the

35. Daybook, 15, 20, 29, 105, 189, 198, 229, 234.

36. U.S. Census, Alabama, 1850 Manufactures Schedule, Autauga County, Lowndes County; U.S. Census, Alabama, 1850 Population Schedule, Autauga County, Lowndes County; Church Register, First Methodist Church of Prattville, Ala., 1849–1866, ACHC, 37–38; Larry W. Nobles, ed., *The Journals of Ferdinand Ellis Smith* (Prattville, Ala: by the editor, 1991), 53; Larry W. Nobles, ed., *The Journals of George Littlefield Smith* (Prattville, Ala: by the editor, 1991), 106, 110–11.

time, Mims suggested that Pratt make another attempt to come to terms with the owners. He indicated that the Cox heirs were primarily interested in maintaining possession of the ferry. As for the warehouse, he supposed that "they would not be reluctant to part with it at a fair compensation in view of all the circumstances." Mims cannily noted that if Pratt established "a warehouse at any point above [Washington Landing] it would finally break up that place and make the property valueless," whereas "should a good warehouse be put up [at Washington Landing] & well conducted, it would divert a good deal of the travel from the upper routes & thereby enhance the value of the Ferry property." Perhaps exercising such leverage over the Cox family, Pratt reached an agreement with them by 1850. Under its terms, the owners received $10,000 for the land that their father had held. Pratt and Jesse Cox, a prominent Alabama River steamboat captain, shared control over the ferry.[37]

Having secured the landing, Pratt began improving its facilities and constructing a plank road between it and Prattville. On a visit to Prattville in February 1851, James De Bow wrote: "A plank road of easy grade, upon which it is calculated a team of four mules will have a load of six tons, will soon be built by Mr. Pratt, connecting his place with the [Alabama] river. He is now building a good wharf and warehouse on the river landing which will compare with the best." Pratt completed the plank road by July at a cost variously estimated at $5,000 to $10,000. He placed Norman Cameron, a young North Carolinian, in charge of the warehouse, a position he would hold until the outbreak of the Civil War.[38]

37. Shadrack Mims to Daniel Pratt, 15 March 1849, Folder 44, Pratt Papers, ADAH; Hardy, "History of Autauga County," 100; Deed Book DE, pp. 509–13, Probate Office, Autauga County Courthouse. For more on Shadrack Mims, see chap. 3. On Jesse Cox, see the *Tuskegee Republican*, 19 May 1859.

38. *De Bow's Review* 10 (February 1851): 228; Nobles, *Journals of George Littlefield Smith*, 17; Hardy, "History of Autauga County," 99; Alabama, 2: 12, R. G. Dun & Co. Collection. On July 20, 1851, George Smith, the eldest son of Amos Smith, wrote that he and his brother "took a ride down toward Washington on the plank road. It was very pleasant." Nobles, *Journals of George Littlefield Smith*, 17. Seventy years after the event, one man recalled that "the making of a railroad was never talked about more than the building of that plank road." That his family left Autauga before Pratt completed the road counted as "a disappointment of my life," he declared. Washington Bryan Crumpton, *A Book of Memories, 1842–1920* (Montgomery, Ala.: Baptist Mission Board, 1921), 11. On the national plank road fad of the 1840s and 1850s, see George Rogers Taylor, *The Transportation Revolution, 1815–1860* (Armonk, N.Y.: M. E. Sharpe, 1951), 29–31.

The 1850 census makes clear why Pratt needed the plank road. In addition to gin and textile factories, Prattville had a sawmill, a gristmill, a foundry, a tin shop, a carriage and wagon shop, and a horse-mill shop. The eight establishments employed 185 people and produced products worth $191,155. The gin factory itself employed twenty-eight men and made 500 gins worth $50,000, while the foundry and sawmill employed six men and made castings and lumber worth $10,700.[39]

From his modest start in Alabama in 1833, Pratt by 1850 had built one of the country's most important cotton-gin factories. He had also helped demonstrate that industry could flourish below the Mason-Dixon Line. Moreover, at fifty-one, he remained an energetic and determined individual, and soon he would launch an ambitious course that would make him, by 1860, the largest cotton-gin manufacturer in the world and one of the South's most accomplished and celebrated businessmen.

39. U.S. Census, Alabama, 1850 Manufactures Schedule, Autauga County.

2

Manufacturing Cotton Gins: 1850–1861

In 1850, James De Bow, tireless booster of southern industry, launched a new series in his *Review,* in which he chronicled the exploits of the South's great industrialists and entrepreneurs. His second installment told the story of Daniel Pratt. De Bow decreed Pratt not only a talented businessman but also "an ornament to human nature, and worthy to be held up as an example for the respect and admiration of mankind." Pratt, wrote De Bow, now manufactured about 600 gins a year and had made some 8,000 since 1833. Noting the strong waterpower of Autauga Creek, the abundance of fine quality yellow pine in the countryside, and Pratt's improvements in and around Washington Landing, De Bow concluded that "no place in Alabama is so well adapted to manufacturing purposes as Prattville. The site could easily support a population of 6,000 inhabitants."[1]

James De Bow's confidence in Daniel Pratt was well placed. By the end of the decade, Pratt had become the largest cotton-gin manufacturer in the world, shipping gins via a complex distribution network all over the South and even to other parts of the world, including Mexico and Russia.

1. *De Bow's Review* 10 (February 1851): 225–28.

He employed dozens of mechanics, the majority of whom were native white southerners. As De Bow had hoped, Daniel Pratt's mammoth cotton-gin factory stood as a monument to what a determined and resourceful industrialist could accomplish, even in the agrarian South.

Despite Pratt's ultimate accomplishments, his road to success was not without potholes. Indeed, Pratt found himself mired in one of the greatest difficulties of his career in 1852. This trouble arose out of Pratt's dissolution of Daniel Pratt and Company and his formation of a new business with Samuel Griswold and Griswold's son Elisha, Samuel Griswold and Company, in 1850. Pratt likely took this step because he hoped that with Samuel Griswold's capital behind him, he could offer a stronger challenge to his main competitors, the Carver and Eagle gin companies.

Carver and Eagle gin companies, both of Bridgewater, Massachusetts, were the North's only major cotton-gin factories. They did a strong business in the Mississippi River Valley and posed a significant obstacle to Pratt in his quest to dominate the gin trade in this area. Griswold, for one, doubted that Samuel Griswold and Company could compete successfully against Carver for the patronage of the great Mississippi Valley planters. "Carver pretends his gins will pick very fast," Griswold noted skeptically, but he nevertheless believed their wily adversary had convinced most big Mississippi Valley planters that the Carver gin was the ideal machine. Griswold noted that while he had sold all his gins "for the last five or six years," Pratt had on hand a "large number" of unsold gins. Rather than try to compete for a larger share of Carver's market, Griswold urged that he and Pratt aim for the smaller, more inaccessible planters by maintaining a large network of traveling agents: "With a reasonable number of good agents I think a fair number of gins can be sold . . . but few of our gins can be sold without traveling agents to call on the small planter back in the country for Carver sells most of the large planters gins on the rivers."[2]

For Griswold, expansion appears almost to have held more peril than promise. Why then did he finally consent to enter the venture? For one thing, Pratt and Griswold had remained good friends since the time they worked together in the early 1830s. Moreover, Griswold's eldest son, Elisha, who had written so favorably about Prattville on his 1842 visit,

2. McMillan, "The Manufacture of Cotton Gins," 3; Moore, *Emergence of the Cotton Kingdom,* 58–59; Samuel Griswold to Daniel Pratt, 29 January 1850, Folder 44, Pratt Papers, ADAH.

strongly supported Pratt, and Griswold seems to have had great faith in his son. In fact, in a letter to Pratt, he authorized Elisha "to enter into any agreement or bargain to purchase or sell any article or property connected with the gin business at Prattville." Griswold declared that Elisha's actions "shall be binding on me as partner of the firm S. Griswold & Co."[3] In a few years, Griswold would regret that he wrote these words, for Pratt's aggressiveness and his own cautiousness doomed their partnership.

Samuel Griswold and Company came into existence on January 1, 1850. The new company consisted of four partners: Pratt, the two Griswolds, and Amos Smith. Elisha Griswold moved to Prattville in the spring, accompanied by his wife and young son, Samuel. Elisha quickly became an integral member of the Prattville community, and the partnership seems to have gone smoothly for about two years.[4] But in the spring of 1852, Pratt, still determined to expand his market share among the large Mississippi Valley planters, made a decision concerning the newly invented "Parkhurst gin" that caused friction with Samuel Griswold and the dissolution of the partnership less than a year later.

Stephen Parkhurst of New York invented a new type of gin that created a sensation in the South in 1852. Proponents of the Parkhurst gin boasted that the machine was entirely superior to the Whitney gin. The Parkhurst was a roller gin, not a saw gin, and its boosters claimed that it did "not cut or destroy the staple as is the case with the saw gin." As a result, cotton ginned with a Parkhurst machine would "bring in the market from one or two cents more per pound than [cotton] produced by the Whitney gin." One writer declared that "Gen. Wade Hampton and Gov. Hammond, of South Carolina, speak in the highest terms of the new gin. Gen. Hampton has thrown away the Whitney gin, and will use no other than Parkhursts."[5]

Riding on this wave of favorable publicity, Parkhurst formed a corporation in 1852 to sell rights to market his gin in Alabama, Georgia, and Louisiana. His price was $40,000 for each state. Two prominent Mont-

3. Samuel Griswold to Daniel Pratt, 29 January 1850.

4. Nobles, *Journals of Ferdinand Ellis Smith,* 64–65; Mollie Ticknor to Merrill Pratt, 9 June 1853, Folder 30, Pratt Papers, ADAH.

5. *Mobile Daily Advertiser,* 24 August 1852, reprinted from the *Savannah Republican; Mobile Daily Advertiser,* 7 November 1852, reprinted from the *Savannah Courier.* Other supposed advantages of the Parkhurst gin were that it was less likely to get out of order, that it required half the horsepower to work it, and that it ginned faster.

gomery businessmen snapped up the Alabama right, but Pratt purchased the Louisiana right. In March, George Smith, Amos Smith's eldest son and a mechanic in Pratt's gin factory, wrote in his journal: "Father says that the gin shop company are going to manufacture the Parkhurst gins for the New Orleans trade." A week later, George's cousin Ferdinand Smith, another Pratt gin mechanic, noted in his journal that "Mr. Parkhurst has been over from Montgomery today to make some arrangement about the construction of his gins." All seemed well, but in a few days an uncertain note crept into Ferdinand's journal: "Messrs. Pratt and Griswold have been in the shop most of the time today engaged on the new gin, trying to make some improvements in the construction of the machine."[6]

By May 1852, the situation had definitely taken a bad turn. On the eighth, Ferdinand wrote: "One of the new Parkhurst cylinders came to the shop. George and I then took hold of [the gin] and took out the old [cylinder] and put in the new [one]. We then started [the gin], but it did not operate satisfactorily." On May 11, Ferdinand complained that the gin "still cuts the seed." Pratt and his best mechanics worked on the Parkhurst cylinders all through May and into June, to no avail. On June 4, Ferdinand wrote: "Mr. Pratt has been in the shop all day at work on those new cylinders, trying them. H. K. Carter got here this morning; he has been in the shop a good part of the time." Finally, on June 11, George Smith recorded ominously that "W. O. Ormsby [Pratt's secretary] having prepared a statement in accordance with the facts in reference to the operation of the cylinders, Ferdinand and I went with him to Esquire Reid's office and testified on oath to the truth of the same."[7]

Trouble was brewing between Pratt and Samuel Griswold during this period. The latter was horrified when he learned that Pratt, with Elisha's consent, had bought the Louisiana right. "My age and health admonish me that I have more business in Georgia than I can do justice to and it would be unwise [for] me to branch out & incur further liabilities," he insisted in a letter to Pratt in May. Griswold also was "unwilling for Elisha to take an interest in [the Parkhurst gin]." He blamed Elisha "for consenting to a trade of that magnitude without consulting me," but he

6. *Mobile Daily Advertiser*, 24 August 1852; Daniel Pratt to Samuel Griswold, 14 June 1852, Folder 44, Pratt Papers, ADAH; Nobles, *Journals of Ferdinand Ellis Smith*, 116–17; Larry Nobles, *Journals of George Littlefield Smith*, 43.

7. Nobles, *Journals of Ferdinand Ellis Smith*, 122, 124–25; Nobles, *Journals of George Littlefield Smith*, 51.

found Pratt more at fault: "I, however, suppose the reason for [Elisha's] not consulting me was owing to the precipiticy with which the trade was entered into, and not having time to consult me, [he] relied entirely on your judgment and consented for you to do as you pleased." Although Pratt had promised to release the Griswolds from the contract and assume the entire liability, Griswold wanted the promise in writing. It was mostly a formality, Griswold claimed, for Elisha, he argued, could not have bound him to the transaction. He included with his letter a release form that he wanted Pratt to sign.[8]

Pratt apparently wrote Griswold a heated letter in response, for on June 7, Griswold again wrote Pratt, declaring he "was much pained to discover that my letter had given you offense by [your] construing its meaning into a threat for the purpose of scaring you into measures." Nevertheless, he insisted that Elisha simply had not possessed the authority to bind him to the Parkhurst deal. In reality, his son had not been "authorized to go beyond or do anything in my name not strictly relating to the manufacture of saw gins and the gin business as then conducted." Moreover, Griswold argued, "Our articles of agreement fixt us limits by saying that no change should be made in the business without consulting me . . . so that no matter how unlimited my letter might have been the articles of agreement superceed that." Suggesting that it would be best to dissolve the partnership rather than continue in an atmosphere of recrimination, Griswold wrote: "I would at once propose to sell out to you both Elisha's interest and mine in the firm of S. Griswold & Co., for unless we can all be friendly, the firm better be closed if it can be done on fair terms." Moreover, Griswold said he did not "see how you can manufacture the new gin while the firm of S. Griswold & Co. goes on."[9]

Pratt set out his position in a letter he wrote to Griswold on June 14. He apologized for giving offense to Samuel: "I cannot believe that the time will ever arrive when I shall not cherish the friendship toward you which has so long existed in my breast." Claiming that at the time he had agreed to release the Griswolds, he had believed that Samuel was "equally bound with the rest of us," he wrote that he had merely wanted from Samuel "the credit of being liberal in this unfortunate affair." Vehemently opposed to dissolving the firm, Pratt argued that "if three out of a firm composed of four should think it to the intrest of the firm to make

8. Samuel Griswold to Daniel Pratt, 29 May 1852, Folder 44, Pratt Papers, ADAH.
9. Samuel Griswold to Daniel Pratt, 7 June 1852, Folder 44, Pratt Papers, ADAH.

some changes or introduce an improvement into their stile of work or contract to build gins of another stile or pattern and these three the persons who superintend and manage the business," they should not "be deprived of doing so" by the remaining member. However, he concluded that "if you or Elisha are dissattisfyed and wish to be released from the concern of S. Griswold & Co., I certainly shall not insist on your remaining."[10]

Pratt vigorously defended himself from Griswold's charges that he had overawed Elisha into consenting to the transaction and that he had been too hasty in entering into the contract. "Mr. Parkhurst sold the right of Ala. to a wealthy company in Montgomery," he wrote, "then went immediately to New Orleans and created a great excitement there." Pratt claimed that he was unmoved, but that Elisha worried that "our gin business was about to be ruined." After learning that a company was being formed to purchase the Louisiana right, Pratt took the matter before Elisha and Amos Smith. The two men advised him "to go over and said they would be willing to take an intrest and would abide by any contract I thought propper to make." In New Orleans, Pratt found that "there was [not] nearly any thing talked about but the Parkhurst gin"; and after seeing an impressive demonstration of the machine, he concluded that it "would go into pretty janeral use especialy amongst the large planters." Under pressure from the rival company, he finally decided to purchase the right. Pratt, representing Samuel Griswold and Company, took a third; H. Kendall Carter and Company took a third; and it was hoped that Alabama businessman James Gilmer would take a third upon his return to New Orleans. Gilmer, however, declined.[11]

Gilmer's refusal to participate left Samuel Griswold and Company and H. Kendall Carter and Company in a difficult position. If the Griswolds backed out, this position would become even worse. Coupled with the failure of the Parkhurst gin, these occurrences threatened to throw Pratt into great financial distress. Pratt ruefully admitted to Griswold that he had made a serious mistake: "Now I will say that the gin they had running in New Orleans was the same they had in Montgomery and the only gin as far as I can learn that ever did perform sattisfactory. I supposed all their gins performed as well as the one they had running and from Mr. Parkhurst's tale they were then making supperior ones. I had

10. Daniel Pratt to Samuel Griswold, 14 June 1852.
11. Ibid.

not got aquainted with Mr. Parkhurst and believed what he said was true. . . . It will probaly take some four or five years to work through it but should my life be spared I intend dooing so."[12]

Despite Pratt's glum assessment of the Parkhurst gin, Ferdinand Smith worked on it in the fall of 1852 and through 1853 in an effort to improve its performance. Moreover, Pratt did sell some of the machines, for Ferdinand's brother Frank and his cousin George made trips to Louisiana and Mississippi to "alter" Parkhurst gins. That Pratt's mechanics had to make such trips, however, belies the claim of Parkhurst's boosters that the gin was unlikely to get out of order. Ferdinand Smith was still working on the faulty cylinder in late 1853, and his last entry concerning the Parkhurst gin was not promising: "Mr. Pratt called in today a little out of patience in not seeing the gin going on as fast as he wished."[13]

Writing years later, both Samuel Hardeman Griswold and Shadrack Mims acknowledged the Parkhurst gin's dismal failure. Griswold cited his grandfather's refusal to become involved with the gin as an example of his astute business judgment. Mims wrote that Pratt lost $40,000 on the gin, but he found a silver lining in the sorry episode. He claimed that Pratt "could by puffing the gin in the papers [as Parkhurst had done] have sold every dollar of the stock, but he was too honest for that. The loss of $40,000 was nothing compared to a clear conscience with him."[14]

Not only had Pratt lost $40,000; he lost the Griswolds as business partners. The firm Samuel Griswold and Company officially dissolved on January 1, 1853. Shadrack Mims, Pratt's cotton-mill agent, became a partner in the new firm, which now consisted of Pratt, Mims, and Amos Smith. Pratt did, however, retain the friendship of the Griswolds despite the rift caused by the unfortunate Parkhurst affair. Indeed, Elisha likely would have remained a partner if his father had allowed him to do so. In the 1850s, he named his third son Daniel Pratt after the man he so clearly admired. Elisha made a friendly visit to Prattville in 1853, and Pratt wrote him a warm letter in 1856, a year before Elisha's untimely death at the age of thirty-eight. Even Samuel Griswold seems to have patched

12. Ibid.
13. Nobles, *Journals of Ferdinand Ellis Smith,* 152, 158, 172; "Journal of Benjamin Franklin Smith," typescript, ACHC. Even as late as September 1855, George Smith wrote, "Mr. Tuttle, patentee of an improved method of making the Parkhurst gin cylinder, is here." Nobles, *Journals of George Littlefield Smith,* 105.
14. Griswold, "The Cotton Gin—An Interesting History"; Shadrack Mims, untitled ms. (1873), 8, Box 37, McMillan Collection.

up his relationship with Pratt, for Samuel and his wife visited Prattville in 1855.[15]

Although Pratt managed to salvage his friendship with the Griswolds, his business position suffered as a result of their defection. Shadrack Mims bought Elisha's interest in the company, but Pratt presumably bought out Samuel, thus incurring another large expense as a direct result of the Parkhurst debacle. In addition, Pratt's attempted masterstroke against Carver and Eagle completely backfired, for Parkhurst's machine was the Edsel of cotton gins.

Despite these problems that beset Pratt in 1852, he launched during 1853 an ambitious expansion campaign that made Daniel Pratt and Company the world's largest cotton-gin manufacturer and himself into one of Alabama's wealthiest men. In the late 1850s, Pratt's expansion program encompassed the production of a gin model that actually matched or even surpassed Carver and Eagle gins in popularity among the great planters of the Mississippi River Delta. These developments would likely have been impossible as long as the rather timorous Samuel Griswold had a voice in the business.

Even during the existence of Samuel Griswold and Company, Pratt had made a major improvement in the Prattville industrial complex. In 1851, he replaced the gristmill with a three-story brick building, 232 feet long and 29 feet wide. This building housed a machine shop; a carpenters' shop; and a sash, door, and blind shop. While small by comparison with the gin and textile factories, the sash, door, and blind shop, leased by Ephraim Morgan, became a promising establishment in its own right. In 1859, a Prattville paper boasted that the sash, door, and blind shop had "acquired an enviable notoriety on account of the superior make and finish of all its work." The paper predicted that "if its business continues to increase the next two or three years as it has the past two, it will soon become the largest [such factory] in the South."[16]

15. (Prattville) *Autauga Citizen*, 10 February 1853; Frank M. Abbott, *Genealogies*, vol. 1, *History of the People of Jones County, Georgia* (Macon, Ga.: National Publishing, 1977), 101–2; Nobles, *Journals of George Littlefield Smith*, 63–64; Daniel Pratt to Elisha Griswold, 11 March 1856, Folder 44, Pratt Papers, ADAH.

16. Daniel Pratt to [Elijah] Chandler, 19 July 1854, Pratt Papers, ADAH; Nobles, *Journals of George Littlefield Smith*, 14; (Prattville) *Autauga Citizen*, 10 February 1859. The sash, door, and blind factory was operational by May 1851, for in that month George Smith noted in his journal that "Mr. Lide from Carlowville [a planter community in southern Dallas County] was at Prattville this evening. He came for the purpose of procuring some sash and doors." Nobles, *Journals of George Littlefield Smith*, 14.

From 1853 to 1855, Pratt greatly expanded the production capacity of the gin factory. He put up a new three-story brick building, 220 feet long and 50 feet wide, with a three-story wing 35 feet long and 40 feet wide. The structure cost Pratt, at a minimum, $60,000 to $80,000. Pratt's new buildings adjoined each other, lining the western bank of Autauga Creek for some 450 feet. A large waterwheel drove the machinery in both structures. Pratt proudly wrote his old friend Elijah Chandler that he expected "to put in the best of machinery and to have the best cotton gin factory in the world." He noted that he now would be able to "turn out in the shop 1500 gins annually if necessary." Pratt hoped that these great edifices would be something "permanent, something that will induce those who come afterward to keep up the place." He admitted that he was "getting old (55 tomorrow)," and he declared that he "must quit building."[17]

Noah Cloud toured Pratt's new buildings in 1857 and enthusiastically wrote of them in an article in his *American Cotton Planter and Soil of the South*. Cloud described for his readers what occurred on each floor of the gin factory. On the first floor, workers constructed the various gin parts, while on the second floor, they assembled the parts into gins and tested them with seed cotton. "Fifty pounds are run through each gin and a note made of the time required to gin it," noted Cloud. "If the speed is not sufficient, or there is any defect found in the performance, it is remedied at once. No gin is allowed to leave the shop until it performs satisfactorily." On the third floor, workers painted and varnished gins before boxing them for shipping. A large elevator moved the gins from floor to floor. A railway connected the lumber house, where wood used to make gin stands was seasoned, and the iron foundry, where smiths made the gin castings, to the gin factory. The entire complex greatly impressed Cloud, who declared, "With all [Mr. Pratt's] late improvements and the advantage afforded by his large factory arrangements, he is able to furnish the neatest, most complete and best cotton gin stand in America."[18]

17. Contract of Daniel Pratt with T. B. Goldsby, A. J. Mullen, and Hiram Granger, 28 September 1853, CECP; Daniel Pratt to [Elijah] Chandler, 19 July 1854. The waterwheel was working by late January 1855, and the gin factory's elevator was in service by late February. Pratt completely transferred operations from the old building to the new one by the end of March. Nobles, *Journals of George Littlefield Smith*, 91–97.

18. *American Cotton Planter and Soil of the South* 1 (May 1857): 156. Pratt completed the lumber house in October 1855 and the railway in December. Nobles, *Journals of George Littlefield Smith*, 106, 116.

Cloud was not alone in singing Prattville's praises. Johnson J. Hooper, the Alabama humorist and editor of the *Montgomery Daily Mail,* toured Prattville the same year as Cloud and came away equally impressed. Hooper was struck by everything he saw in Prattville, but he took particular notice of the gin factory. "The Gin Manufactory," he exclaimed, "is a mammoth concern, great in extent and massive in structure. Each of its three stories is neatly filled with cotton gins in the process of construction." Through "a great variety of most ingenious mechanical contrivance[s]," Hooper continued, Pratt was able "to secure perfect accuracy and uniformity in the gin saws." Moreover, not only were Pratt's gins mechanically sound, they were aesthetically pleasing. According to Hooper, the gins were "very frequently got up in the most elegant and finished style, resembling, more, furniture in the parlor, than a machine for the plantation. We saw many with polished mahogany covers and engraved plates."[19]

Pratt continued expanding production in the late 1850s. In 1856, he manufactured almost 800 gins. At the end of that year, he bought out his partners Amos Smith and Shadrack Mims. By 1859 (after the panic of 1857 had subsided), Pratt manufactured 1,200 gins; and in 1860, his factory produced at full capacity 1,500 gins. The 1860 output was valued at nearly $289,000. Sales, however, did not match production. In 1856, Pratt complained to Elisha Griswold that "the gin business is overdone. I think I have done rong in building my new shop. I cannot go on to advantage . . . to make less than 800 gins annually. I think that is more than I can sell." In 1857, the year of the panic, Pratt sold only 341 gins, while in 1858, he sold 494. Yet in 1859 and 1860, sales jumped significantly, reflecting the late 1850s cotton boom. In 1859, Pratt sold 780 gins; and in 1860, he sold 858. Moreover, these figures probably underestimate Pratt's effective sales since they likely do not include purchases of the extremely popular Eureka gin (see below). Prospects appeared quite bright for the gin factory as the country neared war. Since he had arrived in Alabama, Pratt had built more than 14,000 cotton gins, and he now manufactured 28 percent of the gins produced in the South and one-quarter of all gins produced in America.[20]

19. *Montgomery Daily Mail,* 22 August 1857.

20. Daniel Pratt to Elisha Griswold, 11 March 1856, Pratt Papers, ADAH; *American Cotton Planter and Soil of the South* 4 (April 1860): 192, 195; Ibid., 5 (January 1861): app.; Fred Bateman and Thomas Weiss, *A Deplorable Scarcity: The Failure of Industrialization in the Slave Economy* (Chapel Hill: University of North Carolina Press, 1981), 211. Amos

In 1860, Prattville's various businesses employed more than 200 people and produced output worth $491,991. In the gin factory, the 66 men employed made 1,500 gins valued at $288,730. The factory had a capitalization of $200,000, almost twice that of the cotton mill. Pratt clearly had outdistanced his competition in the cotton-gin industry. The U.S. Census of 1860 listed fifty-two gin manufacturers. Of these, four were major rivals: Samuel Griswold and Clemson, Brown, and Company in Georgia; and Carver and Eagle Gin Companies of Bridgewater, Massachusetts. Griswold's factory, which had been moved to Griswoldsville (several miles south of Clinton) around 1850, and Clemson, Brown, and Company of Columbus each manufactured about 1,000 gins per year. The two Massachusetts companies, Carver and Eagle, made 410 and 580 gins, respectively. The only other factories that built more than 200 gins annually were in Mississippi. Turpin G. Atwood's factory at Bluff Springs in Attala County made 350 gins per year, and Beckett and Tindall of Aberdeen made 250 gins per year.[21]

Though Pratt enjoyed great success in the 1850s, he never penetrated the markets in Georgia (except in the Chattahoochee River Valley) or the Carolinas, where Samuel Griswold and Clemson, Brown, and Company predominated. Moreover, he continued to receive stiff competition in the lower Mississippi Valley from the Massachusetts firms, Carver and Eagle. Pratt improved his situation, however, when he erected his new factory building. In a report on his 1857 visit to Prattville, Johnson J. Hooper noted that Pratt supplied "a large proportion of the gins used by the heavy planters of Mississippi and Louisiana." No doubt many of these gins were the "parlor gins" that caught Hooper's eye. Also destined for the Mississippi Delta were "Eureka gins," which planters bought for a more substantial reason than appearance. Pratt manufactured Eurekas under a contract with their inventor and patentee, D. G. Olmsted of Vicksburg, Mississippi. Eureka gins had sixty to eighty saws and cost, because of their special construction, $6 a saw (or $360 to $480 a gin). D. G. Olmsted specially developed his Eureka machines to gin "swamp cotton" of the Mississippi Delta region, so these gins were "superior for cotton of that peculiar description, to those of any other manufacture." The

---

Smith moved with most of his family to Philadelphia in 1857. His son George took over as gin factory superintendent in 1857 and 1858. Daniel Pratt Smith, untitled ms., 5.

21. U.S. Census, Alabama, 1860 Manufactures Schedule, Autauga County; McMillan, "The Manufacture of Cotton Gins," 18–19.

model clearly did very well with wealthy Delta planters; in 1864, Pratt and Olmsted had $54,000 in uncollected sales alone.[22]

Some lowland planters, however, continued to favor Pratt's regular make of gin. Wade Hampton, for example, ordered six regular eighty-saw gins at $300 apiece in 1860 for his vast Mississippi plantations. Hampton powered his gin houses with steam engines, and Pratt had adapted his large gins to steam power. Similarly, in 1861 David Hunt of Rodney, Mississippi (a small town near Natchez), another extremely wealthy planter, ordered three regular Pratt gins, one of seventy saws and two of sixty-five.[23]

The boom experienced by Pratt's gin business in 1859 and 1860 had led to sharply increased sales, but it also made marketing a more complex process. At age sixty, Pratt decided to hand this worry over to others. Hence, on September 3, 1859, he concluded a contract with Samuel Ticknor and his own nephew and ward, Merrill Pratt (who had lived in Pratt's household since 1841), under terms that had the duo take over the marketing of all gins manufactured by Pratt, except the Eureka model, as the firm Pratt and Ticknor. The contract excepted from its operation the area of Texas west of the Trinity River, over which William Saunders had jurisdiction in accordance with a contract concluded with Pratt in 1856. The Pratt and Ticknor contract was to commence January 1, 1860 and run to January 1, 1865. Ironically, Pratt, as it turned out, had saddled his kinsmen with the crushing legal responsibility for collecting notes during the Civil War on gins held by planters across the South.[24]

22. *Montgomery Daily Mail*, 22 August 1857, 1 August 1859; McMillan, "The Manufacture of Cotton Gins," 6; *Weekly Vicksburg Whig*, 11 August 1858; Summary of Daniel Pratt's Ledger, 1 March 1864, CECP; Eureka Gin Sales to Daniel Pratt, 1 January 1861, CECP. Although the Pratt-Olmsted contract has not yet been located, clear references to it occur in the following: Daniel Pratt Contract with Samuel Ticknor and Merrill Pratt, 3 September 1859, and Daniel Pratt Contract with Samuel Ticknor, 23 January 1866, both ACHC. Under the terms of the contract, two-thirds of the profits went to Pratt and the rest to Olmsted.

23. S. Mims Jr. to Col. Wade Hampton, 4 March 1861, Daniel Pratt to David Hunt, 29 May 1861, both in Pratt & Ticknor Letterbook (1861), ACHC; Moore, *Emergence of the Cotton Kingdom*, 69.

24. Daniel Pratt Contract with Samuel Ticknor and Merrill Pratt, 3 September 1859, ACHC; Daniel Pratt Contract with William Saunders, 5 December 1856, Box 31, McMillan Collection. The Pratt-Saunders contract ran from 1 January 1858 through 1 January 1863. The two principals agreed in 1860 to extend the operation of the contract to 1 January 1865. William Saunders Jr., an Alabama native, had been an agent for Mather, Robinson, and Company, the Hayneville gin factory that burned in 1855. In 1856, he and

A surviving 1861 letterbook yields considerable information on Pratt and Ticknor's marketing practices and agent network. Pratt and Ticknor employed at least seventeen agents in the spring of 1861. Each agent claimed an exclusive sales territory. Three agents were based in Alabama, seven in Mississippi, two in Tennessee, three in Louisiana, and two in Arkansas. While large lowland planters tended to order gins directly from Prattville or through commission houses in Montgomery, Mobile, Columbus (Mississippi), Natchez, Vicksburg, Memphis, New Orleans, and Galveston, smaller interior planters relied more heavily on these traveling agents.[25]

Personal information on Pratt and Ticknor's agents is sparse. W. G. Yarborough, born around 1825 in Georgia, lived in a boarding house in Alexandria, Louisiana. The census enumerator listed his occupation as "ginwright," a reflection of the fact that agents had to be able to repair malfunctioning gins on their note collection rounds. Another agent, W. W. Montague, born in Virginia around 1815, boarded with the household of the mayor of Jackson, Mississippi, in 1860. The enumerator listed Montague's occupation as "gin agent" and his wealth as $5,000, not an inconsiderable sum. Daniel Pratt himself put in a good word for Montague in a letter to planter D. B. Douglas of Bastrop, Louisiana, who had complained about his recently purchased gin. "I notice what you say about the gin," wrote Pratt. "In relation to Mr. Riser [presumably another agent] fixing the gin I would prefer Mr. Montague as he understands fixing gins better than Mr. Riser."[26]

Like W. W. Montague, agent W. Jack Smith received commendation from his employers. Pratt and Ticknor's bookkeeper, Shadrack Mims Jr., wrote another agent that "we think [Smith] will make a good agent as he seems to have a great deal of energy and 'goaheadativeness.'" Agent A. M. Prothro did not win much favor, however. Prothro, an apparent "sub-

---

Thadeus Mather, a New York native, started a commission house in Galveston, Texas, that sold Pratt gins. U.S. Census, Alabama, 1850 Population Schedule, Lowndes County; Nobles, *Journals of George Littlefield Smith*, 108; *Tuskegee Republican*, 19 February 1857.

25. Letterbook, ACHC; *American Cotton Planter and Soil of the South* 5 (January 1861): app.; *Tuskegee Republican*, 19 February 1857. Pratt continued to maintain a commission house in New Orleans, having bought out H. Kendall Carter in 1858 and installed Jacob J. Link of Canada to run it. U.S. Census, Louisiana, 1860 Population Schedule, New Orleans Parish.

26. U.S. Census, Louisiana, 1860 Population Schedule, Rapides Parish; U.S. Census, Mississippi, 1860 Population Schedule, Hinds County; Daniel Pratt to D. B. Douglas, 9 March 1861, Letterbook, ACHC.

agent" of W. G. Yarborough, was dismissed by Yarborough in April 1861. In March, Mims had written Yarborough that "you may use your discretion about discharging A. M. Prothro. If you do not think he is doing a paying business you had better discharge him." As part of the final settlement, Prothro received a $108 gold watch, the cost of which Yarborough passed to Daniel Pratt.[27]

Pratt and Ticknor's agents earned set salaries, plus commissions (10 percent on gin sales and 5 percent on note collections). Pratt and Ticknor also reimbursed its agents for such incidental expenses as travel. William Gaillard of Aberdeen, Mississippi, a particularly valued agent, received a yearly salary in 1861 of $1,200. A. M. Prothro, obviously not so highly valued, received his final settlement in July 1861, $775 for the period from January 1860 to mid-April 1861 ($50 per month), plus traveling expenses of $614.85. In his accounting with Daniel Pratt, W. G. Yarborough charged for a pair of boots and a hat, as well as a subscription to the *Prattville Southern Statesman,* his lodging for eleven and one-half days at the Merchant's Hotel in New Orleans, and the gold watch he gave Prothro.[28]

Pratt and Ticknor valued good agents like Gaillard so highly because they vested their agents with a great deal of responsibility. Any negligence or incompetence on the part of an agent could cause the firm great difficulty, given the slowness of transportation and communication. Sometimes, agents failed to send complete shipping information with their gin orders. In March 1861, Shadrack Mims Jr. reminded H. H. Brooks to be careful on this score: "In giving your orders for gins you did not give the address of the parties we are shipping gins to." In April, Mims instructed H. R. Cummings to "be particular in your letters to give the post offices of the parties you order gins for. Also be very particular about what point the gins are to be shipped to and always what River or Bayou."[29]

Although Pratt and Ticknor provided sales contract forms, the agents evidently had authority to draw their own contracts, a power that could

27. S. Mims Jr. to William Gaillard, 25 March 1861, S. Mims Jr. to W. G. Yarborough, 5 March 1861, Letterbook, ACHC; W. G. Yarborough account with Daniel Pratt, 25 January 1862, CECP.

28. S. Mims Jr. to A. B. Hill, 11 March 1861, Letterbook, ACHC; W. G. Yarborough account, 25 January 1862; A. M. Prothro settlement with Daniel Pratt and Pratt & Ticknor, 7 July 1861, CECP.

29. S. Mims Jr. to H. H. Brooks, 25 March 1861, S. Mims Jr. to H. R. Cummings, 10 April 1861, Letterbook, ACHC.

lead to trouble. Mims had occasion to reprimand H. R. Cummings concerning a contract the latter made with planter Ben Offat of Greenville, Mississippi. Mims complained that the contract was "not drawn up satisfactory, as nothing is mentioned as to the time when due, and according to the way the contract reads we cannot compel [Offat] to pay for the gin at all." Mims demanded, "You must try to get [the contract] in different shape." Two days later, perhaps after having consulted Samuel Ticknor, Mims wrote a letter to Merrill Pratt—who was himself in Greenville, Mississippi—in which he enclosed the flawed contract. "We do not exactly like the way the contract reads as nothing is said about the time when due," he told Merrill. "We should be glad if you would call on Mr. Offat and get [the contract] in different shape and see Mr. Cummings about it." After considerable delay, the concerned parties found their way to a solution, and Pratt and Ticknor shipped a seventy-five-saw gin to Offat's plantation in May.[30]

Even when the agent included the necessary shipping information and drafted a solid contract, he could be undone by penmanship. In May 1861, Shadrack Mims Jr. informed Zack Rogers of Tuskegee that "we could not tell whether [William Finch's] order was for a 45 or 65 saw gin, as it was written rather indistinctly." He added that with another of Rogers's orders "we could not make out the [customer's] name, as it was signed so badly. . . . Have we got the name right? We are close."[31]

On one occasion in Mims's correspondence, the frightening specter of fraud arose. An agent sent an order for a fifty-saw gin for Stephen Thunkild of Mississippi to Prattville, followed by a signed contract. After receiving this gin, Thunkild wrote Pratt and Ticknor denying that he had agreed to buy any gin. Mims appears to have seriously entertained the possibility of forgery, requesting the planter to "please let us know if your name has been falsely signed to the contract, as we wish to enquire into the matter." Less seriously, William Gaillard evidently once fell victim to a misunderstanding, sending in an order for a fifty-saw gin when the planter claimed he had ordered only a horse mill. Mims asked Gaillard to "please look into the matter."[32]

A recurring problem in 1861 was the failure of Pratt and Ticknor's

30. S. Mims Jr. to H. R. Cummings, 10 April 1861, S. Mims Jr. to M. E. Pratt, 12 April 1861, Letterbook, ACHC.
31. S. Mims Jr. to Z[ack] Rogers, 24 May 1861, Letterbook, ACHC.
32. S. Mims Jr. to Stephen Thunkild, 30 May 1861, S. Mims Jr. to William Gaillard, 18 March 1861, Letterbook, ACHC.

agents to desist from taking planters' orders for Eureka gins, which D. G. Olmsted had the exclusive right to market. Faced with demand and undoubtedly anxious to secure commissions on this expensive model, Pratt and Ticknor's agents continued to send orders for Eureka gins to Prattville despite Mims's contrary instructions. On March 12, Mims told agent W. S. Thurston, "You must not sell any more Eurekas as we are not authorized to sell them." On April 19, he sent the same reminder to W. W. Montague and Frank Shelton, apparently to no avail. On May 29, Mims wrote Montague, "We cannot furnish the Eureka gin order for Mr. J. B. Beard as we are not authorized to sell them." The next day, Mims wrote Beard himself, telling him that they could not sell him a Eureka but would gladly provide him "one of our best gins, which we warrant to perform equal to any other gin now in use."[33]

Despite the importance of traveling agents, planters sometimes bypassed them, making gin inquiries directly to Pratt and Ticknor. One planter, B. L. Armstrong of Memphis, expressed interest in a Eureka gin, but Mims disappointed him: "We have nothing to do with [the] Eureka Gin. They are manufactured here by Mr. Pratt for the patentee alone and his sales are restricted to the section of the country where he can personally attend to them." H. H. Irwin of Arkansas asked about payment terms and was answered: "Our terms are payable after 1st crop. . . . When an account runs without being paid . . . we expect interest." Mims sent Messrs. Wallis and Wynn of Mississippi blank contracts giving "our terms and conditions and from which we do not vary." He admitted to these possibly thrifty planters that Pratt made "a gin that is fine furnished and more durable than our $3.00 gins, but [I] do not think it performs any better as to speed and superiority of samples."[34]

Daniel Pratt deemed some of these planter inquiries worth replying to personally. To the extremely wealthy David Hunt of Rodney, Mississippi, Pratt wrote assuringly: "I will send you [gins] of my best make and such as I think you will be pleased with." To Linton Lee of Barnwell District, South Carolina (like Wade Hampton an absentee landlord in Mississippi), Pratt answered a detailed question as to whether he could furnish Lee with a cotton gin that would "gin 3 bales of 500 lbs each in eight

33. S. Mims Jr. to W. S. Thurston, 12 March 1861, S. Mims Jr. to W. W. Montague, 19 April 1861, S. Mims, Jr. to Frank Shelton, 19 April 1861, S. Mims Jr. to W. W. Montague, 20 May 1861, S. Mims Jr. to J. B. Beard, 30 May 1861, all in Letterbook, ACHC.

34. S. Mims Jr. to B. L. Armstrong, 16 May 1861, S. Mims, Jr. to H. J. Irwin, 12 June 1861, S. Mims, Jr. to Messrs. Wallis & Wynn, 15 April 1861, all in Letterbook, ACHC.

hours, one that will make good cotton and gin the seed clean." Pratt explained that if Lee gave one of Pratt's sixty-saw gins three hundred revolutions a minute and had it well-tended, it would perform as requested. He also promised Lee that he could make a gin brush conforming to the specific plan Lee had provided.[35]

On his own initiative, Pratt wrote Hopkins Rice of Clinton, Alabama, concerning a forty-five-saw gin Rice had ordered. "I notice you want to gin 1500 lbs. lint per day, to have the gin run light and pick the saws very clean," he wrote, adding that "1500 lbs. is more than I calculate for a 45 saw gin to do in a day. . . . That is as much as we calculate for a 50 saw gin with good speed and attention." Pratt advised Rice to purchase a fifty-saw gin at either $3 or $4 a saw. "I warrant both [makes] to be good gins," he declared, adding, however, that "the $4 is finely finished and a very superior gin"—thus placing a different emphasis on the relative merits of the two makes than did Mims in his letter to Wallis and Wynn. On March 18, Rice ordered a fifty-saw gin, as Pratt had advised, but because it is not apparent whether it was the $3 or the $4 make, we do not know if Pratt's sales pitch worked.[36]

Daniel Pratt made sure that Pratt and Ticknor took particular care with the gin sent to Francis Strother Lyon, a rich planter and important Alabama politician. Lyon had ordered an eighty-saw gin for his plantation near Demopolis. Shadrack Mims Jr. wrote Lyon informing him that the particular model sent him "was sent to the [agricultural] fair last year at Demopolis and Mr. Pratt wished us to let you have it, as it is a superior gin." Mims closed by expressing his hope that the gin "will arrive safely and prove satisfactory."[37]

Pratt and Ticknor sold to customers who varied widely in wealth, from such great planters as David Hunt, Wade Hampton, and Francis Strother Lyon, to men of more modest means. For example, on June 18, 1861, Pratt and Ticknor shipped a sixty-five-saw gin to Lucian Coco and a sixty-saw gin to Jane Woods, both of Avoyelles Parish in the Red River Valley of Louisiana. Coco was worth $103,500, but Woods was worth considerably less, $37,000. Earlier in the year, Bertin A. Robert, also of

35. Daniel Pratt to David Hunt, 29 May 1861, and Daniel Pratt to Linton Lee, 12 June 1861, Letterbook, ACHC.
36. Daniel Pratt to Hopkins Rice, 11 March 1861, Letterbook, ACHC.
37. S. Mims Jr. to Francis Strother Lyon, 21 March 1861, Letterbook, ACHC.

Avoyelles Parish, had received a sixty-saw gin from the factory, and he was worth still less, $21,200.[38]

Similarly, the wealth of Pratt and Ticknor's customers in southeastern Alabama varied considerably. William J. Bickerstaff of Russell County and R. T. Hudspeth of Henry County, both orderers of sixty-saw gins, were worth $35,000 and $35,880, respectively. On the other hand, Joseph W. Guilford and Green H. Guilford (also of Henry County), orderers of forty-five-saw gins, were worth only $11,150 and $14,465, respectively. At the farthest end of the spectrum from great planters such as Hampton and Hunt was Samuel Shiver of Coffee County, Alabama, a county just entering the commercial cotton market in the 1850s. Shiver, who ordered a gin of only forty saws, was worth a modest $5,260.[39]

Judging by the 1861 letterbook, Pratt and Ticknor at the end of the antebellum era sold gins ranging in size from thirty to eighty saws. In general, gins of forty-five saws or fewer were sold to smaller planters, while those of fifty to sixty saws went to modestly to very wealthy customers. Sales of gins of more than sixty saws (which included the Eureka gin) were made to the wealthiest planters.

Of the 195 gins Pratt and Ticknor sold in the spring and summer of 1861, the majority were of fifty and sixty saws, 37.4 percent and 17.4 percent, respectively (nearly 55 percent together). Gins of sixty-five to eighty saws made up 29.3 percent of sales, while gins of thirty to forty-five saws made up 15.9 percent. Eighty-saw gins made up merely 10.8 percent of the total. Admittedly, the results are somewhat skewed against the largest models because Eureka gins are excluded. Nevertheless, the figures indicate that the great planter did not dominate Pratt's market. Rather, Pratt had a very broad market, encompassing both the Samuel Shivers and the Wade Hamptons of the cotton kingdom, with many men in the middle.

38. S. Mims Jr. to Lucian Coco, 18 June 1861, S. Mims Jr. to Jane Woods, 18 June 1861, S. Mims, Jr. to B[ertin] A. Robert, 23 April 1861, all in Letterbook, ACHC. Bertin A. Robert was likely a relative of Mary (Robert) Epps, the wife of Avoyelles planter Edwin Epps, made notorious in Solomon Northup's *Twelve Years a Slave*.

39. S. Mims Jr. to W. J. Bickerstaff, 23 March 1861, S. Mims Jr. to Samuel Shiver, 25 March 1861, S. Mims Jr. to B. F. Hudspeth, 25 March 1861, S. Mims Jr. to D. W. Guilford, 25 March 1861, S. Mims Jr. to Green H. Guilford, 25 March 1861, all in Letterbook, ACHC; U.S. Census, Alabama, 1860 Population Schedule, Russell County, Henry County, Coffee County.

In the 1850s, Mississippi's developing railroad network greatly eased Pratt and Ticknor's job of delivering gins to planters in that state. Pratt and Ticknor hastened to divert its traffic from rivers to rails where possible. In doing so, it relied particularly on the Mobile and Ohio, which by 1861 extended from Mobile to Columbus, Kentucky. Gins that before would have been sent down the Alabama River to Mobile and up the Tombigbee River to Columbus, Mississippi, and other destinations now were shipped downriver to Mobile, then via the Mobile and Ohio to the numerous towns that had sprouted along the line. The Mobile and Ohio also made southern Mississippi more accessible to Pratt and Ticknor, which accordingly shipped gins to railroad towns in this area.[40]

The Mobile and Ohio altered Pratt and Ticknor's transportation pattern in Alabama as well. The railroad had a branch line to Gainesville, Alabama, that crossed Sumter County, and Pratt and Ticknor sent gins to two Sumter planters via this line. In addition, the Mobile and Ohio made sales possible in Alabama's Tennessee River Valley, which had remained physically isolated from southern Alabama since the state's formation. In March, for example, Pratt and Ticknor shipped a fifty-saw gin to a planter in Lauderdale County. The gin was carried by the Mobile and Ohio to Corinth, Mississippi, and then east on the Memphis and Charleston to Florence, the seat of Lauderdale.[41]

Other Mississippi railroad lines used by Pratt and Ticknor were the Mississippi and Tennessee, the Mississippi Central, and the New Orleans, Jackson, and Great Northern in eastern Mississippi; and the Southern in central Mississippi. The only area of the state where Pratt and Ticknor still relied on river transport was the Delta. For that region, the company continued to send gins by boat from Mobile to New Orleans and from there, up the Mississippi River.

In Louisiana, Pratt and Ticknor mostly shipped gins from New Or-

40. On the development of Mississippi's railroad network, see Moore, *Emergence of the Cotton Kingdom,* chap. 7. On the Mobile and Ohio Railroad specifically, see James F. Doster and David C. Weaver, *Tenn-Tom Country: The Upper Tombigbee Valley* (Tuscaloosa: University of Alabama Press, 1987), 87–91.

41. Doster and Weaver, *Tenn-Tom Country,* 90–1; S. Mims Jr. to S. F. Pool, 5 April 1861, S. Mims Jr. to Elnathan Tartt, 5 April 1861, S. Mims Jr. to Col. H. D. Smith, 25 March 1861, all in Letterbook, ACHC. Mississippi-based agent W. Jack Smith evidently operated in the western Tennessee Valley as well, for when Mims could not reach him at Fulton in northeast Mississippi, he sent a letter to him in Tuscumbia, Alabama. S. Mims Jr. to W. Jack Smith, 21 May 1861, Letterbook, ACHC.

leans up the Mississippi and Red Rivers to various towns and landings. The company did, however, use the New Orleans, Jackson, and Great Northern to ship to points in the Florida Parishes. In some cases, treacherous navigation conditions may have militated against river transport. Mims wrote Jacob Link that he should ship Abram Eddins's gin to Floyd Bayou (in the Mississippi Delta region of Louisiana) "if navigable." If not, he was to ship the gin by rail to Delhi, Louisiana, via Jackson and Vicksburg, Mississippi.[42]

Despite Pratt's efforts to prod Alabama toward a more vigorous internal improvements policy in the 1850s, Pratt and Ticknor could take little advantage of the state's underdeveloped railroad system in 1861. Instead, the firm still largely relied on the Alabama and Tombigbee Rivers. For the expanding cotton-growing region of southeast Alabama, Pratt and Ticknor sent gins by the Montgomery and West Point railroad from Montgomery to Columbus, Georgia, then down the Chattahoochee River.[43]

In sending gins to planters, Pratt and Ticknor sometimes made errors. In May 1861, Pratt and Ticknor sent J. J. Hooker of Mississippi a sixty-saw gin, but the notice it sent him separately stated that the gin had only fifty saws. After Hooker, who had received the notice before the gin arrived, complained that he would be receiving the wrong make of gin, Mims wrote Hooker, explaining and apologizing for the mistake. Hooker fared better than William A. Coppedge of Arkansas, who actually did receive the wrong make of gin. In notifying Coppedge of the mistake, Mims claimed that "the only difference between the two [gins] is price and finish." Coppedge had ordered a gin twenty-five dollars more expensive than the one he had, in fact, received. Mims assured him that the gin sent would "gin equally as fast and give as good a sample as the other [make] and no doubt will please you as well," and he requested Coppedge to let him know whether he would keep the gin or wanted the actual make he had ordered.[44]

Mims blamed some of Pratt and Ticknor's logistical problems on the

42. S. Mims Jr. to Mrs. Mary Addison, 3 May 1861, S. Mims Jr. to John Magee, 3 May 1861, S. Mims Jr. to J. J. Link, 18 June 1861, all in Letterbook, ACHC.

43. S. Mims Jr. to Alexander Weynes, 29 March 1861, S. Mims Jr. to Hopkins Rice, 29 March 1861, S. Mims Jr. to Campbell & Co., 15 April 1861, S. Mims Jr. to King, Allen & Camack, 25 March 1861, S. Mims Jr. to Wolfolk, Warner & Co., 25 March 1861, all in Letterbook, ACHC.

44. S. Mims Jr. to J. J. Hooker, 13 May 1861, and S. Mims Jr. to William A. Coppedge, 1 April 1861, Letterbook, ACHC.

postal system. "You are mistaken about our not answering your letters," he declared to W. G. Yarborough. "We have replyed to every one that required attention." Mims suggested that "the difficulty has been in the mail." In a letter to planter Levi Wray of Copiah County, Mississippi, Mims claimed Wray's "order was nearly 3 weeks reaching us." He put the blame on "some irregularity in the mails."[45]

Once Pratt and Ticknor had successfully distributed gins to customers, it faced the challenge of collecting the money owed for them. The financially distressed Peyton B. Smith of Cass County, Texas, reached an amicable settlement with Pratt and Ticknor. "We note your remark [in your letter] concerning your inability to pay for your gin this year," wrote Mims. "We are willing to abide by your proposition, that is to close the [account] by note with 10% interest from January." Mims enclosed a blank note for Smith to "sign and return to us by mail." In another case, Mims was much less nonchalant. Replying to a letter from an agent, he wrote, "If W. T. McDaniel is not honest enough to pay a just balance due on his gin, we shall have to loose it." He pointedly added: "So you can 'let him rip.'"[46]

Pratt's 1850s expansion necessitated not only an increase in the number of agents selling cotton gins, but also in the number of mechanics manufacturing them. Census data show that Pratt's gin workforce more than doubled from 1850 to 1860, growing from 28 men in the former year to 66 in the latter. Pratt also increased the number of men employed in his foundry from 3 in 1850 to 8 in 1860. On the other hand, Pratt had employed 3 men in his sawmill in 1850 but did not list a sawmill as a separate entity in 1860. Overall, therefore, employment in the gin factory complex went from 34 in 1850 to 74 in 1860.[47]

As the gin factory workforce expanded in the 1850s, its racial composition altered. While slaves accounted for at least half Pratt's workers in the early and mid-1840s, by 1852 only about 22.5 percent of his gin factory workforce was enslaved. This figure likely held steady for the rest of the decade. Eighty-two white men are identifiable from the 1860 census as probable workers in the gin factory and foundry or the various Prattville shops, which leaves only 23 of approximately 105 job slots open for

45. S. Mims Jr. to W. G. Yarborough, 27 April 1861, and S. Mims Jr. to Levi Wray, 24 May 1861, Letterbook, ACHC.

46. S. Mims Jr. to Peyton B. Smith, 27 February 1861, and S. Mims Jr. to W. Jack Smith, 8 April 1861, Letterbook, ACHC.

47. U.S. Census, Alabama, 1850 and 1860 Manufactures Schedules, Autauga County.

slaves. If Pratt is assigned a proportional share of workers, he would have had 16 black workers, or just 22 percent of his workforce. He did not, as one influential historian has concluded, use "scores" of slaves in his gin factory in the 1850s.[48]

Pratt's slaveholdings did expand markedly in the 1850s, but most of this expansion resulted from his purchase of a large plantation in 1858. In 1855, the number of slaves held by Pratt came to 59, only 12 more than in 1840. In January 1855, however, Pratt bought a large tract of land and 32 slaves. Two years later, he owned 107 slaves, 77 males and 30 females. But while the number of male slaves had doubled since 1850, the number of female slaves had tripled.[49]

Obviously, Pratt by 1860 must have worked many of his slaves on his large landholdings. Even in 1850, he had owned 2,200 acres of land (400 improved) worth $13,000. In 1860, his holdings had increased to 4,050 acres of land (1,000 improved) worth $22,500. In addition, Pratt surely employed a large retinue of domestic servants, as he owned a big house with extensive grounds, including a garden, orchard, and vineyard, and his household was a large one.[50]

By the 1850s, Pratt not only had reduced his reliance on slave labor, but he also appears to have relegated many of his slave workers to tasks

48. State Property Tax Assessment, Autauga County, 1852; U.S. Census, Alabama, 1860 Population Schedule, Autauga County; Starobin, *Industrial Slavery*, 19. Starobin's source, Noah Cloud, does not in fact support his contention that "scores" of slaves worked in the gin factory. After a visit to Pratt's gin factory in 1857, Cloud wrote that Pratt employed "many" slaves in the factory, a much less precise term than Starobin's. *American Cotton Planter and Soil of the South*, 1(May 1857): 156. According to the 1852 state property tax assessment, Pratt had 7 slaves working in the gin factory. Since only two years earlier, the census listed the total number of workers in Pratt's gin factory and foundry as 31, the surmise that 22.5 percent of his gin workforce in 1852 was enslaved seems reasonable. Pratt expanded his workforce after his mid-1850s factory enlargement, but even then he likely employed less than a score of slaves. Of course, the assumption that Pratt had a proportional share of Prattville's slave mechanics is speculative, but the resulting assignment of 16 out of 23 slaves to the gin factory and foundry in 1860 is probably not far off the mark. The Prattville shop owners Enoch Robinson, Ephraim Morgan, and James Clepper all were wealthy, slaveowning men, and it is likely that they would have employed at least a few slaves in their own businesses.

49. U.S. Census, Alabama, 1850 and 1860 Slave Schedules, Autauga County; Alabama 1855 State Census, Autauga County; Deed Book DC, 131–33, Probate Office, Autauga County Courthouse.

50. U.S. Census, Alabama, 1850 and 1860 Agricultural Schedules, Autauga County; *American Cotton Planter and Soil of the South* 1 (May 1857): 156.

involving less skill, performed under white supervision. In his brief comments on Pratt's black workforce, Noah Cloud did not specify their type of work, although he did deem their performance "well-skilled."[51] More specific information comes from the journals of Ferdinand and George Smith.

The slave Jim appears to have worked primarily as a planer in the gin factory. In March 1851, George Smith reported that "we [got] a negro fellow to go to work for us. He gets along pretty well." Jim labored much of his time under Ferdinand and George, at least through 1855. In September 1853, for example, Ferdinand reported that he had "started Jim at work on front plank this morning. He took two hundred pieces along to the saw and straightened them." In May 1854, Ferdinand noted that he "had Jim to help me [saw box heads]. He worked two days and [a] half and I three days and we got them all sawed out." Jim labored a total of forty days for Ferdinand in 1852. Like the slaves Cloud noticed in 1857, Jim seems to have been "well-skilled." Only once did Ferdinand or George voice a complaint about him, and that dated from his first year. In September 1851, George grumbled that "Jim made bad work hollowing out the rib boards so I concluded to do it myself."[52]

Charles, the mulatto youth purchased by Pratt from Samuel Griswold in 1843, definitely performed skilled work. In 1855, Pratt placed Ferdinand Smith in charge of the second-floor breasting and finishing department. Ferdinand hired Charles, who was now about twenty-five years old, for $600 and put him to work at "breasting [and] putting on saws and ribs."[53]

Although Pratt successfully used slave labor in his gin factory, it nevertheless presented its own peculiar difficulties. In September 1855, George Smith reported that "Jim ran away this evening." Jim may have resented the treatment to which he was subjected in the factory. Ferdinand Smith recorded in his journal in August 1851 that "Mr. Carrol came into the shop this morning to settle with Jim for some misdemeanor Saturday night. He gave him a few sharp stripes, but I fear not enough, for his benefit in the long run." There was also trouble concerning a slave planer named Joe. On June 23, 1856, George Smith went to Montgomery to get

51. *American Cotton Planter and Soil of the South* 1 (May 1857): 156.

52. Nobles, *Journals of George Littlefield Smith*, 6, 26; Nobles, *Journals of Ferdinand Ellis Smith*, 115, 166, 183.

53. Nobles, *Journals of Ferdinand Ellis Smith*, 199.

Joe released from the jail where he was being held. The next day, the irritated mechanic recorded that he had "got Joe out, in which operation I was bothered considerably."[54]

George Smith had left Pratt's employ and set up a machine shop with Thomas Ormsby by 1860, but white northerners continued to labor in Pratt's gin factory as the Civil War loomed near. Prattville in 1860 claimed fifteen northern-born mechanics, all but one of whom came from a New England state, usually New Hampshire. Another mechanic, William Beckwith, was born in Georgia but had northern parents. If Pratt is assigned a proportional share of northern mechanics, he would have had eleven such workers, or 15 percent of his workforce. Not surprisingly, given the proximity of their nativity, many of these mechanics were related to each other. Particularly extensive were the kin connections among the Smith family. Amos Smith had three nephews, Ferdinand, Frank, and John, who worked as gin mechanics. Daniel Pratt himself had artisanal relatives in town: Ashby Morgan, the husband of Pratt's niece Augusta; Augustus Grayle Morgan, Ashby's younger brother; and Freeman and Lewis Holt, nephews of Daniel Holt, the husband of Daniel Pratt's sister Eliza. Another local mechanic, C. P. Morgan, was likely a brother of Ephraim Morgan. Moreover, most or all of the remaining New England mechanics were probably old acquaintances of other Prattville Yankees.[55]

Judging by the 1860 census, several of Prattvilles northern mechanics earned fairly large incomes. Frank Smith, Ashby Morgan, and John Smith were worth $8,000, $7,700, and $5,000, respectively. Ferdinand

54. Ibid.; Nobles, *Journals of George Littlefield Smith,* 102, 117. Jim had returned, however, by December 1855. Nobles, *Journals of George Littlefield Smith,* 110. Ethelred Carroll, a Virginia-born painter, owned two slaves in 1850. Perhaps, then, Jim belonged to Carroll, not Pratt. U.S. Census, Alabama, 1850 Population Schedule, 1850 Slave Schedule, Autauga County.

55. U.S. Census, Alabama, 1860 and 1900 Population Schedules, Autauga County; Louise Taylor Nelson Boal, *The History of the Smith-Riggs Families* (Prattville, Ala.: by the author, 1990); Cooke, *Genealogy of Daniel Pratt;* Nobles, *Journals of Ferdinand Ellis Smith,* 113; Nobles, *Journals of George Littlefield Smith,* 117; (Prattville) *Autauga Citizen,* 5 October 1854. George Smith gives us an example of how this "New England network" worked in a journal entry from 1851: "About eight o'clock this morning we were agreeably surprised by the arrival here of an old friend of father's, who had worked in the shop with him at Meredith, Mr. Talford Taylor. I showed him around the shop and took him over and introduced him to Mr. Morgan. He concluded to hire him to go to work in the [sash, door, and blind] shop." Nobles, *Journals of George Littlefield Smith,* 14.

Smith did not have a wealth listing, but from his journal it is evident that he was probably the highest-paid mechanic in town. He started working for Pratt in January 1847, contracting for $30 a month. Because he did not work every day in 1847 and 1848, his actual annual pay amounted to $345 and $362.66, respectively. In 1849, his annual pay increased to $451.50. From 1850 to 1853, his salary jumped drastically, to more than $1,000 a year, so that he earned more than twice the average individual wage in 1850. In 1855, Pratt placed Ferdinand in charge of the second-floor breasting and finishing department, increasing his pay accordingly. "Mr. Pratt pays me nine cents per saw," Ferdinand noted. Under his arrangement with Pratt, Ferdinand hired Pratt's slave Charles and employed him "at breasting [and] putting on saws and ribs." Ferdinand now may have earned more than $2,000 a year, matching or even surpassing the gross annual incomes of such prominent Prattvillians as attorney William H. Northington and physician Samuel Parrish Smith.[56]

Amos Smith and his kin became pillars of the Prattville community. Of the Smiths, Shadrack Mims recalled: "This family were remarkable for their steady, quiet, and orderly lives. Honest, industrious, punctual, and economical, they were all successful in business." Even though not all of Prattville's Yankee mechanics did as well as the Smiths, the mean wealth of the northern mechanics with listed wealth in 1860 was $4,480, a significant sum.[57]

Despite the presence of northern-born mechanics in Prattville's factories and shops, most Prattville mechanics in 1860 were actually white southerners, a point worth emphasizing in the face of claims by contemporaries and historians that antebellum white southerners were not a mechanical people. With slaves making up approximately 22 percent of Prattville's mechanics, northerners 15 percent, and foreigners merely 2

56. U.S. Census, Alabama, 1860 Population Schedule, Autauga County; Nobles, *Journals of Ferdinand Ellis Smith,* 1–2, 30, 58, 115, 199; State Property Tax Assessment, Autauga County, 1852. Ferdinand finished 275 gins in the first six months of 1855. If he finished 550 gins for the whole year and these were, on average, fifty-saw gins, then at nine cents per saw and subtracting the $600 he would have paid for the services of Charles for the year, he would have earned $2,150 in 1855. According to the state property tax assessment for 1852, William H. Northington earned an income that year of $1,700, while Samuel Parrish Smith earned $1,600. Less successful professionals such as physicians C. A. Edwards and James Townsend earned only $400 and $500, respectively.

57. Mims, "Autauga County," 265. Most of the Yankee mechanics lodging with the Prattville families had no wealth listing, probably because they were for the most part only temporary residents sending money home.

percent, white southerners accounted for the remaining 61 percent. If Pratt is assigned a proportional share of these men, he would have had 46 gin mechanics who were southerners.

James Clepper, who owned the carriage and wagon shop, was the wealthiest southerner in Prattville engaged in a mechanical occupation. Clepper, a native Tennessean, was worth an impressive $46,000, making him comparable in wealth to Yankees Enoch Robinson and Ephraim Morgan, owners of, respectively, the horse mill and sash, door, and blind shops. James Wainwright of Alabama, the owner of the tin shop, was worth rather less, $8,300, but he solidified his position when he married Daniel Pratt's niece Melissa Holt. Wainwright's wealth compared favorably with that of machine-shop owners Thomas Ormsby and George Smith, who owned property valued at, respectively, $8,000 and $4,000.[58]

The wealthier southern mechanics who worked in Prattville's shops were in roughly the same economic position as George Smith. The six best-off men were Pratt's ward Henry DeBardeleben ($5,000), B. W. Rogers ($5,000), Joshua White ($4,800), Benjamin Gaines ($3,725), Nathan Morris ($3,300), and Asbury Jones ($2,000). Ten other southern mechanics were worth between $1,000 and $1,700, while 12 were worth less than $1,000 but more than $500, and 9 were worth from $100 to $500. Two were worth only $60 each. Twenty-five other men had no wealth listing. The mean wealth of southern-born mechanics with listed wealth in 1860 was slightly more than $1,200, three times the figure for mill operatives. Only one mechanic recorded family members working in the cotton mill, and that was John N. Cook, who was worth $1,500.[59]

Washington Lafayette Ellis became Prattville's most successful southern mechanic in the nineteenth century. "Fate" Ellis (as he was known to his friends) was the son of Elisha and Mary Ellis, who migrated with their family before 1830 from South Carolina to Autauga County, where they farmed in the eastern section. By 1850, they had moved to Prattville, where Elisha worked as a "manufacturer" (probably in the picker room of the cotton mill), and his sons Jacob and Fate worked as mill operatives (likely as spinners). In 1860, the fifty-seven-year-old Elisha worked as a laborer and listed his wealth at $100. Both he and his wife were illiterate.

58. U.S. Census, Alabama, 1860 Population Schedule, Autauga County; Cooke, *Genealogy of Daniel Pratt.*

59. U.S. Census, Alabama, 1860 Population Schedule, Autauga County. The mean wealth of *all* mechanics with listed wealth in 1860 was $1,578.

A fifteen-year-old daughter, Mary, worked as a spinner in the mill. Jacob and Fate now worked as mechanics in the gin factory, however, and were worth $500 and $1,000, respectively. By 1870, their younger brother Abram had joined them in the gin factory. While his brothers did fairly well for themselves, Fate, a highly skilled mechanic, patented several important improvements in the cotton gin in the 1880s. After the Civil War, he became superintendent of the frame and brush department, a member of the town council, vice-president of the Prattville Cotton Mill and Banking Company, and last but not least, mayor of Prattville. Without doubt, Shadrack Mims found this native son as worthy of emulation as the various Smiths from New England. Ellis, Mims recalled in the 1880s, was "a Southern boy raised in the Ginshop" who "made money, and has raised and educated a respectable family besides taking care of an aged father and mother."[60]

William Ward and William Jones also had sons "raised in the gin shop." William Ward and his family migrated from South Carolina to Georgia in the 1830s and from Georgia to Alabama in the 1840s. By 1850, the family had moved to Prattville. Disaster quickly ensued, with both William and his son Milton dying that same year, leaving behind William's widow, Patience, and their remaining six children. In 1850, four sons worked as "manufacturers." In 1860, Robert Ward and Isaac Ward were respectively employed as a gin painter and an iron moulder. The latter brother married Nancy Ellis, a sister of Fate Ellis, while the former wed mill girl Frances Hoyle. George Ward worked as an overseer in the cotton mill. He married Clementine Houston, who, like Nancy Ellis, came from one of the more prominent mill families. All three sons had done well for themselves, judging by their 1860 wealth listings, which were $1,200 for Robert and $1,000 each for George and Isaac.[61]

William Jones, a native South Carolinian and Prattville miller worth

60. U.S. Census, Alabama, 1830, 1850, and 1860 Population Schedules, Autauga County; Tarrant, ed. *Hon. Daniel Pratt,* 17, 96; Charles A. Bennett, *Saw and Toothed Cotton Ginning Developments* (Dallas: Texas Cotton Growers Association, n.d.), 42–43; *Memorial Record of Alabama . . . Together with the Personal Memoirs of Many of Its People* (Madison, Wis.: Brant & Fuller, 1893), 1: 350; *Prattville Progress,* 11 September 1903; Mims, "Autauga County," 266.

61. U.S. Manuscript Census, Alabama, 1850 and 1860 Population Schedules, Autauga County; *Alabama Mortality Scheudle 1850, Seventh Census of the United States, . . . Persons Who Had Died during the Year Ending June 30, 1850,* compiled by Marilyn Davis Hahn (Easley, S.C.: Southern Historical Press, 1983), 1.

$1,000 in 1850, had three sons who probably worked for Pratt in that year: Asbury, an iron moulder; William, a machinist; and Joseph, a looms overseer. In 1860, Asbury Jones was a mechanic worth $2,900. A younger brother named Henry, who lived in Asbury's household, was also a mechanic. Joseph Jones had become the boss of the wool mill. William Jones Jr. died around 1856, however, leaving a widow, Isabella, and two small daughters, Ida and Calista. In 1860, thirty-one-year-old Isabella worked in the cotton mill (one of the few mothers in Prattville to do so) and was worth $200.[62]

Most Prattville mechanics, whether southern or northern, fared well in terms of wealth compared to Prattville's mill operatives. Already in 1850, the gin-factory mechanics received significantly higher pay than their counterparts in the textile factory, and the disparity only increased over the course of the decade. From 1850 to 1860, the average yearly wage for Pratt's mechanics increased sharply, by about 60 percent, about three times the wage increase of mill workers.[63]

Unlike mill-operative households, which usually consisted of a middle-aged parent or parents and a large number of children, gin-mechanic households tended to consist of younger, more recently married parents and smaller numbers of children. This disparity in family size makes the disparity in wealth even more significant. Simply put, gin mechanics supported smaller families with larger salaries. Thirty-five-year-old Samuel Patillo, for example, was worth $1,500 in 1860 and had a wife and two daughters. John Wesley Glass, only twenty-two, was worth $1,000 and had a wife and an infant son. Both Patillo and Glass contrast sharply with Thomas Hale, a fifty-six-year-old butcher worth $400 with a wife and seven children to support. His four oldest daughters worked in the cotton mill, and his older son was employed as a laborer. Even with six wage-earners in the family, the Hale household was considerably less well off than those of Glass and Patillo.[64]

At first glance, the wages of Prattville mechanics appear low by the national standard, but to draw this conclusion would be an error. Highly skilled workers in the North earned as much as $12.00 a week during the 1850s. If we divide the average monthly wage of Pratt's gin and foundry

62. U.S. Census, Alabama, 1850 and 1860 Population Schedules, Autauga County.

63. U.S. Census, Alabama, 1860 Manufactures Schedule, Autauga County. Prattville's rising wage disparity in the 1850s between skilled and unskilled workers mirrored national trends. See Taylor, *Transportation Revolution*, 294–95.

64. U.S. Census, Alabama, 1860 Population Schedule, Autauga County.

workers in 1850 by the number of employees, we get $25.00, or about $6.25 a week. Wages rose substantially over the decade, however. In 1860, Pratt's gin and foundry workers received an average weekly wage of $10.13, a large increase over 1850. While these Prattville wages seem low when compared to northern wages, we must remember that the census enumerator only gave the total number of employees in Pratt's factory and foundry without distinguishing between slaves and free men. This omission depresses the average individual wage figure since the total average monthly wage must be divided by the *total* number of workers, black and white; and slaves did not receive wages, except for overwork (and even yearly overwork received by a slave would have been much smaller than a white mechanic's salary). If 7 slaves are excluded from the 1850 workforce, the average individual weekly wage increases to $8.07 ($387.50 a year, or $32.29 a month). Similarly, if 16 slaves are excluded from the 1860 workforce, the average individual wage increases to $12.93 ($620.68 a year, or $51.72 a month). It would seem, then, that the average wage of Pratt's gin workers was very high by 1860. Moreover, these workers also enjoyed low-cost rental housing.[65]

Prattville's wealthier mechanics probably owned their own homes, but most surely rented houses from Pratt, just as most (perhaps all) operatives did. Judging from a memo book for the years 1852 to 1854, Pratt continued to charge many of his workers nominal rents. For example, John Hearn paid Pratt $75 a year, while James Tunnell paid only $36, and William Healy paid the very modest sum of $24. For men who likely made between $400 and $600 a year in the early 1850s, these rents probably consumed from 5 percent to, at most, 20 percent of their annual incomes. Less fortunate workers around the nation sometimes paid nearly a third of their income in rent.[66]

The estate settlements of Thomas Ormsby and another mechanic, James R. Glass, provide us a closer glimpse of the economic positions of two Prattville mechanics who occupied opposite positions on the economic scale. Ormsby, a Pratt mechanic (and relative) who became a shop owner in the 1850s, died in a skirmish outside Corinth, Mississippi, in 1862, leaving an estate valued at more than $8,400. His estate inventory

65. Taylor, *Transportation Revolution,* 296–97.
66. Pratt Memo Book No. 2, Microfilm, Box 1, Reel 180-C, McMillan Collection; Taylor, *Transportation Revolution,* 296. Gin painter Ethelred Carrol paid higher rents in 1853 and 1854 ($120 and $125), but the house he rented was a fine structure, later purchased by George Smith. See note 67.

included his $2,500 house and lot, as well as two house slaves valued at $1,050. Ormsby also had two shares of stock in the cotton mill worth $2,000, $750 in cash, $1,500 in notes, and eighty acres of land worth $28.20. In addition, he owned a $75 buggy, a $20 Colt pistol, and four bottles of brandy worth $16. Before his death, he had furnished his house with a sofa, eleven parlor chairs, a rocking chair, a carpet rug, a Mexican blanket, a pair of brass andirons, two looking glasses, four framed pictures, four window curtains, five bedsteads, two washstands, a dining table, a pine table, a desk, a United States map, and a bookcase with ninety books. The inventory did not include the value of Ormsby's interest in the machine shop that he and George Smith leased.[67]

James R. Glass left a far humbler estate after his death in 1856. Glass and his wife, Theodosia Pratt (no relation to Daniel), had moved in 1854 from adjacent Bibb County to Prattville, where Glass worked for Pratt and rented a house. After his death, his administrator valued his estate at $409.41. By the time the estate was finally settled in 1858, only $83.51 remained to be turned over to Theodosia.[68]

Although not generally as wealthy as the elite of the Yankee mechanics, southern mechanics such as James R. Glass formed the essential backbone of the gin factory in the 1850s. Surviving records show that mechanics had a much lower attrition rate than Pratt's mill operatives, with whom rapid turnover was a problem. Twenty-one of Prattville's approximately 82 white mechanics, or almost 26 percent, are traceable in Prattville over a ten-year period, from 1860 back to 1850. Fully 19 of them were southerners.[69]

Ten of Prattville's 1860 mechanics who were not present in the town

67. Reports and Wills, Book RL 12, 1862, 330–32, Probate Office, Autauga County Courthouse. Like Ormsby, George Smith was a homeowner, having purchased a house that he called "Mulberry Cottage." This house was a handsome Greek-Revival structure of one and one-half stories with a central hall and six rooms. Nobles, *Journals of George Littlefield Smith*, 89; *Birmingham News/Age Herald*, 2 June 1935. Ferdinand Smith purchased a two-story house in 1854 worth $2,400. Nobles, *Journals of Ferdinand Ellis Smith*, 184.

68. Reports and Wills, Book RB 10, 1858, 235–37, Probate Office, Autauga County Courthouse; Church Register. A few mechanics owned clocks or watches in 1852, including Ashby Morgan (silver watch), George Perlette (gold watch), Harris Ware (clock), and Marcus Cicero Killet (clock). More mechanics, however, gave no such listings. Shop owners did much better in this regard. Western Franks owned a silver watch and a clock, while George Tisdale owned a gold watch and a clock. State Property Tax Assessment, Autauga County, 1852.

69. U.S. Census, Alabama, 1850 and 1860 Population Schedules, Autauga County.

in 1850 appeared there as early as 1854, for their names are on a petition published that year in the (Prattville) *Autauga Citizen*. Four of these men were Yankees, but the other six all came from southern states. Moreover, two of the petitioners had sons who worked for Pratt in 1860. When these four sons and the ten 1854 petitioners themselves are added to the 21 mechanics who had lived in Prattville since at least 1850, we have 35 mechanics (43 percent of all Prattville's white mechanics in 1860) who persisted in Prattville for at least a six-year period. Significantly, fully 29 of the 35 men came from the South. Many, perhaps most, of these mechanics worked for Pratt. It would seem that Pratt did not have trouble finding and keeping a white skilled-labor force in Alabama in spite of the problems he had building a stable corps of operatives for his cotton mill. Thus, when Pratt expanded his gin factory in 1855, he found himself under no great pressure to bring down more northerners or to buy more slaves.[70]

With slave mechanics liable to attempt flight, one essential task performed exclusively by white mechanics was gin repair. Although traveling agents fixed gins too, Pratt mechanics made many repair trips themselves. Amos Smith, his son George, and his nephews Ferdinand and Frank all undertook such missions at one time or another. Typically, the Smiths made local trips, either in Autauga or to such neighboring counties as Lowndes and Montgomery. On October 2–3, 1851, for example, George Smith reported that he and his father had traveled "down to the lower part of the county to fix two gins belonging to Messrs. Hall and Chappel." Setting out at 11:00 A.M. down the Indian Hill Road, the pair reached Autaugaville at 2:00 P.M., where they stopped to tour the new cotton mill. Taking the Selma Road out of Autaugaville, they arrived at Hall's plantation "about night." Hall put the father and son up and provided them "a good supper." The next morning, they "went to work on [Hall's] gin," succeeding by 9:00 A.M. "in making it perform to suit him." The Smiths then set off for Chappel's plantation, "a mile or two" away. Upon reaching it, they "took dinner," then fixed Chappel's gin. Leaving at 2:00 P.M., they finally made it home at 8:30 P.M., "tired enough." George complained that "the roads were extremely dry and dusty making it very unpleasant traveling."[71]

70. (Prattville) *Autauga Citizen*, 5 October 1854; U.S. Census, Alabama, 1850 Population Schedule, Coosa County, 1850 and 1860, Population Schedules, Autauga County.

71. Nobles, *Journals of George Littlefield Smith*, 27–28.

The Smiths on occasion went farther afield in Alabama, traveling down the Alabama River and up the Tombigbee to various Black Belt counties. In 1848, Ferdinand and his uncle Amos also made an unusual two-day overland trip to Talladega County (northeast of Autauga), of which Ferdinand left a fairly detailed record. He and his uncle set out on October 18. They reached Talladega on October 20 but missed their road and got lost for two hours. Finally, they found the plantation of Oliver Welch, fixed his gin, and spent a pleasant night at his house. Ferdinand found Welch, a large planter and prominent Baptist minister and educator, a "very intelligent and well informed" host. The Smiths spent the next day repairing the gins of two other customers and finally left for home on October 22. They "found the roads very rough," obliging them "to travel after dark about four hours before we could find a place of entertainment and that was a miserable log cabin, but we were glad to get that." In the morning, however, the pair "had some excellent venison for breakfast," which they "devoured with a degree of satisfaction." They reached Wetumpka in the afternoon, where they visited the new state penitentiary and a political forum at Coosa Hall. Spending the night at Wetumpka, they finally reached Prattville on October 24, ending a week-long journey.[72]

As if such Alabama trips were not arduous enough, the Smiths made several expeditions to southwestern states as well. On June 6, 1853, Ferdinand Smith noted that George Smith had left on a two-month trip to the Shreveport, Louisiana, area. George did not actually return until August 20. Ferdinand attributed George's delay to "sickness in Arkansas at two of the places where [he] had gins to fix." In March and April of the same year, Frank Smith made trips to New Orleans and Columbus, Mississippi, to work on Parkhurst gins stored at local warehouses. Frank spent three weeks at Pratt's New Orleans warehouse on Notre Dame Street before returning to Mobile by steamboat on April 14. From Mobile, he traveled up the Tombigbee to Columbus, Mississippi, where he "commenced to alter two P. Gins in Lange Warehouse." The next day, April 19, he took the stage to Selma, Alabama, arriving in that city on April 21. At Selma, he boarded the steamboat "Messenger," which reached Washington Landing later in the day.[73]

---

72. Nobles, *Journals of Ferdinand Ellis Smith*, 23–24; E. Grace Jemison, *Historic Tales of Talladega* (Montgomery, Ala.: Paragon Press, 1959), 269.

73. Nobles, *Journals of Ferdinand Ellis Smith*, 158, 164; "Journal of Benjamin Franklin Smith."

Pratt himself occasionally made a repair trip in the 1850s. On September 17, 1853, George Smith wrote that "Father and Mr. Pratt started this morning on a tour fixing gins. Father is going out on the Bigby and Mr. Pratt down in some of the counties south of the Alabama River." Perhaps by this time, Pratt and Smith (who was two years older than Pratt) were not up to the physical strain of such trips. Both men returned home sick.[74]

Daniel Pratt could well have sometimes been exhausted during the 1850s, for his efforts in that decade had been herculean. By 1861, he had positioned himself as the largest gin manufacturer in the world, a colossus of the cotton-growing region. Moreover, Daniel Pratt and Company served as the economic cornerstone of Prattville. It gave Pratt wealth and prestige, which he in turn expended lavishly in a campaign to industrialize the South. Perhaps Pratt's boldest move in this campaign was the launching of a cotton mill in Prattville.

74. Nobles, *Journals of George Littlefield Smith*, 106–6.

3

Manufacturing Textiles: 1846–1861

By the mid-1840s, Daniel Pratt had established himself as an equal in the cotton-gin world to his mentor Samuel Griswold. But in 1846, he did something that Griswold never attempted: he established a textile factory. In the fifteen years from the incorporation of Prattville Manufacturing Company (PMC) to the outbreak of the Civil War, Pratt became one of the guiding lights of the cotton-mill movement in the antebellum South. Somewhat ironically, Pratt, the world's greatest cotton-gin maker, has received much more attention from historians as a manufacturer of cotton textiles. Yet Pratt's accomplishments as a textile manufacturer admittedly are impressive. The cotton mill he started soon became one of the most important in Alabama. Moreover, Prattville's mill had heavy symbolic import, for it demonstrated that a factory with a workforce composed primarily of unskilled white southerners could achieve great success.

The prolonged agricultural depression that followed the panic of 1837 rekindled interest in the textile industry throughout the South, including Alabama. Prior to the 1840s, Alabama had only two major cotton mills, but by 1850, the number had increased to twelve. Prattville claimed the largest mill, and the owners of another mill, Autauga Manufacturing

Company, located only fourteen miles west of Prattville at Autaugaville, modeled their operation after Pratt's.[1]

Given the economic conditions of the 1840s, Pratt probably found it potentially more lucrative to invest in a cotton mill than to undertake a more rapid expansion of his gin business. His motivation for starting PMC, then, may not have been so altruistic as his contemporaries often claimed. Nevertheless, Pratt's writings make clear that he sincerely viewed the development of the textile industry as necessary for the South's economic salvation. The Yankee industrialist hoped PMC would serve as inspiration for fellow Alabama citizens.

The Alabama legislature incorporated PMC on January 13, 1846. PMC had three incorporators: Daniel Pratt, James Allen, and Jesse Perham. Allen, born in upstate New York around 1798, served in 1847 and 1848 as the mill superintendent, but in this capacity he proved a failure. After leaving this job, he became a successful Prattville merchant, passing on his business to his two sons when he returned to New York in the 1850s.[2]

Jesse Perham made a more important contribution to the textile factory, but he left Prattville not long after PMC began operating. Perham served in 1846 as PMC's first superintendent. Yet another New Hampshirite, Perham had been employed in Prattville in 1845 both as a machinist in the gin factory and as minister of the Methodist church. As a public speaker, he was considered something of a spellbinder. One Prattvillian recalled him as "a true orator, having as a revivalist . . . no superior." In the 1850s, the silver-tongued Perham entered politics, becoming a popular stump speaker for the Know-Nothing Party. Sympathetic newspapers carried long excerpts from his speeches on economic issues. Selma news-

1. On the resurgence of southern interest in the textile industry during the 1840s, see Robert Royal Russel, *Economic Aspects of Southern Sectionalism, 1840–1861* (Urbana: University of Illinois Press, 1924), chap. 2; Patrick J. Hearden, *Independence and Empire: The New South's Cotton Mill Campaign, 1865–1901* (DeKalb: Northern Illinois University Press, 1982), chap. 1. On specific states, see Brent D. Glass, *The Textile Industry in North Carolina: A History* (Raleigh: Division of Archives and History, North Carolina Department of Cultural Resources, 1992), 1–23; Ernest McPherson Lander Jr., *The Textile Industry in Antebellum South Carolina* (Baton Rouge: Louisiana State University Press, 1969), pass.; Miller, *Cotton Mill Movement* (Alabama), pass.; Moore, *Emergence of the Cotton Kingdom* (Mississippi), 220–31.

2. *Acts . . . of the General Assembly of the State of Alabama* (1846), 22–23. On the Allen family, see the William C. Allen Papers, Southern Historical Collection, University of North Carolina, Chapel Hill.

paper editor John Hardy, a political ally of Pratt from these years, viewed Perham as a very able debater and "a whole-souled, clever fellow."[3]

This restless, talented man, like Pratt possessed with great entrepreneurial zeal, soon sought other fields to conquer. In 1848, he established, with the help of several wealthy planters in Autauga and Lowndes Counties, Autauga Manufacturing Company in nearby Autaugaville. The factory had not even gotten off the ground, however, when Perham moved to Selma in 1849 and started the Alabama Manufacturing Company, "the first manufacturing establishment of any consequence in the city." Perham superintended the factory, which did "casting and all kinds of foundry and machine work," for several years. He also acted as an agent for the Alabama and Tennessee River Railroad, collecting subscriptions and attending railroad conventions. Despite his successes in Selma, Perham moved, probably in 1853, to the nearby village of Plantersville and started a sash, door, and blind factory. In 1857, he traveled much farther west, settling in Texas, where he bred mustangs. Here he remained until his untimely death in his early fifties in 1867.[4]

In contrast to Allen and Perham, Shadrack Mims, whom Pratt hired as the company agent in 1845, proved a durable figure in Prattville. Mims labored at this post for fifteen years, returning for a short stint at the end of the Civil War. In this capacity, Mims had a wide range of essential tasks to perform. Cotton-mill agents, explains historian Jonathan Prude, "were responsible for determining production schedules, for maintaining adequate stocks of raw materials and adequate numbers of operatives, for supervising shipments of finished products and for helping to shape and promulgate the'rules and regulations' of their establishments."[5]

Shadrack Mims stood out from his business associates even more significantly in being a native southerner, born in Lincoln County, Georgia, in 1804. Orphaned at a young age, Mims moved in 1820 from Georgia

3. Mims, "History of Prattville," 32–33; Miller, *Cotton Mill Movement*, 60; (Selma) *Alabama State Sentinel*, 19 May, 10 July 1855; John Hardy, *Selma: Her Institutions and Her Men* (Selma, Ala.: Times Book and Job Office, 1879), 108.

4. Hardy, *Selma*, 114; Miller, *Cotton Mill Movement*, 79–80; *De Bow's Review* 12 (March 1852): 306–8; (Selma) *Alabama State Sentinel*, 24 April 1855; (Montgomery) *Alabama State Sentinel*, 21 July 1867; Adelaide Smith to Mary Smith, 13 September 1867, ACHC. The Alabama Manufacturing Company operated until 1862, doing "a flourishing and a profitable business," when it became the nucleus of the Confederate Naval Foundry of Selma. Hardy, *Selma*, 114.

5. Jonathan Prude, *The Coming of Industrial Order: Town and Factory Life in Rural Massachusetts, 1810–1860* (New York: Cambridge University Press, 1983), 78.

to Autauga County, Alabama, to live with his older brother and guardian, Seaborn, who had settled in the Alabama River town of Vernon a year earlier. After operating a mercantile business in Vernon from 1825 to 1835, Mims engaged for the next ten years "in farming, warehousing and ferrying on the Alabama River." In 1845, he sold his Vernon interests, contemplating a move to Texas. After visiting Pratt, however, Mims accepted the post of agent and moved with his family to Prattville. A devout Methodist, Mims recalled that in making his decision, he had been swayed by Pratt's determination "to build a manufacturing village . . . so as to give employment to as many people as he could," with "a special eye to the moral and religious condition of the people."[6]

Pratt, Allen, Perham, and Mims were all shareholders in PMC, which was capitalized at $110,000 with 110 shares valued at $1,000 apiece. Pratt owned the largest number of shares, 31, while the Ticknor brothers, Samuel and Simon, each claimed 17 shares. Together, Allen, Perham, and Mims had 14 shares, while three Autauga planters—Organ Tatum, William D. Smith, and Lewis Whetstone—held 15, 10, and 6 shares, respectively. While the number of shares owned by planters, 31, was by no means insignificant, Pratt and his business associates clearly dominated the company. Because the gin factory gave Pratt a secure financial base, he did not need such a great infusion of planter capital for his cotton mill that he lost effective control of the business.[7]

Pratt cemented his power with PMC's articles of incorporation, under which PMC had the "power to appoint and prescribe the names and respective duties of its officers," as well as to "adopt such a constitution and bylaws for its own government as its members may deem proper, not

6. Mims, "History of the M. E. Church."

7. *Alabama Supreme Court Records* 208 (1857): 40–44. Tatum, Smith, and Whetstone were all large slaveholders, owning, respectively, 70, 40, and 43 slaves in 1850. U.S. Census, Alabama, 1850 Slave Schedule, Autauga County. Randall Miller notes that "no large industrial sector, such as emerged in New England, arose in Alabama to challenge the agrarian social order." Alabama's textile factories, he argues, thus depended on planter capital; and dependence required that the textile manufacturer "bend the knee before the altar of agriculture and slavery, or risk the loss of planter patronage and sanction." Miller, *Cotton Mill Movement,* 101. Miller's argument does not hold for Pratt, though it is true that some southern textile magnates, such as William Gregg of South Carolina and Henry Merrell of Georgia, occasionally felt stymied by their shareholders. See Broadus Mitchell, *William Gregg: Factory Master of the Old South* (Chapel Hill: University of North Carolina, 1928); Henry Merrell, *The Autobiography of Henry Merrell: Industrial Missionary to the South,* edited by James L. Skinner III (Athens: University of Georgia Press, 1991).

inconsistent with or repugnant to the Constitution of the United States, and of the State of Alabama." Taking advantage of the liberal articles of incorporation, the shareholders adopted a constitution that placed great power into the hands of the directorate. Each shareholder received one vote per share. Every year, the shareholders were to gather to elect five "managers" from among themselves. The "board of managers" would, in turn, choose a president and a secretary. The board had extremely broad discretion in the governance of the corporation. Shareholders not on the board had no role to play in corporate business except that of providing "counsel and advice." Such a constitution could easily lead to dissatisfaction among minority shareholders, as it in fact did with planter William D. Smith.[8]

Incorporation on paper did not make Prattville Manufacturing Company a reality; much remained to be done before the factory could begin production. Pratt appears to have completed the construction of dwellings for mill operatives in May 1846, debiting $50.40 for "weatherboarding on new houses." Three months later, PMC debited the cost of hauling two thousand pounds of cotton yarn for sale in Montgomery. Pratt had much bigger plans for his factory, however. In September, he told the readers of De Bow's Review: "[I] am just now putting a Cotton Factory in operation expressly for the purpose of making heavy cotton Osnaburg for plantation use—so that I flatter myself that by the first of October next, I will be able to not only furnish the cotton planter with gin stands, but cotton Osnaburg of as good a quality, and as cheap as they can be procured elsewhere." In October, Pratt traveled to Boston, where he contracted for $40,000 to have machinery for the manufacture of osnaburg sent to Prattville. The next month, PMC made its first cotton cloth, which it again sold in Montgomery.[9]

Despite this successful start, difficulties set in, forcing the mill to remain idle for most of 1847. Shadrack Mims complained that the problem lay with a "want of capacity in the superintendent to manage the establishment." Finally, on January 30, 1848, a small shipment of osnaburg arrived in Mobile aboard the steamboat *Montgomery*. A Mobile newspaper, the *Alabama Planter*, approvingly noted the event as "some of the

8. Acts . . . of the General Assembly of the State of Alabama (1846), 22–23; *Alabama Supreme Court Records*, 208: 40–44. The articles of incorporation, which permitted PMC to hold up to $300,000 worth of property, remained in force until 1876.

9. Daybook (1839–1846), 248, 256, 262, 266; *De Bow's Review* 3 (September 1846): 137–53.

first fruits of our domestic manufactures." The paper added that this shipment was "a small beginning, but ten years hence, with the present progressive disposition of our citizens, it may be of some interest to look back and see how and when the start began in Alabama. The advent of these ten bales [of osnaburg] is, therefore, worth recording."[10]

Notwithstanding the optimistic pronouncements in *De Bow's Review* and the *Alabama Planter,* Pratt faced more serious difficulties in his textile operation. Under Allen's tenure, production again broke down in the summer of 1848. Perham being involved with his own mill project in Autaugaville, Pratt found himself with no one capable of managing the day-to-day operations of the factory. As production ground to a halt, Pratt headed north to New England to find a new mill boss. After stopping in New York to consult his textile factor about osnaburg sales, Pratt continued to Providence, Rhode Island, where he succeeded in obtaining a well-qualified superintendent, Gardner Hale. Pratt also took on Hale's eighteen-year-old son, Jeremiah, placing him in charge of the mill's carding room.[11]

Pratt seemed confident that Hale would get the mill moving again. Back in New York, he wrote Shadrack Mims, informing him of his "regret that the weaving is getting [on] so badly" but assuring him that the weavers would "have work enough" once Gardner Hale arrived in Prattville later that year.[12] Pratt's faith in Hale was well placed. Mill performance improved vastly in the 1850s under Hale's guidance, with the result that PMC became one of Alabama's most successful cotton factories. Hale would stay at PMC until after the Civil War, retiring around 1866.

Like Daniel Pratt, Gardner Hale, who was born in Swansea, Massachusetts, in 1809, married into a New England family of some prominence. Hale's wife, Ann Susan Ballou, of Cumberland, Rhode Island, was a relative of Adin Ballou, the well-known nineteenth-century Universalist minister, spiritualist, and founder of the utopian Christian community of Hopedale. Adin Ballou, who knew the Hale family well, related that Gardner Hale was "a superior man in his sphere of life," possessing "eminent skill, judgment, and moral integrity." Ann he viewed as "the flower of [her father's] offspring" and a "superior woman" possessing "an ad-

10. Mims, "History of Prattville," 26 (Mobile) *Alabama Planter,* 31 January 1848.

11. Mims, "History of Prattville," 26; Daniel Pratt to Shadrack Mims, 13 September 1848, Folder 44, Pratt Papers, ADAH.

12. Daniel Pratt to Shadrack Mims, 26 September 1848, Folder 44, Pratt Papers, ADAH.

mirable physical and mental constitution." Ballou judged their son Jeremiah "intelligent" and "enterprising." Other, younger members of the Hale family, including daughter Susan Frances, also would make good names for themselves in Prattville in the 1850s and 1860s.[13]

Upon arriving in Prattville, Gardner Hale faced the pressing task of instructing the operatives in the fundamentals of cotton manufacture, for these had not taken root under Allen's tenure. Shadrack Mims recalled that the mill hands had been "brought up from the piney woods, many of them with no sort of training to any kind of labor; and in learning many mistakes and blunders were made fatal to success." Hale quickly turned things around, however. By May 1849, Mims was able to write Pratt that operations at the mill were proceeding "smoothly so far as I can learn. Mr. Hale thinks from present prospects that he will consume 100 bales of cotton this month."[14]

Although Gardner Hale got mill production going again, he could not help Pratt with another challenge that the factory faced. The textile operation required more funds than the stock subscriptions provided, in part because some of the shareholders had failed to pay in full for their shares. PMC commenced business in 1846 with paid-in capital of $92,195, from which it purchased machinery and erected buildings. To raise the additional money needed, Pratt found it necessary in 1848 to borrow $20,000 from his partner in the New Orleans commission house, H. Kendall Carter. With the help of Carter's loan, Pratt escaped from what a friend termed "a tight place."[15]

Pratt also had to withstand the onslaught of northern competitors, who consistently undercut the prices charged by PMC and other southern cotton mills. Many Alabama merchants believed that the prices charged by southern manufacturers should have been lower than those charged by their northern counterparts since southern manufacturers

13. Adin Ballou, *An Elaborate History and Genealogy of the Ballous in America* (Providence, R.I.: E. L. Freeman & Son, 1888), 478–79, 1019–20. Jeremiah Hale returned to Massachusetts in 1851 after the deaths in Prattville of his young wife and two infant children.

14. Mims, "History of Prattville," 26; Shadrack Mims to Daniel Pratt, 15 May 1849, Folder 44, Pratt Papers, ADAH.

15. George Cooke to Daniel Pratt, 14 February, 15 May, 19 May, 9 June 1848, Folder 44, Pratt Papers, ADAH; *Smith v. Prattville Manufacturing Company, Alabama Reports,* 29: 503–5; *Tuscumbia North Alabamian,* 24 March 1848. Court records indicate that profits from PMC were applied to the balances due on stock owned by Organ Tatum, Lewis Whetstone, and Shadrack Mims. These balances were $1,014.22, $780.45, and $100.00, respectively, but the applicable date is not given. *Alabama Supreme Court Records,* 208: 28.

had, as Pratt admitted, the advantage of "having the raw material at our door." Pratt rejected this reasoning, however, insisting that "experience has proved that we cannot at present manufacture cotton goods as low here as they can in the Eastern States." Southern factories, he noted, had to purchase their machinery in the North, paying freight and expenses, as well as hire badly needed Yankee superintendents and machinists "at high prices" to lure them south. Moreover, southern operatives were "generally inexperienced, requiring two of them to do the labor of one experienced hand." He insisted, nevertheless, that southern manufacturers "make better goods because we work better stock," and he urged Alabama merchants to patronize Alabama factories to "give new life to our manufacturing business."[16]

Between June and October 1849, the price of raw cotton rose sharply, from seven cents to eleven cents per pound. In October, an angry Mobile merchant wrote the *Mobile Tribune* charging Alabama manufacturers with speculating on the price of cotton and warning that, their state loyalty notwithstanding, Alabama merchants would not suffer such unjust treatment. Pratt fired back, insisting in a letter to the *Mobile Herald* that Alabama manufacturers were, in fact, still selling osnaburg at nine cents per yard—the same price they charged before the rise in cotton. He warned, however, that "should the price of cotton continue as it now is the price of heavy goods must rise," for Alabama manufacturers had to be allowed "to make a living profit."[17]

Because New Orleans offered a larger market and better credit facilities, and perhaps because of his difficulties with Alabama buyers, Pratt favored New Orleans over Mobile in marketing his cloth. In New Orleans, he sold textiles through the commission houses Green and Hazard and H. Kendall Carter and Company. A strong demand for Pratt's goods existed in this city at the time PMC began operations. In February 1848, a friend of Pratt wrote him that both commission houses could not keep up with the demand for PMC cloth. H. Kendall Carter "could have sold

16. *Montgomery Tri-Weekly Flag and Advertiser,* 12 April, 2 December 1848; *Wetumpka Daily State Guard,* 29 October 1849, reprinted from the *Mobile Herald;* George Cooke to Daniel Pratt, 14 February, 9 June 1848, Folder 44, Pratt Papers, ADAH. On the challenge northern competition offered southern textile factories, see Russel, *Economic Aspects of Southern Sectionalism,* 62–63. On the problems of Alabama textile companies, see Miller, *Cotton Mill Movement,* chap. 5.

17. *Wetumpka Daily State Guard,* 29 October 1849, reprinted from the *Mobile Herald;* Russel, *Economic Aspects of Southern Sectionalism,* 60.

nine bales on Saturday for cash," the friend emphasized. Not surprisingly, Pratt soon increased the flow of his textiles to New Orleans, and he noted in 1849 that "I have ten times the interest in New Orleans that I have in Mobile." In 1854, PMC listed among its current assets almost $45,000 in notes and drafts held for collection by H. Kendall Carter and Company and Green and Hazard. Together, these sums accounted for about 45 percent of PMC's current assets.[18]

Pratt also marketed textiles in New York. In November 1848, for example, he sold one hundred bales of osnaburg there. His motive was to capitalize on New York's superior credit facilities. In 1849, he noted that "I am often asked the question, why Southern manufacturers ship their goods to New York." The answer, he declared, was "obvious." The textile manufacturer had to pay cash for "every article he uses," but, at the same time, he found himself "obliged to sell his goods on six months credit." In New York, with its strong financial institutions, a manufacturer could, as soon as a commission firm had sold his goods, "draw for at least three-fourths of their value." Moreover, southern merchants could go to New York and "purchase the same goods on twelve months' credit by paying from four to six months' interest." Pratt noted that if Alabama had the same credit arrangements, "we should not be so dependent on New York merchants."[19]

Despite the challenges offered by northern factories and southern markets, PMC prospered in the 1850s. Already by 1850, it had become the largest textile factory in Alabama, employing 136 workers (63 males and 73 females). The factory consumed 1,000 bales of cotton, valued at $50,000, worked 2,800 spindles and 100 looms, and produced 540,000 yards of osnaburg (worth $54,000) and 324,000 yards of sheeting (worth $30,780). PMC was the second most productive major mill in Alabama, with the value of its output at $623 per worker.[20]

18. George Cooke to Daniel Pratt, 14 February, 19 May 1848, Folder 44, Pratt Papers; ADAH; *Montgomery Tri-Weekly Flag and Advertiser,* 12 April 1849; *Alabama Supreme Court Records,* 208: 30–35, 45. In July 1854, Green and Hazard failed. It had sold a large quantity of Pratt's cloth on credit and was unable to collect the money due. Green and Hazard failed owing PMC $20,007, but under a January 1855 settlement engineered by Shadrack Mims, PMC managed to collect only half this amount.

19. *Montgomery Tri-Weekly Flag and Advertiser,* 31 March 1849.

20. U.S. Census, Alabama, 1850 Manufactures Schedule, Autauga County. PMC also produced a small amount of thread called "spun truck." Henry Tally Crumpton, a Washington resident, peddled PMC thread in Autauga County. After moving to Wilcox County in 1851, he opened a small store, where he continued to sell thread. In October 1854, PMC

PMC's productive workers received good wages by southern standards. The average yearly wage of a PMC worker in 1850 was $147.61, a figure $30 higher than the average for six southern states (Alabama, Georgia, North Carolina, South Carolina, Tennessee, and Virginia). PMC's wages, however, did lag considerably behind the averages for Massachusetts ($199) and the United States ($167).[21]

In 1851, James De Bow wrote with great enthusiasm about Prattville's cotton mill. The building consisted of a large structure of two wooden stories over a brick basement, 150 feet long by 36 feet wide, with smaller wood and brick wings. Pratt had provided the operatives' families with "good houses, neatly painted and of uniform size." De Bow noted approvingly that Pratt had "strictly guarded against" intemperance. In every town deed, Pratt required the insertion of a clause forbidding the sale of "ardent spirits" under the penalty of forfeiture, and the state legislature at his urging had prohibited the sale of liquor within two miles of Prattville.[22]

Prattville closely resembled the model for southern mill towns that William Gregg, founder of the celebrated mill town of Graniteville, South Carolina, presented in 1844 in his influential *Essays on Domestic Industry*. In these essays, Gregg had advocated the development of small factory towns as means of providing useful employment for the South's poor whites. One historian has argued that "Alabama's demographic, economic and social climate in the 1840s" made the Gregg-Pratt model of "industrial urbanism" virtually inevitable in Alabama. Planters' fear that the employment of whites in cotton mills might result in a powerful urban working class required such "social control techniques" as keeping mill towns small, maintaining factory ownership of town lots, and enforcing temperance. This argument neglects the influence on Pratt of his New England heritage. Small factory towns were, in fact, what Pratt had

---

had six bales of thread on hand, valued at $306. Crumpton, *Book of Memories,* 10, 15; *Alabama Supreme Court Records,* 208: 45. PMC may actually have been the most productive major mill in the state because the figure for the leading mill given in the 1850 census is so high as to suggest that it is erroneous.

21. Gavin Wright, "Cheap Labor and Southern Textiles before 1880," *Journal of Economic History* 39 (September 1979): 672, table 2. The wages PMC paid were nearly identical to those paid in 1849 at Graniteville Manufacturing Company, William Gregg's successful South Carolina cotton mill. In 1849, Gregg paid his workers $3.05 per week, while PMC in 1850 paid its workers $3.07. Mitchell, *William Gregg,* 60.

22. *De Bow's Review* 10 (February 1851): 226–27.

known in the New Hampshire of the early 1800s. Moreover, given Pratt's conservative Congregationalist upbringing, strict morality was more to him than a handy club he could wield to keep his workers docile. Illustrating this point is a letter Pratt wrote to his sister and brother-in-law Eliza and Daniel Holt in 1847. Given a few more years, Pratt indicated, he would "accomplish what I have ben striving for. That is building up a respectable vilage such as will compare with your Northern towns in point of good morals and good society." He added that Prattville already compared favorably with New England villages of the same size and that his town boasted three churches, a Sabbath school, and preaching "as good as you have in Milford."[23]

Pratt may have modeled Prattville after Milford, New Hampshire, but in point of fact, Prattville resembled any number of northern mill villages. In contrast to the sprawling manufacturing city of Lowell, Massachusetts, notes an authoritative source, the "typical" New England mill village before the Civil War merely "employed some 100 workers." Indeed, these villages were all part of the "Rhode Island System" pioneered by Samuel Slater in the 1790s. In addition to their smaller workforces, mill villages conforming to the Rhode Island System were characterized by family labor and owner paternalism, manifesting itself in the building of common schools, Sunday schools, and churches. Just like Daniel Pratt and William Gregg, northern textile manufacturers saw their social reform programs as giving uplift to the poor and reliable workforces to themselves. In short, Pratt and Gregg, in establishing paternalistic villages, hardly were following commands handed down by an all-powerful planter elite; rather, they were copying a successful northern model.[24]

James De Bow had declared in 1851 that Prattville had great potential as a factory town. "The water power of Autauga Creek," he enthusiastically informed his readers, "is sufficient at all times to drive 30,000 spin-

23. Laurence Shore, *Southern Capitalists: The Ideological Leadership of an Elite, 1832–1885* (Chapel Hill: University of North Carolina Press, 1986), 32–33; Miller, *Cotton Mill Movement*, 63–64; Daniel Pratt to Daniel and Eliza Holt, 1 June 1847, Folder 44, Pratt Papers, ADAH. William Gregg's essays are conveniently reprinted in Daniel Augustus Tompkins, *Cotton Mill, Commercial Features* (Charlotte, N.C.: by the author, 1899), 207–35.

24. Gary Kulik, Roger Parks, and Theodore Z. Penn, eds., *The New England Mill Village, 1790–1860* (Cambridge: Massachusetts Institute of Technology Press, 1982), xxiii–xxxiii. The best study of a northern mill village similar to Prattville is Anthony F. C. Wallace, *Rockdale: The Growth of an American Village in the Early Industrial Revolution* (New York: Knopf, 1978).

dles and 100[0] looms which with the other business that would naturally follow, would support a population of 6,000 inhabitants." Although PMC remained one of Alabama's most important textile factories throughout the 1850s, it never came close to realizing De Bow's expectations. In fact, the firm in 1860 very much resembled the firm of 1850. It was still capitalized at $110,000, and it employed 141 people (62 men and 79 women), only 5 more than in 1850. The number of spindles operated had grown by only 485.[25] Yet the firm did undergo some significant changes during this period.

For one thing, PMC had diversified by commencing to produce coarse woolen goods called linsey. Pratt set out his strategy in a December 1854 article in the *Prattville Southern Statesman*, "Diversity of Pursuits." Alabama, he declared, "had already engaged in the manufacture of cotton goods as extensively as circumstances would justify, particularly of the coarser fabrics." He warned that "there is great danger of overdoing as well as underdoing." To keep the market from becoming glutted with osnaburg, he proposed starting wool mills. Alabama, he noted, "consumes a large amount of linsey and other coarse woolen goods, for which we are dependent upon other States to supply. We might just as well furnish them ourselves, and save that drain upon our income."[26]

Being a man of deeds as well as words, Pratt heeded his own advice and erected a wool mill. When Noah Cloud visited Prattville in May 1857, he found that Pratt had "fitted up a large two story brick building, in which he has already received and is putting up machinery of the latest improvement for carding and spinning wool . . . in another department of the Cotton Factory." Several weeks later, even Pratt's political enemy William Howell, editor of the (Prattville) *Autauga Citizen,* praised the wool mill: "This factory has just been put in operation. . . . The cloth . . . is of superior quality, and reflects much credit on its manufacturer." Pratt's newest manufacturing concern cost $11,000 and was located one-half mile southeast of the cotton factory near the lower bridge over Autauga Creek. Shadrack Mims recalled that the wool mill "came in very opportunely to assist the cotton mill at a time when it needed assistance. The profit on this mill was enormous for the amount of capital invested."

25. *De Bow's Review* 10 (February 1851): 226–27; U.S. Census, Alabama, 1860 Manufactures Schedule, Autauga County.

26. *Prattville Southern Statesman,* 20 December 1854. Linsey, like osnaburg, was used to make clothes for slaves.

In June 1860, the wool mill operated 585 spindles, about 18 percent of the spindles operated by PMC in that year. Nor did Pratt ignore the cotton factory, putting up in 1859 a new brick building on the eastern side of the creek across from the gin factory at a cost of $45,000. Gardner Hale supervised the construction.[27]

The 1850s also saw changes in the ranks of PMC's shareholders and a lawsuit from one disgruntled investor, William D. Smith. In 1854, PMC had six new shareholders: Harriet Ticknor, who had inherited her husband's shares; Thomas Ormsby; Gardner Hale; Nathaniel Waller, a southern-born Selma merchant; John Lapsley, a southern-born Selma attorney; and Seth Paddock Storrs, a Wetumpka politician and judge who had migrated to Alabama from Vermont in 1835. Pratt and the Ticknors still dominated the company, owning 62 of the 110 shares, although Pratt held 3 shares fewer than in 1846. The planters—Smith, Tatum, and Whetstone—now held only 22 shares, the number of Organ Tatum's shares having declined significantly, from 15 to 6.[28]

In 1854, Pratt served as PMC's president, with Seth Storrs as secretary. Shadrack Mims, Organ Tatum, and Lewis Whetstone completed the board of managers. In the same year, the board refused William D. Smith's request for the declaration of a dividend, and in 1855, Smith brought suit before the chancery court at Wetumpka to compel the board to make a declaration. The chancery judge, James Blair Clark, decided

27. *American Cotton Planter and Soil of the South* 1 (May 1857): 156; (Prattville); *Autauga Citizen,* 21 May 1857; Mims, "History of Prattville," 33–34; U.S. Census, Alabama, 1860 Manufactures Schedule, Autauga County.

28. *Alabama Supreme Court Records,* 208: 40, 48–49, 59; Owen, *History of Alabama,* 3: 1012, 4: 1630–31, 1723. Waller, Lapsley, and Storrs were all prominent urban boosters. Lapsley, in particular, became involved in many manufacturing and internal improvement projects in the antebellum period. In 1855, John Lapsley sold his shares to Dallas County planter William Page Molett, one of Alabama's wealthiest men. U.S. Census, Alabama, 1860 Population Schedule, Slave Schedule, Dallas County. Even after this agrarian magnate invested $5,000 in PMC, however, the planter contingent still owned only 27 out of 110 shares. *Alabama Supreme Court Records,* 208: 38. Organ Tatum moved to Arkansas after 1855, dying there a few years later. At his death, Tatum again owned 15 shares of PMC stock. Benjamin Miles, a Prattville merchant who had married a daughter of Tatum and moved to Arkansas as well, ended up with a three-fourths interest in 12 shares. It is not clear what happened to the remaining 3 shares. Benjamin Miles died in the 1860s, leaving his interest in the shares to his brother Freeman, who owned a store in Prattville. In 1866, appraisers valued the shares at $1,250 apiece. Mims, "Autuaga County," 245; Mims, "History of the M. E. Church"; U.S. Census, Arkansas, 1860 Population Schedule, Union County; Reports and Wills, Book RB-17, 173, Book RB-20, 238, 253, 309.

against Smith, however, and Smith appealed Clark's decision to the Alabama Supreme Court.[29]

Before the supreme court, Smith's lawyers argued that the board was guilty of gross negligence in failing to declare a dividend. They noted that in 1854, PMC had current assets of $89,783.45 and current liabilities of only $29,218.41. The resulting surplus of $60,565.04, they argued, was more than enough to cover expenses, so PMC should have declared a dividend.[30]

In a deposition, Shadrack Mims responded that, in light of the company's anticipated expenses, its financial position was not so secure as Smith contended. Mims estimated that labor, cotton, and "incidental expenses" (oil, freight, hauling, storage, and repairs) would amount to $42,981.84 over the next six months, greatly eating into the current account surplus of about $60,000. "If the products of the mill could be sold for cash it would not require such an amount of surplus cash capital," he noted, "but the custom of the country has fixed the term of credit at six months without interest." PMC, therefore, needed a large amount of cash on hand. Declaring a dividend could threaten PMC's fiscal health.[31]

Even under Mims's calculation, PMC retained $17,583.20 of its current account surplus after subtracting the $42,981.84 in anticipated outlays. If this sum had been declared as a dividend, Smith, who owned ten shares, would have received $1,758.32, a 17.6 percent return on his investment. By comparison, William Gregg's cotton mill at Graniteville began paying dividends in 1849, but it was not until 1855 that its annual dividend rate surpassed 10 percent.[32]

29. *Alabama Supreme Court Records*, 208: 46; *Smith v. Prattville Manufacturing Co.*, 502–9.

30. *Smith v. Prattville Manufacturing Co.*, 505–6. Smith's lawyers indignantly asked: "How [$60,000] can now be necessary to meet the current expenses of his business is not perceived. An outlay might be necessary in starting the business; but after operations have been carried on successfully for nearly ten years, the business ought at least to pay its current expenses by its sales. Where is this accumulation to stop? What is to satisfy the 'enlarged discretion' of the managers?" Ibid. In the course of a typical very favorable report, a Dun credit agent noted of PMC in 1854: "Books show a profit of $60,000, never declared a dividend." Alabama, 2: 5, R. G. Dun & Co. Collection.

31. *Alabama Supreme Court Records*, 208: 45–46. Accidents were another "incidental expense" that Mims might have mentioned. In January 1856, George Smith reported that "Mr. Mims is to go down the river to Mobile tonight," as PMC "had some osnaburgs sunk on a boat." Nobles, *Journals of George Littlefield Smith* (Prattville, 1991), 115.

32. Lander, *Textile Industry in Antebellum South Carolina*, 107.

Unfortunately for Smith, the Alabama Supreme Court showed no interest in such details, and it unanimously upheld the chancery court's decision. The court cited the great discretion that PMC's constitution afforded the board of managers and found that the managers had acted in good faith. Chief Justice Samuel Farrow Rice concluded: "The complainant was, at the time he became a stockholder, competent to contract. . . . If the contract operates harshly upon him, that of itself is no reason why the court should release him from it. . . . [The court cannot] usurp the discretion of a private corporation at the insistence of a member whose complaint is against acts of the managers done in good faith, clearly authorized by his own contract."[33]

In this instance, the courts of a southern state staunchly upheld the legal rights of a manufacturer.[34] Yet, PMC's largest planter-investor clearly chafed under Pratt's leadership. Whereas the single-minded Pratt apparently had determined to sacrifice dividends for the sake of growth, Smith, after waiting nearly a decade, had wanted some return on his investment. Finally, he had felt compelled to sue for it.

That Pratt alienated another Autauga planter in 1854 is revealed in a plaintive letter by Albert James Pickett. Pickett, both a planter and a prominent Alabama intellectual, published in 1851 the first history of Alabama, which became widely celebrated. He also took a great interest in railroads in the 1850s, investing in several companies. After Daniel Pratt, George Goldthwaite, and Charles Teed Pollard began setting up a company to build a railroad through Autauga County from Montgomery to Selma, Pickett made his interest in the project clear to Pratt and Pollard. Thus, complained Pickett, "it was no wonder that I should have been mortified and surprised by the omission of my name in the charter." Pickett reported bitterly: "I had written to Pratt and Pollard and requested the latter to show my letter to that English Jew—George Goldthwaite. To all these men I complained of injustice. . . . As it was expected that I would take considerable stock, all I asked was to be put upon an equal footing with themselves—to have a voice in their deliberations." Clearly, Pickett's letter reeks of resentment against "outsiders" who, in his view, wanted the money, but not the advice, of planters for their industrial

33. *Smith v. Prattville Manufacturing Co.*, 509.

34. On another legal victory by a southern manufacturer, see Tom Downey, "Riparian Rights and Manufacturing in Antebellum South Carolina: William Gregg and the Origins of the 'Industrial Mind,'" *Journal of Southern History* 65 (February 1999): 77–108.

schemes. Both Pickett's letter and Smith's lawsuit suggest that, in practice, Pratt was not quite so obeisant to planters as some have suggested.[35]

The 1860 census figures confirm Smith's contention that PMC was a successful operation. In 1860, PMC produced 608,302 yards of osnaburg, valued at $63,871, and 265,000 yards of linsey, valued at $79,740. Production of osnaburg had increased only slightly since 1850, but by diversifying into wool cloth, Pratt increased the value of PMC's output from about $85,000 to nearly $145,000. PMC was now the most productive major mill in Alabama, with an output per worker valued at $1,019. The factory consumed $46,392 worth of cotton and $22,300 worth of wool. It worked 3,285 spindles (2,700 cotton and 585 wool) and 100 looms. The 62 male workers and the 79 female workers received an average yearly wage of $177.10, an increase of nearly 20 percent over 1850. Wages continued to remain higher than the southern average ($146), though the gap had narrowed. One southern state, Virginia, actually slightly surpassed PMC with its average annual wage ($181).[36]

Despite the increase in the value of the textiles it produced, PMC was eclipsed in 1860 by Pratt's own gin factory, which produced gins valued at nearly $290,000. PMC also had been surpassed by Martin, Weakley and Company (located near Florence in the Tennessee River Valley), which enjoyed spectacular growth in the 1850s. By 1860, this company operated 8,000 spindles and produced osnaburg and yarn valued at $256,000. In Alabama, it was Martin, Weakley, and Company, not PMC, that compared favorably with William Gregg's Graniteville Manufacturing Company, which operated 9,245 spindles in 1860. Moreover, several other factories, such as Garland, Goode and Company (located near Mobile) and Barrett, Micou and Company (located at Tallassee in Tallapoosa County) had pulled close to PMC. Probably in response to higher cotton prices in the 1850s, Pratt had poured relatively more capital into the gin factory, with the result that PMC did not live up to its

35. Albert James Pickett to [Bolling Hall II?], 8 March 1854, Box 37, McMillan Collection. On Pickett, see Frank Lawrence Owsley Jr., "Albert J. Pickett: Typical Pioneer State Historian" (Ph.D. diss., University of Alabama, 1955).

36. U.S. Census, Alabama, 1860 Manufactures Schedule, Autauga County; Wright, "Cheap Labor and Southern Textiles," 672. PMC continued to lag behind the national average ($196) and that of Massachusetts ($203). A few of Pratt's operatives in 1860 were probably slaves. If so, this fact would depress the wage figure slightly because the total wage figure is divided by the total number of employees, free and slave.

early promise. Nevertheless, it clearly remained both a major southern textile factory and Alabama's leading producer of linsey.[37]

Of course, Pratt's mill held significance beyond the number of spindles operated in 1860 versus the number operated in 1850. As one Prattvillian, William H. Northington, recalled in a eulogy delivered at Pratt's funeral in 1873, "the manufacture of cotton goods [in the antebellum South] was an experiment." Already enjoying great success with his gin business, Northington noted, Pratt hardly needed "to invest so large a portion of his capital, and devote so much of his valuable time" to this risky endeavor, the outcome of which was very uncertain. Pratt, he argued, was motivated to a great extent by "a desire to benefit the laboring poor, and to develop the resources of the State of his adoption." In Pratt's view, if he could put a successful textile factory into operation in Alabama, others would follow in his footsteps, and a vital new sector of the southern economy would be opened, providing employment for the region's hard-pressed poor whites and enriching the state.[38]

On the whole, Pratt's textile "experiment" should be judged a success. He provided employment and what he viewed as "uplift" to Alabama's rural poor, while they, in turn, proved a capable workforce. That Pratt experienced some difficulties with his workers cannot be denied, but by 1860 he could, with ample justification, view Prattville Manufacturing Company as a model for aspiring southern textile manufacturers.[39]

In 1860, Prattville had forty-six households that included persons employed in the cotton or woolen mills. Two were headed by a mechanic worth $1,500 and a whitewasher worth $4,200, and thus were not mill

37. U.S. Census, Alabama, 1860 Manufactures Schedule, Lauderdale County, Mobile County, Tallapoosa County; Lander, *Textile Industry in Antebellum South Carolina*, 80. On the Alabama textile industry in the 1850s, see Miller, *Cotton Mill Movement*, chap. 5. On the South generally, see Russel, *Economic Aspects of Southern Sectionalism*, chap. 8.

38. William H. Northington, "Eulogy," in *Hon. Daniel Pratt*, 167–68. Pratt's views on southern economic development are discussed in detail below.

39. For more negative views, see Randall Miller's *Cotton Mill Movement* and his articles "Daniel Pratt's Industrial Urbanism," 5–35 and "The Fabric of Control: Slavery in Antebellum Textile Mills," *Business History Review* 55 (winter 1981): 471–90; and Wayne Flynt's *Poor but Proud: Alabama's Poor Whites* (Tuscaloosa: University of Alabama Press, 1989), 19–23. But see also Flynt's more recent, positive portrayal, "Daniel Pratt, Poor Whites, and Evangelical Paternalism on the Alabama Frontier," in *The World of Daniel Pratt: Essays on Industry, Politics, Art, Architecture, Reform, and Town-Building in Alabama* (Montgomery, Ala.: Black Belt Press, 1999), 57–69.

households proper. The remaining forty-four households likely constituted about 27 percent of the total for all of Prattville. Poor white farm
families, most originally from the piney woods region north of Prattville,
composed these households. Widows headed approximately 39 percent
of the mill families. Ninety-six people, 54 males and 52 females, listed
manual jobs associated with a mill. Twelve males worked as mill bosses/
overseers; 8 males (mostly adults) worked as "manufacturers," presumably in the picker room; 9 males (mostly teens) were spinners, 9 males
(mostly teens) were carders, and 2 adult males were cloth trimmers. Four
other males respectively held the jobs of dresser, washer, oiler, and lap-
per, presumably in a mill. Thirty-two females, most aged from seventeen
to twenty-five, worked as weavers, while 12 females, most aged from fifteen to eighteen, labored as spinners. Five other females, aged from eighteen to twenty-three, worked as warpers. In addition, 1 female worked
as a cloth trimmer, 1 as a spreader, and 1 drew thread.[40]

The actual number of whites who labored for PMC in 1860 certainly
must have exceeded the figure of 96. In only two instances were adolescents younger than fifteen recorded as working in a mill, but it seems inconceivable that almost no children aged twelve to fourteen—or even
eight to eleven—worked at PMC. At virtually all American mills at this
time, children twelve and older worked as spinners or carders. Often,
children eight and older did so as well. We know at least one boy eight
or nine years old actually did work at PMC in 1858, for the boy died that
year in a workplace accident at the cotton mill. When William Howell,
editor of the (Prattville) *Autauga Citizen,* reported the fatality in his
paper, he expressed no surprise that such a young child worked for
PMC.[41]

Of the 52 work-aged adolescents (age eight to fourteen) not listed as
employed, 14 attended school. If the remaining 38 worked in the mill in
1860, only 9 job slots, all female, would have been left at PMC, meaning
that, at most, merely 6 percent of PMC's workforce could have been
black. Even if children under twelve are excluded from this calculation,
merely 21 job slots, 5 male and 16 female, are left open. In this event,
slaves would have accounted for 15 percent of the workforce at PMC in
1860. Factoring in some of this group of children is important because
without them, only 68 percent of the PMC operatives would have been

40. U.S. Census, Alabama, 1860 Population Schedule, Autauga County.
41. Ibid. (Prattville) *Autauga Citizen,* 30 September 1858.

white. If this calculation is correct, slave labor played only a minor role at PMC in 1860.[42]

One historian has noted ironically that "Pratt, who had spearheaded the earlier mission to employ and uplift local poor white labor through cotton manufactures, switched to a [racially] mixed labor force during the 1850s," but the significant fact to keep in mind is that black workers probably accounted for a small percentage of Pratt's operatives. Having mistakenly assumed that all of Pratt's slaves were kept at Prattville, this scholar inevitably overstated the significance of slave labor in the town's mills. In actuality, Pratt probably employed most of his slaves on his plantations and in his home. Moreover, Noah Cloud, who toured the cotton mill in 1857, merely noted that "several" of the operatives there were slaves. "Several" certainly does not indicate more than a few. In 1854 and 1855, just two slaves, females named Catherine and Eliza, worked for PMC. If Pratt did make a shift toward slave labor in the late 1850s, it was likely a modest one.[43]

Two main reasons have been advanced to account for Pratt's alleged switch to a racially mixed labor force: "the fluidity of local white labor and the desire to balance white class interests against slave labor." The latter point is strictly conjectural, for no evidence exists of labor unrest per se in antebellum Prattville. The point concerning labor fluidity, does, however, carry some force. What has been called by one scholar "the white workers peculiar habit of moving on after a few months on the job" likely occurred with some frequency in Prattville—though more probably after a few years, not a few months. Pratt himself once grumbled regarding his operatives that "changes [in locale] seem to be necessary to some persons." Certainly, the five- and ten-year persistence rates among mill families had room for improvement. Of the thirty-three operative households in Prattville in 1860 not headed by a mill boss, only four can be traced back to 1850, while three more are traceable back to 1855. Thus, the five-year operative household persistence rate was only 21 per-

42. U.S. Census, Alabama, 1860 Population Schedule, Autauga County. To add another possible variable, if mill children aged twelve to fourteen who attended school in 1860 are included among the PMC workforce, the number of open job slots drops to 7. If mill children eight to eleven who attended school in 1860 are added as well, the figure sinks to 1.

43. Miller, *Cotton Mill Movement*, 211; *American Cotton Planter and Soil of the South* 1 (May 1857): 156; *Alabama Supreme Court Records*, 208: 45; Alabama 1855 Census, Autauga County.

cent, half the six-year persistence rate for individual Prattville mechanics (about 43 percent).[44]

One mill family, the Butlers, clearly illustrates the problem of labor fluidity in Prattville. Nehemiah Butler and his family came to Prattville early in 1852 and went to work in the textile factory. Two years later, however, the promise of higher wages at Garland, Goode, and Company lured them to that factory, located near Mobile. An outraged Shadrack Mims wrote Price Williams, the Garland, Goode, and Company agent, accusing his company of unscrupulous behavior. "[These] people we have been at the care & expense of training thus far," Mims complained, "[and] almost the time they are prepared to render us service we find another Factory sending an irresponsible agent amongst our people making false impressions as to wages which I am sure you will not as agent acknowledge." The "irresponsible agent," a man by the name of Owen, had promised Butler that "one of his daughters can get $16 per month for warping," and Mims insisted this could not be true "if your Superintendent knows his business." Mims admitted that "Butler's girls are good hands for the practice they have had," but he insisted that they were not yet worth $16 per month.[45] Nevertheless, he was obviously sorry to lose them.

According to most scholars, southern mill workers frequently left their jobs because of dissatisfaction with mill-town life. Proud but landless southerners reduced to factory work suffered great "psychological torment" according to this view. But rapid labor turnover in textile factories was hardly an exclusively southern phenomenon. Mills in Massachusetts and Pennsylvania suffered from the problem as well. Nor does labor turnover necessarily indicate unhappiness with mill life. Some southerners—as did some northerners—bought farms with their saved factory wages, but many others simply would appear to have been using their leverage as a valuable labor source to obtain the best mill jobs possible. Moreover, mill towns held allurements not available in the country-

44. Miller, *Cotton Mill Movement,* 212, 219; *Prattville Southern Statesman,* 25 May 1855; U.S. Census, Alabama, 1850 and 1860 Population Schedules, Autauga County; Alabama 1855 Census, Autauga County. Four of the twelve mill bosses can be traced back from 1860 to at least 1855.

45. Shadrack Mims to Price Williams, 15 February 1854, in Randall M. Miller, "Love of Labor: A Note on Daniel Pratt's Employment Practices," *Alabama Historical Quarterly* 37 (summer 1975): 148–49.

side. As historian Richard Griffin has argued, for poor whites "drawn from the pine hills and sand barrens, the cotton mill and its cash wage meant decent food, clothing, and shelter for the first time in their lives."[46]

Two historians have asserted that Pratt's white operatives were so disenchanted with mill life that they proved very poor workers. In advancing this assertion, both men rely on complaints about white operatives made by Shadrack Mims. Pratt's longtime agent certainly found fault with white operatives, but his most critical statements invariably concerned *new* workers. Mims recalled that *initially,* operatives made many mistakes that were "fatal to success," adding: "When [the cotton mill] *first* started [emphasis added], [the workers] were of the very poorest class with very few exceptions and withal ignorant people from obscure parts of the county—many of them having never enjoyed any religious privileges. They were wild, and many of the fathers were drunken and abandoned men whose children had never been trained to work of any kind." But Mims believed that training in the factory, temperance, schooling, and religious instruction greatly improved the condition of these people. His testimony (the merit of which can be debated) certainly fails to support the contention that southern white labor was inherently ineffective.[47]

Indicating his commitment to white labor, Pratt, like William Gregg and many northern counterparts, launched an ambitious program to mold mill workers into an effective workforce. First, he vigorously enforced temperance.

This temperance campaign appears to have met with some success. By 1847, Prattville claimed a temperance society with seventy-two mem-

46. Miller, *Cotton Mill Movement*, 217–18; Miller, "The Fabric of Control," 478–81; Wallace, *Rockdale*, 63–65; Prude, *The Coming of Industrial Order*, 144–45; Richard W. Griffin, "Poor White Laborers in Southern Cotton Factories, 1789–1865," *South Carolina Historical Magazine* 61 (January 1960): 30. See also Tom E. Terrell, "Eager Hands: Labor for Southern Textiles, 1850–1860," *Journal of Economic History* 36 (March 1976): 84–99, and Mitchell, *William Gregg*, 58–60.

47. Miller, *Cotton Mill Movement*, 202; Miller, "The Fabric of Control," 478–81; Starobin, *Industrial Slavery*, 155; Mims, "History of Prattville," 26; Mims, "Autauga County," 266–67. For critiques of PMC's white workers influenced by Miller, see Flynt, *Poor but Proud*, 22–23; W. David Lewis, *Sloss Furnaces and the Rise of the Birmingham District: An Industrial Epic* (Tuscaloosa: University of Alabama Press, 1994), 17; Harvey H. Jackson III, *Rivers of History: Life on the Coosa, Tallapoosa, Cahaba, and Alabama* (Tuscaloosa: University of Alabama Press, 1995), 115.

bers.[48] J. Slater Hughes, a temperance advocate, held Prattville up as a beacon of sobriety, declaring no drunkards lived there. Yet, only a year after Hughes's visit to Prattville, Pratt's New Orleans friend George Cooke wrote Pratt that he regretted that "the demon of alcohol has access to your village." And during an 1851 election, George Smith complained of the antics of "a number of partly inebriated young men" in Prattville and indicated that Gardner Hale had fired a hand for "drinking too much liquor." Nevertheless, Pratt himself affirmed in 1860 that his town was "unusually free [of] the vice of *loafing* and dissipation." Significantly, Pratt lifted his more coercive temperance measures. In 1859, he removed the liquor ban from the town deeds he granted; and in the same year, a grocer offered a wide range of liquor, including whiskey, for sale.[49]

Pratt also strongly encouraged church and Sunday school attendance so that operatives and their families would receive proper moral instruction. By 1846, Prattville had Baptist, Methodist, and Presbyterian churches, all of which were located near the western side of Autauga Creek on land donated by Pratt. Both Pratt and his wife, Esther, became personally involved in church matters. "As long as he was physically able," recalled Shadrack Mims, Pratt "superintended the duties of sexton, doing much of it with his own hands." Moreover, he "would go round the village visiting families, and urging the importance of punctual attendance on Sunday-school and church." For her part, Esther Pratt supplied "suitable clothing" for mill children so that they would not be too embarrassed to attend Sunday-school classes.[50]

While apparently only one mill family, the Houstons, joined the Presbyterian church in the antebellum period, large numbers of mill folk joined the Methodist and Baptist churches. Between 1848 and 1852, at least 55 of the 224 whites who joined or already belonged to the Method-

48. Deed Books, Probate Office, Autauga County Courthouse; *Acts . . . of the State of Alabama (1846)*, 115–16; *Acts . . . of the State of Alabama (1848)*, 165; *Tuscaloosa Independent Monitor*, 9 November 1847, reprinted from the *Temperance Watchman*.

49. *Tuscaloosa Independent Monitor*, 9 November 1847, reprinted from the *Temperance Watchman*; George Cooke to Daniel Pratt, 15 May 1848, Folder 44, Pratt Papers, ADAH; Nobles, *Journals of George Littlefield Smith*, 19; (Prattville) *Autauga Citizen*, 15 December 1859, 16 August 1860.

50. Karen A. Stone, *Prattville Baptist Church: Sharing Our Past with a Vision for the Future, 1838–1988* (Montgomery, Ala.: Brown Printing, 1988), 13–18; James K. Hazen, *Manual of the Presbyterian Church* (Richmond, Va.: Shepperson & Graves, 1878); Church Register; Mims, "History of Prattville," 47, 58.

ist church came from mill families. Although membership rolls for the Baptist church evidently have not survived, it is likely that many of this church's members came from mill households as well. In 1846, the year Pratt started his mill, the church baptized 35 new members, most of whom likely were mill operatives. By 1850, the Baptist church claimed a congregation with 69 white adherents.[51]

Mill families attending the Methodist church included the Buies, the Butlers, the Carnlines, the Ellises, the Grays, the Grants, the Hugheses, the Holstons, the Joneses, the Methanys, the Searcys, and the Williamses. Nehemiah Butler, his wife, Juliana, and four of their daughters were admitted to the church on probation in October 1852. Juliana Butler "died right" on November 26, and the other five Butlers became fully connected members of the church on June 26, 1853. Earlier, in March, Nehemiah, all seven of his daughters, and his son, Matthew, had received baptism. For the Butlers, church attendance was a new experience. Mims wrote in his 1854 letter to the agent for Garland, Goode and Company that "no one [of Nehemiah Butler's] large family of children, some of them grown, had ever heard preaching before coming to Prattville." Mims sternly informed the agent that "Mr. Pratt . . . has incurred a heavy expense in order to supply these people with a regular pastoral oversight," and he charged his rival "as a Christian gentleman to take care both souls & bodies of this family."[52]

Among Prattville mill families, women apparently heard more preaching than men. In the period from 1848 to 1852, 71 percent of the members of the Methodist church from mill families were female. Mary Ellis and Catherine Hale belonged to the church, but their husbands did not. Similarly, widow Hannah Holston and her eldest daughter were church members, but her eldest son was not. However, in many cases, husbands and wives, as well as sons and daughters, were church members. Hatter Abram Carnline belonged to the church, as did his wife, Barbary, his operative sons John and George, and his daughter Visa.[53]

Both males and females occasionally got into trouble with the church. At least half of the fourteen people expelled from Methodist church membership from 1849 to 1852 came from mill families. Fate Ellis, his

51. Stone, *Prattville Baptist Church*, 13–8; Hazen, *Manual of the Presbyterian Church*; Church Register.
52. U.S. Census, Alabama, 1850 Population Schedule, Autauga County; Church Register; Shadrack Mims to Price Williams, 15 February 1854, in "Love of Labor," 148–49.
53. Church Register.

cousin John Ellis, Tilman Jones, and Rebecca Searcy were expelled for neglect of religious duties, while Eliza Gray, Susan Gray, and Sarah Methany were expelled for dancing. All seven individuals were young people, either in their teens or early twenties. Moreover, that two mill girls had out-of-wedlock children in Prattville in 1848 is inferable from an entry in Ferdinand Smith's journal: "Another birth occurred in the Level [the mill operatives' neighborhood] today without a father, poor thing." Neither the journal of Ferdinand Smith nor that of his cousin George, which both run through the mid-1850s, makes another such reference, however. Nor are there recorded Methodist church expulsions after 1852.[54]

Prattville's interdenominational Union Sunday School (an affiliate of the American Sunday School Union) had as its goal the inculcation of virtue in the town's youth. In 1847, Prattville's Sabbath school had twenty teachers, 120 students, and a library of one thousand volumes. Shadrack Mims proudly declared of the institution: "We have one of the best Sabbath schools in the State." Judging from an incomplete 1854 library record, mill children did attend this school, which was divided into male and female departments. The names of children from twelve identifiable mill households appear in the membership record. Probably at least 14 of 80 boys (17.5 percent) in the school in 1854 came from mill families, while 21 (52.9 percent) of the 40 girls (a partial listing) in the school in that year belonged to mill families. In part, this gender disparity probably reflected the general gender disparity in mill families. Nevertheless, Shadrack Mims recalled that mill girls were less resistant to Sunday school than mill boys. Mims asserted that initially, mill children "seemed to have an aversion to Sunday School." Fortunately, however, through the efforts of Mrs. Pratt and other ladies who visited the families and furnished them with proper clothes, "many of the girls, and some few of the boys of the better class were induced to enter the school." Those "boys who did not enter Sunday School," grumbled Mims, "were roaming about over the country robbing orchards and melon patches, and they would do this at night as well as on Sundays."[55]

Pratt sought to provide the children in mill families with a secular edu-

54. Ibid.; Nobles, *Journals of Ferdinand Ellis Smith*, 10. Despite the stigma of church expulsion, Lafayette Ellis became one of Prattville's great success stories.

55. *Tuscaloosa Independent Monitor*, 9 November 1847, reprinted from the *Temperance Watchman*; Prattville Sunday-School Library Record, ACHC; Mims, "Autauga County," 266.

cation as well as a religious one, for he insisted that "it is just as necessary for successful operatives to have a plain, practical education, as it is for them to operate with the hands; the intellect ought to be educated as well as the hands." As early as 1845, Pratt had started a school for village children. The frame schoolhouse cost about $1,000 and "was situated in a cool sequestered place completely surrounded by a forest growth of young oaks and a cool spring." Pratt employed New Hampshire-born Thomas Avery as the school's first teacher. Mims remembered Avery, who later became Pratt's bookkeeper, as "an accomplished scholar and gentleman." By 1847, Prattville had two schools, one of which was a "Ladies School" for children.[56]

Throughout the 1850s, several learning institutions existed in Prattville. In 1860, Pratt put up a fine Italianate brick building that housed the Prattville Male and Female Academy. Pratt also served as the president of the academy's board of trustees. The academy was prohibitively expensive for the children of mill families, who attended a free school that opened in 1857. This school was established expressly for the "education and moral training of the children of factory operatives." Pratt's niece Augusta [Pratt] Morgan taught the school, with assistance from Eliza Abbot, a young woman from New Jersey. Merchant Hassan Allen, formerly secretary of the Sons of Temperance and a current sales agent for a northern piano company, gave music lessons to the students. The editor of the (Prattville) *Autauga Citizen* gave Augusta Morgan and her school qualified praise: "Considering the raw and unlettered material which she has had to operate upon, we think she deserves the greatest credit for the progress she has made in the moral and mental culture of the children under her supervision." From forty to fifty children attended the school, exceeding expectations of twenty to thirty. In fact, attendance was so great that the schoolhouse became overcrowded, and many children had to bring their own seats. In addition, Augusta Morgan received only a "pittance" for her "onerous duties." The editor of the *Citizen* implored "the wealthier class of our citizens to remedy these problems."[57]

The "wealthier class" of Prattville's citizens may not have been as

---

56. *Prattville Southern Statesman*, 20 December 1854; Mims, "History of Autauga County," 266; Daniel Pratt to Daniel and Eliza Holt, 1 June 1847, Pratt Papers, ADAH.

57. (Prattville) *Autauga Citizen*, 18 June 1854, 4 March 1857, 16 August, 20 September 1860. A photograph of the academy building appeared in the *Prattville Progress*, 11 November 1898. Hassan Allen was a son of James Allen.

forthcoming as hoped, for only twenty-one children from mill families were listed as attending school in the 1860 census. A household like that of Toliver Golden, where no fewer than four children went to school, was a rarity. Nevertheless, this number was still 30 percent of the school-age children (six to fourteen years) in the mill families. Augusta Morgan and Eliza Abbot apparently no longer taught at the school, but Mary Sheldon, Augusta Morgan's and Merrill Pratt's stepsister, and Mary Walker, a young New York woman who lodged with a mill family, were listed as teachers in the 1860 census. It appears, then, that although the free school, like the Sunday school and the church, reached only a portion of the operative community, it nevertheless remained a viable institution. Moreover, some mill children who did not attend common school surely learned reading and writing in the Sabbath school.[58]

While the evidence at hand does not permit extravagant affirmations of the success of Pratt's efforts concerning his factory workers, neither should it allow scholarly conclusions that they ended in failure. Many operatives attended Prattville's churches and sent their children to the Union Sunday School and the common school. That others failed to do the same does not negate Pratt's accomplishment in fashioning a capable labor force.[59]

Poor whites hardly shunned Prattville. Especially for families with many daughters and few sons, mill work could hold appeal. Indeed, some families traveled long distances to get to Prattville, surely a major commitment of scarce resources. Two families (in both of which daughters substantially outnumbered sons) offer excellent examples of this phenomenon. In 1850, Toliver Golden and his family lived in Walker County, located in hilly northern Alabama; Nehemiah Butler and his family resided in Coffee County, part of the "wiregrass" region of southern Alabama. Both Walker and Coffee Counties were as insulated from

58. U.S. Census, Alabama, 1860 Population Schedule, Autauga County; Cooke, *Genealogy of Daniel Pratt*. "Designed not merely to impart spiritual truths," notes historian Kenneth Startup, "the Sunday schools also provided pupils with basic literary skills." Kenneth Moore Startup, *The Root of All Evil: The Protestant Clergy and the Economic Mind of the Old South* (Athens: University of Georgia Press, 1997), 102.

59. Although in his early work Randall Miller concedes that Pratt's efforts met with some success, he concludes in a later article that southern whites "were, on the whole, an unreliable workforce who clung to the preindustrial work habits and values of rural and village culture." See Miller, "The Fabric of Control," 478. His latest assessment, while less uncompromising, still leans toward the negative side. See Randall M. Miller, "Daniel Pratt: A New England Yankee in King Cotton's Court," in *The World of Daniel Pratt*, 25.

the market economy as any counties in the state, yet the Goldens and Butlers both moved to Prattville in the 1850s.[60]

Other families offer less dramatic examples of distance migration.
Probably after the death of her husband, Sarah Chatwood brought her
family to Prattville from Tallapoosa County, located one county to the
east of Autauga. Also likely after her husband's death, Elizabeth Royals
moved with her family to Prattville from Pike County, located to the
southeast of Autauga. Two other families, the Griffins and the Glenns,
came to Prattville from adjacent Coosa County.[61]

More commonly, however, the hilly Autauga districts to the north of
Prattville, particularly Milton and Pine Flat, served as Pratt's sources of
operatives. The families of Susan O'Neal, Elnora Killian, and Diah Spurlock all traveled to Prattville from Pine Flat in the 1850s, while Elizabeth
Ross's and Seaborn Carter's families came from Milton. Some of these
families may not have been unfamiliar with manufacturing, for the
O'Neal, Killian, and Spurlock families—as well as mechanics Ebenezer
Killough and James Tunnell—all lived in 1850 in close proximity to Nor-
fleet Ivy, who owned a Pine Flat sash, door, and blind shop, a smithy,
and a gristmill. Ivy retired to Prattville after 1850 (possibly a casualty of
competition with Pratt) and opened a boardinghouse. Both Killough and
Tunnell probably transferred from jobs with Ivy to jobs with Pratt, and
members of the other families may have as well.[62]

The financial condition of these households does seem to have improved, at least moderately, in Prattville. In 1860, thirty-four of the forty-
one mill families with listed wealth had wealth ranging from $100 to
$800. Twenty-two owned property valued at from $100 to $400, while
twelve owned property worth from $500 to $800. Only four families
owned $1,000 or more, while merely three owned less than $100. The
mean wealth among the mill families with wealth listings was slightly
more than $400.[63]

Many households went from having no wealth listing before they
came to Prattville to one amounting in 1860 to $400 or $500. The Spur-

60. U.S. Census, Alabama, 1850 Free Schedule, Coffee County, Walker County, 1860
Population Schedule, Autauga County.

61. U.S. Census, Alabama, 1850 Population Schedule, Coosa County, Pike County, Tallapoosa County.

62. U.S. Census, Alabama, 1850 Population Schedule, 1850 Manufactures Schedule,
Autauga County.

63. U.S. Census, Alabama, 1850 and 1860 Population Schedules, Autauga County.

lock family offers a good example of this occurrence. Diah Spurlock continued to find employment as a laborer in Prattville; Ferdinand Smith noted in his diary in 1855 that he had had over "Mr. Spurlock to hoe my potatoes." Spurlock's teenaged daughters, Frances and Missouri, worked in the mill as a warper and a weaver, respectively, while his fourteen-year-old son, Wilmont, labored as a spinner. Through their joint efforts, the family increased the household's wealth from no listing in 1850 to $400 in 1860.[64]

Another example of economic gain among Prattville mill families can be seen with the Griffin household. William Griffin brought a sprawling family consisting of a wife, Rosanna, and thirteen children from Coosa County to Prattville between 1855 and 1859. His death from cancer in 1859 could well have spelled disaster for the family, but in 1860 at least two of Rosanna's children worked in the mill, one as a spreader and the other as a carder, and Rosanna listed her household wealth as $500.[65]

Rosanna Griffin's case reveals that factory work, while far from offering an easy life, could mean economic survival for widows and orphans. Widows Susan O'Neal, Elnora Killian, and Elizabeth Ross buttress this point. O'Neal, Killian, and Ross went from having no wealth listing in 1850 to listings in 1860 of $600, $250, and $500, respectively. All these women had daughters working variously as spinners, weavers, or warpers. Killian, age forty-nine, also worked in the mill.[66]

Prattville had a few clear cases of impressive upward mobility. The Ellis family, discussed in the last chapter, had children who worked in the cotton mill. Two other mill families, the Matthews and the Houstons, also fared well from their move to town. Shadrack Mims remembered Rachel Houston as a widow "who had seen better days and society, but had been reduced to poverty." Moving to Prattville, she found work for her sons William and Thomas as mechanics in the gin factory and for her daughters Mary and Margaret as weavers in the cotton mill. The family also regularly attended the Presbyterian church. By their industry, they made a good living and built a "comfortable house." In 1860, the sixty-

64. Ibid.; Nobles, *Journals of Ferdinand Ellis Smith*, 212.
65. U.S. Census, Alabama, 1850 and 1860 Population Schedules, Autauga County; *Alabama Mortality Schedule 1860, Eighth Census of the United States, Original Returns of the Assistant Marshalls, Third Series; Persons Who Died during the Year ending June 30, 1860*, compiled by Marilyn Davis Barefield (Easley, S.C.: Southern Historical Press, 1987), 2.
66. U.S. Census, Alabama, 1850 and 1860 Population Schedules, Autauga County.

year-old Houston was worth $1,400, much of which must have come from her two unmarried mechanic sons, who still lived with her.[67]

Martha Matthews was, as Shadrack Mims wrote of Rachel Houston, a widow who had seen better days before she came to Prattville. Her uncle Martin Burt was a successful Autauga planter; her uncle-in-law Henry Hunt worked for a while as a mechanic for Daniel Pratt; and her father, John Coleman, was, she recalled, an enterprising "Jack-of-all-Trades" who provided scarce services in the newly settled county. Besides making such diverse items as shoes, chairs, spinning wheels, breast pins, and steel traps, he repaired gins and built houses.[68]

In 1826, Coleman was making arrangements to start a gin shop near McNeil's Mill, but his health rapidly declined, and he died in April. Coleman's daughter Martha married Henry Matthews in 1831. Matthews, a plantation overseer, died in 1843, leaving a widow and four young children. Martha Matthews, left alone with four children and nothing to depend on for support but her own exertions, moved to Prattville, where she did sewing for townspeople. When the cotton mill started operations in 1846, "she found ready employment for all her children," allowing her "to make a good living" and to achieve for them "very good advantages in the way of education." In addition, Matthews, a member of the Prattville Baptist Church, made certain that her offspring attended church and Sunday school. Eldest son Jesse served as a Sunday-school class leader as well. In 1860, Jesse was a mechanic, while younger son James worked as a spinner in the mill. Both sons lived at home, contributing to the wealth of the Coleman household, which was listed at $1,300 that year. After the Civil War, Jesse became a bookkeeper and then a prominent Prattville merchant. In 1872, at the age of thirty-nine, he married Lily Horn, a stepdaughter of New Hampshire-born gin mechanic C. P. Morgan. Martha's other son, James, moved to Monroe, Georgia, where he started a jewelry shop; and her daughter Mary married Hugh Narramore, a Prattville saddle and harness shop owner.[69]

67. Mims, "Autauga County," 267; Hazen, *Manual of the Presbyterian Church,* 5; U.S. Census, Alabama, 1850 and 1860 Population Schedules, Autauga County.

68. Samuel Parrish Smith, "Burts and Colemans" [1885], *Autauga Ancestry* 5 (May 1995): 21–22, 27.

69. Ibid., 23–25; Prattville Sunday-School Library Record. In his journal Ferdinand Smith records: "This evening went up to Mrs. Matthew's and got my shirts." Nobles, *Journals of Ferdinand Ellis Smith,* 11.

No doubt the family of Martha Matthews, like that of Rachel Houston, was an atypical mill family. While Martha Matthews's husband did not own a farm, he was a well-respected plantation overseer. Moreover, some of her kin, such as her uncle Martin Burt, were undeniably well-off. In addition, her own father, John Coleman, resembled Daniel Pratt in his undoubted mechanical ingenuity.[70] In short, Martha Matthews and Rachel Houston headed formerly middle-class families that regained and even advanced their social and economic status in Prattville. They were not, like the Ellis family, people who had always been poor; and their success stories are not so dramatic. Nevertheless, it is clear that Prattville's cotton mill did offer a ladder for these determined widows to climb.

As a group, Pratt's mill bosses did not do as well financially as Houston or Matthews. Twelve men, all southern-born, worked as mill bosses in 1860. Of these, four were worth from $500 to $1,000, three from $100 to less than $500, one was worth $50, and the remaining four had no wealth listing. However, it is worth noting that all these men were much younger than the typical operative household head, ranging in age from twenty-four to thirty-two. Moreover, the bosses had married much more recently and had smaller families.[71]

Gardner Hale stood at the top of the factory echelon in 1860, followed by the two mill agents, William Fay and A. J. Thompson. Fay, a thirty-three-year-old native of Vermont, succeeded Shadrack Mims in 1860 as the cotton-mill agent. He was a nephew of Edwin Fay, a long-time Autauga resident who had migrated to Alabama as a schoolteacher and eventually become a successful planter. William Fay himself had once taught school, but at the time of his election as Mims's replacement, he had an agency in Prattville for the Montgomery Insurance Company. The background of the twenty-eight-year-old Thompson, a native of Alabama, is not clear, although it appears he was a brother of Clinton Thompson, a Prattville restaurant owner. A. J. Thompson had wealth valued at $1,000, much less than Fay, who was worth $10,000.[72]

Whatever their financial condition, Prattville's mill workers surely

---

70. John Coleman's brother Thomas had talents similar to those of John. Thomas Coleman owned a wagon shop in the 1820s and also made gins on special order. Smith, "Burts and Colemans," 25.

71. U.S. Census, Alabama, 1860 Population Schedule, Autauga County.

72. Ibid.; Alabama, 2: 5, R. G. Dun & Co. Collection. On the Fay family, see Bell Irwin Wiley, ed., *"This Infernal War": The Confederate Letters of Edwin H. Fay* (Austin: University of Texas Press, 1958).

found appealing the quality low-rent housing Pratt provided. De Bow declared that Pratt's operatives had for a small rent "good houses, neatly painted and of uniform size." Some operatives' households in Prattville supplemented their income by taking in lodgers, typically young adult males or females who worked in the gin or textile factories. Widows Cynthia Mason and Mary Davis evidently did particularly well as landladies. Mason, worth $700, lodged four young male adults: a mechanic, a blacksmith, an operative, and an overseer. Mason's daughters all worked in the mill, while her son attended school. Davis, worth $800, lodged five individuals, including three operatives. None of Davis's children had occupations listed in the census, but a daughter who died from typhoid fever in 1859 had worked as a weaver.[73]

Mill families had a wide choice of Prattville stores in which to spend their hard-earned cash. Since Prattville was not a company town, it had no company store. In any given year in the 1850s, some half-dozen mercantile concerns operated in Prattville. Perhaps the most popular was W. C. Allen and Company, a firm owned by New York natives W. C. Allen and his brother Hassan, sons of James Allen. In 1854, the Allen brothers advertised such diverse items as clothing, hardware, utensils, foodstuffs, toiletries, jewelry, toys, books, and tobacco—all "at the lowest prices."[74]

While housing and access to stores, churches, and schools likely offered strong incentives to some families to come to work in Prattville's mills, poor working conditions and long hours may have discouraged others. Operatives labored until 6:00 to 6:30 P.M. Monday through Friday and until 5:00 P.M. on Saturday. In addition, workers had forty-five minutes to an hour to eat their dinner at home after the ringing of the noon bell. Assuming the day began about 6:00 A.M., it would seem likely that mill operatives faced a grueling schedule of eleven hours of work on Mondays through Fridays and ten hours of work on Saturdays.[75]

Due to a paucity of evidence, little can be stated about working conditions in the textile factory. Beyond doubt, however, is that an exceptionally horrible accident in the mill claimed the life of a young boy operative in September 1858. The boy was Probadus Griffin, a son of William and Rosanna Griffin. At the time of his fatal accident, Probadus was probably

73. *De Bow's Review* 10 (February 1851): 226; U.S. Census, Alabama, 1860 Population Schedule, Autauga County; *Alabama Mortality Schedule, 1860,* 2.

74. (Prattville) *Autauga Citizen,* 15 December 1859.

75. *Prattville Southern Statesman,* 16 June 1859.

eight or nine years old. A machine belt in the carding room caught the boy, hurling him to the roofing above, where he was decapitated, his head remaining lodged in the machinery while his "lifeless trunk" fell back to the floor, spattering several of his horrified coworkers with blood. One of Probadus Griffin's brothers ran home to inform his mother, Rosanna, that "her son was dead & his head was off, & she ran as hard as she could [to the mill] screaming every step." Upon seeing the ghastly sight in the carding room, she swooned and "was perfectly crazy for several days." Terrible as this occurrence was, no other operative injuries, not to mention fatalities, are noted in Prattville diaries or newspapers in the antebellum period.[76]

By 1861, Pratt's textiles "experiment" had clearly proven itself successful. Labor turnover undoubtedly caused Pratt some difficulty, and as cotton prices rose in the 1850s, he apparently found it more profitable to divert capital into the gin factory and a plantation, just as potential planter investors may have found it more profitable to invest in land and slaves. As a consequence, the mill never achieved the significance it might have. Nevertheless, Pratt had successfully established one of the South's major textile factories. Moreover, the mill, in conjunction with the gin factory, became the nucleus around which the town of Prattville developed.

76. (Prattville) *Autauga Citizen,* 30 September 1858; Adelaide Smith to Julia Smith, 4 October 1858, in possession of Dora Pratt Smith Haas, Montgomery, Alabama. News of only one other mill accident appeared in the papers during Pratt's lifetime. In June 1868, Andrew Simmons, a twenty-two-year-old carder, "got his right arm shockingly mangled" in a carding machine. As a result, Simmons had to have his arm amputated. Two years later, Simmons worked as a night watchman in the mill, suggesting that Pratt felt obligated to keep him employed in some capacity. *Montgomery Daily Mail,* 20 June 1868.

4

The Man at the Center

Although a place called Prattville first came into existence in 1839, it remained for years a tiny offshoot of Daniel Pratt's cotton-gin factory. Only with the advent of the cotton mill in 1846 did Prattville begin to blossom. In 1850, the village had a free population of 448; by 1860, the free population had more than doubled to approximately 943.[1] On the eve of the Civil War, Prattville had grown into Alabama's premier factory town and the business center of a wealthy Black Belt county. Not content with these distinctions, Prattville's ambitious and enterprising citizenry spoke of making the town the "Lowell of the South." Even as Prattville grew and diversified, however, Daniel Pratt remained at the center of its affairs, so much so that the local Democratic paper took to referring to him as "the Great I Am." To a large extent, Prattville mirrored the man after whom it had been named.

Soon after he had started his cotton mill, Pratt wrote to his New Hampshire relatives in 1847 about what had become his ruling passion: "Should my life be spared a few years longer I think I shall accomplish what I have ben striving for. That is build up a respectable vilage such as

---

1. U.S. Census, Alabama, 1850 and 1860 Population Schedules, Autauga County.

will compare with your Northern towns in point of good morals and good society." Pratt boasted that he was, in fact, "not afraid of a comparison with any vilage in New England of the same population." He listed two things that he felt made life in Prattville especially good, its churches and its schools: "We have regular preaching every Sabath and januraly every Wednesday night and I think as good as you have in Milford. We have a Methodist Church numbering 100 or more members, a respectable Baptist Church and Presbeterian. We also have an excelent school the year round besides a ladies school for small children. We have a Sabath school numbering 120 scholars. We also have a Bible class."[2]

For Pratt, then, Prattville was to be a reflection of the value system inculcated in his New England boyhood, a place of hard work and religious devotion, of, as he put it, "good morals and good society." Until the end of his life, Pratt himself remained almost obsessively concerned with the pursuit of his calling, never resting with the attainment of a goal, but immediately dashing off in pursuit of another one. An R. G. Dun and Company agent approvingly noted of Pratt in 1854 that he was "worth at least half a million in [property] & as anxious to add to it & save as ever." Despite his preoccupation with business, Pratt did not neglect what he conceived as his familial and religious duties. Pursuit of profit for its own sake, he believed, would have been a sin. Through personal and public charity, Pratt sought to fulfill what he saw as his Christian obligations to his fellow man.[3]

Anson West, a minister who had known Pratt, recalled him as a tall, straight-backed man with "large hands and feet, a Roman nose, and eyes the color of the sky." He declared that "not only did [Pratt's] countenance beam with benevolence, but his entire person indicated benevolence." Indeed, he found Pratt the very "embodiment of energy, integrity, and philanthropy."[4] Nevertheless, Pratt's expression also had a serious, even stern quality, suggesting that his philanthropy would be tempered by a clearheaded estimation of the would-be recipient's worth.

2. Daniel Pratt to Daniel and Eliza Holt, 1 June 1847, Pratt Papers, ADAH.

3. Louisiana, 9: 57, R. G. Dun & Co. Collection. Daniel Pratt's upright character was a great business asset, for Dun agents placed heavy emphasis on moral probity in determining an individual's creditworthiness. Pratt never failed to receive the highest encomiums from these visitors: "a 1st rate man in all respects" (1850); "a careful prudent honest industrious man" (1853); "a man of indomitable energy & unwavering integrity" (1856). Alabama, 2: 5, 12, R. G. Dun & Co. Collection.

4. Anson West, A History of Methodism in Alabama (Nashville, Tenn.: Publishing House, Methodist Episcopal Church, 1893), 617.

Pratt's family and friends viewed him as a kind but very reserved man. During the Civil War, when Julia (Smith) Pratt wrote her husband, Merrill (Pratt's nephew and ward), of her experience in joining Prattville's Methodist church, she noted that Daniel Pratt and his wife, Esther, had different reactions to her act: "When I was coming out of church today, M[rs.] P[ratt] met me and said she was so glad to see me take the steps that I had taken today. Mr. P[ratt] also seemed to be very glad although he did not say anything." Two months later, Merrill mentioned in a letter to Julia that "Uncle Pratt" had written him "that Julia Pratt was well and as *pretty* as ever." Of this comment Merrill joked, "Something must be about to happen for I think this about the first time he ever said anyone was pretty." Possibly alluding to the incident Julia had described, he added, "Tho I recon he thought his wife was [even] if he didn't say so, don't you?"[5]

Shadrack Mims, who wrote at great length in the 1870s and 1880s about Pratt's character, agreed that Pratt could be formal and distant. Mims recalled that in conversations, Pratt, "modest at all times," preferred listening to talking. Although enjoying "a pleasant witticism or repartee that gave no offense," Pratt did not condescend to "foolish jesting." Never stooping to "undue familiarity" with men, Pratt "reserved . . . the right to repel it in others toward himself." Not surprisingly, perhaps, "he had few confidants."[6]

Mims also implied that Pratt could have flashes of temper: "When things did not go on [in his business] to suit him, he was impatient and fretful, and sometimes abrupt." An example of this tendency can be seen in Ferdinand Smith's delicate observation that his boss became "a little out of patience" over his mechanics' difficulties with the Parkhurst gin. Mims argued, however, that considering how few men measured up to his standards as a businessman, Pratt actually "exercised great forbearance towards the shortcomings of others."[7]

Mims repeatedly emphasized Pratt's unflagging devotion to business. So much of Pratt's time was "taken up with business during the week," noted Mims, "that he found little time for society." Pratt's friends and even his doctor warned him that he endangered his health by overwork-

5. Julia Pratt to Merrill Pratt, 23 November 1862, Box 21, McMillan Collection; Merrill Pratt to Julia Pratt, 19 January 1863, Folder 34, Pratt Papers, ADAH.

6. Mims, "History of Prattville," 55.

7. Ibid., 45–46; Nobles, *Journals of Ferdinand Ellis Smith*, 172.

ing, but to no avail. "No persuasion . . . could prevail with him to favor himself, even at the near approach of his last illness. Work was his element, and work he would, when he should have been in bed under treatment." Mims related that Pratt had even declared "that if he knew that tomorrow would be his last day on earth, he would continue his regular routine of work."[8]

This assertion, while dramatic, is borne out by Pratt's actions. He continued to drive himself in the 1860s and 1870s, even as his health steadily worsened. In 1872, less than a year before his death, he complained to Mims that he had "ben laid up about two weeks not able to attend to business. My hand is so lame now I am hardly able to hold a pen." Pratt declared that he desired to go to Talladega Springs for a water cure, as friends had urged him, but that his heavy workload would not allow him to do so.[9]

Detailing only Pratt's absorption with his work, however, gives an incomplete portrait of the man. Pratt balanced his devotion to business with a commitment to family, friends, and the community at large. His strong ties to his own family can be traced from his 1827 letter to his father through the rest of his life. In 1827, he told his parent, "You may depend, I respect you as a father and believe that I think of you as often as you do of me." He assured Edward that he felt "under grate obligation to you and feel it my duty to assist you in time of need" and promised "should you be in want of any of the necessaries of life by letting me know it you shall have the last cent before you shall suffer." Pratt's father died in 1829, but as Pratt's own fortunes rose in the late 1830s and 1840s and those of his siblings declined, he repeatedly expressed his concern and offered help.[10]

By the time Pratt moved to Alabama in 1833, all his siblings had wed. His oldest sister, Asenath, married Joseph Chandler, likely a brother of Pratt's good friend Elijah Chandler. After Asenath died in 1836, leaving three children, Joseph married Pratt's forty-one-year-old sister Dorcas. Joseph himself died the next year, however, leaving the widowed Dorcas $50 and a clock. Daniel's two younger sisters, Abigail and Eliza, wed local farmers of modest means, Artemas Howard and Daniel Holt, re-

8. Mims, "History of Prattville," 46.

9. Daniel Pratt to Shadrack Mims, 3 June 1872, Box 37, McMillan Collection.

10. Daniel Pratt to Edward Pratt, 19 June 1827, Pratt Papers, ADAH; Cooke, *Genealogy of Daniel Pratt*.

spectively. Daniel's only brother, Edward, married Dorcas Pevey, a daughter of Peter Pevey, a well-respected farmer who lived in the nearby township of Greenfield. Edward appears, like Daniel, to have worked as a carpenter.[11]

Edward Pratt had consumption (from which he would die in 1838), and in 1835 he accepted Daniel's invitation to come to Alabama to improve his health. While noting in a letter to his wife that "my Brother works like a slave," Edward reported that Daniel and Esther "are very kind to me. They do everything in their power to make me comfortable." In the gin shop he had his "choice out of all the work," and he could work when he pleased. Dorcas replied that it "brought great joy to my heart that you was placed in a situation where you have everything to make you comfortable." She expressed "much gratitude to Brother and Sister for their kindness."[12]

Despite his kind treatment, Edward fretted about his separation from his family. A particular worry of his concerned the education of his two children, ten-year-old Augusta and seven-year-old Merrill. "I feel very badly that the children were deprived of going to the village school [during summer]," he informed Dorcas. "If you can persuade them to go to Greenfield or anywhere else [during winter] by paying their board and tuition I should be very glad." In his 1838 will, Edward reiterated his desire that his children attend school, specifically directing that Dorcas provide Augusta and Merrill with "a good common school education."[13]

Dorcas did her best to fulfill her dead husband's wish by sending thirteen-year-old Merrill to live with his Uncle Daniel in Prattville in 1841. Merrill would in some respects become the son Daniel never had, serving him as his right-hand man in the gin business and eventually taking over the reins after his uncle's death. In 1842, Daniel wrote his sister Dorcas of his pleasure with Merrill, evidently a virtuous and dutiful teenager: "Merrill appears to injoy himself very well. He is a very good boy. [He] is always willing to do all that I want him to." Probably recalling

11. Cooke, *Genealogy of Daniel Pratt*; Livermore and Putnam, *History of the Town of Wilton*, 467; Blood, *History of Temple*, 242; Will of Joseph Chandler of Wilton, Hillsborough County Courthouse. Much of the information in the above sources was verified from a visit to Wilton Cemetery.

12. Edward Pratt to Dorcas Pratt, 25 September 1835, Box 37, McMillan Collection.

13. Edward Pratt to Dorcas Pratt, 2 September 1835, and Dorcas Pratt to Edward Pratt, 28 October 1835, Box 37, McMillan Collection; Will of Edward Pratt of Wilton, Hillsborough County Courthouse.

his brother's wish, he added that Merrill "has ben at school since he was with me."[14]

Pratt also helped his sister Dorcas, a childless widow with no means of her own. When in New York City on a business trip, he sent Dorcas a $50 check, apologizing for sending her "so small a trifle." He explained that he "would have sent more but could not well spare it at this time" because of his difficulty in obtaining "northern funds." Nevertheless, he implored her not to think him unable or unwilling "to do more," insisting that it would "be a great pleasure to me to furnish you with all you need." Pratt's obvious guilt at not doing more at the time to help Dorcas poured out at the end of the letter when he prayed that "the Lord support you under all of your afflictions" and signed as "unworthy brother Daniel."[15]

By 1847, Dorcas had moved in with her sister Eliza and her husband, Daniel Holt. Visiting the Holts that year, Pratt found Daniel in poor health. Distressed by this discovery, he wrote the Holts from Prattville in June, informing them of his concern. After describing his village in glowing terms, he invited the Holts and Dorcas to move to Prattville: "Now if you would like to live in such a vilage . . . , I will build a house for you and will give you imployment in the mills, say to attend to my flouring and grist mill. Your children can go to school as long as necessary and can work in the Factory if you wish them to do so. I would build large enough for Sister Dorcas to live with you." Admitting that the Holts nevertheless "might not be sattisfyed here," he insisted they must be their "own judges." He assured them that if they did "not feel disposed to come," he would help them as soon as he possibly could. Again he pled the difficulty he had in obtaining ready cash: "Although I have a large property in this place I have allways had as much as I could do to get along and meet my payments and it is yet so."[16]

Pratt's proposal apparently met with some reluctance, but Dorcas, the Holts, and their six children finally did move to Prattville in 1850, accompanied by Merrill's sister, Augusta, and her husband, Ashby Morgan. Instead of going to work in one of Pratt's factories or shops, Daniel

14. Tarrant, ed., *Hon. Daniel Pratt,* 174; Daniel Pratt to Dorcas Chandler, 12 October 1842, Box 37, McMillan Collection.

15. Daniel Pratt to Dorcas Chandler, 12 October 1842, McMillan Collection.

16. Daniel Pratt to Daniel and Eliza Holt, 1 June 1847, Pratt Papers, ADAH. To Dorcas, Pratt included a separate note, urging her "to exercise your own judgment and decide the way you think would be most conducive to your future happiness."

Holt took over the operation of a farm Pratt owned. "Mr. Pratt thought he would build him a house about a mile out of the village and get someone to go on it and raise hogs and fouls and take his cows to make his butter," Daniel Holt wrote to some relatives back home, "but he could not get anyone to go on to his farm that he could trust. . . . Eliza said she guessed he had better send us. . . . I told him I was willing to go there or to the mill whichever would be best for him. He concluded that it was best for us to go on his farm." Both Daniel Holt and his wife declared themselves very pleased with their new situation. Daniel wrote that Pratt "has built us a very good house. It is on a hill so that we can see into the village of Prattville and see the city of Montgomery, and we have the best of water." In addition, Holt had "1 1/2 acres to plant with corn," and Pratt promised to build him "a Yankee barn."[17]

Eliza reported that "as yet we feel perfectly contented." The farmhouse she found "very neatly finished and convenient." It had one story with six rooms and a "piazza" extending around three sides. Moreover, she had charge of the "nicest dairy room" she had ever seen. Eliza also asserted that she went calling "much more [in Prattville] than at the North," describing in particular a fine Thanksgiving celebrated at Daniel Pratt's mansion. A great many relatives, including Merrill's visiting mother, had attended, making the event "quite a party."[18]

Pratt's remaining sister, Abigail, and her family never moved to Prattville. Pratt did not forget these relatives, however, lending each of Abigail's three children, Artemas, Eliza, and Esther, $500 in 1860. Pratt's bookkeeper listed the amounts as payable "1 day." Records indicate that Pratt lent large sums to other in-laws as well. Both Daniel Holt and Dorcas (Pevey) Pratt received sizable amounts from Pratt, the former $3,000 in 1858 and the latter $1,000 in 1860. Again, both amounts were entered as payable "1 day."[19]

Although Pratt had promised the Holts a house large enough for his sister Dorcas, she actually resided at the Pratt mansion, along with Mer-

17. Nobles, *Journals of Ferdinand Ellis Smith,* 80; Daniel Holt to Abiel and Betsy Holt, 10 February 1852, Box 37, McMillan Collection.

18. Eliza Holt to Abiel and Betsy Holt, 10 February 1852, McMillan Collection. Eliza Holt's commendation of Pratt's dairy room was apparently correct; she won a $1 premium for best fresh butter the next year at the Robinson Springs Agricultural Fair. (Prattville) *Autauga Citizen,* 24 November 1853.

19. Esther Howard to Merrill Pratt, 11 November 1863, Folder 34, Pratt Papers, ADAH; Pratt's Bills Payable, 1 March 1863, CECP.

rill; Esther's twice-widowed mother, Edith Kingsbury; Julia Bill, a young first cousin, once-removed, of Esther; and the widowed Mary DeBardeleben and her three children, for whom Pratt became guardian after the death of Mrs. DeBardeleben's husband. Pratt had room for all these people in part because his immediate family comprised only himself, Esther, and their daughter, Ellen, born in 1844.[20]

Daniel and Esther evidently did not attempt to start a family until the early 1840s. In all likelihood, the prudent Yankee couple had waited to do so until their successful move to Prattville had put them on a stable financial footing. Esther, who married Pratt at the age of twenty-four, did not give birth to her first child until 1843, when she was forty years old. The child, Mary, died that same year. In addition to Ellen, the Pratts had another daughter, Maria, who was born in 1847 and died in 1849.[21]

At the same time Daniel and Esther were attempting to start a family, Daniel was building a home, the first real one the couple would have. Designed by Pratt and completed early in 1843, the house stood on the western bank of Autauga Creek some 200 feet northwest of the gin factory. Though its academic classical facade strongly resembled one of Pratt's earlier houses, Pratt's new home had a far less ornate interior than any of those he had built in Georgia. An architectural expert who toured the house in 1935 found the decorative moldings "severe" and the mahogany stairway "conservative," yet he admired the great house's "lack of strain toward pretentiousness" and its "utilitarian aspect." According to Pratt, he and Esther did not so much want a lavish house as to "have every thing very convenient about us and room a plenty." Outbuildings included a sunken brick wine cellar and brick stables. In addition, a large two-story brick wing housed servants' quarters, a laundry, a bathroom, a kitchen, and serving rooms. Later in the decade, Pratt added an orchard, a vineyard, and an art gallery to his estate. James De Bow described the house in 1847 as "a splendid structure, with beautiful neighboring grounds."[22]

20. U.S. Census, Alabama, 1850 and 1860 Population Schedules, Autauga County; Hunnewell, *Ticknor Family*, 37, 43. Mary DeBardeleben was the widow of a planter from the Dutch Bend area. Since she was a native of upstate New York, she may have been a distant relation of Pratt or his wife. Her eldest son, Henry, later married Pratt's daughter, Ellen, and became one of the founders of Birmingham.

21. Mims, "History of Prattville," 20–21; Gandrud, *Autauga County,* 3. It is possible that the Pratts may have had medical difficulty conceiving a child.

22. Gamble, *Alabama Catalog,* 194; *Birmingham News Age-Herald,* 28 April 1935; Daniel Pratt to Dorcas Chandler, 12 October 1842, McMillan Collection; *De Bow's Re-*

Pratt believed that a man and his family should enjoy the fruits of his labor. In his 1852 *American Cotton Planter* article, he had chided miserly planters living in miserable abodes. The same year, Pratt listed the value of his jewelry, plate, and furniture at $2,000, ranking second in his county only to planter John Steele. Distantly following Pratt were planters Absalom Jackson ($1,000) and Benjamin Fitzpatrick ($950).[23] Pratt doubtlessly presided over one of the finest estates in Autauga County.

Pratt's home and its grounds reveal him as a man of culture and refinement. He had a myriad of interests beyond business, including art, music, viticulture, and pomology. Susan Frances Hale Tarrant, Gardner Hale's oldest daughter and a music teacher, testified to Pratt's love of music, which dated from his days at Temple Meeting House. In one parlor he had a grand piano, in the other, a large music box, and in the library, an organ. Still not content, Pratt kept installed in his art gallery a made-to-order hand organ that "contained cylinders for seventy tunes, all sacred music." Tarrant remembered that Pratt had particular fondness for this specially constructed item: "It was Mr. Pratt's pleasure on Sunday afternoons to sit down before this instrument, and soon the grand old tunes of 'Dundee,' 'Mear,' 'Old Hundred,' and others, would be heard, pealing out their hallowed strains, delighting him and other listeners."[24]

As Pratt purchased musical instruments to place in his mansion, he began planting a vineyard on the hillside behind it, evidently distinguishing wine-drinking from the consumption of whiskey and other hard liquors, of which he strongly disapproved. In the spring of 1849, Pratt, while in New Orleans on a business trip, wrote Englishman James Noyes, who owned the celebrated Hollywood Vineyards outside Natchez, Mississippi, requesting the latter man's help in starting a vineyard in Prattville. Aware that Noyes would be visiting Mobile in the summer, Pratt invited him to come to Prattville during the trip. Noyes doubted he would have time to make such a journey upriver, but he hoped to meet Pratt in Mobile so that the novice winemaker might "taste a thimbleful of Hollywood Tokay and a little talk about the wine cause in the south." Pratt decided to order 320 Roanoke grapevines, and in the fall he again wrote Noyes, asking for detailed instructions on planting. Pratt informed the

---

view 4 (September 1848): 137. Continental Eagle Corporation razed Pratt's house in 1962. Gamble, *Alabama Catalog,* 194.

23. Alabama State Property Tax Assessment, Autauga County, 1852, ACHC; *American Cotton Planter* 1 (January 1853): 23. The figure of $2,000 was surely a drastic underestimate.

24. Tarrant, ed., *Hon. Daniel Pratt,* 85.

viticulturist that he hoped to travel to Natchez from New Orleans to visit
Hollywood vineyards in the winter, causing Noyes to respond enthusiastically: "I should feel heartily pleased to receive a visit at any time from
a citizen of your state but a visit from Mr. Pratt, the Father of the manufacturing interest of Alabama, will make me more than proud."[25]

The next year, Pratt requested advice from Noyes on the hiring of a
gardener. Noyes recommended against hiring a white man for the post:
"There is very little chance of procuring such as I could recommend for
all that pretend to know anything will not engage but for very high wages
and do nothing but look on while others do the work." Instead, Noyes
advised Pratt "to select from among your servants a likely negro and send
him to me for about 18 months." Noyes himself would teach "him all
that is necessary for the vineyard and kitchen garden." He assured Pratt
that he had "2 such hands either of which I would not give for the services of the best white gardener." Although he feared Pratt might "think
such a plan an expensive one," Noyes insisted that "in the end it is the
cheapest and most satisfactory one you can adopt." Despite Noyes's admonition against hiring a white man, Pratt, demonstrating his thriftiness
and/or a partiality toward white labor, did just that, for living in the Pratt
household in 1850 was John Welch, a Scottish gardener.[26]

In the mid-1850s, Pratt began patronizing Charles Axt, a German viti-
culturalist living in Washington, Georgia, whose list of customers included prominent Autauga planters and Montgomery businessmen. R. G.
Dun and Company estimated that Pratt spent $5,000 on his vineyard. In
1860, he produced five hundred gallons of wine, almost half the wine
produced in Autauga County that year. Pratt's wine making efforts won
notice in the pages of the *Montgomery Daily Mail* and Noah Cloud's
American Cotton Planter and Soil of the South. Cloud, one of the South's
most accomplished agricultural reformers, gave the most detailed description of Pratt's vineyard. According to Cloud, the vineyard was composed of "three to five acres of scuppernongs and catawbas, terraced in
the most picturesque style to the summit level of a high and very steep
hill, perhaps one hundred feet or more perpendicular." Cloud noted that
the vineyard contained "in all twenty-five acres of land" and was "en-

25. James Noyes to Daniel Pratt, 26 March, 19 April, 15 November 1849, Folder 44,
Pratt Papers, ADAH.

26. James Noyes to Daniel Pratt, 31 August 1850, Folder 44, Pratt Papers, ADAH; U.S.
Census, Alabama, 1850 Population Schedule, Autauga County.

closed by a substantial brick and pickette fence." After his tour, Cloud enjoyed "several specimens of fine Autauga wine" with Esther Pratt's "elegant dinner." Cloud also praised Pratt's "beautiful orchard," declaring that it had "fine, large fruit trees, embracing various varieties of the apple, peach, pear, plum, and fig, all healthful and thrifty."[27]

Perhaps Pratt's most intriguing outside interest was art. Pratt, insisted Susan Tarrant, "was an artist as well as an artisan."[28] Though he continued to dabble in architecture in the 1840s and 1850s, Pratt's known structures—his house, the Prattville Methodist Church, and the rejected plans for the Alabama Capitol—show little of the flair of his work in Georgia. Pratt's real contribution to southern art during this period occurred when he became, in 1844, the patron of painter George Cooke.

Born in Maryland in 1793 as the son of a lawyer, George Cooke in his twenties embarked on a career as a painter after having worked in "the mercantile trade as a partner in a china and grocery business." Spending several years in Europe with his wife, Maria, where he pursued his artistic education, Cooke returned to America fired with the ambition to become a "history and landscape artist in the grand manner" but instead found himself wandering across the South "in pursuit of portrait commissions."[29]

George Cooke and Daniel Pratt appear to have hit it off almost immediately. For one thing, as one writer has noted, the pair "seemed to agree about everything: they were both political conservatives who deplored Jacksonian populism; they were devout Methodists; and they were aesthetic traditionalists." But even more important, the two friends were intelligent, sensitive, and driven men who shared an occasional sense of impatience with a South that did not always live up to their highest hopes and fondest dreams. Indeed, one could argue that Cooke and Pratt had

27. *American Cotton Planter and Soil of the South* 1 (May 1857): 156–57; Alabama, 2: 12, R. G. Dun & Co. Collection; U.S. Census, Alabama, 1860 Agricultural Schedule, Autauga County. See also *Montgomery Daily Mail*, 17 July, 22 August 1857. Scattered references to Charles Axt are found in Folder 44, Pratt Papers, ADAH, and in the Continental Eagle Corporation Papers. The second largest wine producer in Autauga County in 1860 was Daniel Holt, who made 364 gallons. Together, Pratt and his brother-in-law accounted for 80 percent of Autauga's wine production. (Prattville) *Autauga Citizen*, 17 November 1853.

28. Tarrant, ed., *Hon. Daniel Pratt*, 85.

29. Donald D. Keyes, *George Cooke 1793–1849*, with additional essays by Linda Crocker Simmons, Estill Curtis Pennington, William Nathaniel Banks. (Athens, Ga.: Georgia Museum of Art, 1991), 7–15, 23, 27.

their own "sacred circle" of sorts, not altogether unlike that of William Gilmore Simms, James Henry Hammond, Nathaniel Beverly Tucker, Edmund Ruffin, and George Holmes.[30]

Soon after meeting Cooke in 1844, Pratt agreed to rent to him for use as an art gallery the top two floors of his four-story commission house at 15 Saint Charles Street in New Orleans. In December 1844, Cooke opened his National Gallery of Paintings, which became "a fixture" in the city's cultural life. Upon the National Gallery's opening, one New Orleans paper declared its "admiration and surprise that so large a number of most excellent paintings should be now in existence among us." In addition to his own work, Cooke displayed paintings by such prominent artists as Thomas Cole, Thomas Doughty, John Gadsby Chapman, and Thomas Sully. Sully's copy of Gilbert Stuart's famous full-length portrait of George Washington sold for $600.[31]

For the next four years, Cooke would open the gallery every winter, leaving New Orleans in the summer, but his bold project did not live up to its early promise, despite the favorable attention it had won in the press. In 1846, Cooke bemoaned: "There is no prospect of selling paintings here. . . . I despair of success with my Gallery. This winter it has only averaged 60 $ per week, just covering expenses." Although wealthy New Orleans financier James Robb attempted to bolster the tottering gallery, Cooke's most steadfast supporter proved to be Daniel Pratt. In November 1845, Pratt gave Cooke a challenging commission to make an enlargement of his painting *Interior of St. Peter's, Rome* for an art gallery Pratt had decided to build (at the cost of $10,000) on the grounds of his Prattville estate. Pratt intended that Cooke's huge painting would serve as the centerpiece of the gallery. Cooke explained: "Mr. Pratt is building a gallery adjoining his house in Alabama to be lighted from above and I am to paint St. Peter's Church to fill one end of it, fifteen by twenty-three feet, so that when you enter the door the whole church with its arches and colonnades in perspective will appear as in nature." Cooke (with his wife) spent two summers at Pratt's home, completing his masterwork in 1847. The same year, he also painted a group portrait of Esther Pratt, little Ellen, and her mulatto nursemaid. Cooke and his wife spent some of early 1848 in Prattville as well, during which time Cooke traveled to

---

30. Ibid., 41–42; Drew Gilpin Faust, *A Sacred Circle: The Dilemma of the Intellectual in the Old South, 1840–1860* (Baltimore: Johns Hopkins University Press, 1977).

31. Keyes, *George Cooke*, 18–19, 42.

Selma and executed a painting of John Lapsley, a prominent Selma businessman and a soon-to-be shareholder in Prattville Manufacturing Company, as well as a memorial portrait of Lapsley's deceased son.[32]

When the ailing Cooke traveled north to take water cures during the summer of 1848, he carried with him another Pratt commission, this one to paint full-length portraits of John C. Calhoun and Daniel Webster. Pratt already owned a copy of Cooke's full-length portrait of Henry Clay, and he hoped to have the complete "great triumvirate" for his gallery. He wrote Calhoun, explaining that he had authorized Cooke "to call on you and request of you to sit for a full-length portrait should it comport with your many important duties to afford him the time." In the end, Cooke only managed to execute the Calhoun portrait. Cooke reported that Calhoun, though preoccupied by political issues, "appeared much flattered by the invitation to sit for his portrait," but that Webster, pleading fatigue, repeatedly prevaricated. Sympathetically noting the recent deaths of two of Webster's children, Cooke wrote that the statesman "appeared very depressed and somewhat worn with care. Yet his fine black eye has not lost its lustre."[33]

In July, Cooke reported to Pratt that he had "had only *three* sittings from Mr. Calhoun," as the statesman "had been unusually occupied with questions of great interest to the South." Cooke compared Calhoun to "the fabled 'Atlas carrying the world on his shoulders,'" for he sustained "the whole weight of the South on the slavery question in the acquired territories." Cooke complained that Calhoun illustrated "a certain character in the Bible, who when told to do something, said 'Sir, I go'—but went not," but he hoped that Webster would "be like the other who refused, but afterward went and did it." In August, having finished the head of Calhoun and sketched his figure, he and Maria went to take the waters at Saratoga and Sharon Springs. From there he wrote Webster, offering to paint him in Boston, but Webster wrote back refusing, again pleading ill health.[34]

The Cookes returned to New Orleans in the fall, determined to close his failing National Gallery and move to Athens, Georgia, where they

32. Ibid., 19–20, 42–43, 76–79; Alabama, 2: 12, R. G. Dun & Co. Collection.

33. Keyes, *George Cooke*, 20, 43; Daniel Pratt to J. C. Calhoun, 22 May 1848, John C. Calhoun Papers, Clemson University, Clemson, S.C.; George Cooke to Daniel Pratt, 9 June 1848, Folder 44, Pratt Papers, ADAH.

34. George Cooke to Daniel Pratt, 21 July, 6 September, 19 October 1848, Folder 44, Pratt Papers, ADAH.

had lived previously and preferred both the climate and the people. In the spring, Cooke had tried renting the gallery out as a lecture hall. One "Dr. Colton" had drawn crowds of 150 to 200 persons nightly to his lectures, but, Cooke complained, "in this warm weather, there is not sufficient ventilation, nor is the room large enough." In March 1849, however, before the couple could complete the move, Cooke contracted cholera and died. Daniel Pratt (along with James Robb) served as one of Cooke's executors. Also indicative of the trust Cooke placed in Pratt is the fourth item of his will: "Any amount due me by Daniel Pratt, Esq., after deducting the rent for rooms in his building, and also for any other painting he may wish to purchase, may remain in the hands of said Pratt at legal interest until he may prefer paying it over to my wife."[35]

Pratt purchased more than a dozen Cooke paintings, transferring them to his Prattville gallery. His collection included, in addition to the Clay and Calhoun portraits, Cooke's copy of Stuart's portrait of George Washington, a portrait of Cooke's wife, Cooke's self-portrait, and an 1847 portrait of Bishop Joshua Soule of the Methodist Church. In addition, Pratt also bought for his collection American and European landscape paintings (of such subjects as Rome, Naples, Niagara Falls, and Natural Bridge, Virginia) and Cooke's copies of religious works by European masters, including Federico Barocci's *Christ Appearing to Mary Magdalene in the Garden,* Govert Flinck's *Annunciation to the Shepherds of the Birth of Christ,* Raphael's *The Transfiguration,* and Leonardo Da Vinci's *The Last Supper.* Art historian Jessie Poesch ranks Pratt's art collection as among the finest private collections in the antebellum South.[36]

The gallery, which could be entered from the flower garden or from the house's back piazza, had skylights in the ceiling, arranged so that "the paintings could be seen to best advantage." At one end of the gallery, en-

35. George Cooke to Daniel Pratt, 14 February 1848, Folder 44, Pratt Papers, ADAH; Marilou A. Rudolph, "George Cooke and His Paintings," *Georgia Historical Quarterly* 44 (June 1960): 148–49.

36. Rudolph, "George Cooke," 149; *Descriptive Catalogue of Paintings in the Gallery of Daniel Pratt, Together with a Memoir of George Cooke, Artist* (Prattville: n.p., 1853); Jessie J. Poesch, *The Art of the Old South: Painting, Sculpture, Architecture, and the Products of Craftsmen, 1560–1860* (New York: Harrison House, 1983), 301. See also Laquita Thompson, "Daniel Pratt's Picture Gallery," *Alabama Review* 48 (July 1995): 166–74 and "Daniel Pratt and George Cooke: Developing a Gallery," in *The World of Daniel Pratt,* 107–19.

tirely covering the wall, was Cooke's *Interior of St. Peter's, Rome.* Above the door of the piazza entrance, taking up the full width of the room, was Cooke's copy of *The Last Supper.* Visitors to Prattville came away very impressed with the gallery. One guest of Pratt was particularly enraptured by *Interior of St. Peter's, Rome,* calling it "the finest painting in Alabama." This painting, he wrote, had "received the highest commendations" from professional artists. He added: "The coloring is exceedingly fine and the perspective is most admirable. Every object appears to stand in bold relief from the canvass [*sic*], and as you look upon it you can easily imagine yourself standing in the entrance of the grand old cathedral, gazing upon the beauties of the magnificent altar."[37]

Cooke's widow, Maria, decided that his body should lie in the town where his work was really honored, so she had it moved from Saint Louis Cemetery in New Orleans to Pratt's private cemetery in Prattville, where an impressive obelisk was erected over his grave. Pratt's reverent treatment of Cooke after his death indicates the closeness of his relationship with the Cookes, as does his and Esther's naming one of their daughters after Maria Cooke.[38] Cooke's seven surviving letters to Pratt, dating from February to October 1848, are further evidence of this closeness.

In his letters to Pratt, Cooke does not treat him as a provincial patron he must patiently humor, but as an intellectual equal with whom discourse was enjoyable. Cooke clearly felt on familiar terms with Pratt and his family. "Mrs. Cooke and myself were very much gratified to hear of your pleasant trip on your *name-sake* [the Alabama River steamboat *Daniel Pratt*], and of the good health of your little family," he wrote in February 1848, "and however flattered [we are] by the name of your little Maria, I think it will be difficult for her to rival Ellen in our affections." In another missive, Cooke announced that he greatly looked forward to visiting Prattville in the fall. He wanted to see all of Pratt's "improvements" in the town, as well as "make a group [portrait] of little Ellen and Maria and once again enjoy the hospitality of yourself and family." He also expressed his wish to "once more 'sit together in heavenly places'" with Pratt, Jesse Perham, and Shadrack Mims.[39]

37. Tarrant, ed., *Hon. Daniel Pratt,* 84–85; *Montgomery Daily Mail,* 8 September 1855.

38. Keyes, *George Cooke,* 42, 44. Another Prattville couple, Llewellyn and Elvira Spigner (both of whom were staunch Methodists) named a son George Cooke Spigner in 1849. Church Register.

39. George Cooke to Daniel Pratt, 14 February, 21 July 1848, Folder 44, Pratt Papers, ADAH.

In addition to discussing at length with Pratt matters of national politics ("With you I am utterly disgusted with [the] Democracy and fear we
shall have to endure its abuses to the last"), world affairs ("All that I predicted of the French is coming to pass, and the worst is yet to come"),
and religion ("I can but think there is more real religion at the South than
at the North. . . . [In the North] there is more formality than spiritual
worship, and hence every kind of -ism prevails from Universalism to
Millerism"), Cooke, the former merchant, discoursed on financial issues
and the intricacies of Pratt's newly launched business. "I am greatly gratified at the success of your enterprise and hope the stockholders will be
able to pay up the amount due, but have fears under the existing pressure
of money matters they cannot," he lectured in one letter. "I do not pretend to have your foresight in business, but I certainly did forsee the scarcity of money and reduced price of cotton when I advised you not to lay
in your stock of cotton at the prices then given and although the prospect
of peace [in Europe] and advanced state of the season may relieve the
money market a little, you may rely upon money will be scarce for a long
time whether Cass or Taylor be the next president." Cooke also gave
Pratt the benefit of his discussions with the energetic Selma merchant
John Lapsley, who recently had sat for a portrait and whom Pratt hoped
would actively take up the cause of Alabama industry. "I have not heard
from Mr. Lapsley since we left Selma," Cooke confided, "but I have no
doubt of his intention to engage his friends in the manufacturing interest.
It requires, however, time and opportunity for them to make up their
minds."[40]

Cooke's regard for Pratt as a full intellectual equal is especially striking in light of his strong declaration to his brother that he could not be
true friends with a mental inferior, no matter how much he might respect
him. "I am not an aristocrat," he insisted, "and think myself no better
than the man who knows how to plough and live virtuously; but my
mind would never be elevated by such associations." He concluded: "I
should not seek such [a man] for a bosom friend."[41]

With the death of Cooke, Pratt lost a true "bosom friend," one of the
few he appears ever to have had. Even Pratt's great admirer Shadrack
Mims wrote regretfully of his own "misfortune of having known so little

40. George Cooke to Daniel Pratt, 14 February, 15 May, 9 June, 21 July, 6 September
1848, Folder 44, Pratt Papers, ADAH.
41. Rudolph, "George Cooke," 117.

of [Pratt] personally."[42] Indeed, the only other person who can with certainty be viewed as a bosom friend of Pratt is Esther, his wife of nearly forty-six years. Although, sadly, no letters between the two survive, it is discernible from the available evidence that the couple had an uncommonly strong marriage.

All descriptions of Esther Pratt by her contemporaries portray her as Daniel Pratt's virtuous helpmate through all his ups and downs. According to Mims, Pratt placed great faith in the judgment of Esther, "her husband's equal." The pair "were happily made one" and "never pulled at different ends of the rope." In 1833, Pratt actually offered to "return North and settle . . . among their relations if she desired." Fortunately for Prattville, Esther "very wisely decided to remain in the South." Mims found an important moral about the Pratt's marriage in this anecdote, declaring, "Some men are so mannish that they will think it a weak point to consult their wives, when perhaps their greatest weakness lies in not consulting them." Noah Cloud would have concurred with Mims that Esther's opinions were worthy of attention, for he found her "a lady of unusual intelligence and social vivacity" who discoursed interestingly on the Pratt estate's "tastefully arranged shrubbery, fine fruit and vegetable gardens, and terraced vineyards."[43]

Esther Pratt, originally a Presbyterian, converted to Methodism along with her husband in 1832. Like Daniel, she became involved in Prattville benevolence projects, particularly sewing for the needy. Throughout the antebellum period, Esther provided Sunday-school clothing for Pratt's factory operatives; and during the Civil War, she served as president of the Prattville Ladies Aid Society. The society, which made clothing for Alabama soldiers, was, as historian Malcolm McMillan has noted, one of "the more active of the small town societies" in Alabama.[44]

An 1847 portrait of Esther by George Cooke depicts her as a beaming, round-cheeked matron holding her young child, Ellen, on her lap while Ellen's mulatto nursemaid stands by in the background.[45] Esther was

42. Mims, "History of Prattville," 32.

43. Mims, "History of Prattville," 24; Mims, "History of the M. E. Church"; *American Cotton Planter and Soil of the South* 1 (May 1857): 156. Reflecting Cloud's estimate of her, Esther Pratt won $1 premiums for scuppernong jelly and pear preserves at the 1853 Robinson Springs Agricultural Fair. (Prattville) *Autauga Citizen,* 24 November 1853.

44. Mims, "History of Prattville," 58; Mims, "History of the M. E. Church"; Malcolm C. McMillan, *Alabama Confederate Reader* (Tuscaloosa: University of Alabama Press, 1962), 350.

45. Keyes, *George Cooke,* 42–43.

likely pregnant with Maria at the time of the sitting. Judging from this blissfully domestic portrait, it appears that Esther had a cheerful, serene nature that no doubt helped clear Pratt's more tempestuous moods.

Both Daniel and Esther Pratt doted on Ellen, their only child to survive infancy. Of Ellen, Pratt wrote his relatives in 1847 that "she . . . is a sweet little girl. We think a good deal of her but not enough to spoil her." Pratt's judgment that he and Esther did not spoil Ellen may have been in error, however. In February 1863, the eighteen-year-old Ellen eloped with Henry DeBardeleben, another of Pratt's wards, provoking a major scandal in the town. Receiving news of the event from his wife at Port Hudson, Louisiana, Merrill Pratt reacted angrily, branding Ellen a willful young girl who had "had her own way too long." Merrill had worried in Prattville that Henry and Ellen might be up to something, and he had discussed the matter with his Aunt Esther, but she did not believe Ellen would marry without her parents' consent. Now that Ellen indeed had run off with Henry, Merrill feared the scandal would "ruin" his uncle, who was "getting old and feeble." He suspected that Henry DeBardeleben, who was "not calculated for any good girl," had actually "seduced" Ellen prior to the elopement.[46]

Daniel Pratt's relatives in Prattville fully shared Merrill's outrage over the behavior of Ellen and Henry. Indeed, many of them initially refused even to speak to the couple when they returned to Prattville in March. The reaction to the affair by Merrill and the rest of Ellen's kin would appear to stand in marked contrast to that of Ellen's parents, who seem to have been extremely forgiving of their daughter's rash action, given the remarkable discipline and self-control they had exercised in their own lives. Certainly, Pratt's treatment of Ellen in this instance was not that of a stern, cold man.[47]

Pratt's life, in fact, is characterized in part by charitable acts, not just toward family, but toward friends and even strangers. As early as 1820, the young Daniel Pratt used the money he had earned in Savannah to re-

46. Daniel Pratt to Daniel and Eliza Holt, 1 June 1847, Pratt Papers; ADAH; Merrill Pratt to Julia Pratt, 18 February 1863, Box 34, Pratt Papers, ADAH. According to Merrill, some of the blame for the elopement rested with one Eliza, who was clearly a slave and in fact may have been the mulatto nursemaid in George Cooke's portrait. In Merrill's view, Eliza was a "bad woman" who exercised a negative influence on Ellen. He had informed his uncle and aunt of his worries, even going "so far as to tell Aunt to keep Ellen away from her," but to no avail.

47. Merrill Pratt to Julia Pratt, 30 March 1863, Box 34, Pratt Papers, ADAH.

deem the mortgage on Aaron Kimball Putnam's home. As late as 1863, Pratt wrote a $1,000 check to Shadrack Mims, who suffered from poor health and financial troubles. "As you have four sons in the army and I have not the pleasure to have any I think it nothing but right for me to contribute this much towards their expenses," he wrote in the accompanying letter. Mindful of Mims's pride, he added, "I do not contribute this because I think you are not able and willing to do all that is necessary for your sons, but because I think you deserve it and that it is a pleasure to me to do so."[48]

Shadrack Mims recorded several instances of Pratt's benevolence to down-at-the-heels strangers. Pratt's charity, wrote Mims, was not "spasmodic"; rather, a "constant stream" ran "from his heart and purse." To a Prattville man whose home had burned, Pratt gave $500 to assist in rebuilding. In Hot Springs, Arkansas, Pratt gave $50 to a "poor, afflicted and penniless" man who "was being improved by the water but had no means either to stay or get away." Years later, upon meeting a Prattvillian traveling in Arkansas, the man informed him of Pratt's kind act, declaring that "Mr. Pratt is one of the best men I ever met."[49]

Sometimes, strangers had to content themselves with advice, which Pratt, a successful, self-made man, never hesitated to dispense. For example, a young widow wrote Pratt asking whether she could procure jobs for her children in Pratt's mill. Discovering from her letter that the woman "was an educated lady," Pratt wrote her back "advising her and encouraging her to take a school." Several years later, Pratt "received a letter from this lady thanking him for his advice" and informing him "that she had succeeded so well in her calling as [a] teacher" that she had been able to purchase a home that served as "a fine building for an academy" and to save "a surplus of money besides."[50]

Pratt penned some heartfelt "good advice" to an old friend he had not seen in years, Elijah Chandler, the New Hampshire carpenter who had lent Pratt much of the money he had used to purchase Joseph May's land in the 1830s. By 1854, Chandler, now in his sixties, had migrated to Pope County, Arkansas, in search of new economic opportunities. Noting

48. Mims, "History of Prattville," 42–43; Daniel Pratt to Shadrack Mims, 5 September 1863, Box 37, McMillan Collection.

49. Mims, untitled ms., McMillan Collection. According to Mims, Daniel Pratt's bookkeeper once remarked to him "that he could not keep up with Mr. Pratt's expenditures" on charity. Mims, "History of Prattville," 53.

50. Mims, "History of Prattville," 53.

Chandler's "feeble" health and likely recalling his own hard struggle in frontier Alabama, Pratt intimated that Chandler's move perhaps had been imprudent. Asserting that Chandler had "enough of this world's goods to permit all the comforts of this life," Pratt urged him: "Live the balance of your days on what you have labored hard for." Pratt declared that "there are none of us that can be perfectly happy in this life, [so] let us make ourselves as happy as circumstances will admit and live in a constant preparation for perfect happiness hereafter." Pratt suggested to his friend that when he tired of living alone, he should move to Prattville, where, Pratt said, he and his wife would do "the best we can to make you comfortable." Despite his advice, however, Pratt wrote that he was eager to read "a history of that far-off country [and] a description of your place and improvements." Should he pass through Arkansas himself, Pratt added, he would "stop and spend a night" at Chandler's abode.[51]

Pratt also expended exceedingly large sums of money on Prattville churches and schools, which he expected to benefit the townspeople in general. According to an R. G. Dun and Company agent, Pratt had by 1853 already given "away to charity purposes as much as $100,000." In probably his most expensive projects, he spent $20,000 on the Prattville Methodist church building (completed in 1853) and nearly $9,500 on the Prattville Male and Female Academy (completed in 1861). In addition to the church, the Methodist church building housed the town's interdenominational Sunday-school room and library. The academy served for years as Autauga County's best school. Pratt also "contributed largely" to the building of the Autauga County Courthouse (completed in 1870). When he did not give money, he often gave land, providing lots for Prattville's Baptist and Presbyterian churches and the town cemetery. Pratt also likely conceived of his cotton mill to some extent as a charitable project for poor whites, but though his contemporaries repeatedly made this assertion, there is no direct evidence from Pratt's pen concerning it.[52]

Viewing even his art gallery as a public benefit, Pratt opened the building to visitors. Middle-class citizens of Prattville fondly remembered their visits there. Susan Tarrant recalled spending hours in the gallery, "inspired by the revelations on canvas and always grateful that there was

51. Daniel Pratt to [Elijah] Chandler, 19 July 1854, Pratt Papers, ADAH.
52. Alabama, 2: 12, R. G. Dun & Co. Collection; Mims, untitled ms.; Prattville Academy Expenses from May 1859 to June 1861, Folder 54, Pratt Papers, ADAH.

one man—I've never seen his like—who was willing to spend money for the fine arts, and make the same accessible to those who otherwise had no opportunity to gratify their love for the beautiful." When after the Civil War the art gallery building became infected with dry rot and had to be torn down, Pratt donated the two largest paintings, *Interior, St. Peter's* and *The Last Supper,* to the University of Georgia, whose president, Andrew Adgate Lipscomb, had been a friend of Pratt's since the 1850s when he was president of Tuskegee Female College, a Methodist school that Ellen Pratt possibly attended. *Interior, St. Peter's* was placed at one end of the Greek Revival university chapel, where it still stands. An Athens newspaper contrasted "the taste and liberality of the generous donor" with the "niggardliness" of the state legislature. Pratt, it noted, had endowed the university "with a magnificent work of art" worth some $15,000 to $18,000, while the "solons" in the legislature had provided the university with an annual stipend of only $8,000.[53]

Not confining his benevolence projects to Prattville's white population, Pratt extended aid of a sort to blacks before and after the Civil War. His white admirers, at least, agreed that Pratt did many fine things for African Americans. Shadrack Mims declared that Pratt as a master "was free and generous" with his slaves, "providing fully for all their physical wants and comforts." Pratt, Mims insisted, bought "the best quality food and clothing" for his bondsmen and built them "comfortable and commodious houses." After the Civil War, Pratt donated a two-story building and lot worth $1,500 to the freedmen to serve as a church and day school. In his 1873 eulogy to Pratt, Charles Doster, a white Prattville Republican, declared that the town's black inhabitants "should honor and revere his memory, because he was their friend, and did for them many acts of charity." Mims fully concurred, asserting that Pratt "never failed to assist [his former slaves] to the last when called on" for help.[54] Testi-

53. Tarrant, ed., *Hon. Daniel Pratt,* 85; Andrew Adgate Lipscomb to Daniel Pratt, 17 August, 1 September 1868, Folder 46, Pratt Papers, ADAH. Lipscomb enclosed the quoted newspaper article in one of his letters. On one occasion, the art gallery served as the location of a triple wedding. Thomas Ormsby married Gardner Hale's daughter Hannah, George Smith married Esther Ticknor's cousin Mary Ormsby, and Ferdinand Smith wed Martha Riggs. After the weddings, Pratt served the party "a most sumptuous dinner." Ferdinand Smith wrote appreciatively that Pratt's "kind proposal indicated his true feelings towards the young men of Prattville." Nobles, *Journals of Ferdinand Ellis Smith,* 170, 175.

54. Mims, untitled ms.; Charles Doster, "Eulogy," in *Hon. Daniel Pratt,* 138. An intriguing example of one of Pratt's kind acts concerns his slave Eliza. According to his bookkeeper, Pratt lent the sum of $700 (payable "1 day") to Eliza on October 26, 1861. Eliza,

monials of whites notwithstanding, however, Pratt became a loyal Democrat after the war and staunchly opposed black social equality.

In addition to performing benevolent acts in Prattville, Pratt became involved in statewide projects of the Methodist Church. Passionately devoted to the cause of education, he served as a trustee for two important Methodist schools in south Alabama, Centenary Institute in Dallas County and East Alabama Male College in Auburn. Nor did Pratt's service end there. Not surprisingly, given his business success, the Methodist Alabama Conference included him among the nine lay members it appointed in 1850 to its newly created Joint Board of Finance.[55]

Pratt extended a philanthropic hand to other institutions besides those of the Methodist Church. The University of Alabama, the East Alabama Masonic Institute of Oak Bowery, and Howard College of Marion all received donations from Pratt, who soon found himself an honorary member of such scholastic clubs as the University of Alabama's Philomathic Society, Howard's Adelphic Society, and the East Alabama Masonic Institute's Irving Literary Society. To the unlettered Pratt, it is clear that these honorary memberships held great significance. Each institution received an appreciative, humble (and poorly spelled) letter of acceptance from him. To the corresponding secretary of the Adelphic Society, Pratt wrote with great feeling of his belief in education: "Unfortunately I never had the advantage of an Education. I am probaly more thouraly convinced of its importance than I should have ben had I received it, as every days experiance shows me the necessity of it. I am a friend to all literary and moral institutions or societies. . . . It must certainly be very great consolation to a man in his old age to look back and see that his life has ben spent in binefiting the condition of others and the improvement of Society. If we can do this we shall feel that we have not lived in vane."[56]

Pratt's greatest honor probably occurred in 1846, when the trustees of the University of Alabama conferred upon him "the honorary degree of master in the mechanic and useful arts." The highly complimentary letter

---

whom the bookkeeper listed as a servant, is likely the "bad woman" Merrill Pratt referred to in his letter concerning Ellen Pratt's elopement. Furthermore, it seems possible that Eliza was the mulatto nursemaid of Ellen in George Cooke's 1847 painting. What became of Eliza after the war, however, is not known. Pratt's Bills Payable, 1 March 1863, 1 January 1864, CECP.

55. West, *History of Methodism*, 611, 681, 736.

56. Daniel Pratt to W. D. Lee, 21 December 1850, Folder 44, Pratt Papers, ADAH. See also Daniel Pratt to Thomas Bugbee, 19 December 1850, Folder 44, Pratt Papers, ADAH.

written by his admirer Basil Manly, president of the university (and a Baptist minister), informing Pratt of the degree bestowed on him, gives an idea of the esteem in which Pratt was held in Alabama as early as that year:

> Without having devoted your life to literary pursuits, you have attained . . . that which is the end of all letters and all study, the art of making men around you *wiser, better,* and *happier.* You have shown, in a substantial manner, . . . that you value, and know how to promote, the industrial and economic virtues among men, rendering your own intelligence and honestly acquired wealth a blessing to all that come within the sphere of your influence: You have shown yourself the friend & supporter of schools for the son of the laboring man, as well as of the rich; that all the rising generation may be fitted to that ambition of republican freedom which it is the peculiar privilege of American citizens to enjoy: above all, you have shown that you discern what is the great source of all virtue and happiness, of all knowledge and success, by your efficient maintenance of the Institutions of the religion of our Lord Jesus Christ, among your people.[57]

Entering Pratt's office shortly after he received Manly's missive, Shadrack Mims witnessed the deep effect it had on his friend. "As he handed me the letter," recalled Mims, "the tear-drop stood in his eye." Pratt quickly penned Manly a heartfelt response, in which he confessed himself "at a loss to know how to answer" Manly's letter, for it had filled him with "supprise and astonishment." Pratt insisted that he felt "unworthy of the honour and unworthy to receive such a letter as you was pleased to address to me." If he had "done anything to benefit others, or to benefit society," Pratt humbly added, credit lay with God: "Had not the means and disposition ben derived from a purer source than poor, erring, and degenerate man, I should never have deserved any applause for any good deed." Pratt hoped that the honor bestowed upon him by the University would "be the means of awakening me to a higher sense of duty, that I may be more 'diligent in business, fervant in spirit, serving the Lord.'"[58]

As such words indicate, Daniel Pratt clearly felt obligated by his religious faith to do more than simply pile up money. To that end he used

57. Basil Manly to Daniel Pratt, 4 January 1847, Folder 46, Pratt Papers, ADAH.

58. Mims, "History of Prattville," 30; Daniel Pratt to Basil Manly, 21 January 1847, Folder 45, Pratt Papers, ADAH.

his wealth to improve, as he saw it, the lives of his family, friends, and fellow men and women. In particular, Pratt hoped to make Prattville a model town—a "shining city" on the banks of Autauga Creek that incorporated the virtues he held dear. In this endeavor, he once again enjoyed great, though not complete, success.

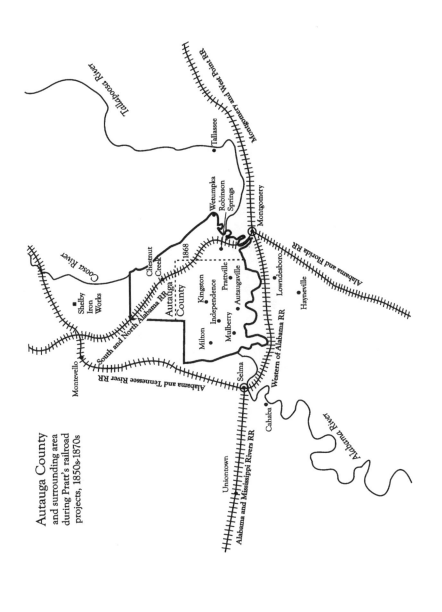

Autauga County
and surrounding area
during Pratt's railroad
projects, 1850s-1870s

Tallapoosa River

Montgomery and West Point RR

Tallassee

Wetumpka
Robinson
Springs

Montgomery

Coosa River

Chestnut
Creek

1868

Alabama and Florida RR

Shelby
Iron
Works

Autauga
County

Kingston

Pratsville

Autaugaville

Lowndesboro

Hayneville

Independence

Milton

Mulberry

South and North Alabama RR

Western of Alabama RR

Montevallo

Alabama and Tennessee River RR

Selma

Cahaba

Alabama River

Uniontown

Alabama and Mississippi Rivers RR

5

BUILDING A TOWN: PRATTVILLE, 1846–1861

In accordance with Daniel Pratt's desire, Prattville expanded in the fifteen years before the Civil War from a company village into a diversified marketing and manufacturing center. Like the citizens of other towns across the United States, Prattvillians in the late 1850s enthusiastically embraced boosterism, trumpeting the economic and social advances that their town had made during the decade and urging the necessity of doing even more. Toward the goal of improving their town economically, the people of Prattville launched vigorous campaigns to capture the county courthouse and to get railroads routed their way. At the same time that Prattvillians pursued economic advancement, they also sought social improvement through the establishment of churches, schools, and voluntary associations promoting virtuous behavior in Prattville's populace. Despite their efforts, however, Prattville did suffer moral lapses—drinking and brawling, for example, occasionally broke out in the town's normally quiet streets. Moreover, the desired courthouse and railroads did not materialize until after the Civil War, in part because of political squabbles that broke out between Pratt and his supporters on the one side and Autauga's Democrats on the other. Nevertheless, Daniel Pratt and the people of Prattville by 1860 had largely succeeded in making, as Pratt had put it, a town of "good morals and good society."

Most historians ignore antebellum southern towns, and those who do take notice of these communities tend to be dismissive. One scholar, for example, concedes that there "were, of course, towns and cities in the Old South," but then he proceeds to describe them in terms that cancel the significance of his concession: " 'Mere trading posts,' W. J. Cash called the best of them, and that is precisely and only what they were. . . . White-painted towns dozing in the summer sun, strewn about with hogs, dogs, and a few people; a languid populace briefly awakening with the arrival of a steamboat—that smoking, belching monster that likely provided the only excitement for a day or a week, unless a revival was in town—and then quickly resuming its 'at ease' posture waiting for nothing more than supper." With good reason, the people of Prattville would have been appalled at such a description. But for slavery, Prattville was not readily distinguishable from northern towns of the same period. Antebellum Prattville in truth challenges the prevailing scholarly opinion that a hegemonic premodern planter class stunted the economic and cultural vitality of the southern town. Much of what was supposedly new about the New South of the postbellum years already existed in Prattville in the 1850s.[1]

1. David R. Goldfield, *Cotton Fields and Skyscrapers: Southern City and Region, 1607–1980* (Baton Rouge: Louisiana State University Press, 1982), 32. Goldfield's statement, while more colorful than most, is representative in perspective. There are exceptions to this general view, however, including the earlier work of Goldfield. See Blaine A. Brownell and David R. Goldfield, eds., *The City in Southern History: The Growth of Urban Civilization in the South* (Port Washington, N.Y.: Kennikat Press, 1977); David R. Goldfield, *Urban Growth in an Age of Sectionalism: Virginia, 1847–1861* (Baton Rouge: Louisiana State University Press, 1977); James Michael Russell, *Atlanta, 1847–1890: City Building in the Old South and the New* (Baton Rouge: Louisiana State University Press, 1988); Lisa C. Tolbert, *Constructing Townscapes: Space and Society in Antebellum Tennessee* (Chapel Hill: University of North Carolina Press, 1999); Kenneth A. Wheeler, *To Wear a City's Crown: The Beginnings of Urban Growth in Texas, 1836–1865* (Cambridge, Mass.: Harvard University Press, 1968). Also important are political histories that stress the societal tensions allegedly provoked by the embrace of the market revolution by many southerners in the 1850s. See Lacy K. Ford Jr., *Origins of Southern Radicalism: The South Carolina Upcountry, 1800–1860* (New York: Oxford University Press, 1988); Marc W. Kruman, *Parties and Politics in North Carolina, 1836–1865* (Baton Rouge: Louisiana State University Press, 1983); J. Mills Thornton III, *Politics and Power in a Slave Society: Alabama, 1800–1860* (Baton Rouge: Louisiana State University Press, 1978). For a major new revisionist work on antebellum southern social history, see John W. Quist, *Restless Visionaries:*

Prattville grew markedly in the fifteen years before the Civil War. In 1850, the town had a free population of approximately 448. By the end of the decade, Prattville's population had more than doubled to about 943. The town's significant population growth was in large part due to Daniel Pratt's efforts to make his creation something more than a company town. Pratt encouraged new businesses by renting factory space to enterprising mechanics. He also liquidated his company store, enabling independent merchants to start their own concerns. Moreover, by constructing his four-mile plank road from Prattville to Washington Landing on the Alabama River, he made Prattville Autauga County's main trade portal to the outside world.[2]

Prattville's increasing importance as Autauga's marketing center in the 1850s is made clear by comparing the number of merchants in the town in 1850 and 1860. In 1850, Prattville had six merchants, one hatter, and one tailor. By 1860, Prattville boasted fourteen merchants, more than twice the number it had ten years earlier. In addition to its general merchants, Prattville claimed three druggists, a dentist, and a shoemaker. Seven clerks were employed by these various shopkeepers.[3]

The two drugstores in Prattville give some idea of the variety of goods stocked by local shops. Joseph Hurd's establishment carried such exoticly named items as Eau Lustrale Hair Renovator ("a charming article for the Toilet . . . which . . . renders [hair] beautifully soft and glossy"), Lemon Rouge De Sorgho ("a permanent and beautiful carnation for the

The Social Roots of Antebellum Reform in Alabama and Michigan (Baton Rouge: Louisiana State University Press, 1998). For a revisionist study by pioneering social historians that indicates that the size of the noncountry population of the antebellum South has been seriously underestimated by scholars, see Darrett B. Rutman, with Anita H. Rutman, "The Village South," in *Small Worlds, Large Questions: Explorations in Early American Social History, 1600–1850,* edited by Darrett B. Rutman and Anita H. Rutman (Charlottesville: University of Virginia Press, 1994), 231–72.

2. U.S. Census, Alabama, 1850 and 1860 Population Schedules, Autauga County. Only after Pratt's death did the board of managers of Prattville Manufacturing Company launch a company store in direct competition with Prattville merchants, a "departure," Shadrack Mims noted in an angry petition he drew up, that did "not reflect credit upon the illustrious founder of this place." In a private letter written at the same time, Mims complained bitterly that Pratt's "immediate representatives [Henry DeBardeleben, Merrill Pratt, and Samuel Parrish Smith] have thought best to pursue a different policy than the one he pursued, that of 'live and let live.'" Shadrack Mims, "Petition of Objections to Prattville Mfg. Board" [June 1873?], typescript, Box 37, McMillan Collection; Shadrack Mims to Esther Pratt [June 1873?], Box 37, McMillan Collection.

3. U.S. Census, Alabama, 1850 and 1860 Population Schedules, Autauga County.

cheeks and lips"), Lorillard's Maccaboy Snuff, Cotton King Cigars, Moffat's Life Pills, and Phoenix Bitters. Not to be outdone, Hurd's competitor, Spong and Root, boasted of its supplies of Frangipanni ("an everlasting perfume for the handkerchief and sachets for the Ladies Wardrobe"), butter and soda crackers ("fresh from the bakery"), and valentines (pointedly but unromantically designated "*Cheap as Dirt*").[4]

In addition to its merchants, Prattville also had six physicians, three attorneys, six teachers, and eight men employed in building trades. Travelers to Prattville in the 1850s could stay at the Tennessee House and Stables and dine at Casimir and Jacob Krout's restaurant. Neither of these businesses was in operation in 1860, yet the town that year did have two boarding houses (run by widows of shop owners) and a lively "oyster saloon" that stocked, besides the requisite oysters, cigars, tobacco, whiskey, brandy, cordials, ale, porter, champagne, cider, wines, bitters, and "snuff of all kinds." Teetotalers seeking to quench their thirst could look to Spong and Root's "soda joint," with its "cool soda water served up with the most delicious syrups."[5]

In 1860, only 52 of Prattville's approximately 173 households are linkable to Pratt's gin factory or to a shop, while 47 households can be linked with a mill. Thus, 74 of Prattville's households, or 43 percent, were headed by someone not employed in manufacturing. Of these non-manufacturing families, 26 were headed by planters, but the remaining 48 were almost all headed by men or women employed in the various trades and professions described above. Clearly, this segment of Prattville's population, which did not depend directly on Pratt for its livelihood, had significance.

While recognizing that Prattville was not some sleepy southern hamlet, one may question whether it was really "southern" at all or instead a northern transplant. Numerically, Prattville's Yankee element was not dominant. Of the town's approximately 173 households in 1860, only 13 (7.5 percent) were headed by northerners. Foreign-born residents headed another 3 (1.7 percent) of the households. Out of Prattville's free population of about 943, 65 persons (6.9 percent) came from the North, while merely 5 (.5 percent) came from foreign countries.[6] Thus, nonsoutherners

4. *Prattville Southern Statesman*, 15 October 1857, 4 March, 8 April 1858, 10 February, 28 July, 10 November 1859.

5. U.S. Census, Alabama, 1850 and 1860 Population Schedules, Autauga County; (Prattville) *Autauga Citizen*, 10 February 1853, 15 December 1859, 29 March 1860.

6. U.S. Census, Alabama, 1860 Population Schedule, Autauga County.

accounted for only about 9.2 percent of Prattville's heads of households and 7.4 percent of its free population. Put another way, southerners (mostly Alabamians, Georgians, and South Carolinians) accounted for over 90 percent of Prattville's heads of households and free population. As far as nativity is concerned, then, Prattville can hardly be viewed as some Rockdale mill village picked up and deposited in Alabama.

It is indisputable, however, that Prattville's northerners constituted an extremely important segment of the town's population. Fifteen percent of Prattville's white mechanics in 1860 hailed from the North. Gardner Hale remained Pratt's mill superintendent, while Francis Farnsworth of Connecticut was probably the gin-factory boss. William Fay of Vermont replaced Georgian Shadrack Mims as the cotton mill agent in 1860. Amos Smith's nephews Ferdinand and Frank stood at the top of the gin-factory hierarchy. Merrill Pratt and Samuel Ticknor marketed Pratt's gins, while Thomas Avery kept Pratt's books. The machine shop of Thomas Ormsby and George Smith serviced Pratt's factories. Enoch Robinson made horse mills, and Ephraim Morgan made sashes, doors, and blinds in shops that were next to Pratt's own factories in size and importance to Prattville's economy.

Nor did Prattville's industrious Yankees confine their efforts to the town's factories and shops. Northerners held jobs in white-collar professions as well. Joseph Hurd of New Jersey and William Root of Massachusetts were druggists, while William Bush of Massachusetts served as the town dentist. Jay DeWitt Wheat of New York had employment as a bookkeeper in 1860, while in the late 1850s, he edited the *Prattville Southern Statesman*. William Allen and his brother Hassan were Prattville's leading merchants. Henry Butler of Massachusetts headed the Prattville Academy, while four northern-born women were schoolteachers.[7]

Although the importance of northerners in Prattville is undeniable, the free southern population hardly was confined to absentee planters and poor white mill-operatives. Southern members of Prattville's middle class in the decade of the 1850s included most of the town's merchants, all its physicians and attorneys, teachers William Miles and Jere S. Williams, agent Shadrack Mims, shop owners James Clepper, James Wainwright, David Suter and Llewellyn Spigner, and such highly skilled mechanics as Nathan Morris, Harris Ware, Joshua White, and B. W. Rogers. Several of

7. Ibid.

these men, including physician Samuel Parrish Smith and tinsmith James Wainwright, married into Yankee families.[8]

Other important southerners in Prattville were the town's first newspaper editors. With financial assistance from Daniel Pratt, William Howell and T. S. Luckett started the *Autauga Citizen* in 1853. These two southerners immediately made the *Citizen* a platform for the views of Pratt and like-minded Prattville boosters. According to the editors, Prattville served as an economic beacon for the rest of the South to follow. "As a place of business and industry," they declared, Prattville was unsurpassed "by any other county town of its size in the state." Indeed, they boasted, Prattville's "large and commodious" brick commercial structures presented "an appearance that would do credit to older and larger towns—even cities." If the South, with all its advantages in natural resources, would only follow Prattville's example and turn its energies to "diversified pursuits," she would soon "occupy a position to be envied by the first nations of the earth, in point of commercial greatness." Without the South's abundant natural riches, the editors pointed out, both England and New England had become major industrial centers. Moreover, manufacturing would benefit the South socially as well as economically by giving employment to "thousands" of the region's young men, "who might otherwise drag out a miserable existence in idleness and profligacy." If only "the true sentiments" concerning "*the respectability of labor*" were instilled in the minds of these idle young men, they could be

8. Ibid.; 1855 Alabama State Census. In 1840, Samuel Parrish Smith, a recent graduate of Philadelphia's Jefferson Medical School and a native of Georgia, married Adelaide Allen, the daughter of a Connecticut merchant residing at Washington, Alabama. In 1845, Smith and his family moved to Prattville, where he established a successful medical practice and became one of the village's preeminent citizens. His eldest daughter, Julia, wed Merrill Pratt in 1862, while his son Eugene became Prattville's most renowned intellectual, graduating from Heidelberg University after the Civil War, marrying a daughter of University of Alabama president Landon Garland, and serving as state geologist for more than fifty years. *Prattville Southern Signal*, 3 September 1886; *Prattville Progress*, 3 April, 17 June 1891; Oliver Seymour Phelps and Andrew T. Servin, *The Phelps Family of America* (Pittsfield, Mass.: Eagle Publishing, 1899); Owen, *History of Alabama*, 4: 1579–80, 1595; Stewart J. Lloyd, *Eugene Allen Smith: Alabama's Great Geologist* (New York: Newcomen Society in North America, 1954); Marriage Book, 4: 153, Probate Office, Autauga County Courthouse. James Wainwright, a tin-shop owner, married Melissa Holt, one of Daniel Pratt's nieces, in 1858. Nobles, *Journals of Ferdinand Ellis Smith*, 74; Alabama, 2: 9, R. G. Dun & Co. Collection.

"profitably employed" as shop mechanics and factory superintendents and overseers, just as in Prattville.[9]

Occasionally, a dissenting voice appeared in the pages of the *Citizen*. "A Friend of Agriculture" wrote Prattville's paper complaining of an article by one "Cid Hamet" in the nearby Autaugaville paper, the *Mercury*. Cid Hamet, the writer noted, had evinced "a very commendable zeal for manufacturing in our State," but he had erred in asserting that "manufacturing is more profitable than planting." For the South to become a successful manufacturing region, the writer continued, it first needed two things, population and capital. In order to obtain greater population and capital, the South would have to embark upon a more liberal policy toward railroads and banks. "Why talk about encouraging manufacturing when the few concerns now operating are thrown upon the mercy of brokers operating on Georgia and Carolina funds," he demanded. "It is perfectly preposterous to even dream of success under such disadvantages." Cid Hamet's boast of the South's advantages over New England in waterpower and proximity to raw material meant little when New England had much superior "monied facilities." While the writer was "no enemy to our State and her citizens encouraging the various branches of manufacturing," he insisted that ultimately, "the prosperity of any country depends mainly upon her farming and planting interest for stability."[10] Clearly, Cid Hamet had nettled an Autauga planter by directly challenging the primacy of agriculture over industry, something Daniel Pratt and Prattville boosters scrupulously avoided.

Making "her" point more playfully than "a Friend of Agriculture," one "Dorothy Dump" wrote a letter to the *Citizen* in 1853 satirizing the newspaper's pretensions about Prattville and Autauga County:

> Autauga certainly deserves *one* paper—for it is the next greatest place to anywhere! No matter where *that* is. . . . Then there are the factories, foundries, etc. Bless me! . . . Show me another county in the State that has two such noble cotton mills!—pray, where do you find so much industry, enterprise, competition and excitement, as at Prattville and Autaugaville? . . . The railroad too! We must not forget to take a trip on that. . . . If I had been Albert Pickett, and author of the history of Alabama, I should have left De Soto and his army to wander up and down the Mississippi

9. (Prattville) *Autauga Citizen*, 10 February, 17 March 1853.
10. (Prattville) *Autauga Citizen*, 17 November 1853.

and river beds as they liked and dedicated the volume to the history of Autauga.

Dorothy Dump had a point in poking fun at Prattville's pretensions, for despite the exertions of the town's citizens in the 1850s, Prattville during this decade neither got its railroad nor did it become Autauga's political seat. With justification, Dorothy Dump called the county courthouse, located at the interior village of Kingston, "that long coveted prize—that Eldorado of all you Prattvillians!" The *Citizen* clearly felt frustrated that Kingston had managed to retain this ornament, even though Prattville had far outstripped the piney woods village in population. Describing Kingston in the same 1853 article on Autauga County in which they had sung Prattville's praises, the editors of the paper could not refrain from contemptuous sarcasm: "Kingston . . . is situated in a healthy region, and would be a very pretty place, if there was not quite so much *sand*. But Kingston may yet start to grow—who knows? They have commenced the building of the new brick Jail, which, when finished, is bound to improve the place a little, or at least increase the *population*."[11]

Prattville had succeeded in bringing the site of the county seat to a vote in 1852, but Kingston narrowly bested its larger rival. George Smith noted in his journal on August 2 that an election had been held that day "to decide the location of the Court House. The Prattville folks were very desirous to have it come [here] and voted accordingly." Ferdinand Smith recorded that of 234 votes cast in Prattville precinct, 233 went for Prattville. Unfortunately for the "Prattville folks," Kingston edged Prattville by 55 votes. "The people here feel somewhat depressed," noted Ferdinand as he reported the disappointing result in his journal. Prattville was unable to wrest the seat from Kingston until 1868.[12]

Prattville's railroad campaign proved considerably more intricate than its courthouse fight, and in the end, no more successful. The first big push began in April 1853, when Daniel Pratt published a two-part editorial in the *Citizen*, "Our Improvement and Prosperity as a Nation." From this editorial it is clear that Pratt had become swept up in the Whig vision of

11. (Prattville) *Autauga Citizen*, 10 February, 2 June 1853.
12. Nobles, *Journals of George Littlefield Smith*, 68; Nobles, *Journals of Ferdinand Ellis Smith*, 131; Larry W. Nobles, *Compendium of Old Autauga County History* (Prattville Ala: by the author, 1997), 56.

progress. "This is an age of improvement," he ringingly declared. "There are no people on the face of the earth who possess the same spirit of enterprise as the citizens of the United States. . . . Should peace and prosperity be continued to us twenty-five years longer, we shall far outstrip every other nation."[13]

Pratt insisted that the most important improvement for the country to make was to build more railroads: "That State which expects prosperity will assuredly be disappointed if it fails to connect different parts of its territory and the adjoining States by railroads." Because of superior "natural advantages," Pratt asserted, Alabama particularly stood to gain from railroad construction. Myriad industries would prosper:

> The manufacturing of iron ore can be made equally as profitable as in other States,when we have railroads to carry it to market. If we want fine marble houses, we can have them equal in quality, and build them as cheap as any other State. Our cities can be supplied with coal as cheap as any other State. Lumber of the best quality we have in abundance. Above our home wants we could supply Texas and also the northeastern States, for ship building. We now send to Maine and Philadelphia for thousands of casks of lime, which would be furnished on better terms at home.

Pratt added that "the time is not far distant when we shall grow and manufacture our home supply of wool" and also that he still had hopes for the "cotton manufacturing business, although we have much to contend with." With railroads stimulating all these industries, Alabama would become "the most independent State in the union." To help achieve this great end, Pratt urged "every citizen of our State, who can spare $100, $1,000, or $10,000 to invest at once in railroad stock." Even if investors did not for several years receive a dividend, "they would not be losers" because real estate values would appreciate. Besides, Pratt reminded his readers, "Alabamians ought to consider that it is our duty to pursue that course which will most benefit the rising generation."[14]

Prattvillians were interested in two proposed lines. The first would run from Montgomery to Selma through southern Autauga County, connecting Autauga's planters to major railroads in these two hubs. The second would run from Montgomery north through Autauga to some point on the Tennessee River, opening for exploitation the virtually untapped rich

13. (Prattville) *Autauga Citizen,* 7 April 1853.
14. (Prattville) *Autauga Citizen,* 14 April 1853.

mineral belt of northern Alabama. In July 1853, Pratt traveled on the Alabama and Tennessee Railroad from Selma to Montevallo in Shelby County, where he discussed Autauga's project with local railroad boosters. He also corresponded with Montgomery's Charles Teed Pollard, Alabama's great railroad promoter. On August 13, Pratt brought together a large delegation of Alabama railroad supporters for a conference in Prattville to gain public support for his plans.[15]

The delegation to Prattville's railroad conference included important figures from the Black Belt counties of Autauga, Montgomery, Dallas, Perry, Marengo, and Sumter, as well as the hill counties of Shelby and Jefferson. Having been elected conference president, Pratt opened it with a short speech. The resolutions committee, on which Pratt sat, produced two resolutions: first, that a railroad running through Autauga from Montgomery to Selma and then on to Jackson, Mississippi, would form "an indispensable link in the chain of railroads, which are soon to connect the Atlantic and Pacific oceans," and second, that a railroad line running from Montgomery through Autauga and Shelby to a point on the Tennessee River would be "of the utmost importance in affecting a development of the mineral resources of the State of Alabama." Pratt picked the men to serve on committees charged with securing charters for and promoting the two proposed railroads. He also chose a delegation to attend a railroad convention at Elyton in Jefferson County later that month. Unsurprisingly, Pratt ended up a member of all three groups. The *Citizen* had nothing but praise for Pratt's convention: "Judging from the number who attended . . . and the harmony and unanimity which prevailed throughout the proceedings, we set down the establishment and early completion of the two roads as a fixed fact."[16]

Despite the newspaper's confidence, Prattville never obtained a railroad in the antebellum period. The "harmony and unanimity" of the August railroad convention collapsed under the pressure of personal pique and partisan politics as the 1850s progressed. Only as the sectional crisis

15. (Prattville) *Autauga Citizen,* 21 July, 18, 25 August 1853.

16. (Prattville) *Autauga Citizen,* 18 August 1853. Among the notable Alabamians attending the convention were Charles Teed Pollard, Francis Strother Lyon, Thomas Hill Watts, George Goldthwaite, John Lapsley, and William Mudd. Autaugians at the convention included planters Bolling Hall, Absalom Jackson, Crawford Motley Jackson, Charles Malone Howard, William Montgomery, Neil Smith Graham, and Caleb Moncrief, as well as Prattville attorney William H. Northington and Autaugaville minister and textile manufacturer David Smedley.

brought Autauga's bickering factions together did Pratt's railroad project get back on track.

Soon after the railroad convention ended, the *Autaugaville Mercury* launched an attack on Pratt, claiming that he had insulted Autaugaville's citizens by not placing someone from the town on the committee charged with promoting the Montgomery-Selma Road, which, were it routed through Autauga County, would surely pass through Autaugaville. Pratt defended himself by claiming that he had "made the best selection" he could have "in the hurry of the moment." Charles Malone Howard, a planter living near Autaugaville, had seemed to Pratt a good choice "to attend to the interests of Autaugaville." The *Mercury* had named Albert Pickett, a highly respected historian and the owner of a large plantation near Autaugaville, as the man Pratt should have chosen, but Pratt pointed out that Pickett actually lived in Montgomery. In any event, de-clared Pratt, Autaugaville's own representatives at the convention had not recommended Pickett. Pratt assured the *Mercury* that he had nothing but the best wishes for Autaugaville. He, for one, was not "of that class of people in our State" who did not desire a railroad unless it ran "by their door." Rather, Pratt avowed that he would take great pleasure in having a line run "through any part of our county," including Autauga-ville. Despite Pratt's conciliatory tone, however, he could not resist chid-ing the *Mercury*'s editors for complaining about the convention's result when they had not attended it. "If the editors feel so great an interest in their flourishing village," he queried, "would it not seem more likely that they were in earnest, if they had attended the convention . . . and given their views of railroads?"[17]

After Pratt's remarks succeeded only in provoking another editorial assault from the *Mercury,* he signaled his desire to let the issue lie, but those who felt slighted continued to air their grievances. Albert Pickett complained in a letter that Pratt, Pollard, and George Goldthwaite ("that English Jew") completely ignored his opinions on the Montgomery-Selma Road. Pratt, he insisted, had been made "fully aware" of his deep interest in the subject, for the pair had made a "tour of observation" to-gether along the railroad's projected route in the fall of 1853. When a railroad company was incorporated early in 1854 under the name West-ern of Alabama Railroad Company (Western Railroad Company), Pick-ett's distress turned to anger on account of the omission of his name from

17. (Prattville) Autauga Citizen, 1 September 1853.

the company's charter. "As it was expected that I would take considerable stock," he told a friend bitterly, "all I asked was to be put upon an
equal footing with themselves—to have a voice in their deliberations."
The Western Railroad Company's board of commissioners did choose
Pickett, along with David Smedley, to oversee the collection in Autaugaville of capital stock subscriptions, but both men summarily declined
these posts. According to Pickett, Smedley gave Charles Pollard, secretary
of Western Railroad Company, two reasons for his action: "1st business.
2nd last summer at Prattville no man about Autaugaville appointed as a
Delegate, no man about Autaugaville named to cooperate in a survey &
none put in the recent charter."[18]

Carping from Autaugaville boosters aside, Pratt's project had much
support, judging by the *Autauga Citizen*. "Progress" wrote a detailed letter in which he proposed a route for the Montgomery-Selma Road, while
"Alabama" sent a long missive asserting the importance of state aid to
railroads. Nor did the editors of the *Citizen* run short of imploring
words: "It is evident to every reflecting mind that it is impossible for this
county to do without a railroad any longer. . . . Let every man put aside
the interests of minor importance—let all forget the petty prejudices
which may have heretofore existed—let all act in perfect unison with
each other."[19]

Ironically, given this stirring plea for unity for the sake of Prattville's
economic advancement, the *Citizen* would tear Prattville apart in the
summer of 1854 by launching a violent assault on the town's founder,
effectively retarding railroad development efforts in Autauga for several
years. Pratt truly must have been dismayed by this unforeseen occurrence. The original *Citizen* editors William Howell and T. S. Luckett professed political neutrality, but like Pratt, they showed a decided sympathy
for Whiggish economic policies. Pratt firmly believed that support for
banks and railroads was not a matter of politics, but of economic ratio-
nality and responsibility. The industrialist simply could not believe that
Democratic politicians sincerely opposed these entities on ideological
grounds. Rather, he was convinced that these designing men cynically
fostered the class resentments of common people in order to advance
themselves politically. Above all, in Pratt's view, the Democrats wanted

18. (Prattville) *Autauga Citizen*, 15 September 1853; Albert Pickett to [Bolling Hall?],
8 March 1854, McMillan Collection.
19. (Prattville) *Autauga Citizen*, 1, 8 September 1853, 2 March 1854.

a political hobbyhorse to ride against the Whigs, no matter the adverse economic consequences. "It is my oppinion [that] had the Whigs as a party ben opposed to Chartered Institutions and Banking then the Democrats as a party would have ben in favor of them," Pratt trenchantly observed in 1847. He had hoped that the *Autauga Citizen* would provide a forum for his enlightened economic views, but his plan completely backfired, for William Howell turned against him in less than two years.[20]

Luckett left the *Citizen* after several months, leaving the paper exclusively in the hands of Howell. True to the newspaper's nonpartisan stance, Howell remained neutral during a political storm that shook Prattville in the late summer and early fall of 1853. The highly partisan dispute concerned the disposition of Prattville's postmastership. In 1846, Pratt had outfitted a post office in one of his brick buildings on the western side of Autauga Creek. After a succession of postmasters, Shadrack Mims, professedly a Democrat, ascended to the position in 1850. When the Democratic Party reoccupied the White House in 1853, local Democrats began agitating for the removal of the post office across the creek into Prattville proper and for the appointment of a fully loyal party man as postmaster.[21] Trouble quickly ensued.

In August 1853, shortly after Prattville's railroad convention, William Ormsby (who was Esther Ticknor Pratt's cousin and the bookkeeper for Ephraim Morgan's sash, door, and blind shop) precipitated an out-and-out political firefight over the postmastership by savagely attacking the Democratic agitators in a piece in the *Citizen* titled "A Reverie." In this, Ormsby lauded Pratt's accomplishments: building a gin factory and a cotton mill (the latter of which gave employment to "poor and destitute families" and guaranteed them "at least an easy subsistence and comfortable homes"), building the Methodist church and Union Sunday School and contributing to Prattville's other churches and schools, and giving "impetus to other branches of industry" besides his own, thus developing a "lovely village" with "merchants, doctors, and lawyers." Having built up Pratt as a sort of moral colossus, Ormsby then knocked down the

20. Daniel Pratt to Dixon Hall Lewis, 21 September 1847, Lewis Papers, University of Texas Library, Austin. In his letter to Lewis, Pratt went on to urge that "the two parties unite for the intrest of our State. Not ask as is now the custom what will be for the intrest of our party but ask what will be for the present and future intrest of our State."

21. Information on the Prattville postmaster fight is found in the following issues of the (Prattville) *Autauga Citizen:* 11, 18 August, 1, 8, 15, 22, 29 September, 6, 13 October 1853.

moral pygmies who would challenge this great and good man. Addressing them directly, he angrily lectured: "You are daily reaping the results
of his energy, but you are not satisfied. Judging from your actions, you
would, cormorant-like, pluck him from his high position and devour his
substance. . . . He has endeavored to merit your good will—but you are
ready to spit upon him. He has been the instrument, in God's hands, of
adding to your substance—but you would have all that he possesses. He
has been a public benefactor in your midst, while you have heaped cal-
umny and abuse upon him. Would that himself and his effects could be
transplanted to another locality: you then would wish for his return."[22]

Ormsby sought to shame these Democrats for conspiring to seize the
postmastership, but in so extravagantly praising Pratt and condemning
his opponents, he overplayed his hand. Democrats angrily objected to
what they viewed as the antirepublican tone of Ormsby's "Reverie."
Ormsby assumed "that whatever does not have its conception, its birth
and its maturity in the *particular junto* composed of himself, his master
and company must necessarily be wrong," huffed a Democrat in a letter
to the *Citizen*. "What presumption! Proper subordination is commendable, but a cringing parasite is detestable." Surely such "fulsome praise"
from "a loaf and fish sycophant" must have nauseated Pratt himself,
"a man of known modesty and sensibility." Pratt, argued the writer,
deserved "the highest encomiums for his eminent services to his community—his Christian benevolence—his indiscriminate charity and bound-
less liberality." Nevertheless, the Democrats had complete justification in
seeking to have the postmastership transferred to Benjamin Durden, a
sixty-year-old carpenter and staunch Democrat. This "aged and infirm
old citizen, honest, faithful and capable," desired the post not merely out
of partisanship but also out of the hope that it would help him better support his "large and dependent family."[23]

Pratt remained aloof from this fracas, but Shadrack Mims soon lent
Ormsby some support. Democratic activists in Autauga County had put
up Durden to seek the postmastership solely "on party grounds," according to Mims, who complained that Durden simply did not have the necessary qualifications to serve as postmaster. Members of both parties,
Mims asserted, had requested him not to relinquish the job. Unfortunately for Mims, he, like Ormsby, had left himself open to charges of elit-

22. (Prattville) *Autauga Citizen,* 11 August 1853.
23. (Prattville) Autauga Citizen, 18 August 1853.

ism, and Benjamin Durden promptly leveled such charges in a letter to the *Citizen* that Prattville attorney and leading Autauga Democrat William H. Northington actually scripted. "Notwithstanding I am not very expert at writing Reminiscences," the humble "Durden" jabbed at Mims, whose "Old Citizen" column appeared regularly in the Prattville newspaper, "I am not so vain, presumptuous and arrogant as to think I am the only man about Prattville who can give permanency to the Post Office." Durden did not believe that such a claim would "find much favor among the plain republicans of old Autauga." Moreover, he belittled Mims for his professed political independence as well as his elitism. The carpenter viewed trimmers such as Mims as "objects of distrust and suspicion." Who could tell where he stood with such a creature? Durden asserted a right to the office both as a loyal party man and as a "poor" artisan with "a large and dependent family," many of whom, he noted, worked as "honest and faithful laborers" in Pratt's gin factory.[24]

Despite protests from Ormsby, Mims, and their supporters, some thirty to forty Prattville Democrats petitioned for a transfer of the postmastership to Durden. While waiting word from Washington, D.C., both sides escalated their rhetorical attacks. The rather mild Mims found himself compared to such despots as Tsar Nicholas, Alexander the Great, Napoleon Bonaparte, and Julius Caesar. Writing in his own name, William H. Northington proved particularly scathing. Mims, he cried, had stepped forward "as the peculiar champion of *wealth* and the *one man power*," regarding "all who do not sacrilegiously bend the knee of reverence at the *shrine* of his *monied God* as unworthy of a participation in the management of or control in our government." With such bombast, Northington effectively silenced his enemies, and in January 1854, Durden ascended to the postmastership, a position he would hold for nearly seven years.[25]

The heated political contest for the Prattville postmastership fractured the town at a time when, as William Howell had noted, a unified effort was needed to bring railroads to Autauga County. Judging from the names signed to a petition of support for Durden, Pratt's most vocal opposition came from a group of Democratic planters and attorneys living in Prattville and its vicinity. Of the twenty-five names on the petition, only six belonged to men currently or formerly employed in trades in

24. (Prattville) *Autauga Citizen*, 1, 8 September 1853.
25. (Prattville) *Autauga Citizen*, 15 September, 13 October 1853.

Prattville: Llewellyn Spigner (previously owner of Prattville's carriage shop but now engaged in farming), A. K. McWilliams (merchant), George Tisdale (owner of a tin shop), Casimir Krout (restauranteur), William Morgan (proprietor of the Tennessee House and Stables), and Daniel Suter (blacksmith). By no means did all local planters belong to this group, however. Absalom Doster and his sons Charles and Edward (respectively a Prattville attorney and a Prattville physician), for example, did not sign the petition. Nor did Thomas Smith, the father of Samuel Parrish Smith, Pratt's friend and physician. Nevertheless, Autauga had a very strong Democratic organization, basically a cog in Benjamin Fitzpatrick's political machine, the "Montgomery Regency." Fitzpatrick, one of Alabama's U.S. senators, claimed as his domicile his Autauga plantation, Oak Grove. Two of his most important lieutenants, Bolling Hall and Crawford Motley Jackson, also resided in Autauga. To challenge Autauga's powerful Democratic Party over the postmastership, as Mims and Ormsby had done, risked alienating these powerful planters from Pratt's railroad projects. No doubt keenly aware of this, Pratt had kept his own counsel during the brouhaha.[26]

Unfortunately for Pratt, the Democrats, not content to leave bad enough alone, began agitating over a new issue in 1854—the incorporation of Prattville—and this time they had the vocal support of the *Autauga Citizen,* William Howell having defected to their side. Pratt would now find himself under venomous personal attack from a serpent in his "lovely village." The circumstances surrounding the cancellation of the incorporation election are somewhat unclear. On August 24, the *Citizen* announced that an election was to be held on that Saturday, but on August 31, the paper tersely noted that the "election for the incorporation of Prattville did not take place, as it was considered unnecessary to hold said election." In their journals, the Smith cousins, Ferdinand and George, are more explicit. George noted that an election was to be held in Prattville concerning incorporation, but that "the managers would not hold it." George and some of his friends "considered that the same as a defeat and fired 35 guns and were going to fire 15 more but backed out." Ferdinand made clear why they "backed out": "In the afternoon the boys fired the cannon and came near to getting into a fight."[27]

26. (Prattville) *Autauga Citizen,* 13 October 1853. On Benjamin Fitzpatrick's Montgomery Regency, see Thornton, *Politics and Power,* 365–98.

27. (Prattville) *Autauga Citizen,*24, 31 August 1854; Nobles, *Journals of George Littlefield Smith,* 79; Nobles, *Journals of Ferdinand Ellis Smith,* 189.

Pratt likely feared two things about incorporation: property taxes and loss of personal power. Opponents of incorporation claimed that it could result in an additional tax of 1 percent on real estate, as well as a $2 poll tax. As for the issue of power, Prattville's board of managers appears to have been unelected. Pratt probably feared that free elections simply would give the Democrats more opportunity for "trouble making" in his own backyard. To refuse even to hold an election concerning the matter, however, certainly made him vulnerable to charges of despotism.[28]

William Howell, having thrown in his lot with Autauga's Democratic Party, now hurled such charges. He claimed that Pratt had precipitated the break by attempting to have his paper proscribed in Prattville. Howell declared that the scales had dropped from his eyes. "Here, right here, in the heart of the Sunny South," he exclaimed in horror, "has sprung up one of those little *one horse* despotisms so peculiar to the manufacturing towns of the North." Pratt, whom Howell now cleverly dubbed "the Great I Am" (an allusion to Yahweh in the Old Testament), had even gone so far as to threaten one of his workers, "a respectable citizen," with expulsion from Prattville if he voted for the Democratic ticket. "Truly, the man who can utter such sentiments, in a republican government," declared the outraged Howell, "is fit to wear the diadem of a Czar." Howell suggested that Pratt organize a band of adventurers, conquer Cuba, and proclaim himself a monarch.[29]

Despite Howell's insistence that the proscription of his newspaper was the work of a tiny clique of wealthy Prattvillians, it appears that the move met with wide approbation in Prattville. Howell's boast of having picked up at least two hundred new subscriptions from such Democratic precincts as Pine Flat, Chestnut Creek, and Milton suggests that he had lost a large number of subscriptions from Whiggish Prattville. George Smith spent a day gathering sixty signatures to a document defending Pratt from Howell's charges, which he requested Howell to publish in the *Citizen*. Howell consented to do so, but he sneered at the signers for having lost their manly independence by having "*voted* and *acted* with Mr. Pratt on every occasion, ever since they have been in his employ." Admittedly, Pratt employees filled the ranks of the signers. Only a few, such as James Allen, Henry Thigpen, Ephraim Morgan, James Wainwright, and Western Franks, had their own business concerns. Yet of the forty-four men

28. (Prattville) *Autauga Citizen*, 24 August 1854.
29. (Prattville) *Autauga Citizen*, 5 October 1854.

who listed their party affiliation, sixteen (or 36 percent), including Shadrack Mims, Amos Smith, and such humble mechanics as Washington Lafayette Ellis and Marcus Cicero Killet, listed their party affiliation as Democratic, suggesting that Pratt, contrary to Howell's insistence, had left his workers some measure of political autonomy.[30]

Suddenly facing a vigorously partisan Democratic paper in their midst, Prattville's Whigs threw their support in December 1854 behind a new Prattville newspaper, the *Southern Statesman,* edited by no less than T. S. Luckett, Howell's former partner, and William Ormsby, the man who had done so much to aggravate Prattville's political schism. The description of the *Statesman* on the front page indicated that it would be quite in line with Pratt's way of thinking: "An Independent Family Journal, Devoted to Southern Industry, Agriculture, Manufactures, Mechanics, Internal Improvements, Current News, etc." The illustration on the masthead was a man (rather resembling Pratt) standing beside cotton bales and a cotton gin with Prattville's great factories looming in the background. During the next two years, as the American, or Know-Nothing, Party rose and fell in Alabama, the *Statesman* and the *Citizen* constantly traded blows with each other.[31]

The railroad cause suffered an even more serious setback in Prattville in 1855 when state Democrats, following the lead of Governor Winston (who was running for reelection), came out vigorously against state aid for internal improvements. Pratt ran as the American Party candidate for the state senate seat for Autauga and Montgomery Counties that year, and he found himself pilloried by Howell for his strong support of state aid. Howell, who in 1853 had shown sympathy to proponents of state aid, now denounced it as a "wild and reckless system of taxation for the construction of railroads." The editor of the *Citizen* brutally ridiculed Pratt's performance in the debates with his Democratic opponent, Judge Adam Felder of Montgomery, which took place in Autauga County during the summer. Howell concluded that Pratt was "a man unfit" to serve in the state senate.[32]

In the end, Howell's rough tactics seem to have worked. The movement of Autauga's up-country yeoman Democrats into the American

30. (Prattville) *Autauga Citizen,* 20 September, 5 October 1854.

31. *Prattville Southern Statesman,* 20 December 1854. This is the only known surviving issue from 1854 to 1859. The *Statesman* published until the outbreak of the Civil War.

32. (Prattville) *Autauga Citizen,* 5, 12, 19 July 1855.

Party came to an abrupt halt by mid-July. By the August election, traditional party alignment had reasserted itself as Autauga's up-country yeoman election districts voted heavily Democratic and its low-country planter districts voted American. While Pratt won Montgomery County by 110 votes, he lost his home county by 140 votes, resulting in a narrow loss to Felder.[33]

The bitter election campaign only worsened feelings between Pratt and Prattville's Democrats. Already in March 1855, an R. G. Dun agent had noted that Pratt was "not popular, will have his own way & monopolize everything." During the summer, Howell brandished a new epithet for Pratt, "the Grand Sachem." He again accused Pratt of despotism, claiming that he used "all manner of low chicanery to induce" subscribers to cancel their subscriptions to the *Citizen*.[34]

Events in 1856 did nothing to improve the situation. In this year, Autauga's twenty-four-year Democratic incumbent probate judge, Henly Brown, faced opposition from the nominally independent but, in fact, Know-Nothing-supported James Clepper, a Prattville carriage maker. Once again Democrats feared they might lose a political race due to defections from disaffected up-country yeomen. "The fact is," wrote a panicked William Howell to Bolling Hall only four days before the election, "Major Brown is beat, to a certainty, unless we do something soon." Howell noted fretfully that "at least 30 Brown men have gone to Clepper in Chesnut [Creek precinct]." Howell urged Hall to visit "Chesnut Creek as soon as possible" to get the precinct's wayward Democrats back into line. "Unless we do something soon we are beaten—There is no denying the fact," he reiterated. The last-minute Democratic efforts proved successful, for Brown, "the old war horse," defeated Clepper by 142 votes, virtually the same margin Felder had achieved over Pratt.[35]

Seeing the Democrats win a victory at the very last minute proved galling to Prattville's "Independents," some of whom apparently sought to extract vengeance in a highhanded and petty fashion. In June 1856, several Know-Nothing Methodists brought charges of falsehood against Edward Doster, a physician and son of prominent local planter Absalom

33. (Prattville) *Autauga Citizen*, 19 July, 2, 9 August 1855. For more detail on Pratt's 1855 state senate race, see chap. 7.

34. Alabama, 2: 12, R. G. Dun & Co. Collection; (Prattville) *Autauga Citizen*, 19 July 1855.

35. William Howell to Bolling Hall, 1 May 1856, Folder 4, Box 4, Bolling Hall Papers; (Prattville) *Autauga Citizen*, 24 April, 8 May 1856.

Doster, claiming that he had stated during the recent campaign that he would vote for Clepper but then, in fact, voted for Brown. Furthermore, according to the *Citizen,* these men attempted to have the physician's practice boycotted. With much pathos, Howell begged Autaugians not to allow these cruel conspirators to reduce "Dr. Doster, his wife and little ones to houseless, homeless wanderers" and to "show to the world that a man cannot be crushed in old Autauga" merely for staking out his own political course. Among the men testifying against Doster stood Thomas Ormsby, the brother of William, and Samuel Parrish Smith, a former Whig. Of Ormsby, Doster angrily declared that he had "not had a conversation with him in five years of more than one minute's duration." The Methodist Quarterly Conference found for Doster, leaving his opponents discredited and both sides even farther apart than previously.[36]

Finally in May 1857, Pratt, who had long ago pulled his advertising from the pages of the *Citizen,* made Howell a sort of peace offering. Pratt's mill boss Gardner Hale sent his son George over to Howell's office with a bundle containing "a pattern of three and a half yards of cloth for a pair of pants," made at Pratt's recently launched wool mill. Howell facetiously wrote that on seeing the young man ("a descendant of a 'bloody Know Nothing'") entering his "sanctum" with a "very mysterious looking bundle under his arm," he at first feared that the Know-Nothings had devised "some infernal machine . . . for the purpose of blowing us 'sky high.'" On seeing the cloth, however, he deemed it of a "superior quality" that reflected "much credit on its manufacturer." Howell even went so far as to tender his "sincere thanks for this very handsome and substantial present." Pratt's move probably helped repair relations between the two men. By early 1859, Howell began to print complimentary pieces on Prattville businessmen, marking his return to his 1853–1854 role as a Prattville booster. He enthusiastically predicted that it would not be long "before our thriving village will become the Lowell of the South."[37]

Howell's reanimated magnanimity toward Pratt and his friends was not simply the result of a young man bearing a gift of woolen cloth. With the collapse of organized opposition to the Democratic Party in Alabama in the late 1850s and the rising sectional tension in the country, the conservative Montgomery Regency for which the *Citizen* spoke began to

36. *Autauga Citizen,* 19 June, 7 August 1856.
37. *Autauga Citizen,* 21 May 1857, 10 February, 10 March 1859.

worry much more about the insurgency of William Lowndes Yancey and the fire-eaters within the Democratic Party than about the machinations of former Whigs and Know-Nothings. Pro-railroad men of different political persuasions now found it easier to cooperate on economic projects.[38]

As the Civil War loomed closer, Howell and other Prattville Democrats helped Pratt get one of his railroad projects moving again. In February 1860, the *Citizen* informed its readers that Lowndes County, located across the Alabama River from Autauga, was "making great exertions" to have the Western Railroad routed through its area. Howell emphasized to his readers the great importance of Autauga getting the line instead of Lowndes. With a railroad rumbling through its midst, Howell speculated, Prattville's population would explode to "seven or eight thousand." The *Citizen*'s editor approvingly noted that "Mr. Pratt, our enterprising townsman . . . has made most liberal offers to the managers of the road, to induce them to locate the route through Prattville."[39]

In April, railroad boosters held a convention in Kingston, Autauga County's seat, to raise subscriptions for the Western Railroad. Informing readers of the upcoming convention, Howell again emphasized that "the people of Lowndes are making desperate efforts to get the road" and pleaded with "the people of Autauga" to "arouse themselves to their true interests" and buy $100,000 worth of stock. If they would only do so, the road would "be *certain* to pass through Autauga," Howell avowed.[40]

The Kingston railroad convention, held on April 2, gathered a remarkable collection of old political enemies, united by their desire for a railroad through Autauga. Charles Doster, a Prattville attorney and the brother of Edward, served as convention secretary, while Daniel Pratt, Bolling Hall, and William H. Northington all served on the resolutions committee, Pratt as its chair. Pratt, who brought with him books of subscription, made the opening speech, followed by declamations from Hall and Northington. The *Statesman* complimented Pratt's "plain common sense" style of speaking, while the *Citizen*, which had ridiculed his 1855 campaign stump performance, found Pratt's speech "able and forcible" and "earnest and practical." The convention appointed Pratt to its county subscriptions committee. Howell reported that the convention

38. Thornton, *Politics and Power*, 365–98.
39. (Prattville) *Autauga Citizen*, 16 February 1860.
40. (Prattville) *Autauga Citizen*, 29 March 1860.

concluded that Autauga actually needed a total of $150,000 in stock sub-
scriptions, but only $60,000 had been raised; and he fretted that if Au-
taugians did not raise this extra amount, the county would lose the road,
leaving the people "to jog along in the same old fogy manner" of "the
last forty years." The *Statesman*, however, took assurance from Autauga's dependable Daniel Pratt: "We have a man among us who always
foots the bill in raising what may be necessary to carry forward worthy
public enterprises."[41]

On April 7, another railroad convention took place, this time at Prattville. Daniel Pratt, along with such wealthy planters as Bolling Hall, John
Steele, Absalom Jackson, and John Wood, made large subscriptions. Despite such efforts, however, Lowndes County won the contest over the
Western Railroad. Prattville now had to pin its hopes on the South and
North Alabama Railroad Company (South and North), which had incorporated in November 1858 and had raised $75,350 in stock subscrip-
tions at a Montgomery convention held the same month. Unfortunately,
the Civil War disrupted progress on the line, and Prattville had to wait
until Reconstruction to renew the railroad struggle.[42]

By the late 1850s, progress had again become the gospel throughout
Prattville, but precious time had been frittered away in fruitless political
squabbles, and the Civil War would bring all development schemes to an
abrupt halt. Yet while Prattville did not live up to the grandiose economic
expectations of the early 1850s, Prattvillians could still look proudly on
their town's renowned gin and textile factories, as well as its smaller
shops and stores. Moreover, Prattville had made significant cultural advances since the 1840s with the establishment of churches, schools, and
voluntary associations. Just as he had seen his tiny company village grow
into a major manufacturing and marketing center, Pratt witnessed the realization of his vision of a town of "good morals and good society" in
the last decade before the Civil War.

41. (Prattville) *Autauga Citizen,* 5 April 1860; *Prattville Southern Statesman,* 7, 14
April 1860.
42. (Prattville) *Autauga Citizen,* 4 November 1858, 12 April 1860.

Daniel Pratt's home in Temple township, New Hampshire.
From Henry Ames Blood, *History of Temple, N.H. (1860)*

Daniel Pratt in *De Bow's Review*, 1851.
Courtesy of Auburn University

Portrait of Esther Ticknor Pratt with baby Ellen and nursemaid
(Eliza?), by George Cooke, 1847. The oil portrait burned in a
house fire in 1958.
By permission of Virginia Neal Almand and the National Society
of the Colonial Dames of America in the State of Alabama

PRATTSVILLE, ALABAMA.

View of Daniel Pratt's house (1843), original cotton mil (1846),
original cotton gin factory (1839), and grist mill (1841) in *De Bow's
Review*, 1851. Most of the actual town is omitted from the
engraving, creating a misleadingly pastoral impression.
Courtesy of Louisiana State University Library

1856 advertisement for Daniel Pratt cotton gins displaying the
Methodist church building (upper right); original cotton mill
(upper left); sash, door, and blind shop (lower left);
foundry and smithy (lower center).

Courtesy of Tommy Brown

View of second cotton gin factory (1855) and sash, door,
and blind shop (1851).
From Henry Ames Blood, *History of Temple, N.H.* (1860)

Shadrack Mims, partner in the
cotton gin factory from 1853 to
1856, agent of PMC from 1846
to 1860, and longtime chroni-
cler of the exploits of Daniel
Pratt.
Courtesy of Larry Nobles

Henry Debardeleben, son-in-
law of Daniel Pratt and one of
the major figures in late
nineteenth-century southern
industry.
Courtesy of the Bessemer Area
Chamber of Commerce

Ellen Pratt Debardeleben.
Courtesy of the Bessemer Area
Chamber of Commerce

Daniel Pratt's nephew and ward Merrill Pratt, who with Samuel Ticknor took over the marketing of Pratt's gins in 1860 and became the leading figure in Prattville industry after his uncle's death.
Courtesy of Merrill and Suzanne Pratt

Amos Smith, superintendent of and partner in Pratt's gin factory from 1839 to 1856.
Courtesy of Maria Lamb

Daniel and Esther Pratt, c. 1870.
Courtesy of Ernest Johnson

Daniel Pratt, c. 1870.
Courtesy of Larry Nobles

6

BUILDING A SOCIETY: PRATTVILLE, 1840–1861

Like their counterparts in northern towns and villages, middle-class Prattvillians knew that a railroad alone would not suddenly usher in the blessings of material prosperity. To participate fully in the market revolution sweeping the country, they needed to improve themselves as well as their town. Only a virtuous populace would be able to take real advantage of the expanding economic opportunities offered them by the dynamic age in which they lived. Mindful of the imperative of self-improvement, Prattvillians sought in the 1850s to inculcate virtue in themselves through churches, schools, and voluntary associations. They succeeded so well that Daniel Pratt felt able to proclaim in 1860 that Prattville was "unusually free [of] the vice of *loafing* and dissipation" and was peopled by an "industrious, intelligent and refined" citizenry. Quoting his biblical namesake, Pratt contentedly declared, "How good and how pleasant it is for brethren to dwell together in unity."[1]

Churches were, perhaps, the key institutions fostering middle-class

---

1. (Prattville) *Autauga Citizen*, 16 August 1860. While the literature on the development of the northern middle class in Jacksonian America is voluminous, historians have paid scant attention to the southern middle class in the same period, though it most certainly existed. See, however, Quist's pathbreaking *Restless Visionaries* and Paul D. Escott,

values in Prattville. Pratt himself had written in 1850 of the positive social effect he thought religion had on Alabama in a letter to the secretary
of the Adelphic Society of Howard College, a Baptist school located in
Marion, Alabama. Noting that Howard's student body was "composed
of young men such as must soon take the responsipal stations in our
state," he declared: "They ought not only to be Literary but Religious
men such as will reform society by their instructions and example."[2]

Given Pratt's conviction, it no doubt gratified him that churches began
appearing in Prattville during the 1840s, the first decade of the village's
existence. Missionary Baptists organized a church in 1840 soon after
Pratt's arrival at May's Mill. Pratt built a small frame church on a lot on
the west side of Autauga Creek, and he deeded the church and lot to a
board of trustees composed of himself and several local planters. Like the
building itself, the congregation in the beginning was tiny, merely fourteen members. By 1842, membership stood at only thirty-seven persons,
twenty whites and seventeen blacks. In 1846, however, the church baptized thirty-five new white members. By 1850, the congregation claimed
eighty-two adherents, most of whom (sixty-nine) were white. Almost certainly, this influx of white members in 1846 resulted from the arrival in
Prattville that year of families Pratt had recruited to work in his new cotton mill.[3]

The Prattville Presbyterian church claimed a far more elite congregation. In 1846, thirteen individuals from three local planter families organized the church. By 1858, thirty-eight white persons had joined the
congregation, increasing its size to about fifty. In 1860, a dynamic new
minister, James King Hazen of Massachusetts, began serving the church.
His tenure as pastor would last nearly seventeen years. Hazen, who had
come to Prattville in 1858 to work for Daniel Pratt, married Samuel Ticknor's only child, Mary, and became, after the Civil War, a director of the
Prattville Manufacturing Company and the guiding spirit behind the
Presbyterian Orphan's Home at Tuskegee, Alabama. During the energetic Hazen's first month in office in 1860, no fewer than twenty individuals joined the congregation. Yet even in 1860, members of the three
founding planter families made up a large segment of the church's mem-

---

ed., *North Carolina Yeoman: The Diary of Basil Armstrong Thomasson, 1853–1862* (Athens: University of Georgia Press, 1996).

2. Daniel Pratt to W. D. Lee, 21 December 1850, Pratt Papers, ADAH.

3. Stone, *Prattville Baptist Church,* 13–18.

bership. The church also served over the years as the spiritual home for a significant portion of Prattville's Yankee population. Relatively few southern artisans and operatives belonged, however. Overall, the Prattville Presbyterian Church should be viewed as a middle- and upper-class institution.[4]

While the Baptist church enjoyed, as Pratt had written, a "respectable" membership, and the Presbyterian church experienced substantial growth on the eve of the Civil War, the most important church in the antebellum period was that of Pratt's own faith, Methodist. Pratt found that Autauga was fertile ground in which to plant a vigorous Methodist church, a major Methodist revival having swept the county in the 1820s. In 1822, Graves' Ferry (located near Washington, then Autauga's seat) became the site of a great Methodist camp meeting, "largely attended from far and near." Among those who converted to Methodism at this time was Thomas Smith, father of Samuel Parrish Smith. The elder Smith was, according to Shadrack Mims, "a man in whom everyone had confidence" and who "did much good in influencing others to do right. Every member of his family became religious." Mims himself first professed religion in 1821 as a result of a revival in Vernon, the village founded by his elder brother, Seaborn. During a visit from a Methodist circuit rider, Seaborn Mims's wife suddenly became overwhelmed by the Holy Spirit. "Her ecstasy was so intense that she could not restrain herself," reported church historian Anson West, "and soon she made the entire premises resound with her shouts." A revival resulted, winning over "nearly the entire population" of Vernon, including Seaborn and Shadrack, to Methodism.[5]

With devoted Methodists such as Shadrack Mims and Samuel Parrish Smith at Pratt's side, it is not surprising that Prattville had a strong Methodist church. Elvira Ramsey Spigner, wife of Llewellyn, also played a part in putting Prattville Methodism on sure footing. She was the daughter of James Ramsey, a "Georgia Methodist of the old stamp." As a result of

4. James M. Graham, *A Brief History of the First Presbyterian Church of Prattville, Alabama* (Prattville: by the author, 1935), 4–8, 17; Hazen, *Manual of the Presbyterian Church,* 4–6.

5. West, *History of Methodism,* 174–79; Shadrack Mims, "Autauga County," 249. When Mims moved to Alabama in 1820, he "had never heard nor seen but few Methodist preachers." But only a few months after having arrived in Vernon, he found "there was no getting rid of them." Shadrack Mims to T. O. Semmes, October 1873, Box 37, McMillan Collection.

the persuasion of this "most estimable lady whose seat in the church and S[unday] School was never vacant when she could attend," her husband and their two daughters joined the church.[6]

In 1844, Pratt outfitted the upper room of Benjamin Miles's store to serve Prattville Methodists as a place of worship. Perhaps influenced by the heavenly voices above, Miles himself "soon afterwards embraced religion, joined the church, and became a useful and exemplary working member." In 1846, Pratt arranged to have one of his machinists, Jesse Perham of New Hampshire, serve as pastor of the church. Perham had joined the Methodist Church at Livingston, Alabama, in 1839 and was licensed to preach the next year. Mims deemed Perham, who served through 1847, a fine minister and a "true orator by nature." He noted that "as a revivalist [Perham] had no superior." Anson West concurred in Mims's assessment of Perham's eloquence, finding his speaking "gushing and enthusiastic." Under Perham's leadership, "a large church was formed of young people, mostly engaged in the manufacturing departments." Jacob Slater Hughes, a Methodist minister and temperance advocate, visited Prattville twice in 1847 and found its populace well-churched and virtuous, with the exception of "a *few* youngsters [mill children?] who have not learned to be decent in the house of God."[7]

The Prattville Methodist church continued to enjoy growth in the next several years after Hughes's visits. By 1852, the church claimed 251 members (137 white and 114 black), making it about three times as large as the Baptist church and eight times as large as the Presbyterian church. By this time, the room above Miles's store surely had become rather cramped. In 1853, Pratt completed construction of a new church from his own design. The imposing two-story brick battlemented Gothic building cost him about $20,000. Pratt felt great pride in the church he had raised, believing it no less than "probably the best brick building in Alabama." The upper story encompassed the church itself (75 feet by 60 feet) and the Sunday-school room (75 feet by 40 feet), while the lower story housed stores and offices, the rentals of which went to pay church expenses. Pratt hired a prominent New Orleans fresco painter, Charles

6. Mims, "History of the M. E. Church."
7. West, *History of Methodism,* 545, 547; Mims, "History of the M. E. Church"; Mims, "History of Prattville," 32–33; *Tuscaloosa Independent Monitor,* 9 November 1847, reprinted from the *Temperance Watchman.*

Potthoff, to embellish the walls and ceiling of the church with trompe l'oeil decoration. Several "young ladies" of Prattville made an "elegant carpet" for the church as well as a table cover and a pulpit rug. Spittoons were thoughtfully supplied for "gentlemen" who were habitual tobacco chewers. Pratt invited a correspondent from the Methodist newspaper the *Southern Christian Advocate* to attend the church dedication. His impressed guest reported to the *Advocate* that the building stood as a "monument" to "the liberality of one noble heart—Daniel Pratt, Esq. has done it all." This was, he noted, "just one of [Pratt's] many liberal acts," but out of respect for his host's "humility and delicacy of feeling," he refrained from adding more detail.[8]

Pratt and his family were, of course, the leading members of the Methodist church, but the surviving register kept by recording steward Samuel Parrish Smith shows that a wide spectrum of townspeople belonged to the congregation in the 1850s. Especially striking are the significant gains the church made among households headed by mechanics and operatives. At least eighteen mechanics, fifteen of them southern, joined the church in this period. Mill worker membership in the Methodist church (discussed in chapter 3) also was substantial.[9]

While people from many different ranks in life joined the Methodist congregation, however, the leadership was confined to members of the middle or upper class. Besides Daniel Pratt, Shadrack Mims, and Samuel Parrish Smith—the usual trinity—those who served as church stewards included southern physician Hugh Hillhouse, southern attorney Thomas Sadler, southern merchant Benjamin Miles, northern bookkeeper William Ormsby, southern clerk Norman Cameron, northern shop owner Thomas Ormsby, southern shop owner James Wainwright, and southern

---

8. Church Register; (Prattville) *Autauga Citizen*, 14 July 1853; (Montgomery) *Alabama State Journal*, 20 August 1853; Daniel Pratt to [Elijah] Chandler, 19 July 1854, Pratt Papers, ADAH; Mims, "History of the M. E. Church." A photograph of the later-razed Methodist church building appeared in the *Prattville Progress*, 11 November 1898. On the fresco painter Charles Potthoff, see John A. Mahé II and Rosanne McCaffrey, eds., *Encyclopedia of New Orleans Artists: 1718–1918* (New Orleans: The Historical New Orleans Collection, 1987), 313. In the 1850s, Potthoff also frescoed the interiors of the First Presbyterian Church and Trinity Episcopal Church in New Orleans.

9. Church Register; U.S. Census, Alabama, 1850 and 1860 Population Schedules, Autauga County. In one case, persistent feminine pressure apparently won over a lagging husband. Mechanic George Duckworth finally joined the church in 1865, seven years after his wife and daughter Elizabeth, four years after his daughter Nancy, and one year after his daughter Rosanna.

mechanic James Tunnell. Tunnell was the humblest member of this group, but even he was worth $1,050 in 1860.[10]

One might have thought that Amos Smith and his family, as well as his nephew Ferdinand, might have fared poorly in the estimation of some Prattvillians, including Daniel Pratt himself, for although the Smiths regularly attended services at Prattville churches, they were partial to Universalism, a faith that has as its central tenet the belief in universal salvation. Moreover, the Smiths even dabbled in Spiritualism for a short time. Religious conservatives like Pratt and Mims tended to classify Universalism and Spiritualism among such radical northern "isms" as abolitionism, feminism, and socialism. Yet though the Smiths entertained itinerant Universalist ministers and held "table tippings" in their home, they apparently suffered no social ostracism for their unorthodox beliefs. To the contrary, Shadrack Mims, a staunch southern Methodist, gave the family unqualified praise, declaring: "If the world was fitted up with just such people, we should have a comparatively happy world." Mims saved his sectarian scorn for rural hard-shell Baptists, whom he derided for their alleged ignorance and opposition to "Sunday Schools and all other institutions."[11]

Prattvillians of different faiths joined together on Sunday in the Union Sunday School, which was affiliated with the American Sunday School Union, a national organization formed in Philadelphia in 1824 to promote Sunday schools in the United States. The school was divided into male and female departments. A surviving Sunday-school library record reveals that in 1854, the male department claimed about 80 students in any given month, as well as sixteen teachers.[12]

The sixteen teachers of the male department were merchants Henry Thigpen and James Allen; planters Washington Pollard, John Shelman,

10. U.S. Census, Alabama, 1860 Population Schedule, Autauga County.

11. Mims, "Autauga County," 265–66. On Universalism and Spiritualism in Prattville, see Curtis J. Evans, "Daniel Pratt of Prattville: A Northern Industrialist and a Southern Town" (Ph.D. diss., Louisiana State University, 1998), 324–38.

12. *Tuscaloosa Independent Monitor*, 9 November 1847; Daniel Pratt to Daniel and Eliza Holt, 1 June 1847, Pratt Papers; ADAH; Prattville Sunday-School Library Record, ACHC. On the American Sunday School Union, see Ann M. Boylan, *Sunday School: The Formation of an American Institution, 1790–1880* (New Haven, Conn.: Yale University Press, 1988). Prattville's school probably purchased its library from the American Union, which sold "Sunday School Libraries" of varying size and price in the 1850s. Boylan, *Sunday School*, 49, 51, 56. The Sunday-school library record has "American Sunday School Union" and its Philadelphia address stamped on front.

and Daniel Holt; bookkeeper (and later agent) William Fay; bookkeeper William Ormsby; mill overseer George Ward; and mechanics George Smith, Ferdinand Smith, Frank Smith, James Wainwright, Ashby Morgan, Jesse Matthews, James Tunnell, and Nathan Morris. Half these men were northerners, while the other half were southerners. Most of them were of fairly modest means, having wealth ranging in 1860 from $1,000 to $10,000. The three wealthiest, planter Washington Pollard ($24,100), planter John Shelman ($16,700), and merchant Henry Thigpen ($13,070), had no connection to Pratt. Pollard owned a plantation near Washington Landing, while Shelman owned one in northern Montgomery County. Both men lived in Prattville for several years in the 1850s, apparently preferring the amenities of village life. In addition to serving as a Sunday-school teacher, Shelman worked as an agent for the Alabama Bible Society.[13]

Shelman, Tunnell, Thigpen, Wainwright, and Ormsby belonged to the Methodist Church in 1854; Matthews, Holt, and Frank Smith were Baptists; and Fay and Morgan were Presbyterians. Ferdinand Smith and George Smith inclined toward Universalism, although later in the decade the former would become a Methodist and the latter an Episcopalian. The religious affiliations of Allen, Pollard, Ward, and Morris are unknown, though it seems likely that the latter two men, who came from more humble backgrounds, were Baptists.

The teachers of the male department of the Prattville Union Sunday School, then, represented a variety of religious, regional, and economic backgrounds. Again, northerners were disproportionately involved, but southerners held their own. Most of the men had some connection to Prattville industrial occupations, but a few did not. Intriguingly, at least three of the male Sunday-school teachers, Ormsby and the Smith cousins Ferdinand and George, even dabbled in Spiritualism.

13. Prattville Sunday-School Library Record; U.S. Census, Alabama, 1860 Population Schedule, Autauga County, Montgomery County; Nobles, *Journals of George Littlefield Smith*, 44. Another planter involved in Prattville church life, Methodist George Noble, later became manager of the Alabama Bible Society's Bible Repository in Montgomery. In 1854, Ferdinand Smith married Martha Riggs, one of Noble's in-laws and wards. Owen, *History of Alabama*, 3: 1283; Boal, *History of Smith-Riggs Family*. In the 1840s, Pratt and Mims taught Sunday-school classes as well. Malcolm Alexander Smith, a local planter's son born in 1840, wrote that his "earliest recollection of Mr. Pratt dates back to the time when I first, as a small child, attended the Union Sabbath-School in Prattville." Pratt was Smith's teacher, and Smith recalled "being drilled by him in questions touching the historical portions of the Scriptures." Smith praised Pratt's "care, kindness, and solicitude" as a teacher. Malcolm Alexander Smith, "Eulogy," in *Hon. Daniel Pratt*, 118.

The students of the Sabbath school came fairly evenly from families across Prattville's social spectrum. Out of the boys' and girls' divisions of the school, a total of sixty-four children from thirty-four households are identifiable. Ten of these households (to which sixteen children belonged) were headed by merchants, planters, or professionals. The other twenty-four households (with forty-eight children) belonged to the operative and artisan communities. Five of these artisan households (accounting for twelve children) stood at the apex of Prattville society, being those of shop owners or high-ranking factory management. Yet we also find three dozen children from nineteen households of artisans and operatives.[14]

Though rich and poor children rubbed shoulders on Sunday, they had far less interaction on weekdays, attending different common schools. In the 1850s, mill children attended a free school (discussed in chapter 3), while youths from wealthier families enrolled at Prattville Male and Female Academy, a private institution conducted by a succession of men, including southerners William Miles and Jere S. Williams and northerner Henry Butler. Prattvillians, however, wanted a bigger and better school, one that would not only pull the town's young people away from established academies in other towns, such as Selma and Lowndesboro, but also attract students from across Autauga and adjacent counties. The *Autauga Citizen* was emphatic on the importance of education, declaring: "It is still true and ever will be, that 'knowledge is power.'" Rather than "ranting about northern influence," the paper urged, "let us go to work in earnest and work out our own disenthrallment by diffusing knowledge universally among our people." The *Citizen* suggested that the people of Prattville disenthrall themselves by erecting a male and female academy. Beyond providing a finer education to young Prattvillians, the school "would be the means of greatly increasing the growth of our town." Daniel Pratt fully shared the sentiments expressed by the *Citizen*, declaring in a private letter that "no man holds [education] in a higher estimation than myself."[15]

Pratt made his commitment to education quite apparent when he ex-

14. Prattville Sunday-School Library Record; U.S. Census, Alabama, 1850 and 1860, Population Schedules, Autauga County. A list in the Sunday-school library record includes the names of thirty-nine female students in the Sunday school, but it does not give any teachers. It seems likely that this is only a partial listing of students, for there is no reason to think that only half as many girls attended as boys.

15. (Prattville) *Autauga Citizen,* 7 September 1854; Daniel Pratt to Thomas Bugbee, 19 December 1848, Pratt Papers, ADAH.

pended more than $9,000 on a new Male and Female Academy, erected between 1859 and 1861. The substantial brick Italianate structure itself cost almost $8,000, its furnishings more than $1,000, and the school bell in the ornate bracketed cupola almost $400. Pratt served as president of the academy's board of trustees, which included Shadrack Mims; attorneys William H. Northington, Charles Doster, and Henry J. Livingston; physician C. A. Edwards; mechanic Joshua White; shop owner George Smith; planter John Merritt; and factory agent William Fay. The board secured as the school's principal a native southerner, the Reverend E. D. Pitts of Auburn Female College. Pratt proudly declared that Prattville now had "the most elegantly furnished school building, of the size, in the State." A visiting newspaper correspondent reported that "in putting up this fine school," Prattvillians had "added another to the many evidences of their public spirit, and of their attention to the necessities of the rising generation." For his part, Pratt believed that the new Male and Female Academy would considerably advance "the mental and moral culture of [Prattville's] youth."[16]

In addition to churches and schools, voluntary associations played an important role in building the "industrious, intelligent, and refined" citizenry of which Pratt proudly wrote in 1860. Over the antebellum period, Prattville claimed chapters of the Sons of Temperance and the American Bible Society, a fire-engine company, a singing society, a marching band, a debating society, a masonic order, and a lyceum. The Sons of Temperance directly engaged a problem that greatly concerned both Daniel Pratt and his supporters. By 1847, Prattville had a Sons of Temperance chapter with seventy-two members, all pledged to abstain from alcohol. Pratt's gin-shop superintendent Amos Smith served as president of the organization; John Mills, a blacksmith from Georgia, was its vice-president, and merchant Hassan Allen served as secretary. William Ormsby and merchants James Allen and Benjamin Miles made up the business committee. In 1848, the group enjoyed considerable strength in Prattville, holding monthly meetings and organizing marches. The group may have declined after 1850, yet temperance remained a pressing moral concern through-

16. (Prattville) *Autauga Citizen*, 10 March, 12 May 1859, 16 August 1860; *Tuskegee Republican*, 19 May 1859; "Prattville Academy Expenses from May 1859 to June 1861," Pratt Papers, ADAH; *Prattville Progress*, 25 August 1927. The new school certainly was more expensive than other Prattville schools, costing $32 to $132 per year. By contrast, Butler's school in 1860 cost only from $18 to $26 per year. (Prattville) *Autauga Citizen*, 5 January, 20 September 1860.

out the decade, judging from its popularity as a sermon and lecture topic. For example, a Mr. Hewlett, "the grand lecturer for the Sons" in Alabama, spoke twice in Prattville in 1852.[17]

Temperance no doubt was an indirect concern of the Prattville Bible Society, which had organized by 1846. The Prattville Bible Society, an offshoot of the Alabama Bible Society and the American Bible Society, had as its goal the distribution of Bibles to indigent households. In 1846, Prattville's society included among its members at least a half-dozen Pratt employees, including three gin mechanics. By the next year the society was "flourishing," according to a visiting Methodist minister corresponding with the *Temperance Watchman*. Moreover, agents from both the Alabama Bible Society and the American Tract Society, a related organization, spoke in Prattville churches. One speaker, a Mr. King, collected $27 in contributions from local citizens in 1848.[18]

Other Prattville voluntary associations may not have had explicit moral goals such as temperance or Bible distribution, but they helped "improve" members in some way. Prattville's Fire Engine Company obviously had a broader public purpose, but it also strove to instill character and responsibility in those men who belonged. As members of the engine company, young men were given control over an organization charged with protecting the lives and property of their fellow citizens, an especially important task in Prattville, where a conflagration in a factory could destroy thousands of dollars worth of property, take dozens of lives, and throw scores of people out of work.

Forty-six men organized the engine company in 1846, the same year Daniel Pratt started his cotton mill. Under its constitution and bylaws, the engine company held monthly meetings and an annual supper in December. Most of the fifteen identified members were middle-class me-

17. *Tuscaloosa Independent Monitor,* 9 November 1847, reprinted from *Temperance Watchman;* Nobles, *Journals of Ferdinand Ellis Smith,* 5–6, 8, 26, 78, 114, 120; Nobles, *Journals of George Littlefield Smith,* 41, 47, 49. On Sons of Temperance chapters in other southern communities, see Quist, *Restless Visionaries,* 192–230, pass.; W. J. Rorabaugh, "The Sons of Temperance in Antebellum Jasper County," *Georgia Historical Quarterly* 64 (fall 1980): 263–79. For temperance efforts in the Old South in general, see Ian R. Tyrrell, "Drink and Temperance in the Antebellum South: An Overview and Interpretation," *Journal of Southern History* 48 (November 1982): 485–510.

18. Daybook (1839–1846), 227; Nobles, *Journals of Ferdinand Ellis Smith,* 4; Nobles, *Journals of George Littlefield Smith,* 44.

chanics, mill bosses, merchants, and clerks. Only four—mill boss George Ward, merchant James M. Smith, and shop owners Llewellyn Spigner and James Wainwright—were southerners.[19] Still, many more men belonged to the engine company, and no doubt quite a few of these unknown members hailed from the South.

The engine company clearly had a purely social dimension, the annual suppers being hotly anticipated events. Indeed, at the 1852 supper, held at William Morgan's Tennessee House, "a part of the company," according to a condemnatory Ferdinand Smith, "tarried awhile and went into some pretty rough performances." Several men, presumably inebriated, had to be "put to bed." This embarrassing incident propelled the members the next year into formally suspending "the by-laws referring to the annual supper." Officially or not, the supper again took place later that year, but Ferdinand, no doubt relieved, reported that everything "passed off finely."[20]

The majority of the engine company frowned on both drunkenness and absenteeism. In 1852, two members resigned after "some pretty warm discussion" concerning the expulsion of "members absent from a called meeting." The engine company was first and foremost a public-service organization that needed men who would take their responsibilities seriously. It thus served as an engine of modernization, not a roadblock in its path, helping to prepare young men for responsible roles in the market economy.[21]

When called on to serve, the engine company performed well, putting out fires in John Shelman's kitchen, the "gin plank kiln," and most memorably, the picker room located in the basement of the cotton mill. On June 28, 1854, a day when the thermometer reached ninety-seven degrees, several bales of cotton ignited in the picker room. Fortunately, the engine company "was out in short order" and soon had "a stream of

19. *Prattville Southern Signal*, 21 December 1872; Nobles, *Journals of Ferdinand Ellis Smith*, 1, 9–10, 29, 31, 83, 111, 145, 175, 199; Nobles, *Journals of George Littlefield Smith*, 1, 67, 91; U.S. Census, 1850 Population Schedule, Autauga County.

20. Nobles, *Journals of Ferdinand Ellis Smith*, 142, 169, 172; Nobles, *Journals of George Littlefield Smith*, 30–3.

21. Nobles, *Journals of Ferdinand Ellis Smith*, 25, 127; Nobles, *Journals of George Littlefield Smith*, 54. For a contrary view of volunteer engine companies as "organizations deeply embedded in traditionalist communities" see Bruce Laurie, *Working People of Philadelphia, 1800–1853* (Philadelphia: Temple University Press, 1980), 58–61.

water going on the fire." The *Autauga Citizen* showered the "excellent engine company" with praise for arriving "on the spot in double quick time" and extinguishing the blaze "with but little difficulty."[22]

Although rendering far less dramatic service, the Prattville Band also proved an enduring institution that provided young men with both camaraderie and responsibilities. Band members, including Ferdinand Smith, George Smith, George Tisdale, Merrill Pratt, Norman Cameron, and Thomas Ormsby, adopted a constitution and bylaws on February 8, 1848.[23] Though members tried to uphold strict standards of personal behavior, the band, as did the engine company, had its lapses. In 1848, for example, the band resolved that Thomas Ormsby "had forfeited his membership in consequence of bad conduct." Despite this punitive action against Ormsby, a "scuffle came off" at an 1852 band meeting, resulting in the bandying of "some profanity." Ferdinand piously concluded that the unpleasantness was "a fair specimen of what accompanies gambling."[24]

Such events as Ferdinand Smith condemned seem to have been rare, however. Like the engine company, the band became a polished organization that acquitted itself well on several important occasions. Perhaps the band's most notable performance took place in 1854, when the organization played a prominent role in Prattville's Fourth of July celebration. On June 20, 1854, "the people of Prattville . . . offered the band $100 to play for them" on the big day. "We are going to meet at five o-clock every evening until the Fourth," Ferdinand determinedly declared. On July 4, the band marched three-fourths of a mile down the plank road to the "barbecue ground," where a "strong stand" had been raised for the band and the speakers. Once the band arrived, they gave, according to the *Citizen,* "an excellent performance," finally closing the celebration with a rendition of "Hail, Columbia." Buoyed by this success, "the members of the band concluded to send to the North for some music[al instruments] through [Hassan] Allen," the local agent for Boardman and Gray of Albany, New York. In August, George Smith reported that "the instruments had arrived from New York . . . in good order." George received a bary-

22. Nobles, *Journals of Ferdinand Ellis Smith,* 12, 96, 186; Nobles, *Journals of George Littlefield Smith,* 74; (Prattville) *Autauga Citizen,* 29 June 1854.

23. Nobles, *Journals of Ferdinand Ellis Smith,* 4, 6, 11, 13. With the exception of Cameron, all these men were northerners.

24. Ibid., 13, 139–40.

ton, and the next day he put his carpentry skills to use by fashioning a case for the instrument.[25]

Unlike the band and the engine company, the Prattville Singing Society was open to both men and women. Formed sometime before 1851, the society was headed by chorister Samuel Parrish Smith until 1854, when he was succeeded by Ashby Morgan, a Yankee gin mechanic and Merrill Pratt's brother-in-law. Its most fervent member was quite possibly George Smith, who in 1854 decided to conduct a singing school in his spare time to improve the quality of the society's singing. After buying a blackboard and borrowing a copy of *Lowell Mason's Large Musical Exercises* from a friend, Professor P. A. Towne of Montgomery, George set up school in the Baptist Church, teaching eight sessions in November and December.[26]

Like George Smith's school, Prattville's lyceum served to disseminate useful knowledge among the town's population. As befitted a manufacturing town, lectures often centered on science and technology. On December 4, 1848, Ferdinand Smith attended a "very interesting" lecture on electricity, which included an "apparatus to make experiments." George Smith, his sisters Mary and Sarah, his brother Daniel, and William Ormsby also attended. On November 17, 1853, Ferdinand Smith and his uncle Amos attended a lecture on education by a phrenologist. After the doctor's talk, Ferdinand reported, he "examined some heads." On other occasions, one man discussed physiology, while another displayed a panorama, *New Orleans and the Bank of the Mississippi,* and a diorama, *The Crystal Palace by Gaslight.* Ferdinand Smith declared the exhibit "a splendid entertainment," while his cousin George noted that the "very fine" presentation "elicited a good deal of admiration from the audience." Not all lectures revolved around science and technology, however. In 1854, A. P. Dietz, head of Prattville Academy, declaimed on "A Vindication of the American Revolution." In September and October 1853, one Professor Morris gave a series of talks on "his new and much improved system of grammar." The *Citizen* urged Prattvillians to attend Morris's lectures, noting that "his grammar has been approved by scores of men of talent, and introduced into many schools." The paper reminded its readers that "this is a progressive age, and that advancement

25. Nobles, *Journals of Ferdinand Ellis Smith,* 185–86; (Prattville) *Autauga Citizen,* 13 July 1854; Nobles, *Journals of George Littlefield Smith,* 76, 78.

26. Nobles, *Journals of George Littlefield Smith,* 2, 4, 85–88.

and simplification can as easily be made in the English language as anything else." The Smith cousins heeded the *Citizen*'s call, attending thirteen of Morris's fourteen lectures, missing the one only on account of rain.[27]

One southern mechanic, Benjamin A. Rogers, did more than attend lectures—he delivered one. Unfortunately, Rogers's talk, given in May 1853 and titled "Southern Improvements," met with considerable ridicule. The *Autauga Citizen*, which reprinted the talk verbatim, snickered at the poor grammar and spelling of "the erudite lecturer," comparing the written text to "hieroglyphics and other dead languages." Ferdinand Smith allowed that Rogers had "labored hard," but he concluded that he had never seen "a more laughable and ridiculous affair. . . . There was not the least particle of sense in any of it." (Ferdinand did grudgingly admit that Rogers had drawn a large audience of "boys and young men," as well as "a few ladies," and that "his brass bore him through").[28]

Such snickering aside, Rogers's speech is a striking testament to the middle-class view of society espoused by the very people who snickered. Though poorly educated, Rogers wholeheartedly endorsed the Whiggish view of industrial and social development that was being forcefully advanced in the North at this time. In "Southern Improvements," Rogers pointedly asked: "Why are thay not as enterprising men in the south as in [the] north?" One explanation, he asserted, was the comparative lack of voluntary associations in the South. "I say in a place like this we ned

27. (Prattville) *Autauga Citizen*, 26 October 1854; Nobles, *Journals of Ferdinand Ellis Smith*, 27, 75, 94, 123, 149, 167–70; Nobles, *Journals of George Littlefield Smith*, 14, 49, 64; (Prattville) *Autauga Citizen*, 6 October 1853. Dietz, a New Orleans native, had recently moved from Montgomery to Prattville. He was the nephew of Professor Alexander Dietz of New Orleans. (Prattville) *Autauga Citizen*, 28 September 1854.

28. (Prattville) *Autauga Citizen*, 19 May 1853; Nobles, *Journals of Ferdinand Ellis Smith*, 156. While Prattville's skilled artisans most certainly were included in the town's middle class, the contempt displayed by Ferdinand Smith and the editor of the *Citizen* for Rogers does suggest the existence of social divisions based on education and manners. On the division between a white-collar middle class and a blue-collar working class in nineteenth-century America, see Stuart M. Blumin, *The Emergence of the Middle Class: Social Experience in the American City, 1760–1900* (New York: Cambridge University Press, 1989); and John F. Kasson, *Rudeness and Civility: Manners in Nineteenth-Century Urban America* (New York: Hill & Wang, 1990). One writer in a New England mechanics' journal complained "that at most lyceums workingmen were frowned on or treated sarcastically if they tried to speak on an issue." Teresa Ann Murphy, *Ten Hours' Labor: Religion, Reform, and Gender in Early New England* (Ithaca, N.Y.: Cornell University Press, 1992), 62.

a gentalmen and ladis' society." Associations, Rogers declared, "are matters of importance with us in the south. . . . If we gain nothing [else] by those asociations we have som consolation of its doing thoase some good that may come after us." Later in his rambling discourse, he returned to this theme: "We need societes as well as churches by which asociating with each other, we will gain information."[29]

Rogers fervently believed that he lived in an age of expanding opportunity. Drawing inspiration from the life of Prattville's founder, he declared: "I am a pore man, But I do not rest content with the thought of Remaining so as long as I live." Daniel Pratt, he noted, "was once a pore man" himself, but he had made a fortune through his hard work. Moreover, Pratt used his great wealth to benefit others, not just himself. Indeed, asserted Rogers, Pratt had "done more for Atagy Co[unty] and the residers . . . than anney man in [the county]." Nor did Pratt do such things as starting a cotton mill "Because he had captal for no other use." Rather, Pratt did so "because he felt the importance of this interprize to the South." Rogers declared that "danl Pratt" deserved "the honor and Praise as well as Popularity of this co[unty] and State."[30]

After asserting that the great fault of most Alabamians was that "we sleep to much," Rogers concluded that if people would only emulate the admirable Pratt and apply themselves in productive endeavors "from dark to respectable bed time," there was no telling what they might accomplish. "Whare was our fathers 40 years ago?" Rogers asked. "What convayance had they to traval? Hors carts. How did they send news from one place to another? On hors Back. . . . [I]f [any] one had said hav a telagraf thay would of confind him for a crazey man. But now thay are not startled at men starting Perpetual motion." In the 1850s, he added, some visionaries dared to conceive of such things as "a flying Boat to cary 2 hundred Persons to calefonia and Back [twice] a week." Rogers himself hoped to "invent a wagon to run plank roads By Steam."[31]

Prattvillians did not rely on lyceum lectures alone for information. Townspeople had ready access to books, newspapers, and journals as well. Books were available both in Prattville, where, for example, W. C. Allen and Company boasted of its "sole agency [in Autauga County] for the subscription works published by D. Appleton and Company," the

29. (Prattville) *Autauga Citizen*, 19 May 1853.
30. Ibid.
31. Ibid.

New York City publishing firm, and in nearby Montgomery, which had a large book and music store owned by Armand Pfister, a transplanted Barbadian and Alabama's grandmason. The Smith cousins made numerous trips to Pfister's store, purchasing a wide variety of literature, history, and geography, and they subscribed to a large number of journals, from *De Bow's Review* and the *New York Journal of Commerce* to *Harper's* and *Blackwood's*.[32]

The Smiths were not the only readers in Prattville. Two of the more skilled southern mechanics, Nathan Morris and Lafayette Ellis, subscribed to *Harper's* as well. Moreover, the Ormsby brothers, bookkeeper William and shop owner Thomas, had good-sized libraries, which were partially inventoried after their deaths in 1859 and 1862, respectively. William owned, among other things, *Aunt Phillis's Cabin, Cotton Is King,* a two-volume biography of John Randolph, the collected works of Byron, De Bow's *Industrial Resources,* and John Lloyd Stephens's *Incidents of Travel in Egypt, Arabia Petraea, and the Holy Land.* His brother Thomas's collection included *Livingstone's Travels and Researches in South Africa,* a fifteen-volume *Evangelical Library,* the fifteen-volume collected works of Washington Irving, and appropriately enough for a Confederate officer, William Hardee's *Rifle and Light Infantry Tactics.* Purchasers of the Ormsbys' books at estate sales reflected a wide spectrum of Prattville society. Among them we find Daniel Pratt, Enoch Robinson, Samuel Parrish Smith, George Smith, Gardner Hale, Henry Hale, James Clepper, James Wainwright, William Root, William Spong, teacher C. Whit Smith, physician J. D. O'Bannon, merchant Samuel Booth, attorneys Charles Doster, William H. Northington, and John L. Alexander, and mechanics Jacob Ellis and Harris Ware.[33]

If they read nothing else, Prattville mechanics likely at least perused the pages of the *Citizen* and the *Statesman.* Before breaking with Pratt, the *Citizen* occasionally ran stories clearly aimed at mechanics. Literary pieces such as "The Two Carpenters: A Sketch for Mechanics" instructed artisan readers that material prosperity followed virtuous living as naturally as day followed night. In "Two Carpenters," Charles Brackett and

32. Nobles, *Journals of George Littlefield Smith,* 61, 63, 73, 79, 101, 121.

33. Reports and Wills, Book J 10, 1858, pp. 378–79, Book RL 12, pp. 330–32, Probate Office, Autauga County Courthouse; Nobles, *Journals of George Littlefield Smith,* 121. Prattville also had a reading room, probably located in the gin-factory building. Nobles, *Journals of Ferdinand Ellis Smith,* 120, 133, 151; (Prattville) *Autauga Citizen,* 6 October 1853.

Ludlow Watson are carpenters' apprentices with very different attitudes toward work. While Ludlow spends his free time enjoying a variety of frivolous pastimes, the sober Charles reads *The History of Architecture* ("dry stuff," snorts Ludlow) and takes special lessons in "mensuration" from a professor at the local academy ("Oh, bother mensuration," Ludlow cries). Instead of joining Ludlow and his girlfriend in a boating party on the pond, Charles and his equally sober girlfriend Mary Waters spend their Sabbath visiting her ailing aunt. Ludlow marries his sweetheart at the age of twenty-one, and the newlyweds lodge with the bride's mother. Charles and Mary, however, prudently postpone their nuptials until Charles "can get a house to put a wife into." The story ends with Charles triumphantly winning the competition for the design of the state capitol. Charles becomes a great architect, "known throughout the Union," and he and his new wife soon "own one of the prettiest houses in his native town." The chastened Ludlow declares to Charles that he had never "thought that a carpenter could be such a man," to which Charles responds: "And why not a carpenter as well as any one? It only requires study and application." Ludlow protests that "all men are not like you," but Charles cuts him to the quick: "Because all men don't try."[34]

Another story, "Wouldn't Marry a Mechanic," draws a similar moral. In this tale, a frivolous young lady thoughtlessly rejects a mechanic because he has to work for a living and she dislikes "the name of a mechanic." Instead, she marries a man of leisure, who, to her dismay, soon becomes "a regular vagrant about grog shops." To support herself and her children, she is reduced to taking in washing. Meanwhile, the hardworking mechanic she so casually rejected becomes "a worthy man" with "one of the best women for a wife."[35]

Prattville women did not have their own formal associations in the antebellum period. Nevertheless, the free women of Prattville did not live out their lives isolated in individual households. While formal female associations in Prattville were a legacy of the Civil War, townswomen did come together in the female department of the Union Sunday School, as

34. (Prattville) *Autauga Citizen*, 1 September 1853. The paper supported by Pratt, the *Statesman*, surely ran such stories as well, but few issues are extant.

35. (Prattville) *Autauga Citizen*, 10 November 1853. Such newspaper stories are at odds with Stuart Blumin's assertion that magazines at this time told the mechanic "to know, be content with, and keep, his rather humble place." On the contrary, they urged mechanics (realistically or not) to scale the heights of success. For Blumin's discussion of this issue, see *Emergence of the Middle Class*, 121–33.

well as in quilting and sewing circles. Daniel Pratt's sister Eliza Holt wrote relatives in New Hampshire that she did not find life at her brother's farm, located near Prattville, at all lonely. "I have been out here much more than at the North," she declared. "I get along very well with the folks without, but instead of tea, we often go to dinner." Eliza concluded, "The society here is very pleasant." If she and her family became "dissatisfied" with farm life, she added, they could always move "back to the village."[36]

It is misleading to suggest that all Prattvillians piously spent every free moment engaged in character-building endeavors. Indeed, moral lapses, manifested in brawling and drinking, certainly were not unknown in the town, even among the "respectable" middle class. On Christmas Day 1850, a nasty fight occurred between Thomas Ormsby and Frank DeBardeleben, a planter and relation of Pratt's ward Henry DeBardeleben. The enraged Ormsby pulled a knife on DeBardeleben, badly cutting him. Ferdinand Smith labeled the fight a "very disgraceful affair."[37]

Evidently much more common than fights between townspeople were fights between country people visiting town. In 1856, a man named McGruder struck a man named Long over the head with a hickory stick and then attempted to shoot him during an altercation at the store of A. K. McWilliams and Company. Long managed to get the pistol away from McGruder and then attempted to throttle his enemy, but the pair were separated. When upon the issue of a warrant, Justice of the Peace Llewellyn Spigner attempted to arrest McGruder, the latter fired two shots at Spigner (which missed) and attempted to escape. In hot pursuit, the dauntless Spigner "put a ball through McGruder's leg" and captured him. The next evening, the constable and a party of men took McGruder

36. (Prattville) *Autauga Citizen*, 23 July 1853; Adelaide Smith to Julia Smith, 4 April 1858, Box 96, McMillan Collection; Eliza Holt to Abiel and Betsy Holt, 10 February 1852, McMillan Collection. Elizabeth Fox-Genovese asserts that the "predominantly rural character of southern society [she includes "small towns and villages" in her definition of "rural"] excluded southern women from many of the opportunities that were opening up for their northern sisters," such as developing "sustained female networks beyond the household" and forming "voluntary associations of various kinds." Elizabeth Fox-Genovese, *Within the Plantation Household: Black and White Women of the Old South* (Chapel Hill: University of North Carolina Press, 1988), 70. For a recent revisionist view that sees southern women as having much more of a public role in the Old South, see Elizabeth R. Varon, *We Mean to Be Counted: White Women and Politics in Antebellum Virginia* (Chapel Hill: University of North Carolina Press, 1998).

37. Nobles, *Journals of Ferdinand Ellis Smith*, 82.

to the county jail in Kingston. The wheels of justice evidently moved swiftly in Prattville.[38]

No doubt liquor played a role in some of these tussles. Ferdinand Smith related several incidents of excessive drinking in his journal. In 1848, he mentioned that he "was pained to hear that Doct[or] Townshend [a member of the Sons of Temperance] has returned to his intoxicating cup." In 1849, he noted that "the subject of conversation [in the gin shop] this morning was the oyster treat that some of the young men helped themselves to on Saturday and its consequences." Rather dryly, Ferdinand reported on July 16, 1855, that "Mr. Killet has not got over his Fourth of July yet." Marcus Cicero Killet was one of Pratt's longest-serving mechanics.[39]

Probably the most embarrassing example of middle-class drunkenness in Prattville was reported by Adelaide Smith in a letter to her daughter Julia in 1858. "Mr. Miles has been seen typsy once or twice lately," she informed her daughter. "I was sorry to hear it. I do not think he would get many scholars next session . . . if the patrons should know he drank." William Miles, the head of Prattville Academy from 1856 to 1858, moved to Texas soon after Adelaide Smith penned her pointed letter.[40]

What really distinguishes these examples of middle-class inebriation in Prattville, however, is their rarity. While it appears that many middle-class Prattvillians imbibed, they did not do so to excess. In this respect, these people followed the example of the town's leading citizen, Daniel Pratt, who, it will be recalled, produced wine from the Catawba grapes he cultivated in his vineyard. Pratt's fondness for wine dates back at least

38. Nobles, *Journals of George Littlefield Smith*, 116. In 1859, two planters' sons got into a "shooting scrape" on the upper bridge over Autauga Creek in Prattville. After getting into a fistfight with Arch Wilson, Bill Rice pulled out a gun and shot his opponent, inflicting a slight wound. Adelaide Smith to Julia Smith, 17 April 1859, Box 96, McMillan Collection. Judging by accounts of the South from contemporaries and modern-day scholars, if this portrayal of Prattville is correct, it was a unique oasis of relative peace in the Old South. See Bertram Wyatt-Brown, *Southern Honor: Ethics and Behavior in the Old South* (New York: Oxford University Press, 1982); Dickson D. Bruce Jr., *Violence and Culture in the Antebellum South* (Austin: University of Texas Press, 1979); Edward L. Ayers, *Vengeance and Justice: Crime and Punishment in the Nineteenth-Century American South* (New York: Oxford University Press, 1984); Daniel S. Dupre, *Transforming the Cotton Frontier: Madison County, Alabama, 1800–1840* (Baton Rouge: Louisiana State University Press, 1997), 139–54.

39. Nobles, *Journals of Ferdinand Ellis Smith*, 8, 54, 211.

40. Adelaide Smith to Julia Smith, 4 April 1859, Box 96, McMillan Collection.

to 1836, when he purchased three gallons of Málaga wine at a store in Washington. Even the abstemious Smith cousins tipped a glass on occasion. One Saturday in 1854, for example, George Smith and his wife Mary (Ormsby) attended an oyster party hosted by William and Isabella Ormsby. A generous host, Ormsby served his guests claret with their oysters. George and Mary had a "delightful" time, not getting home until 11 P.M.[41]

Such restrained social drinking evidently did not violate the moral standards of Prattville's middle class. A wedding charivari in 1852 and an 1851 political demonstration, in both of which liquor likely played a role, were different matters entirely. Both events became pretty wild, to the great disgust of those middle-class Yankee mechanics, the cousins Ferdinand and George Smith. On February 26, 1852, Nathan Morris, one of Daniel Pratt's best southern gin mechanics, married Eliza Franks, a daughter of Western Franks, an original Pratt mechanic who had become a shop owner. That evening, "a good number" of Prattville's citizens, including the Smith cousins, attended the weekly singing society meeting. Later that night, Ferdinand recorded in his diary that the society had "had a good sing," but he complained that "the goings-on of ragamuffins out celebrating Miss Eliza Franks' wedding supper" had "somewhat disturbed" the singers. In the same key, George Smith declared in his diary, "The Cowbellians were out in full force and made [the] night hideous with their horrid noises." He added irritably that on his way back from the "sing" to his father's house, Mount Airy, the noisy mob "frightened my horse considerably."[42]

The Smith cousins had been similarly nettled by a political demonstration by Southern Rights Democrats in August 1851. That month saw the culmination of a hard-fought, heated campaign between Southern Rights and Unionist candidates in the races for the U.S. and state houses of representatives. On election day, August 4, George reported that "two fights were begun, but were promptly put a stop to." Ferdinand noted that

41. Richard Allen Account Book, 1836–1841, ACHC; Nobles, *Journals of George Littlefield Smith*, 68. In contrast to Pratt, mechanic Western Franks regularly purchased whiskey at Allen's store in the 1830s. Whether he took the pledge after he became a successful shop owner is unknown.

42. Nobles, *Journals of Ferdinand Ellis Smith*, 115; Nobles, *Journals of George Littlefield Smith*, 42. On the charivari in the nineteenth-century South, see William F. Holmes, "Charivari: Race, Honor, and Post Office Politics in Sharon, Georgia, 1890," *Georgia Historical Quarterly* 80 (winter 1996): 759–84 and Wyatt-Brown, *Southern Honor*, 435–61.

"there was considerable excitement in town and a little attempt at fighting, but the disturbance soon ended." He added that he "was sorry to see some drunkenness."[43]

The atmosphere in the town remained volatile for three days, as anxious partisans awaited the election results. On August 5, Ferdinand wrote, "There has been a little excitement among the Fire Eaters, growing out of the election." He added the next day that "considerable excitement" again occurred in the town, "mostly occasioned by a few drunken fellows." George Smith gave more explicit detail: "Some of the Southern Rights crowd are mad because Mr. Hale turned a [mill] hand off who voted that ticket." He added his opinion that at bottom, "the great trouble with this is getting and drinking too much liquor." When news came in on August 7 of a Southern Rights victory in Autauga, Prattville's Southern Rights men staged what an outraged George Smith called "a very ridiculous affair." He described the unseemly celebration at length: "A number of partly inebriated young men procured a skeleton and placing it on a table in the middle of the street, named it Jesse R. Jones, the Union candidate for [state] representative, and then performed the funeral ceremonies over it. . . . Old man Killet presided and Mr. William Cox delivered the funeral address."[44]

Judging from extant letters and diaries, most middle-class Prattvillians seem to have engaged in much less boisterous activities. Besides attending society sings and lyceum lectures, they played card games such as whist and smut, pulled candy, and attended dances and traveling circuses. Dances most typically occurred in conjunction with Fourth of July celebrations and, naturally, at commencements of the dancing academy. On July 4, 1851, a cotillion took place at Alida Hall. The arrangers hired three musicians to make music and local restauranteur Casimir Krout to provide supper. Ferdinand and George Smith attended, accompanied by George's sisters Elizabeth and Sarah. While Ferdinand deemed the cotillion "a rather ordinary affair," George declared enthusiastically that he

43. Nobles, *Journals of Ferdinand Ellis Smith*, 98; Nobles, *Journals of George Littlefield Smith*, 19. For background on the bitter 1851 Alabama election, see Thornton, *Politics and Power*, 164–204.

44. Nobles, *Journals of Ferdinand Ellis Smith*, 98; Nobles, *Journals of George Littlefield Smith*, 19–20. "Old man Killet" was probably John Killet, a farmer born around 1785 in South Carolina who lived in Prattville in the household of his son Marcus Cicero Killet, a (hard-drinking) gin mechanic. U.S. Census, Alabama, 1850 Population Schedule, Autauga County.

had "a fine time" and "danced as much as I wished and had good partners." Festivities did not end until 2:30 A.M. The next day, George "remained in bed until nine." He then got himself over to the shop to do some work, but he complained that he "did not feel very smart."[45]

Prattvillians also attended celebrations held in the county by various planters. In March 1853, George noted that "a large party went from Prattville to attend a soiree at Mr. John DeJarnette's tonight." Similarly, Prattville citizens, including Ferdinand and George's sister Mary, attended a big wedding party at planter Martin Burt's place in 1850. Although Burt's two-story dogtrot house was not large enough to accommodate everyone, the planter did provide his guests with a "rich and bountiful supper." Ferdinand noticed distinct differences between the town and country guests. "In one corner [of the room]," he noted, "sat a group of old women, with one or two of the more plain sort of girls who did not have the advantage of a boarding school education, with their pipes smoking and eagerly watching the maneuvering of the rest of the company." Ferdinand contrasted these rustic pipe-smoking women with the "more polished and fashionable ladies" in another corner, who entertained "their selves with the novelty of the scene, perhaps at the expense of some of the peculiarities of some of the more plain and simple sort of folks."[46]

As this anecdote of Ferdinand Smith indicates, Prattvillians of the 1850s saw a vast cultural difference, not between North and South, but between their "sophisticated" town and the "primitive" Autauga countryside.[47] Indeed, the Smith cousins, who unlike such opinionated and influential northern observers of the South as Frederick Law Olmsted, actually lived in the region they wrote about, made no invidious compari-

45. Nobles, *Journals of Ferdinand Ellis Smith,* 96; Nobles, *Journals of George Littlefield Smith,* 16. George also reported making a trip to New Orleans with William Ormsby in 1851, during which the pair visited the Placide Varietes Theater to see a play with "The Water Witches Singing and Dancing interspersed." The awed George revealed that "one of the lady dancers took time to exhibit a part not often exposed to the vulgar gaze." He found this exhibition "of course quite interesting." Nobles, *Journals of George Littlefield Smith,* 12. In addition, the relatively adventurous George defended "the merits of the circus as an honorable occupation" in a discussion with his skeptical cousin Ferdinand. Nobles, *Journals of Ferdinand Ellis Smith,* 36.

46. Nobles, *Journals of George Littlefield Smith,* 65; Nobles, *Journals of Ferdinand Ellis Smith,* 63.

47. For other examples of antebellum southern villagers mocking "country ways," see Rutman, "The Village South," 270–71.

sons between North and South in their journals. As Pratt had hoped so fervently, Prattville had become much like those "respectable" New Hampshire towns of Milford and Wilton that he recalled from his youth. In one area alone did Pratt's town differ drastically from those in the North. What made Prattville peculiar was the institution of slavery. When Pratt entered the political arena to spread more effectively his economic and social gospel, he found that he had to learn the language of the politics of slavery if he hoped to make himself a political force. His political career in antebellum Alabama reveals both the opportunities and the obstacles that an industrial missionary faced in the Old South.

7

THE POLITICS OF DANIEL PRATT, 1847–1856

By 1847, Daniel Pratt had established himself as one of the South's most important manufacturers. After fifteen years in Alabama, the New Hampshire farm boy had become a wealthy and influential man. Planters from Georgia to Texas used his gins, and Pratt expected to duplicate this success with his recently launched cotton mill. He evidently decided that the time had come for him to start expressing publicly his opinions on pressing political issues in Alabama. From 1847 until his death more than a quarter century later in 1873, Pratt played an active role in Alabama politics. In the period before the Civil War, he forcefully advocated southern economic diversification, urging southerners to promote banking, internal improvements, and manufacturing. Pratt also opposed the efforts made by southern fire-eaters to sunder the nation, all the while making clear his support for the South's "peculiar institution." Slavery, he insisted, could be maintained within the Union. Nor did Pratt confine his political opinions to the pages of newspapers. In the 1850s, he became actively involved in the Whig and American Parties. His prewar political activities culminated in a campaign for a seat in the Alabama senate in 1855.

The important role played by Daniel Pratt in antebellum Alabama politics belies the contention historians have made for more than thirty years that Pratt and other southern manufacturers were muzzled by a hegemonic, premodern planter class. Eugene Genovese presents this argument in its most uncompromising form in his influential 1965 essay "The Industrialists under the Slave Regime." Insisting that "the cause of Southern industrialism demanded, above all, the destruction of the slave regime," Genovese derides Pratt and other southern industrialists for their alleged impotence in the face of determined planter opposition to large-scale industrialization. In order to be "permitted" by planters "to operate in the South," manufacturers "had to accept the prevailing social system despite the restrictions it had imposed on the expansion of their wealth as a class." Dependent on a planter market for cotton gins and textiles, Pratt did not dare challenge the economic primacy of plantation agriculture. Although Pratt was, along with William Gregg, the famous South Carolina textile manufacturer, "the most thoroughly bourgeois of the industrial spokesmen of the Lower South," he, like Gregg, "bowed to the slaveholders and accepted their terms." Increased manufacturing would not be allowed to lead to "a general industrialization."[1]

Later historians have followed in Genovese's footsteps. Like Genovese, Randall Miller concludes that Pratt capitulated to the South's planter class. Miller, however, argues that Pratt did so not because of a failure of class will, but because he sincerely adopted planter ideology. In Miller's view, Pratt was far from being "thoroughly bourgeois." Rather, Pratt evinced "an attachment to Southern principles that went beyond mere expediency." Pratt, argues Miller, advocated "modest industrialization" and "positive state action to support internal improvements, education, and banking" in order "to protect the racial and social order in the South, not destroy it." Although Miller rescues Pratt from Genovese's charge of class cowardice, his basic conclusion is much the same: Pratt failed to offer any significant challenge to the South's agrarian social order.[2]

Miller asserts that hostile Alabamians effectively silenced Pratt's political voice in 1850. Other scholars have relied on Miller's assertion in arguing that southern political culture proved unfriendly to vocal

1. Genovese, *Political Economy of Slavery*, 181, 183–84.
2. Miller, "Daniel Pratt's Industrial Urbanism," 16–17, 31–32, 34. Similar material on Pratt is also found in Miller's *Cotton Mill Movement*. For a contrary view of southern planters, see Shore, *Southern Capitalists*.

advocates of industrialization. In reality, however, Pratt did not fall silent. On the contrary, he became more actively involved in Alabama politics during the decade of the 1850s. Moreover, while Pratt suffered some sniping from Democrats and fire-eaters, he always received strong support from Whigs and Know-Nothings, who found his economic and social views appealing. Indeed, to the chagrin of his traditionalist Jacksonian Democrat opponents, much of Pratt's economic agenda came into being in the 1850s. By the end of the decade, Alabama's government had created a statewide system of private banks and enacted a general program of assistance to private internal improvement projects. As J. Mills Thornton has noted, "in the realm of internal improvements as with banking, the doctrines of Whiggery triumphed [in Alabama] as the Whig party died."[3] In short, antebellum Alabama provided a mostly receptive environment for Pratt and his ideas. There is no evidence that he felt compelled to temper his convictions.

In June 1847, Pratt made his first known attempt to shape Alabama public opinion. That month the *Montgomery Tri-Weekly Flag and Advertiser* published a letter from Pratt ambitiously addressed "TO THE PEOPLE OF ALABAMA." In this missive, the Yankee industrialist enthusiastically detailed Alabama's potential as a manufacturing state. "Alabama does not know her means of wealth," he declared. "She does not know the advantages she possesses over other states." Pratt predicted that the textile and iron industries would both flourish in Alabama. "No estimate can be made of what our Iron manufacturing will amount to," he insisted. As for textiles, Pratt could "see no good reason why Alabama 20 years hence, should not manufacture all the cotton grown in the State." Alabama, he noted, had "more good water power" than Massachusetts, home of the celebrated Lowell. Admittedly, Alabama could not boast of a wonderful railroad network like Massachusetts, yet his adopted state did "have fine navigable rivers in the vicinity of a great portion of our water power, from the banks of which we can, at small expense, ship to Mobile and New Orleans, and thence to any part of the world."[4]

3. Thornton, *Politics and Power*, 45–52. For works following Miller, see Bateman and Weiss, *Deplorable Scarcity*, 162; John Ashworth, *Slavery, Capitalism, and Politics in the Antebellum Republic*, vol. 1, *Commerce and Compromise, 1820–1850* (New York: Cambridge University Press, 1995), 100; Wiener, *Social Origins*, 144–45.

4. *Montgomery Tri-Weekly Flag and Advertiser*, 5 June 1847. Shortly after Pratt composed this letter, Michael Tuomey, professor of geology at the University of Alabama, commenced Alabama's "first systematic geological survey." Lewis S. Dean, "Michael Tuomey

Pratt urged planters to help Alabama fully exploit its industrial capacity by investing in manufacturing. Too many planters put all their money into land and slaves, which in most cases did nothing to permanently benefit the state. A planter, Pratt noted, "will continue his planting business probably for some number of years, until he exhausts the soil. . . . He will then take his negroes and what other property he may have accumulated and leave the State. The worn out plantation is all that Alabama has for her share. Thus we see that instead of his enriching our State, she has been impoverished as much as the plantation thus abandoned has been sunk in value." In contrast, he maintained, investment in manufacturing permanently enriched Alabama. The greater portion of the investment went into buildings and heavy machinery that would never be removed from the state. If the original owners failed, others would step into their place. Pratt speculated that a million dollars "invested in a village manufacturing cotton" would provide employment for 1,600 operatives. The operatives, along with members of their families who did not labor in the factory (about 400 persons), would, in turn, "bring in 1500 more [people] in other small [businesses]." Such a town (actually a small city), now numbering some 3,500 individuals, "would create a market for all the provisions made to spare from 10 to 20 miles around, encouraging and enriching all our small, industrious farmers."[5]

Pratt's enthusiasm for industry and small, diversified farms is pronounced. Admittedly, Pratt avowed that he did not oppose "the planting interest." Indeed, he thought "agriculturists the bone and sinew of our country." As a manufacturer of gins and textiles, Pratt hardly would have wished ill on large cotton planters. Nevertheless, in lauding "agriculturalists" as the "bone and sinew of our country," he probably had more in mind those "small, industrious farmers" producing "provisions made to spare" for local manufacturing villages. It is clear that Pratt's ideas, if implemented, promised to significantly diversify the southern economy.[6]

Not resting content with urging planters to invest their surplus capital in industry, Pratt placed heavy emphasis in his letter on the importance of "wise legislation." Alabama needed laws "that would keep our capital at home, and induce capitalists to come in from other states." Again looking at Massachusetts as an example of success, he pointed out that

---

and the Pursuit of a Geological Survey of Alabama, 1847–1857," *Alabama Review* 44 (April 1991): 102. Pratt, no doubt, was closely following Tuomey's activities.

5. *Montgomery Tri-Weekly Flag and Advertiser*, 5 June 1847.

6. Ibid.

"her liberal course of legislation—the inducements that she held out to capitalists, that were not offered by other states," had made Massachusetts "immensely wealthy, having about one eighth of her population employed in the different branches of manufacturing." Pratt noted that "Massachusetts has always granted liberal charters to manufacturing companies." Other states were following Massachusetts' example and were thereby "rapidly increasing in wealth and population." Unfortunately, complained Pratt, Alabama, "instead of encouraging capitalists to invest in manufacturing has rather thrown obstructions in their way." Pratt declined to say anything further on the subject, but his next letter made clear that by "obstructions" he was referring to Alabama's tax on capital invested in manufacturing. Pratt viewed such "obstructions" as wholly misguided. "It is thought by most persons in our Southern States, that manufacturing benefits the capitalists, but is of no advantage to persons in moderate circumstances," Pratt asserted, but he insisted that this belief was mistaken. When capitalists lent money "to merchants, or to Government, or to some persons living out of State, or to planters, who invest it in negroes and land," no "advantage" accrued "to the community generally." But when capital was invested in Alabama businesses, the "whole community" benefited.[7]

Pratt's letter to the *Flag and Advertiser* contained bold and forceful arguments that reached audiences presumably not only in Montgomery but in much of the state. Nineteen days after the publication of this letter, the *Flag and Advertiser* published a second letter from Pratt, in which the Yankee industrialist leapt into the great debate over banking in Alabama that then gripped the public forum. After the panic of 1837, during which people suffered severe, even devastating, financial losses, nationwide reaction had set in against state-run banks, which had extended loans to great numbers of people, only to call them in during the panic. In Alabama, the legislature responded to the will of an angry public by

7. Ibid. In his forceful critique of antebellum southern industrialists, Eugene Genovese places great emphasis on the point that the "strongest voices of southern industrialism, with those of [William] Gregg and Pratt in the lead, pleaded with planters to invest in industry." See Genovese, *Political Economy of Slavery,* 188–91. The use of the word "pleaded" strongly connotes cringing helplessness on the part of industrialists. In my reading, however, Pratt's writings are deliberately provocative, daring, for example, to compare Alabama unfavorably to Massachusetts (something few Alabama politicians would attempt even today). Moreover, Pratt went beyond "pleading" for the money of Alabama planters, emphasizing the importance of attracting out-of-state investment with "liberal" legislation.

liquidating the state-run Bank of Alabama in 1842. Since that action, Alabamians had had to manage almost entirely without banks in their state.[8]

Arguing that the absence of banks imposed great difficulties on Alabama capitalists, Pratt urged in his second letter that the legislature charter a bank with $250,000 capital in Montgomery. Several days earlier, correspondents from Dallas County had sent a clipping to the *Flag and Advertiser* containing the 1837 testimony before the Pennsylvania state legislature of one Charles Hagner, a textile manufacturer at Manayunk who had called for the abolition of all banks in the United States. Of Hagner's testimony Pratt wrote witheringly: "I presume there is no intelligent, thinking man in our State, who would say he expected to live to see the day when banks will be done away with throughout the United States." In any event, it was obvious, Pratt declared, that banks were a positive good. "Notwithstanding there was such clear proof given by Mr. Hagner ten years ago" that banks were ruining Pennsylvania, Pratt noted sarcastically, "they still continue them—their State is also improving."[9]

Until Pratt called for a restoration of banks in Alabama, the *Flag and Advertiser,* a Democratic paper, had shown considerable sympathy for his views. The paper agreed with him that Alabama was "well adapted to manufacturing of all sorts" and looked to such men as Pratt to take the lead in developing "productive industry" in the state. Nevertheless, the paper rejected Pratt's argument that banks were essential to the development of "productive industry" in Alabama. "We dissent *toto caelo* from Mr. P's notion as to the necessity of banks of issue for the successful prosecution of manufacturing," declared the editors.[10]

In his second missive, Pratt also explicitly attacked Alabama's tax on capital invested in manufacturing. He reminded readers of the *Flag and Advertiser* that textile manufacturers labored "under many disadvantages. We have to get all our machinery from the North, with a very heavy expense for its transportation. When we get our machinery set up, we have to run it with inexperienced hands." Given the problems faced by textile manufacturers in Alabama, Pratt asked whether it would not be wise for the state "at least to tax manufacturing capital no higher than property otherwise invested?" Under the current system, Pratt asserted,

8. Thornton, *Politics and Power,* 45–47.
9. *Montgomery Tri-Weekly Flag and Advertiser,* 14, 24 June 1847.
10. *Montgomery Tri-Weekly Flag and Advertiser,* 24 June 1847.

"the tax on capital invested in manufacturing is about one fifth higher than on most other property." Pratt warned that if Alabama did not change its policy, it would "drive the most of our capital out of the State." On this issue the *Flag and Advertiser* agreed with Pratt. Indeed, the editors even suggested that the "public interest" might "be promoted by entirely excepting capital thus invested from taxation for a limited time." The editors declared that their own "notions of political economy" led them "to oppose all taxation by which productive labor is hampered." Moreover, noted the editors, taxation increased production costs, thereby increasing consumption costs. In short, they concluded, "taxation retards the development of the industrial pursuit to which it is applied."[11]

Despite having made some headway with his letters (judging by the editorial responses in the *Flag and Advertiser*), Pratt nevertheless felt very pessimistic about the prospects for banking in his adopted state. In September 1847, he wrote a despondent letter to his friend U.S. Senator Dixon Hall Lewis of nearby Lowndes County. At this time, Lewis was one of the most important politicians in Alabama. Pratt enclosed with his letter several newspaper clippings from the *Flag and Advertiser,* including his own letters, and he requested Lewis to share with him Lewis's views of the subjects he had addressed. "I must confess that I am dishartned and frequently regret that I have expended so much in trying to do what there is so little prospect or probability at this time of dooing," Pratt darkly declared. He found it "verry disscouraging and dishartning to any man or set of men to make improvements in this State as it is now situated and as it seems our leading men are detirmined it shall be." In Pratt's view, demagogic politicians riding the antibank hobbyhorse were driving Alabama into the ditch. Pratt complained that the Democratic Party in Alabama did not "consider the intrest of the State." He insisted "that it must be evident to every reflecting unpredjiced man that we can never compeete successfully with other states in the manufacturing business unless we have the same facilities." But instead of working with the Whigs to restore Alabama's financial health by rechartering banks, the Democrats, playing on Jacksonian fears of power and privilege, continued to attempt to make political capital out of attacking them. Pratt denounced Democratic opposition to banks as wholly insincere: "It is my oppinion had the Whigs as a party ben opposed to Chartered Institutions and

11. Ibid.

Banking that the Democrats as a party would have ben in favor of them." Pratt insisted to Democrat Lewis that it was "perfect right we should have two political parties," but he also pleaded that "the two parties unite for the intrest of our State" by bringing back banks.[12]

Pratt's pessimism proved unjustified, for many Democratic members of the state legislature soon came around to his way of thinking. Between 1847 and 1849, the probank forces won the battle for popular opinion, and Democrats came to believe that they could no longer make political hay out of opposition to banks. By 1849, according to J. Mills Thornton, "it had become apparent to most Alabamians that the time had arrived when the state could no longer afford to dwell in a banking vacuum." In that year, Democrats dropped their "intransigent anti-bank governor, Reuben Chapman," and nominated instead probank Supreme Court Justice Henry Collier, a man who had such pronounced Whiggish sympathies that he almost could be viewed as a Democrat in name only. With Collier as their nominee, the Democrats won a close gubernatorial race, but they lost the senate to the Whigs. In 1850, a new state legislature passed bills incorporating a bank in Mobile and, more importantly, permitting free banking in Alabama. Both measures passed with substantial Democratic support. The legislature also defeated a measure to make bank stockholders individually liable for the total debts of a bank. Again, significant numbers of Democrats sided with the Whigs on this issue. On the other hand, the legislature simultaneously enacted a tax on the incomes of officers of corporations (as well as those of public officials) and tabled a bill to prohibit the taxation of "labor or industry."[13]

Despite defeats on the issue of taxes, Pratt could take great satisfaction in the restoration of banking in Alabama. In March 1849, he had revived his letter-writing campaign in the hope of converting Alabamians to his probank position. This time he wrote a letter titled "Present Position of Alabama" to the *Mobile Tribune*. His decision not to send this epistle to the Democratic flagship newspaper in Montgomery is not surprising, given the letter's aggressive, assertive tone. Pratt asked his readers how Georgia, a state "greatly inferior to [Alabama] in natural resources," had gone so far ahead of Alabama in building railroads and factories. "The reason is obvious," he pronounced. Georgia had granted liberal

12. Daniel Pratt to Dixon Hall Lewis, 21 September 1847, Lewis Papers.
13. Thornton, *Politics and Power*, 281–85, 287, 464–65; Quist, *Restless Visionaries*, 74–75, 177–78.

charters and banking privileges, "without which railroads and manufactures cannot prosper." If Alabama refused soon to follow suit, Pratt predicted, she would become a wasted region of "worn out lands" and "dilapidated villages and towns."[14]

Pratt placed responsibility for this dire state of affairs directly on the shoulders of Alabama's elected representatives and their "narrow, contracted and short sighted policy." He complained that their goal appeared to be "to cramp our State in every possible way." So long as the state legislature continued such foolish behavior, he warned, "we shall continue to sink, until finally our enterprising citizens will seek other places to make investments and engage in manufacturing of the different branches."[15]

Pratt's *Mobile Tribune* letter caught the attention of the editors of the *Tri-Weekly Flag and Advertiser,* who reprinted it in their paper, along with unfavorable editorial comment. Admitting that Pratt was "an honest and sincere friend of the best interest of the State," the editors rejected his contention that banks were vital to Alabama's economic prosperity. Banks, they asserted, had had nothing to do with the success of Prattville itself. Rather, "*labor* did it all, aided by the energy and industry of Mr. Pratt himself." The editors expanded upon this theme, clearly derived from the labor theory of value: "The *labor* of the men and women of Prattville made the town what it is; and *labor* will do the same for any locality. Mr. Pratt settled there comparatively a poor man: he surrounded himself with a working population, and the *profits made from THEIR LABOR is shown in the buildings, the machinery, and the other evidences of wealth which Prattville possesses.*"[16]

Finding such rhetoric intolerable, Pratt quickly fired off a forceful response. "It is true, as you say, that I settled in Prattville comparatively a poor man," Pratt admitted. "But I will state that I had more cash means than I have now, or have had since." Access to "banking facilities" had proven vital to Pratt in building his factories. In 1837, he had borrowed $2,000 from the Montgomery branch of the state bank to help him pay for the land he had purchased from Joseph May. After the state liquidated the bank in 1842, he "got money from Georgia." Upon opening

14. *Montgomery Tri-Weekly Flag and Advertiser,* 31 March 1849, reprinted from the *Mobile Tribune.*

15. Ibid.

16. *Montgomery Tri-Weekly Flag and Advertiser,* 31 March 1849.

his commission house in New Orleans in 1846, Pratt turned to that city for credit. In fact, Pratt observed pointedly, "Louisiana has done as much toward building up Prattville as Alabama." Clearly, Pratt implied, to suggest that labor, not capital, had built Prattville was preposterous. Labor could, of course, *work* the machinery, but it could not provide the credit necessary to *buy* the machinery in the first place. The tough words of this Yankee industrialist forcefully impressed the editors of the *Flag and Advertiser,* who attempted to assure him that they had not had "the remotest idea of trenching in any way upon his personal or private affairs." Indeed, they declared, they had "very great respect" for Pratt, recognizing that he had "made his own fortune" in Alabama and that he was a sterling example of what energy and industry could accomplish.[17]

Relying on the exchange between Pratt and the *Flag and Advertiser,* one scholar has concluded that "positive state notions were not . . . well received in Alabama," but this interpretation is misleading.[18] Although the *Flag and Advertiser* editors opposed banking, they nevertheless sympathized with other views Pratt held, such as his opposition to taxes, and they consistently strove to make clear their great esteem for Pratt and his accomplishments as a manufacturer. In any event, it is erroneous to extrapolate from one Democratic newspaper that *Alabama* rejected Pratt's "positive state notions." It is important to remember that in 1850, the Alabama state legislature adopted Pratt's probank position when it enacted a free banking law. In all likelihood, the resolution of the banking battle lifted Pratt from the depths of his depression and encouraged him to continue publicly to air his opinions in the newspapers. In this episode, Pratt displayed no timidity, nor did he face planter opposition to "positive state notions."

Flushed with success over the banking issue, Pratt evidently felt emboldened to take a public stance on the controversial Compromise of 1850, Congress's attempt to settle the question of whether to allow slavery in the territories won in the Mexican War. The admission of California as a free state proved a bitter pill for many southerners, but in a letter sent to the (Montgomery) *Alabama State Journal* in October 1850, Pratt urged Alabamians to swallow it. While asserting that "this great agitation has arisen solely from the Northern people interfering with our institution of slavery," Pratt nevertheless did not believe that "secession or

17. *Montgomery Tri-Weekly Flag and Advertiser,* 12 April 1849.
18. Miller, "Daniel Pratt's Industrial Urbanism," 15.

a division of our glorious Union" was the proper remedy for the South. Secession would only exacerbate North-South tensions by increasing the incidence of runaway slaves. Nor was the South economically prepared for secession. "Instead of spending our time and resources in calling conventions," Pratt recommended, "let us spend them in encouraging and protecting our own State. Let us show a disposition to encourage home industry and home trade." Only after southerners had built a stronger manufacturing sector would secession be a prudent course. Pratt argued that to foster southern industrial development, southerners should patronize southern manufacturers. "Instead of going to New York and Boston for almost everything we consume," Pratt wrote, "let us encourage our own Tailors, Shoemakers, Farmers, Saddlers, Cabinet makers, Carriage makers, Rail makers, Broom makers, Cotton Gin makers, Cotton and Woolen factories, and many other branches of business."[19]

In his 1850 letter, Pratt also made his first known public utterance on slavery. Long ago he had written rather ambivalently to his father concerning slavery "that to live in anny country it is necessary to conform to the customs of the country in part." Now Pratt expressed no hesitation about slavery's absolute moral rightness, writing of " the blessings resulting from our slave institutions." American slavery, he explained, "was designed by Providence to *christianize* that degraded people [Africans]." Even with his public endorsement of slavery, however, Pratt soon found himself the subject of a blazing attack from William Lowndes Yancey's radical paper, the *Montgomery Atlas*. [20]

The affair began on November 6, 1850 (about two weeks after the *Alabama State Journal* published Pratt's missive), when a letter signed "Charles Pym" appeared in the *Montgomery Advertiser*, along with approving comments from the editors. The letter so outraged Pratt that he mailed a long response to the *Alabama State Journal*. According to Pratt, Pym and the editors of the *Advertiser* had challenged the character and patriotism of northern-born residents of Alabama, many of whom had supported the Compromise of 1850. Pratt was equally incensed by the editors' waspish claim that the typical Alabama Yankee was uncouth and

---

19. (Montgomery) *Alabama State Journal,* 24 October 1850. Pratt's letter was reprinted, along with favorable editorial comment, in the *Fort Smith (Arkansas) Herald* on December 6, 1850. See Richard W. Griffin, "Pro-Industrial Sentiment and Cotton Factories in Arkansas, 1820–1863," *Arkansas Historical Quarterly* 15 (1956): 130.

20. (Montgomery) *Alabama State Journal,* 24 October 1850.

ignorant, having "enjoyed, in the way of education, the benefit of a few quarters in a free school, made some proficiency in church music, and served an apprenticeship to the manufacture of gimlets and fishing-tackle."[21]

Pratt made clear that he would not allow such partisan bombast to silence him. Despite his having been "born in one of the New England states," Pratt wrote, he had just as much right to air his opinions as a native of South Carolina: "I claim to be a citizen of Alabama, and to be much attached to the State, and to feel as deep an interest in its welfare and future prosperity, as either the Editors of the *Advertiser,* or any contributor to that paper who so freely denounces all Northern born citizens." According to Pym, declared Pratt, a man "born North" had "no right to express his opinion." If he dared do so, Pym demanded that the man "be marked." If Pym's view gained general approval in Alabama, concluded Pratt, it would be "best for all persons born in a State or country where slavery does not exist to pull up stakes and start over—for a government where the majority will not tolerate a proper freedom of the press is not worth sustaining." Happily, Pratt did not think such a state of affairs existed in his adopted state. Indeed, he declared that he was "proud of being a citizen of Alabama, where a large majority of the citizens" appreciated the qualities of "honesty, enterprise and industry," even in a Yankee.[22]

Pratt's defense of Alabama Yankees provoked Pym to write another letter, this time aimed specifically at Pratt. Pym's second missive, which appeared in the *Montgomery Atlas,* contained words that were breathtakingly backward: "You [Pratt] have some reputation as a manufacturer of cotton goods, but your skill in that department is no evidence of your ability to mark out a path for the Southern people. . . . Yet you have put yourself forward as an adviser of the people respecting matters which are cautiously and tenderly touched on by the jurists and the statesmen of our land, and by those who have been born and bred upon the land!! The wealth you have acquired has made you step above your *station*." Pym ordered Pratt to confine himself "to the manufacture of cotton goods." If he dared put himself "amid the heat and dust of the present stern struggle among southern men," he would "be marked and treated as a Gentile

21. (Montgomery) *Alabama State Journal,* 13 November 1850.
22. Ibid.

in Israel—the Barbarian among the Romans." It was for "statesmen to blaze out the path for the people of Alabama."[23]

Significantly, Pym's vicious personal attack on Pratt appeared in a radical Montgomery newspaper co-owned by William Lowndes Yancey, one of the South's most preeminent fire-eaters. Yancey and his cohorts can hardly be seen properly as representing mainstream Alabamians, for as William Cooper has noted, "efforts to precipitate secession over the Compromise of 1850 failed miserably."[24] That the *Advertiser,* the Democratic state organ, printed the original Pym letter and also indulged in potshots against Yankees is more significant. Nevertheless, the editors of the *Advertiser* evidently did not mimic the reactionary stance of Pym, nor did they attack Pratt personally. For them to have done so would not have squared with their own praise of Pratt the previous year during the bank fight. Yankee-baiting was, however, a time-honored tactic in southern politics, and by associating himself with the Whig Party on the banking issue in 1849 and on the Compromise of 1850, Pratt had, in some Democrats' eyes, made himself fair political game.

When radicals and Democrats criticized Pratt, Whigs rushed to his defense. Both the (Montgomery) *Alabama State Journal* and the *New Orleans Bulletin* wrote editorials lauding Pratt and denouncing his critics. Pym's outrageous condescension gave Whigs an opportunity to reverse places with the Democrats and pose as defenders of the common man. Pym's "doctrine," declared the editors of the *Journal,* was "dangerous, monarchical and abominable, and repulsive to every feeling and principle of republicanism." How dare Pym presume "to establish and designate stations in our republican institutions, as if there were any station or position that Mr. Pratt, or any worthy citizen, has not the right to aspire to if they wish." For Pratt the *Journal* had nothing but praise: "We would give more for the strong, clear, practical sense of Mr. Pratt in reference to the true interests of Alabama, than that of all the statesmen who could be mentioned.—In fact he has done more to develop the resources of the State and point out its way to wealth and power, than all the demagogues and scheming politicians with which [Alabama] has been cursed from its

23. (Montgomery) *Alabama State Journal,* 22 November 1850. Jonathan Wiener muddles this event considerably in his account of it, attributing the attack on Pratt to the "class-conscious" *Journal.* In reality, the Whig *Journal* steadfastly defended Pratt against his critics. See Wiener, *Social Origins,* 144–45.

24. William J. Cooper Jr. *The South and the Politics of Slavery, 1828–1856* (Baton Rouge: Louisiana State University Press, 1978), 317.

foundation." Not to be outdone, the editors of the *New Orleans Bulletin* diagnosed Pym's statements as evidence of "madness." Yankees such as Pratt, they declared, should be cherished as the South's "very best citizens." The editors went so far as to invite any Yankees who felt shunned in Alabama to come to Louisiana, where they would "find a hearty welcome."[25]

In December 1850, the *Advertiser* returned to the fray, accusing Pratt of turning a cold shoulder to a group of Autauga Southern Rights men who wanted to use some of Pratt's land for a rally and barbecue for Congressman Sampson Harris, a Southern Rights Democrat. The editors of the *Advertiser* retreated from their accusation, however, when it turned out that the group had not even requested Pratt's permission to use his land in the first place. Moreover, Pratt himself had attended the event and suspended operations at his factories so that his workers could attend as well. Once again, a political salvo aimed at Pratt had been deflected.[26]

Pratt became more politically active than ever before during the 1850s. This tough and determined New England Yankee was hardly such a sensitive plant that he could not withstand the blasts of fire-eaters. No doubt he found sustenance in the extravagant praise he received from his Whig friends. In April 1851, the *Journal* published a long piece praising Pratt and flaying fire-eaters. The *Journal* reminded readers of Pym's "articles of studied mockery and contempt" that had "sneered" at Pratt because "he was a practical man, whose hands were soiled by contact with this vulgar manufacturing." In contrast to the sneering Pym, the *Journal* celebrated Pratt, declaring that he had shown Alabamians "the true road to power and prosperity." In the *Journal*'s view, this "true road" was "the policy of diversifying capital and directing it in all the channels where it can be used with profit in developing the mineral wealth with which our lands are teeming." While the *Journal* recognized that "some portions of all the Gulf States are wholly agricultural," it pointed out that "other important portions of all these States" claimed abundant "mineral wealth and manufacturing resources." Just because "some important sections grow cotton and rice," it did not follow that other sections without identical "natural capacities" must "do the same or remain idle, unproductive and unsettled." The *Journal* insisted that all sectional interests

25. (Montgomery) *Alabama State Journal*, 22 November 1850; *Mobile Daily Advertiser*, 4 December 1850, reprinted from the *New Orleans Bulletin*.
26. (Montgomery) *Alabama State Journal*, 14 December 1850.

within Alabama "should be fostered and urged on harmoniously together." Alabama had inside her borders "all the necessary elements of an independent empire." It was folly for her not to develop her resources.[27]

In the 1850s, Pratt became one of Alabama's—indeed the South's—most vocal preachers of the industrial gospel. He realized that he could not single-handedly pave Alabama's "true road to power and prosperity," and he determined to persuade others to join him in the effort. Nor did he refrain from involving himself in overtly political matters. In May 1851, Pratt, along with Elisha Griswold and planter Lewis Whetstone, a shareholder in the cotton mill, attended a fusion convention of Constitutional Union men and moderate Southern Rights men held in Autauga's county seat, Kingston, to choose delegates for a convention to nominate a congressional candidate for the upcoming election. The convention appointed both Pratt and Griswold to the ten-man resolutions committee. The preamble produced by the committee denounced South Carolina for "wild and fearful schemes of secession and revolution" that threatened to "break up this grand and glorious Republic." To help "preserve the Constitution and Union of our beloved Country," the committee proposed seven resolutions, all of which convention members unanimously adopted. In the resolutions, the members declared that the measures included in the Compromise of 1850 did not "afford sufficient cause" for any southern state to secede from the Union and "revolutionise" the government. While the members did "not approve of the whole of the said Compromise measures," they nevertheless recognized them "as the law of the land." As "order-loving, law-abiding citizens," the members intended to abide by those measures.[28]

Although the adopted resolutions clearly embraced the Compromise of 1850, they also bluntly informed the North "that further aggressions upon [southern] rights are to cease." Such "aggressions" included abolishing slavery in the District of Columbia, materially modifying the Fugitive Slave Act, and prohibiting slavery from any U.S. territory. If the North kept up its "aggressions," the South would be justified "in resort-

27. (Montgomery) *Alabama State Journal,* 12 April 1851. Randall Miller has characterized Pym as representing Alabama's "planting interest" and has asserted that a humiliated Pratt withdrew from politics for nearly a decade as a result of Pym's verbal assault. Miller, "Daniel Pratt's Industrial Urbanism," 31. Though Miller's interpretation of this event has influenced other scholars, his conclusions are erroneous.

28. (Montgomery) *Alabama State Journal,* 26 May 1851.

ing to such ulterior measures of resistance and redress as she might think proper to adopt."[29]

Pratt's hand in the committee's work is most evident in the seventh resolution, which declared it the "imperative duty" of "every citizen" of Alabama "to foster and cherish our own commerce, our own manufactures, our own mechanic arts of every kind and description," with the goal of enabling the South "to rely on herself alone for the protection of her rights and honor." Taken together, the adopted resolutions at the Southern Rights Constitutional Union Convention at Kingston embodied Pratt's public political positions: southern rights maintained within the Union and secession as a last resort, to be turned to only after the South had greatly strengthened the industrial sector of its economy.[30]

At the nominating convention, the Union men chose as their congressional candidate William Mudd of Jefferson County, a former legislator and, like Pratt, an active promoter of manufacturing and internal improvements. The opponent Mudd faced was incumbent Sampson Harris, a Southern Rights Democrat. As this election approached, tensions increased between the Unionists and the more radical Southern Rights men. On June 21, a group of fire-eaters held a meeting in Kingston. Two days later, a "bad affray" broke out in the gin factory between two mechanics, Unionist William Healy of New Hampshire and a fire-eater named Jones. Three days after this event, "Jones had Healy arrested," but Elisha Griswold intervened and worked out "an amicable settlement" between his two bickering mechanics. Griswold's mediation did not douse fire-eater enmity toward Healy, however. On election day, August 4, "a report got abroad that [Healy] had [been] making incendiary speeches to the Negroes." A group of local hotheads "determined to tar and feather him or ride him on a rail, but they concluded to defer it until further evidence could be procured." Taking no chances, Healy "armed himself with a revolver." Finally, however, Healy's enemies "concluded to drop it," finding "no foundation in fact for the reports."[31]

Although the Healy affair ended without any tar being spilled, two fights broke out on election day: one between T. J. Tarleton, a Unionist planter from New Hampshire who had chaired the Southern Rights Con-

29. Ibid.
30. Ibid.
31. Thornton, *Politics and Power*, 194; Nobles, *Journals of Ferdinand Ellis Smith*, 95, 98; Nobles, *Journals of George Littlefield Smith*, 19–20.

stitutional Union Convention, and Bolling Hall, one of Autauga's most important Democrats; the other between Unionist O. W. G. Methany, a mill operative from Virginia, and J. T. Hamilton, a prominent Democratic planter. The next day saw more "excitement . . . among the Fire Eaters" over a rumor that Gardner Hale had fired an operative who had voted for the Southern Rights ticket. George Smith noted: "Some of the Southern Rights crowd are very mad." Considerable drinking among the Southern Rights men led to fear that violence might occur, but nothing happened. No doubt Harris's narrow victory helped to calm the extreme Southern Rights contingent in Prattville.[32]

Autauga politics had quite clearly become divisive and bitter by 1851. During this heated political struggle, Pratt had come down forcefully on the side of the Union Party. As Alabama's most celebrated industrialist and a wealthy and articulate man, he automatically became an important political figure in Autauga. Even before 1851, however, his political sympathies had been readily apparent, despite his claims of nonpartisanship. In 1848, Pratt furnished a mule team and wagon, with a banner bearing the words "Rough and Ready" flying overhead, to carry Prattville's Zachary Taylor supporters to the polls; and in 1852, he attended the Whig state convention at Montgomery as a delegate from Autauga County. The nomination by the national Whig Party of Winfield Scott, whom many southern Whigs viewed as soft on slavery and the Compromise of 1850, caused Whig spirits to plummet in Alabama and across the South. Those few men who attended the Montgomery convention must surely have been Alabama's most committed and loyal Whigs. Pratt played an important role at this convention, serving as one of the five vice-presidents and as a member of the Committee of Thirteen, which drafted the convention's resolutions. The Committee of Thirteen put on a brave face, drafting a resolution commending Winfield Scott for his many virtues, including his own southern birth and his "ties of blood and marriage with Southern citizens," and asserting that he would maintain the Compromise of 1850 and protect "the Constitutional rights attaching to our peculiar institution." At the same time, however, the committee drafted a long tribute to Millard Fillmore, the sitting president, whom most southerners had hoped would receive the nomination instead of Scott.[33]

32. Nobles, *Journals of Ferdinand Ellis Smith*, 98; Nobles, *Journals of George Littlefield Smith*, 19.

33. Nobles, *Journals of Ferdinand Ellis Smith*, 25; (Montgomery) *Alabama State Journal*, 4 September 1852. Pratt's efforts were not in vain. Prattville went for Taylor over Lewis Cass by 52 votes. Taylor won the county by 75 votes. One of Taylor's votes came from

Like his southern Whig brethren, Pratt no doubt preferred Fillmore to Scott as the candidate who could better reassure wavering southern voters that he would protect the South's "peculiar institution." Pratt had taken a step in August 1851 to make even clearer his own commitment to slavery when he sent a long proslavery letter to the *Farmer's Cabinet,* a journal "with free soil tendencies" published in Amherst, New Hampshire. Edward and R. Boylston, the editors, held Pratt in high esteem, having reprinted the laudatory 1851 *De Bow's Review* article on the Alabama manufacturer in July. Assuring the editors that he had read and enjoyed the *Farmer's Cabinet* since his childhood days under the "parental roof," Pratt nevertheless declared that he had been troubled to find of late that the Boylstons had started running antislavery articles. Noting that his longstanding business in the South had made him "acquainted with nearly all of the Cotton, Sugar and Rice growing country" and had taken him among the "largest as well as small planters," Pratt asserted that he had become quite knowledgeable about "the character and situation of the Negroes, and the treatment they receive from their owners." Southern slaves, Pratt insisted, were "well off" and "happy." Indeed, he dramatically avowed that "African slavery in North America has been a greater blessing to the human family than any other institution except the Christian religion." Blacks in Africa, Pratt pronounced, were "perhaps the most degraded beings on the face of the earth. Ignorant, indolent and savage, they are but little above the brute creation, and so situated as to have but little chance of their condition being materially improved at present." Given such awful circumstances, then, Africans were much better off as slaves in the United States, where "they are well fed and clothed, taught industry and economy, agriculture and the mechanic arts, and the Christian religion."[34]

Not only did blacks benefit from slavery, Pratt continued, so did "the white population of the world." Slavery had brought into existence the great textile mills of "Old and New England." Without the cotton produced by slaves—here Pratt claimed that the "negro is peculiarly fitted

---

Ferdinand Smith, who, in a rare burst of political enthusiasm, wrote in his diary: "Hurrah for Z. Taylor." Nobles, *Journals of Ferdinand Ellis Smith,* 25. Pratt quite openly discussed his partiality toward the Whigs with his friend George Cooke in 1848. In one of his letters Cooke assured Pratt: "With you I am utterly disgusted with [the] Democracy and fear we shall have to endure its abuses to the last." George Cooke to Daniel Pratt, 21 July 1848, Pratt Papers, ADAH. On Scott's disastrous campaign in the South, see Cooper, *The South and the Politics of Slavery,* and Thornton, *Politics and Power.*

34. *Farmer's Cabinet,* 24 July, 27 August 1851.

for [southern] lands and climate"—less than a fourth of the mills currently in operation would exist. Moreover, since "cotton mills and other manufactories . . . have been the primary cause of most of our internal improvements," the elimination of slavery would have a negative impact on northern canal and railroad projects as well. Clearly, then, Pratt concluded, slavery was vital economically to the North as well as the South.[35]

Given these "facts," Pratt queried, "would it not be folly and madness to break up our happy government on the account of African slavery?" He warned the editors "that the slaveholding States are now on a pivot—a very small weight will turn the scale on whichever side it is thrown." If the North continued to agitate the slavery question, Pratt predicted, the South would secede—"no mistake about it." On the other hand, if the North would only "sustain the Constitution of the United States, and let our domestic institutions alone," both sections would find that they could "unite and live peaceably and friendly in the great family of States." The United States stood poised to become "the most powerful nation on earth," but a fratricidal war would leave both sections of the country weaker.[36]

Over a quarter century after the *Farmer's Cabinet* printed Pratt's proslavery letter, Shadrack Mims recalled that the publication of such a missive "in a New Hampshire paper was like throwing firebrands against a den of rattlesnakes." Mims's memory served him well. During the next five months, the *Farmer's Cabinet* published a half dozen letters that virulently attacked Pratt's proslavery sentiments. The editors of the *Cabinet* set the precedent. Though they published the letter "not only from regard to the writer, but from a desire to promote a free and fair discussion of the 'peculiar institution,'"—here they expressed their "wish that the press, North and South, were open to free discussion"—the editors declared peremptorily: "We cannot contemplate the position of our correspondent but with feelings of horror."[37]

For his part, correspondent L. Chase of Milford (the town the Holt family had recently left to move to Prattville) read the communication of his fellow New England native "with mingled emotions of astonishment, sorrow and shame." In designating slavery a blessing, Pratt advocated a system "repugnant to the principles of republicanism, Christianity and

35. *Farmer's Cabinet*, 27 August 1851.
36. Ibid.
37. *Prattville Southern Signal*, 11 January 1878; *Farmer's Cabinet*, 3 September 1851.

every moral sentiment of our nature." Pratt expected his northern audience "to receive and admit" his assertions concerning slavery "with a very obsequious 'yes massa,'" but, Chase declared, he would not submit. "What are the legitimate fruits of Slavery?" he asked. "Pure, unadulterated despotism." Not only did the slave, who was kept in "profound ignorance" and extinguished intellectually, suffer, so did the slaveholder, in whom slavery induced "indolence" and fostered "the worst passions of the human heart." How else could one explain "the idleness that almost universally prevails at the South? The horse racing, cock-fighting and gambling of every species?" Why else did "almost every paper from the South literally groan with the details of duels, murders, assassinations in every form?" It was true, Chase admitted, that northern prisons were more filled with criminals, but this was because "We at the North punish our criminals, and thus protect society." Southerners, on the other hand, "let their criminals and murderers run at large." Who could deny that these horrors resulted from the "spirit engendered by Slavery"?[38]

L. Chase continued his criticism of Pratt in two more letters, one published in September, the other in October. In his second letter, Chase scoffed at the notion that the lot of Africans was improved by enslavement. "It is of no consequence if they are fed on angels' food and quaff nectar, and [are] clothed in purple and fine linen, and sleep on beds of down," Chase insisted, "so long as they are subject to the vicissitudes of slavery." Slave families could be broken up at the planter's whim, while wives were "liable to suffer the indignities of the most hellish lusts" and husbands were "precluded by the penalty of death" from protecting their wives. Similarly, Chase scoffed at the notion that slaves were taught the Christian faith in the South, pointing to cases he had read about in the newspapers in which individuals were severely punished for teaching slaves to read the Bible. "'He that Knoweth his master's will and doeth it not shall be beaten with many stripes'" was "about the extent of [biblical] texts adapted to slavery," Chase concluded witheringly.[39]

In his final letter, Chase took on Pratt's arguments that slavery economically benefited the country and that southern secession was a real threat. "Could not the stimulus of free labor have accomplished as much or even more in the production of cotton than Slave labor?" he queried. "Yankee enterprise would have found ways and means." Indeed, if more

38. *Farmer's Cabinet*, 10 September 1851.
39. *Farmer's Cabinet*, 24 September 1851.

"Yankees like Mr. Pratt, possessed of his skill and enterprise," migrated to the South, the region could be transformed. As for the threat of secession, Chase sneered that this "senseless cry of the South of 'dissolving the Union,' to frighten the timid of the North to do their bidding, has long since lost all its terror in the mind of every man who has sense to keep out of a fiery furnace (politicians always excepted)." The South was simply bluffing, and in any event, the North itself might soon become so exasperated with the South's "overbearing encroachments" that it would secede.[40]

After this last blast, Chase fell silent, but two more correspondents took up the same cause. In October, the *Cabinet* published a much more temperate missive from one "Franklin," a self-professed laboring man. Franklin declared that he was glad to see Pratt proclaim slavery a blessing, for when "slavery can only stand on the footing of beneficence, we may be assured that it is not far from its fall." How could Pratt declare that slaves were happy when southerners found it "necessary to guard against their escape, by exposing them to the unrestrained cruelties of unmerciful men—to the rage of bloodthirsty dogs?" While Franklin did not assert that slavery excluded "all good or all happiness," he nevertheless argued that it "is hard to graft good on what is essentially evil and corrupt." Whatever "comforts" slaves enjoyed could not compensate for the "degradation, insolence, indignities, ignorance, servility, scars and violations of domestic rights" they suffered. What Pratt did not comprehend was that "the free charge and care of one's self—restrained only by just and equal laws—is the indispensable condition of the highest human culture, progress and happiness." Franklin also rejected Pratt's assertion that slavery had performed economic wonders for the North and the South. New England, he insisted, owed its prosperity to "the general influence of freedom." Nor would Franklin accept Pratt's plea for northerners to cease agitating the slavery question. Every American had not only the right but the duty "to use all fair and lawful means, not only to prevent [slavery's] extension, but to *extirpate* it."[41]

Pratt penned a response to Chase that did not appear in the *Cabinet* until November. In his new missive, Pratt reiterated that slavery was indeed a blessing. Not only had native Africans been "taken from a Savage State" and instructed in Christianity and the "principles of civilization," but now free blacks were leaving the United States to colonize Liberia.

40. *Farmer's Cabinet*, 22 October 1851.
41. *Farmer's Cabinet*, 29 October 1851.

This event, Pratt predicted, would result in "civilizing and Christianizing the African race." Moreover, a civilized and Christian Africa would become a major trading partner with the United States some "fifty years hence." American slaves, he suggested, would join free blacks in colonizing this now-thriving continent: "The facilities between Africa and the United States will be such that the free Negroes will find it in their interest to go there, and a great many who are now Slaves will be sent there. Emigration to Africa will be as large as it now is from Ireland and Germany to the United States . . . if it is not [God's purpose] that slavery should exist, the whole African race will go to South America and Africa."[42]

In the meantime, slavery still very much existed, and Pratt proceeded to rebut the assertion that it was a manifestly cruel and brutal institution: "Such men as [Chase] would say that Negroes at the South are treated like dumb brutes, even worse, but that does not make it so." Pratt did not "deny that there are many families of Negroes who have been badly treated—who have not been provided for as they should have been." Yet, he added, these unfortunate cases were the result of the action of evil individuals, not the institution itself. "There are base men in every State and Country, who live far from the Golden Rule." Slavery placed "a heavy responsibility . . . upon the owners of Negroes," one that not everyone carried well. Nevertheless, Pratt asserted that "there is no situation in which the Slave could be placed . . . where they would be as well off as they now are." Saying this, Pratt was taking into consideration "the manner in which [slaves] have been raised, their natural disposition and many other things."[43]

In closing, Pratt urged that "persons who live in glass houses should be careful how they throw stones." Not only did abolitionists denounce the South for slavery itself, but also for its alleged cultural defects, including "idleness, horse-racing, gambling, duelling, [and] murders and assassinations of every form." This attack must have struck deep in Pratt, who took so much pride in his town "of good morals and good society." However, he pointed to what he viewed as the North's own social ills. "I think if [abolitionists] would note down a list of suicides, house burnings, burglaries, church difficulties, and insanity, together with the *isms* which we [in the South] are entirely exempt from, such as Fourerism [*sic*], Socialism, Owenism, Millerism, Mormonism and spiritual knockings, that

42. *Farmer's Cabinet*, 5 November 1851.
43. Ibid.

they would keep silent on this subject." Daniel Pratt, a passionate believer in "progress," evidently agreed with southern conservatives that the "isms" carried "progress" too far.[44]

After the *Cabinet* printed Pratt's response to his critics, a lull of more than three months occurred; but in late January and early February 1852, two letters, both by J. W. P. of Milford, appeared. Like Chase and Franklin, J. W. P., another self-professed "laboring man," scoffed at the idea that God sanctified slavery because it introduced slaves to Christianity and made them the eventual means of Christianizing Africa: "To represent God in this light, it seems to me is the way to manufacture atheists by thousands. That he has glorious designs upon Africa, I have no doubt, but if he is the being I suppose, he will use more merciful means." Slavery was evil, and even if any benefit did come from it, the "end does not justify the means." J. W. P. mused that a pirate might "will to me his amassed wealth, and with it I may promote education, found asylums, feed and clothe the poor &c. Is piracy therefore a blessing?" J. W. P. doubted that slaves were really well cared for anyway. "The Slave laws . . . make it criminal to teach the Slave the alphabet," he complained. Worse, slave women were sexually exploited by planters: "The great number of yellow-faced Slaves tell a tale of Southern morals." In his second letter, J. W. P. provided a long list of horrors to which slaves were subjected:

> It can be established on the best authority that slaves in our country are overworked, underfed, wretchedly clad and lodged, and have insufficient sleep; that they often have to wear iron collars and weights at their feet while at their work, and to wear yokes, bells and iron horns; that they are made to wear gags in their mouths for hours and days, have their front teeth knocked out, are flogged with terrible severity, and have red pepper, hot brine, spirits of turpentine, &c., poured into their lacerated flesh; that they are mangled by the blows of the paddle, and torn by the claws of cats

44. Ibid. Historians sometimes write as if opposition to the radical "isms" necessarily indicates extreme conservatism. See, for example, Peter Kolchin, *American Slavery, 1619–1877* (New York: Hill & Wang, 1993), 187. Pratt's comments indicate, on the contrary, that even a person who was in many ways progressive could have strong reservations about the wisdom of such movements. On this point, see the perceptive discussion in Quist, *Restless Visionaries*, 462–70. Quist emphasizes that "both communitarianism and female suffrage were considered radical throughout most of the country; in neither Washtenaw [Michigan] or Tuscaloosa [Alabama] county were multitudes eagerly embracing these causes." Quist, *Restless Visionaries*, 470.

drawn across them; that their ears are cut off, their eyes knocked out, their flesh branded with hot iron, that they have been in some instances cut by piece meal and the fragments thrown into the fire and consumed.

Moreover, these atrocities were often done not "in darkness, in secret, but in the light of day," and their perpetrators went unpunished by the law.[45]

The final shot in the letter battle was fired by Daniel Pratt, whose last missive was published in April. Pratt complained of the tough language his critics had used against him: "I have never supposed that the proper way to convince a man when he was in error was to abuse him." Though he feared his arguments fell on deaf ears, he would try one more time to explain his position. Pratt insisted that he had "never denied but Slavery was an evil." Nevertheless, the "blessings" which flowed from slavery outweighed the evils. To the extent that slaves did suffer, Pratt thought much of the blame lay with abolitionists, who had frightened planters into repressive measures, such as prohibiting slaves from learning to read. "I presume there are but few enlightened masters who do not regret this evil," wrote Pratt. "We would not have had any laws against learning slaves to read, had the abolitionists of the North let the subject [of slavery] alone." In spite of the laws, Pratt claimed, "many [slaves] can read and learn their children to read, or their young masters and mistresses do for them." Pratt dismissed J. W. P.'s catalog of atrocities as a wild fantasy. "The instruments of torture . . . mentioned . . . I can confidently state, are not in use; if so, it seems to me, I should certainly have witnessed them, in my extensive travels among the plantations of the South." Pratt the businessman found such accusations extremely improbable. "Healthy negro men" sold for $500 to $1,500, women from $300 to $1,200. What "sane person would cripple one of these servants so that he would not be able to labor, or starve him so that he would not have the strength to labor, or neglect to provide him with suitable clothing in cold weather, to guard against diseases arising from colds?" Even "the most unfeeling wretch in the world" would not so abuse a slave because doing so would fly in the face of his economic interests.[46]

Should he be wrong, Pratt asked, what was the abolitionists' solution? Slaves could not be freed "in their present situation," for they were not "prepared to take care [of] or provide for themselves." Were they "pre-

45. *Farmer's Cabinet*, 5 November 1851, 21 January, 4 February 1852.
46. *Farmer's Cabinet*, 1 April 1852.

pared for freedom," they could never enjoy it in the United States, North or South. Whites would never allow former slaves "equal rights and privileges," for they always had, and likely always would, regard blacks "as an inferior race." But in any event, planters as a matter of right would have to be allowed compensation for their freed slaves, which would necessarily amount to millions of dollars. Pratt strongly doubted that abolitionists would ever support such a measure.[47]

Pratt concluded his epistle with the humble admission that doing "justice to this subject requires a man better educated than myself," and, in truth, his arguments were riddled with logical difficulties. Perhaps most problematically, at the time Pratt was writing his letters, the United States had prohibited participation in the international slave trade for two generations. If slaves were not now sufficiently "prepared" to carry out their sacred mission of Christianizing Africa, when would they be? Pratt's formula, while no doubt sincerely put forth, amounted to prevarication. What is most striking about Pratt's letters, however, is his admission, however halting, that slavery was an evil. This concession is especially interesting in light of the declaration by the editors of the *Farmer's Cabinet* that Pratt "once felt as we do respecting [slavery]."[48] Despite Pratt's ringing declaration that slavery was "a greater blessing to the human family than any other institution except the Christian religion," his stance on the "peculiar institution" in the early 1850s actually was somewhat ambiguous, simultaneously embracing both the "necessary evil" and "positive good" variants of the proslavery argument. Pratt, it seems, had still not quite shaken off the hand of his New Hampshire past.

Although Pratt's proslavery letters received catcalls in the North, his friends at the *Alabama State Journal* applauded his original missive. Pratt, declared the *Journal*, was "eminently a practical man, with a deserved reputation for his large experience and sound observation" and thus his "opinion of the value of the institution of African slavery, not only to the negro race, but to the world" was "unanswerable." The *Journal* expected the letter to have a salutary effect on northerners "of limited information who are grossly deceived on this subject and who know no more of the institution of slavery than they have learned from the misera-

47. Ibid.
48. *Farmer's Cabinet*, 3 September 1851, 1 April 1852. While Pratt scoffed at J. W. P.'s overheated visions of horrific sadism, he seemed blind to the undeniable daily degradation slaves suffered even under the "kindest" of masters.

bly false caricatures in the windows of the Abolitionist print shops."[49] Once again Pratt had scored another political goal, at least as far as Alabama's Whig press was concerned.

Until a newspaper started in Prattville in 1853, the *Journal* served as Pratt's public forum. Not only did the editors shower praise upon the industrialist, they also published his letters. On October 17, 1851, Pratt read a letter authored by "Laborer" that so impressed him that he wrote a response that very day and sent it to the *Journal*. It is not hard to see why Pratt found Laborer's letter so appealing. In his epistle, Laborer complained that too many southern boys were brought up as dandies with no respect for honest labor. The southern dandy did have some skills, admitted Laborer sarcastically: "[H]e can toot a horn equal to a trooper, and glories in the *voice* of a hound—can set a gaff on the heel of a sock with great precision—is an expert dancer—loves to be seen puffing 'the best Havana'—rides admirably with his ivory whip-staff—chats most charmingly on all the nonsensical subjects of general gossip—takes a social glass, and now and then is seen gentlemanly tight—perhaps knows something of cards, and delights in poker." Such a man "is the very beau ideal of the ladies," conceded Laborer, but "what honorable position in society" could he fill? Laborer declared that ways had to be found to impress upon these young men the importance of learning some sort of useful calling. First, he suggested that "industrial publications and scientific works . . . be widely circulated among the people." These worthy items, Laborer hoped, would replace "trashy novels" as the reading material of young men. In addition, Laborer urged that "agricultural and mechanical societies . . . be established in every county." Here Alabama's government "should lend a helping hand, and give suitable encouragement." Finally, the "Legislature should establish agricultural and mechanical schools." When the day came "when all young men were properly educated in some useful branch of industry, be it agricultural, mechanical or science," Laborer eagerly concluded, honest workers "would be more respected and hold a higher rank in the social circle, and many would be both useful and happy who are in a fair way to become vagabonds and outcasts."[50]

In his own letter, Pratt admitted that he had read Laborer's remarks "with much pleasure." He hoped "an interest may be awakened on the

49. (Montgomery) *Alabama State Journal,* 13 September 1851.
50. (Montgomery) *Alabama State Journal,* 17 October 1851.

subject of the future destiny of our young men." Like Laborer, Pratt found it "alarming to see what little interest the young men and their parents seemingly had for their future usefulness and happiness." To these shortsighted people Pratt declared bluntly, "No man is happy who has no useful employment." Pratt admitted he was aware that many people thought it "degrading . . . to be seen following the plow, or with a jack-plane, saw, trowel, hammer, or any other machine tool in their hands." Nevertheless, he stamped such views as mistaken. Labor brought material rewards that would command respect and admiration from others: "Is any man thought less of for having a neat, substantial dwelling, the front yard adorned with shrubbery and flowers, a good vegetable garden, a pleasant wife and cheerful children to welcome a visitor? . . . No man whose society I would wish to cultivate would think less of me for having some occupation . . . provided I attended strictly to [it] and was punctual and honest."[51]

Pratt made clear that his advice applied equally to all social classes in Alabama including—indeed, especially—the most privileged. "Many persons think it outrageous for a man to labor, if he is what they call rich and able to live without it," but, Pratt declared, such people were woefully misguided. He claimed that "if a man is wealthy and has sons, it is much more important that he should raise them to business than if he was poor." Pratt pronounced that "riches prove a curse instead of a blessing to a man who is raised to no business." This maxim was true, according to Pratt, because such an ill-trained man would have no idea how to "make riches not only a blessing to himself but to those around him." Instead, the accursed man would foolishly fritter away his wealth, doing no one, not even himself, any good.[52]

Pratt agreed with Laborer that to instill "habits of industry" in young men, a mechanic's institute was essential. He hoped to finance the school through both private donations and public assistance. Pratt proffered a personal donation of $2,000, plus the site for the school (presumably to be located in Prattville). He also suggested that the institute provide free tuition and lodging "for such as are not able to pay," so that no dutiful young man would have the door to opportunity shut in his face.[53]

Once again Pratt's views found a receptive audience in the *Journal* edi-

51. (Montgomery) *Alabama State Journal,* 22 October 1851.
52. Ibid.
53. Ibid.

tors, who found it "cheering . . . that the importance of the subject of developing the industrial resources of the State is engaging the attention of practical men and able writers." Pratt's specific proposal of starting an industrial school did not capture broad public interest, however. The only response to his letter published in the *Journal* came from an avid phrenologist named Whitfield, who endorsed Pratt's institute as long as it was "conducted on Phrenological principles." Whitfield demanded "that no young man be admitted into the School whose mental developments are not of a high order, considered Phrenologically."[54] In this case, Pratt must have found the popular response to his ambitious ideas rather deflating.

Pratt's major political concern for the next four or five years became internal improvements, specifically railroads; and in this instance, at least, many other Alabamians did share his interest. In February 1853, Pratt helped start a Prattville newspaper, the *Autauga Citizen,* which promptly became the forum for Pratt and other local railroad advocates. Pratt's enthusiastic opinion of railroads and his involvement in Autauga railroad projects have been discussed earlier. Here his role in Alabama's great "state aid" campaign of 1855 shall be considered.

Internal improvements advocates had attempted in the 1851 session of the state legislature to push through a general program of state aid for internal improvements, but their efforts met with defeat. A renewed attempt during the 1853 session was blocked by the new governor, John Anthony Winston, a Jacksonian Democrat who was extremely skeptical of state aid to private railroad companies. When Winston ran for reelection in 1855, state aid accordingly became the great issue in the gubernatorial race.[55]

Pratt must surely have found dismaying the advent of John Anthony Winston, for he believed passionately that rapid railroad development would do more to diversify Alabama's economy than any other measure now that the legislature had restored banking. "That State which expects prosperity will assuredly be disappointed," he asserted in 1853 in the *Autauga Citizen,* "if it fails to connect the differing parts of its territory and the adjoining states by railroads." Pratt laid special emphasis on the point that railroads would unlock the remote mineral resources in northern Alabama. In another 1853 letter to the *Citizen,* he expressed the hope

54. (Montgomery) *Alabama State Journal,* 22 December 1851.
55. Thornton, *Politics and Power,* 321–27.

that Alabama would elect a governor and legislators "friendly to rail-roads."[56] After the disappointing session of 1853, Pratt decided to lay down his pen and run for the legislature himself.

Pratt had already cast aside the mask of nonpartisanship when he played a prominent role at the 1852 Whig state convention. He reaffirmed his devotion to the Whigs by not abandoning them when, in the wake of the tempest over Winfield Scott's nomination, the party's boat began rapidly taking on water. In fact, as the party started sinking into oblivion in 1853, Pratt stood prominently at its helm, having been elected to the Whig state central committee that year. When Know-Nothing lodges began forming in Alabama in 1854, Pratt, along with most of his fellow Whigs, drifted into the new organization, hoping it would serve as an effective foil to the ascendant Democracy.[57] It would be as a Know-Nothing that Pratt would embark on his own political campaign.

In 1853, the (Montgomery) *Alabama State Journal* had floated Pratt's name as a candidate for the state senate seat of Autauga and Montgomery Counties. In 1855, a Pratt candidacy finally materialized when the Know-Nothings chose him as their man to run for the seat against Democrat Adam Felder, a Montgomery attorney and former judge.[58] Pratt's 1855 race for the state senate reveals the error in contentions that Pratt had no political courage, for in his exceedingly close race, Pratt suffered blow after blow from tough, battle-hardened Democrats. A timorous man surely never would have ventured into battle.

Throughout the campaign, which lasted from June until August, the *Autauga Citizen,* which the Democrats had bought out the year before, waged an especially nasty vendetta against Pratt, upon whom editor William Howell had once heaped praise. Howell in 1855 received marching orders from Bolling Hall and Autauga's other Democratic leaders. Along with most planter Democrats in Autauga, Hall had supported Pratt's railroad development plans in 1853 and 1854. Fearing, however, that disillusioned Democrats might turn to the Know-Nothings in the 1855 election, Autauga's Democracy unleashed Howell to bludgeon Pratt with any handy implement, including the state aid issue.[59]

56. (Prattville) *Autauga Citizen,* 7 April, 1 July 1853.

57. (Prattville) *Autauga Citizen,* 9 June 1853. On the collapse of the Whigs and the rise of the American Party in Alabama, see Thornton, *Politics and Power,* 352–55.

58. (Prattville) *Autauga Citizen,* 24 March 1853, 28 June 1855.

59. Pratt's campaign can be followed in the *Autauga Citizen*'s June, July, and August issues. The *Southern Statesman,* Prattville's Know-Nothing organ, has no surviving issues from this period, but the Know-Nothing view of the campaign can be found in the pages of

Only a short time earlier, Howell had enthusiastically supported Pratt's position on railroads, but now he stridently denounced the man and his ideas. Even before Pratt's nomination, Howell had reversed his position on state aid, urgently warning his readers that the policy was a "wild and reckless system of taxation for the construction of railroads" and an "abominable doctrine" that "would bankrupt the most prosperous state in the Union." In June, with Pratt's nomination looming, Howell also played what might be called the "Yankee card," pointing out that the Democratic candidate, at least, would "be one of Alabama's native sons, who has been raised in our midst, and who would be true to the South were he even a resident of the land of wooden nutmegs."[60]

In the campaign, attacks on Pratt's economic agenda likely damaged him more than unsubtle reminders of his Yankee origins. Certainly, Howell directed most of his rhetorical bombast at state aid. Pratt surely was as closely associated with state aid as any Alabamian, while his residence in the South for more than twenty years and his staunch public defense of slavery rendered xenophobic attacks upon him largely ineffective. In short, Pratt's 1855 race for the Alabama state senate turned into a referendum on state aid. Pratt—along with his issue—lost, but only by a slender margin. Although Pratt won Montgomery County and Autauga's wealthy planter-dominated southern precincts and enjoyed vocal support from Selma, he lost Autauga's yeoman-dominated northern precincts by large margins, giving his opponent a very narrow victory. Autauga's planters proved quite receptive to Pratt's economic agenda. Opposition came mostly from small farmers unwilling to pay taxes to support it.

Having previously aired his political views only in print, Pratt found

---

the (Selma) *Alabama State Sentinel*. John Hardy, the editor of the *Sentinel*, took a strong interest in Pratt's race because his paper had a sizeable circulation in Autauga. Moreover, Hardy himself passionately supported state aid and personally despised William Howell. At one point during the heated campaign, Hardy referred to Howell as a "little stinking toad" and "the little lump of feotid matter," epithets that seem strong even by the standards of the time. (Selma) *Alabama State Sentinel*, 5 June 1855. On the close political relationship between William Howell and Bolling Hall, see William Howell to Bolling Hall, 1 May 1856, Bolling Hall Papers. Earlier in the 1850s, Hall had attempted to reach out to mechanics with a letter published in the *Autauga Citizen* titled "To the Mechanics of Autauga County," in which he assured this group that they lived "in an age of progress" that valued inventors such as Arkwright, Watt, Fulton, Ericcson, and Whitney far above writers like Emerson ("with his school of magnificent nonsense") and Irving. (Prattville) *Autauga Citizen*, 31 March 1853.

60. (Prattville) *Autauga Citizen*, 26 April 1855; (Selma) *Alabama State Sentinel*, 26 June 1855.

the necessary transition from essay writer to stump speaker in his 1855 campaign rather difficult. Even such strong admirers of Pratt as the editors of the (Montgomery) *Alabama State Journal* conceded that Pratt was "perhaps a better writer than speaker." His most vocal enemy, William Howell, mocked him for his oratorical shortcomings. About a public debate held at Autaugaville between Pratt and his opponent, Howell sneered that Pratt had made only "a few incoherent and disconnected remarks." Pratt fared no better on his home turf, according to Howell. At a Prattville debate, declared the *Citizen*'s editor, Felder had "acquitted himself with honor," while Pratt "did not even make a point." Howell concluded cruelly that Pratt's debate performance revealed him as "unfit" to serve in the Alabama state senate.[61]

The editors of the *Journal* countered Howell's taunts by pointing out that rhetorical skill did not measure legislative ability: "It is not the fluent talking man, as much as the common sense man of the committees . . . who directs and controls legislation." As a man "eloquent in *deeds,* not words," Pratt possessed better qualifications than Felder "for the duties of faithful, intelligent, [and] practical legislation." Indeed, when Pratt did win a seat in the Alabama legislature in 1860, he confirmed the *Journal*'s maxim, proving himself an effective and important legislator. Felder, on the other hand, seems to have mainly won distinction as a political opportunist of the first order.[62]

Pratt soon recognized that Felder was getting the better of him in public debates. After an encounter at Pine Flat, a hamlet in up-country Autauga, Pratt retired from the field. Howell quickly found another needle with which to prick Pratt, however. He accused the industrialist, whom he now dubbed "the Grand Sachem," of resorting to "all manners of low chicanery to induce" *Citizen* subscribers to cancel their subscriptions. By "low chicanery" Howell presumably meant threats of economic boycotts

61. (Prattville) *Autauga Citizen,* 5, 12 July, 4 August 1855. One of Pratt's employees, Ferdinand Smith, attended the Prattville debate and found the exchanges between Pratt and Felder "very good on both sides." Nobles, *Journals of Ferdinand Ellis Smith,* 211.

62. (Montgomery) *Alabama State Journal,* 4 August 1855. On Pratt's service in the Alabama state legislature, see chapter 8. The sentiments expressed by the *Journal* concerning the proper qualifications for a legislator strikingly resemble those expressed in 1860 by Frederick Law Olmsted: "The valuable men at Washington are not speakers of Greek or aught else, but the diggers and builders of the committees, and the clerks of the departments, and the best of these men are trained in habits of business . . . and . . . have been drawn directly from private business." See Olmsted, *A Journal in the Back Country* (London: S. Low, Son & Co., 1860), 436.

against Prattville tradesmen and professionals who did not do as Pratt willed. Ironically, given his own tactics, Howell took solace in the belief that "the abuse of petty *demagogues* almost invariably effects more good than harm."[63]

Despite Howell's abuse of Pratt, the Know-Nothings seemed to make some headway in Autauga during the early summer, winning converts in up-country precincts, including Chestnut Creek, an area so staunchly Democratic that people had dubbed it "the Gibraltar of Autauga Democracy." As the season passed, however, Howell's mud began to stick to his target. By mid-July, the editor gleefully reported a series of defections from American ranks, as wayward up-country yeomen began returning home to the Democratic Party.[64]

The August election returns revealed that Pratt had lost the race to Felder by a mere 30 votes. While Pratt had won Montgomery County by 110 votes, Felder had bested Pratt by 140 votes in Autauga. Traditional Autauga voting patterns had, in the end, held firm, with the southern precincts generally favoring Pratt and the northern precincts heavily favoring Felder. Pratt won three of Autauga's four low-country precincts, capturing an impressive 71 percent of the vote in Robinson Springs (a veritable planter redoubt), 62 percent in Prattville, and 52 percent in Autaugaville. Pratt did lose Mulberry precinct, yet he did so by the thinnest possible margin—1 vote. In Autauga's central precincts, Pratt suffered fairly narrow defeats. At Independence, Pratt took 47 percent of the vote, while in both Milton and Wetumpka his share dropped somewhat, to 44 percent. In the hilly, yeoman-dominated northern precincts of Autauga, Felder simply plowed under his businessman opponent. Pine Flat returned 32 percent of its vote for Pratt, Kingston delivered 31 percent, and Chestnut Creek, "the Gibraltar of Autauga Democracy," conceded only a paltry 24 percent.[65] Planters in Autauga, it seems, had proved rather receptive

63. (Prattville) *Autauga Citizen*, 19 July 1855. I have found no independent verification of Howell's charge against Pratt.

64. (Prattville) *Autauga Citizen*, 5, 19 July, 2, 23 August 1855.

65. (Prattville) *Autauga Citizen*, 9 August 1855; Hardy, "History of Autauga County," 96–116. When Adam Felder ran for reelection in 1857, he scored a similar victory against his opponent, W. H. Rives. However, Rives ran considerably stronger than Pratt in Chestnut Creek (33 percent) and considerably weaker than Pratt in Prattville (53 percent). (Prattville) *Autauga Citizen*, 13 August 1857. Pratt's stronger performance in Prattville suggests that he had more appeal among the town's formerly up-country mill families, who probably tended to vote Democratic. An 1853 letter from Albert Pickett to Bolling Hall indicates that Autaugaville's mill families, at least, were receptive to the Democrats. In this letter,

to Pratt and his state aid notions. His candidacy had been fatally undermined, not by planters, but by yeoman farmers from the piney woods.

Undaunted by his political setbacks, Pratt continued to play an active role in Alabama's public affairs. He no doubt found considerable solace in the strong support he had received during his campaign from both Autauga planters and the editors of the *Montgomery Mail,* the *Montgomery Journal,* and the (Selma) *Alabama State Sentinel.* John Hardy proved himself an especially fervent acolyte, contrasting the forward-looking Pratt with backward-looking "political demagogues" like Alabama's sitting governor. Pratt and his "thriving" town had shown Alabamians who would but open their eyes what "a liberal progressive spirit" could accomplish for the state. What Alabama needed, concluded Hardy, was more men like Pratt and fewer like Winston. Then she would become "the most prosperous and thriving state in the Union."[66]

Three weeks after Pratt's defeat, Autauga's defiant Know-Nothings held a barbecue and political rally in the Sunday-school room of Prattville's imposing Methodist church building. The *Montgomery Mail,* Alabama's Know-Nothing organ, reported that one thousand people attended the big event. Because the Sunday-school room had a seating capacity of only about five hundred people, many of the attendees had to stand in the vestibule and doorways. Evidently, Pratt had learned something about the "graces of oratory" during the course of the campaign. Noting that at the recent Democratic barbecue at Autaugaville, the crowd had given three cheers for Chestnut Creek as the Gibraltar of Autauga Democracy, Pratt proposed that his fellow Know-Nothings give "three cheers for the ladies, the Gibraltar of the American Party in Alabama." The *Mail* reported that Pratt's "proposition was responded to with three most hearty cheers, and the applause was loud and long." After the barbecue, Pratt, ever the gracious host, invited a number of people to his art gallery, where they viewed his collection of George Cooke paintings. "Everything passed off finely," wrote townsman George Smith in his journal that night.[67]

Pickett informed Hall, a leading Democrat running for the state senate, that "Mr. Stephens a warm friend of yours and a workman in the factory desires that you will visit Autaugaville & give the operatives & children a speech at *night.* I would do so if I were you & would come prepared to make them an elaborate talk." A. J. Pickett to Bolling Hall, 13 July 1853, Folder 3, Box 4, Bolling Hall Papers.

66. (Selma) *Alabama State Sentinel,* 24 May 1855.

67. *Montgomery Daily Mail,* 5, 8 September 1855; Nobles, *Journals of George Littlefield Smith,* 102.

Pratt attended another American Party barbecue in Autauga a couple weeks later. He remained active in the American Party into 1856, when he served as a delegate to the party's state convention in Montgomery.[68] Nevertheless, Pratt's 1855 political race represented the high-water mark of his involvement in the politics of antebellum Alabama. After 1856, slavery—always the central issue in southern politics—swept economic issues such as state aid off the political stage. Pratt, who thought threats of secession precipitous and foolhardy, had little else to contribute to the increasingly acrimonious debates over the extension of slavery in the western territories and the reopening of the slave trade. Moreover, by the late 1850s, he found his time largely occupied with his greatly expanded cotton-gin business. Yet Pratt could look back with some satisfaction on the role he had played in antebellum Alabama politics. Through the example of Prattville, his own cogent newspaper articles, and his 1855 political campaign, Pratt had forcefully advanced proposals for the economic development and diversification of Alabama. The declarations of this Yankee manufacturer fell upon an appreciative and attentive audience (though admittedly hecklers such as Howell and Yancey were present), and many of them ultimately were adopted. Nor, as events turned out, was Pratt's role in Alabama politics over by any means. Indeed, the years of Civil War and Reconstruction would see Pratt reach the apex of his influence in Alabama.

68. Nobles, *Journals of George Littlefield Smith*, 103, 115.

8

SECESSION AND CIVIL WAR: 1857–1865

During the late 1850s, the rift between the South and the North over the issue of slavery widened dangerously. As Alabama neared secession in late 1860, Daniel Pratt, who opposed this drastic step, ironically found himself drafted to run for Autauga's seat in the Alabama House of Representatives; and this time, he won easily. Once in the legislature, Pratt verified the (Montgomery) *Alabama State Journal*'s prediction that he would be "a common sense man of the committees." In addition to authoring several significant bills, he also chaired the important Manufactures Committee, which oversaw bills concerning the chartering of corporations. While Pratt's political career blossomed in wartime, however, his businesses withered. The conflict engulfed his western market, decimating gin sales. Although Pratt's cotton and wool mills initially boomed, the financial collapse of the Confederacy eventually turned this boom into a bust. Ultimately, the Civil War proved a disaster, not only for the South, but for Pratt himself. Pratt attempted simultaneously to advance his personal interests and those of the Confederacy during the war, but in the end, they conflicted. Nevertheless, Pratt survived the war to recoup his business fortunes during Reconstruction, and his political stock remained high until his death.

In the late 1850s, especially after John Brown's raid at Harpers Ferry in October 1859, the same anti-Yankee hysteria that gripped the rest of the South took hold of many people in Prattville, a town that certainly had its share of northerners. In 1858 and 1859, Prattville citizens held public meetings to discuss the supposed danger posed by alleged abolitionist agitators within their midst and to pursue appropriate remedies. At the first of these meetings, which took place in May 1858, the conduct and beliefs of three "New England Yankees"—M. W. Leland, Joseph H. Wentworth, and Edward Slocum—underwent scrutiny. Prattvillians at the meeting accused Leland of "tampering with slaves," Wentworth of harboring "abolition sentiments," and Slocum of "entertaining and promulgating abolition sentiments." Shadrack Mims chaired the meeting, while Daniel Pratt and Samuel Parrish Smith, among others, served on the resolutions committee. After a "short consultation," the committee concluded that the concerns about Leland, Wentworth, and Slocum had validity and that another committee should be formed, this one charged with the duty of calling on Leland and Slocum to request them to leave Alabama. Slocum was to be allowed only forty-eight hours to vacate the state. Wentworth, perhaps because he stood accused merely of harboring "abolition sentiments," got off more easily. The committee was merely to recommend that he leave Prattville. Members of this unwelcoming committee included Shadrack Mims, attorney Charles Doster, physician Charles Edwards, schoolteacher William Miles, and mechanics Nathan Morris, Ferdinand Smith, and George Smith.[1]

The presence of three gin mechanics on this committee suggests that the Yankee outcasts were themselves mechanics. Wentworth definitely claimed this occupation. The 1860 census records him as a twenty-three-year-old mechanic from Maine lodging in the house of Thomas Ormsby.[2] Presumably, Wentworth managed to convince his visiting committee, which included two fellow Yankee mechanics, that he did not hold "abolition sentiments," or else he surely would not have been residing in Prattville two years later.

Although Wentworth managed to elude the clutches of vigilant Prattvillians, other Yankees did not share his good fortune. Daniel Pratt, who

1. William L. Barney, *The Secessionist Impulse: Alabama and Mississippi in 1860* (Princeton, N.J.: Princeton University Press, 1974), 163–70; (Prattville) *Autauga Citizen*, 8 April 1858.
2. U.S. Census, Alabama, 1860 Population Schedule, Autauga County.

admittedly played a role in the ousting of Leland and Slocum, seems to have stood on the sidelines during these other episodes. In November 1859, an itinerant Yankee bookseller became "strongly suspected of unsoundness, and was closely watched." After discovering that he received letters at the Prattville post office that "had been mailed at *suspicious* places north of Mason & Dixon's line," some citizens concluded that he was probably a secret abolitionist agent sent to foment trouble among the slaves. Thereupon, a delegation "requested him to leave, 'immediately, if not sooner,'" which he did. The *Citizen* wrote approvingly of the incident and urged Autaugians "to arrest all suspicious individuals that may be found lurking about our villages and plantations, and compel them to give account of themselves."[3]

Watchful Prattvillians soon snared another suspect Yankee, Luther Cleaveland of Maine, a millwright in his early sixties. Cleaveland had already run into trouble two years earlier at Deatsville, a village in the Pine Flat precinct. In September 1857, a Deatsville citizens' committee had given Cleaveland thirty days to vacate the village. The committee's letter of explanation declared that "from observation and rumor," citizens had come to believe that Cleaveland "opposed . . . Southern interest[s] and institutions," and it advised him "to return to the North," where he could "enjoy the company of *abolitionists* and *negroes* to [his] heart's content."[4]

After Cleaveland's expulsion from Deatsville, the hapless mechanic moved back to Prattville, where he had previously resided. Some Prattvillians, at least, believed him a worthy man. The editor of the *Citizen,* William Howell, complained that before moving to Deatsville, Cleaveland had obtained "some four or five certificates of character from certain [Prattvillians]," despite the fact that Autauga's "best southern citizens" had regarded him right from the start "as a suspicious individual." The citizens of Deatsville, Howell declared, had "very properly disregarded" the imprudently granted certificates. Cleaveland seems to have avoided trouble in Prattville for nearly two years, but in December 1859, the recently formed Prattville vigilance committee reported at a public meeting that Cleaveland was "an unsafe member of a Southern community." Thus informed, the meeting's resolutions committee resolved that another committee be formed "to notify said Cleaveland to leave this

3. (Prattville) *Autauga Citizen,* 1 December 1859.
4. (Prattville) *Autauga Citizen,* 24 September 1857.

county within ten hours." If Cleaveland failed to do so, he would "be forced to leave." The committee resolved further "to sustain the [vigilance] committee in *any course* [emphasis added] they may think proper to pursue in expelling him from our community."[5]

There is no indication that Pratt even attended this meeting, let alone played any part in it. It is clear, too, that some Prattvillians, evidently Yankees themselves, had testified to Cleaveland's good character two years earlier. The prime inside agitators in Prattville seem to have been William H. Northington and Charles Doster, southern-born attorneys and Democrats, as well as William Howell, editor of Prattville's Democratic newspaper. Northington and Doster played prominent parts in both the December public meeting and the formation in November of the Prattville vigilance committee, which was charged with protecting "lives and property from the incendiary attacks of such men as old John Brown, and *nigger stealers* generally." For his part, Howell now turned the rhetorical firepower he had used to cut down Pratt in the 1855 election onto the abolitionist conspirators he saw lurking in village streets and country lanes. Cleaveland he described as a beast incarnate: "short," "thick-set," "bald headed," "ugly features and a hooked nose," "a real Judas countenance." Howell fretted that Prattville "will soon get its name up for fostering abolitionists."[6]

Despite all the fulminations against Yankees from Democratic quarters, many northerners (most of whom were New Englanders) continued to reside in Prattville in 1860. Yankees continued to play a vital role in the town's economy and culture. Daniel Pratt does not appear, for the most part, to have lent his sanction to antiabolitionist agitation, but neither did he attempt to put a stop to it. To the contrary, he reaffirmed his support for slavery in the late 1850s and warned northerners to leave the South alone.

Pratt's home town, Temple, New Hampshire, celebrated its centennial

5. (Prattville) *Autauga Citizen*, 15 December 1859.

6. (Prattville) *Autauga Citizen*, 1 December 1859, 24 September 1857, 8 April 1858. In one case, Howell allowed that some Prattvillians had wrongly suspected Lorenzo Wilder, a recent resident who hailed from Massachusetts, of being an abolitionist. Several letters from reliable northerners to William H. Northington revealed, Howell explained, that back in Massachusetts, Wilder had been "no *abolitionist,* but a *Democrat,*" which, of course, was permissible. (Prattville) *Autauga Citizen*, 5 January 1860. On the formation of vigilance committees in the South in the 1850s and their role in fomenting secession sentiment, see Barney, *Secessionist Impulse*, 171–80, 211–12.

in late 1858. The people of Temple invited their most famous son, Daniel Pratt, to attend, but he declined, pleading that distance prevented him from conveniently doing so. Pratt did, however, send Temple a $50 check, as well as some advice. Americans, Pratt declared, were "a happy, thriving, and prosperous people." Indeed, he opined, a "happier people does not exist on earth." But one thing was "necessary to secure the perpetuity of these blessings: that is for each division of the country to attend to its own individual interests."[7] Pratt put his message delicately, but his meaning was clear: northerners agitating against the South's "peculiar institution" threatened to destroy a happy, prosperous republic.

The next year, Pratt sent a more bellicose missive, "Alabama Improvements and the True Interests of Her People," to Noah Cloud's prominent agricultural journal, *American Cotton Planter and Soil of the South*. In this letter, Pratt indicated that he had tired of debating the question of slavery's moral rightness with outraged abolitionists. "I have no patience to listen to a class of persons, who speak of fencing in or penning up slavery," he declared peremptorily. "It is all talk. Slavery will eventually go where it can be made profitable, and no where else is it wanted." If New Englanders had been able to turn a profit from slavery, Pratt added with a surprisingly nasty thrust against his native people, they "would have a greater proportion of their population slaves than Alabama." Pratt went on to assert strongly the morality of slavery, as he had earlier in the decade. "I am well aware," he admitted, "that a large portion of the present generation in the Eastern States has been educated to believe that African slavery is a curse and a sin against High Heaven." Where these people went wrong, however, was in failing to consider "the degraded state of cannibalism, ignorance and poverty the negro is in [in] his native country." American slavery, Pratt continued to insist, was "the only way" of improving the African "physically, morally and religiously." He no longer left any room for doubt about slavery's inherent correctness, adding rather smugly: "God in his Providence has ordered all things right."[8] The ambiguity of the early 1850s had disappeared.

This interest in slavery was not merely theoretical, for during the 1850s, Pratt's slaveholdings significantly expanded. Between 1850 and

7. Daniel Pratt to Nahum A. Child, 8 September 1858, reprinted in *Hon. Daniel Pratt*, 80–81.

8. *Montgomery Daily Mail*, 25 February 1859, reprinted from *American Cotton Planter and Soil of the South*. The portions of this letter that concern slavery were deleted in Tarrant's book. See Tarrant, ed., *Hon. Daniel Pratt*, 77.

1860, the number of slaves owned by Pratt increased from 47 to 107. One scholar has attributed Pratt's expansion of his slaveholdings at this time to criticism received from the *Montgomery Atlas* in 1850; he argues that Pratt attempted, in effect, to buy his way into the planter class in the hope that this would insulate him from further attacks.[9] There are several problems with this analysis, however. First, during his long career in Alabama, Pratt seems to have been remarkably tenacious in pursuing his own course and doing things his own way, regardless of what others thought. Second, Pratt already owned a large number of slaves in 1850. Third, criticism from the extremist *Montgomery Atlas* was hardly a traumatizing event, for the *Atlas* was hacked apart by cutting countereditorials from Pratt's supporters. Finally, Pratt's largest slave purchase actually took place in 1858, more than seven years after the *Atlas* assaulted him.

State records reveal that Pratt owned 40 slaves in 1852. Between 1850 and 1852, then, the number of slaves that he owned actually dropped. By 1855, Pratt's slaveholdings had increased to 59. Thus the biggest increase in Pratt's slaveholdings occurred between 1855, when he owned 59 slaves, and 1860, when he owned 107. On January 4, 1858, Pratt purchased a plantation with 32 slaves located below Prattville near Washington Landing.[10] The remaining 16 slaves reasonably can be attributed to natural increase. Was Pratt attempting further to solidify his position as a landowner and slaveowner with this purchase in 1858? The answer is much simpler. Pratt, first and foremost a businessman, probably saw a seemingly good investment opportunity and grabbed it.

Pratt was extremely troubled by his low gin sales in 1857. In 1855, he had completed the massive expansion of his gin factory, so that it was now unprofitable for him to manufacture fewer than 800 gins annually. In 1857, the year of the panic, he sold only 341 gins, less than half the number his factory had produced. The year before, Pratt wrote glumly to his friend Elisha Griswold: "The gin business is overdone. I think I have done rong in building my new shop. . . . I think that [800] gins is more than I can sell." Moreover, Pratt viewed the osnaburg market as glutted, so he did not want to expand his cotton mill either—though he did build

9. U.S. Census, Alabama, 1850 and 1860 Slave Schedules, Autauga County; Miller, *Cotton Mill Movement*, 219–20.

10. Alabama State Property Tax Assessment, Autauga County, 1852, ACHC; Alabama 1855 State Census, Autauga County; Deed Book DC, 131–33, Probate Office, Autauga County Courthouse. Pratt's purchase included the McCowly tract and adjoining land. The land and slaves together cost him $25,425.

a small woolen mill in 1857. Under these circumstances, it is wrong to conclude, as one scholar does, that "investments in slaves represented dead capital for manufactures." If Pratt bought his plantation for a low price and then sold it a few years later for a higher one, he could have profitably expanded his manufacturing operations at a more propitious time.[11]

Rather than attempt to become some sort of agrarian aristocrat, Pratt continued to do what he could for southern manufacturing. Understanding the political trends of the 1850s, Pratt attempted to link the cause of southern industry to southern nationalism. As early as his 1855 state senate campaign, Pratt warned southerners that the increasingly strident sectional conflict made it imperative that the South develop the requisite industrial capacity to defend itself in war. Pratt struck this note more loudly in his 1859 letter to the *Cotton Planter*. "I profess to be a Southern rights man, and strongly contend that the South ought to maintain her rights at all hazards," Pratt began belligerently. Nevertheless, he elaborated, "I would . . . pursue a somewhat different course from that of our politicians." Pratt's course was for southerners to stop making "flaming fiery speeches and threats" and, instead, "to go quietly and peaceably to work, and make ourselves less dependent on those who abuse and would gladly ruin us." Southerners should produce their own iron, coal, lime, marble, axes, hoes, spades, firearms, powder, wagons, carriages, saddles, bridles, harnesses, clothing, plows, doors, sashes, blinds, shoes, boots, "and last, but not least," cotton gins. "Give us proper encouragement," Pratt challenged his readers, "and you will be furnished with mechanics and manufacturers." Prattville showed what determined men could accomplish in the South if southerners would but heed the example. "Hitherto we at the South [have] pursued a wrong course," Pratt chastised. If

11. Miller, *Cotton Mill Movement*, 219. In 1856, Pratt offered to pay part of a debt to Elisha Griswold by getting him an Autauga plantation near Washington Landing at a bargain price. He did not use as one of his selling points that the plantation would confer loftier status on Elisha. He seems simply to have viewed the property as a good buy. See Daniel Pratt to Elisha Griswold, 11 March 1856, Pratt Papers, ADAH. Despite its evidentiary weaknesses, Miller's "status thesis" has resurfaced in the new major history of Alabama: "But by the 1850s, with white labor proving unsatisfactory and the secessionists attacking his northern birth and loyalty to the South, Pratt invested heavily in slaves and began to use them in his factories." William Warren Rogers, et al., *Alabama: The History of a Deep South State* (Tuscaloosa: University of Alabama Press, 1994), 125. See also Lewis, *Sloss Furnaces*, 17.

southerners would "attend strictly to . . . business," however, they would be able to make the North yield to their demands.[12]

When the newly formed Wetumpka Dragoons wrote Pratt in February 1860 querying whether his cotton mill could manufacture cloth for their uniforms, Pratt took advantage of the opportunity to reiterate his view on southern preparedness. "Nothing will do more to prevent war than a preparation for it," Pratt pronounced, "and if it does not prevent it, a preparation is absolutely necessary to carry it on." He commended the Wetumpka Dragoons for making a point of seeking to purchase their cloth from a southern concern: "This is the spirit for which I have been an advocate for the past twenty years." Pratt warned that "we of the South are much more dependent than we suppose." Instead of constantly orating, southerners needed to "go relentlessly but earnestly to work" building business enterprises. Pratt also urged state legislators to "encourage internal improvements, such as rail roads and manufactures, by diminishing or removing the tax on capital invested in [such businesses]." Such beneficent legislation would attract outside investment and encourage manufacturers and mechanics. With war looming on the horizon, Pratt insisted that if southerners would only "set about it in the right way," they would be industrially self-sufficient in ten years, "in spite of all the Black Republican forces that can be paraded."[13] The only problem with Pratt's hopeful scenario is that many southerners were unwilling to abide a decade of Republican parading, as events that winter would prove.

12. (Selma) *Alabama State Sentinel,* 24 May 1855, quoting the *Prattville Southern Statesman; Montgomery Daily Mail,* 25 February 1859, reprinted from *American Cotton Planter and Soil of the South.* In a jab at the fierce-talking fire-eaters, Pratt added: "Some prefer to show their works by their faith. I hope to show my faith by my works." He boasted that he purchased all his shafting, pig iron, and lime in the South and that he patronized southern schools, having brought down "eight children from the Northern States [presumably family relations such as Merrill Pratt and Julia Bill] and educated them in Alabama." Despite Pratt's boast about patronizing southern raw material suppliers, however, he continued to remain dependent on English and northern manufacturers for a wide range of items right up to the outbreak of the Civil War, including screws, bolts, nails, tacks, steel plates, bristles, twine, paints, and varnishes. Machinery came from Ball and Williams of Worcester, Massachusetts and Putnam Machine Company of Fitchburg, Massachusetts. See Notes and Bills Payable, 1858–1866, CECP.

13. (Prattville) *Autauga Citizen,* 23 February 1860, reprinted from the *Wetumpka Enquirer.* Admitting to his inquirers that he could not provide cloth "of a suitable color for your purpose," Pratt recommended James Roswell King's factory at Roswell, Georgia.

As the Civil War neared, Pratt continued to enjoy the same good press he had generally received since the 1840s. In 1857, a *Montgomery Daily Mail* correspondent found Pratt a "plain, affable and kind old gentleman, who . . . by dint of his individual exertions alone . . . made Prattville what it is—a flourishing and healthy village, with all the facilities for manufacturing." Similarly, a correspondent for the *Tuskegee Republican* wrote that "Mr. Pratt has many of the traits of a great man. Here upon the arid sands of a pine barren he has built up a seat of industry, wealth and contentment that ought to send his name down to future generations with éclat."[14] Even William Howell, who had mauled Pratt during the 1855 political campaign and who now growled about the Yankee menace, wrote admiringly of Pratt in the late 1850s.

Pratt's popularity only increased during the secession crisis, despite his opposition to sundering the Republic. Pratt remained uncharacteristically mute in the newspapers during much of 1860, but he finally spoke when the *Montgomery Daily Mail* claimed that he supported for president John C. Breckinridge, the candidate of southern Democrats. "I must say," Pratt wrote the *Mail*, "that my preference has been all the time for Bell and Everett." Pratt's support for the ticket of the Constitutional Union Party shows that, like many old southern Whigs, he still believed that the Union was worth preserving and that southern rights could be maintained within it. In October, Pratt attended a meeting of Prattville's Breckinridge and Lane Club at Alida Hall. He "was loudly called for" by "the large crowd in attendance," and he promptly rose to speak, despite laboring "under physical pain and suffering" from a neuralgia attack. He again declared himself for John Bell, yet he added that he believed Breckinridge "a sound and true man." Judging from the report in the *Statesman*, however, Pratt showed greater concern in his Alida Hall speech with industrialization than with secession. He urged the South to "encourage the manufacture of arms, and gunpowder, and everything that the South needed to make her independent and prosperous . . . and show" the North that it was capable of maintaining southern "independence and rights." Such a course, Pratt predicted, would bring northern "fanatics" to heel. If, however, "the worst should . . . come to the worst" and the South was "forced in self defense to withdraw from the Union, she would then be prepared for the emergency."[15]

14. *Montgomery Daily Mail,* 17 July 1857; *Tuskegee Republican,* 19 May 1859.

15. (Prattville) *Autauga Citizen,* 9 August 1860, reprinted in the *Montgomery Mail; Prattville Southern Statesman,* 6 October 1860.

Daniel Pratt and other supporters of the Constitutional Union Party were not alone in opposing Breckinridge. In June, when the Democratic convention at Baltimore split between Breckinridge and Stephen Douglas, the local party in Autauga similarly fractured. Many of Autauga's most prominent conservative Democrats, including Bolling Hall and Charles Doster, had already pledged their support to Douglas in May of that year at a party convention at Kingston. Reflecting sentiments similar to Pratt's, Hall vigorously denounced "the enemies of the Union both North and South." The Democratic Party's Autauga organ, the *Citizen,* thereupon fell into line and declared for Douglas. In September, Howell predicted that the Little Giant would "carry Autauga by a small plurality majority." The *Citizen*'s editor insisted "that all the leading Democrats in this county, with a few exceptions, are strong for Douglas" and "that the old line Democracy all over the county are rallying to his support." Howell also predicted that Bell would place a strong second, as "many old-line Whigs and conservative Know-Nothings are leaving Breckinridge and going over to Bell." Breckinridge, it seemed, would run a poor third, according to Howell's hopeful scenario.[16]

Howell's prognostications proved woefully inaccurate in November. With 49 percent of the vote, Breckinridge nearly won an outright majority in Autauga. Douglas finished second with 31 percent of the vote, and Bell finished a poor third with only 20 percent. Breckinridge won in six precincts, while Douglas won in four, all of them located in the up-country. Bell's best performance (33 percent) was in the planter precinct of Robinson Springs, but even there Breckinridge bested him, winning 47 percent of the vote. Southern Democrats stormed Whiggish Prattville as well. In the precinct that included the "Lowell of the South," Breckinridge won a staggering 65 percent of the vote, while Bell took only 20 percent.[17]

Clearly, contrary to Howell's assertions, many old-line Whigs voted for Breckinridge.[18] Nevertheless, Bell and Douglas together still made up a bare majority of the Autauga vote. If the two groups would work together, they might be able to prevent Breckinridge supporters from sending a delegate favoring immediate secession to the secession convention

16. (Prattville) *Autauga Citizen,* 24 May, 28 June, 20 September 1860.

17. (Prattville) *Autauga Citizen,* 15 November 1860.

18. For a contrary view, see Thomas B. Alexander and Peggy J. Duckworth, "Alabama's Black Belt Whigs during Secession: A New Viewpoint," *Alabama Review* (July 1964) 17: 181–97.

called by the governor of Alabama upon Abraham Lincoln's election in November. Soon Pratt found himself working with Bolling Hall and other conservative Democrats to forestall immediate secession. Just as the two men had cooperated in trying to bring railroads into Autauga County, they would now join in an attempt to prevent secessionists from derailing the Union, at least until Alabama could consult with her sister southern states.

As soon as it became clear that Lincoln had won the election, Autaugians scheduled a public meeting at Kingston on November 28 to choose that county's delegate to the secession convention. William Howell announced before the convention that he supported the cooperationist position: that Alabama should leave the Union only in the company of a "number of States sufficiently strong to form a Southern Confederacy that would give [Alabama] all needed protection." Among the men cooperationist Howell believed should receive consideration as Autauga's delegate to the secession convention were Bolling Hall and Daniel Pratt.[19]

Unfortunately for the cooperationists, their opponents, known as immediatists because they wanted Alabama to secede from the Union at once, gained control of the Kingston meeting. Howell was outraged by the behavior of the immediatists or, as he now bitterly dubbed them, "*the Separate State Action Yancey men.*" He complained that "the Douglas men, and the Bell men, and the cooperation Breckinridge men" had done everything they could "to harmonize the meeting, but all efforts to accomplish this most desirable end proved utterly futile" because "the Yanceyites were determined to rule or ruin." According to Howell, the militant Yanceyites turned deaf ears to the pleas made by Pratt, Hall, Doster, and even Benjamin Fitzpatrick, the respected former governor and U.S. senator, "to keep down the old partisan spirit."[20]

The Kingston meeting quickly degenerated into a noisy, quarrelsome affair. Chairman W. C. Penick stacked the ten-man resolutions committee with seven Yanceyites, in the process completely passing over, as Howell angrily emphasized, such men as Fitzpatrick, Hall, and Pratt. Instead of eminences, Howell reported bitterly, Penick chose "young and inexperienced men, who happened to have voted with the Yancey party before." The bitterly divided committee produced two reports, a majority report that "embodied Yancey's rash and precipitate doctrine, Indepen-

19. (Prattville) *Autauga Citizen*, 22 November 1860.
20. (Prattville) *Autauga Citizen*, 29 November 1860.

dent Separate State Action," and a minority report that endorsed cooperation. When an attempt was made to vote on whether to adopt the majority report, chaos ensued in the packed courtroom, where between five hundred and six hundred men had gathered. To restore order, the crowd "retired to the street and formed two lines." At this point, "the conservative cooperation men" decided to keep walking. This group marched into an adjacent building and held its own meeting, at which it adopted the cooperationist minority report and nominated its own man, Bolling Hall. Howell reported that Hall "delivered one of the most able, logical, impressive and eloquent speeches we have ever listened to in favor of cooperation and in opposition to the Yancey doctrine of *Independent Separate State Action*." Doster, Fitzpatrick, and Pratt also made speeches "strongly urging cooperation" and declared themselves ready "to use all fair means to secure the election of Major Hall as the Delegate to the [Secession] Convention" from Autauga County.[21]

At this juncture, Autauga's representative in the lower house of the state legislature abruptly died. On December 11, two hundred to three hundred cooperationists came together to nominate a candidate for the suddenly vacant seat. This time, the cooperationists nominated a former Whig, Daniel Pratt. "Mr. Pratt is a gentleman of large experience, is a clear thinker, and is considered one of the best financiers in the State," William Howell wrote effusively, adding that "he is just such a man as the people of Autauga desire to represent them in these troublesome times." To oppose Pratt, the immediatists chose a Dr. Robinson of Chestnut Creek. Pratt, perhaps recalling his difficult 1855 race, proved reluctant to accept the proffered nomination, but he finally relented at the urging of a delegation of "old and respectable citizens." Pratt insisted, however, that under no circumstances would he "canvass the county" or leave his business affairs to "electioneer with any man for the purpose of getting his vote." William Howell, the man who had ridiculed Pratt in 1855, declared confidently that the precincts of Autauga, especially "that glorious old box, Chestnut Creek . . . will roll up such tremendous majorities for Hall and Pratt as will astonish the immediate secession . . . party."[22] Howell proved correct in only one man's case.

For Hall and Pratt to best their rivals, they had to hold together a co-

---

21. Ibid. William Barney provides a good concise summary of the battle between cooperationists and immediatists in Autauga County. See Barney, *Secessionist Impulse*, 251–52.

22. (Prattville) *Autauga Citizen*, 6, 13, 20, December 1860.

alition of Douglas Democrats and Bell Whigs. To be on the safe side, they also needed to detach some Breckinridge Whigs from Prattville and Breckinridge Democrats from Chestnut Creek. The Hall and Pratt pairing seemed uniquely suited to accomplish this goal, for Pratt, of course, was popular in Prattville, while Hall, a Robinson Springs planter, had cannily built strong personal ties with the men of Chestnut Creek and enjoyed great influence in that large piney woods precinct. In the end, however, the plan worked only halfway. Pratt decisively defeated his opponent, 57 percent to 43 percent, while Hall failed by a razor-thin margin, 49 percent to 51 percent. The official precinct tally makes clear why the two results turned out differently. Chestnut Creek Democrats followed Hall's lead and voted for Pratt as well, but Prattville Whigs did not extend the same favor to Hall. Hall and Pratt won 88 percent and 85 percent, respectively, of the vote in Chestnut Creek. Yet, while Pratt was able to win nearly half (49.6 percent) of the vote in Prattville (where Bell and Douglas together had taken only 35 percent of the vote), Hall could only muster less than a fourth (24 percent) of the votes cast in Pratt's home precinct.[23]

The magnitude of Pratt's victory was impressive. Besides Prattville, he lost only two other precincts, Robinson Springs (where he still managed to gain 48 percent of the vote) and Autaugaville (where he garnered only 23 percent of the vote). In no other precinct did his share of the vote drop below 55 percent. As at Chestnut Creek, his victory tallies were astounding, given his 1855 track record: Mulberry, 82 percent; Milton, 79 percent; Kingston, 63 percent; Wetumpka, 59 percent; Independence, 58 percent; and Pine Flat, 55 percent. Nor should Pratt's sudden popularity in the piney woods be viewed as entirely the result of his sharing the political spotlight with a popular Democrat such as Bolling Hall. After all, Pratt's opponent actually hailed from Chestnut Creek. By 1860, Pratt had a longtime reputation as a man of prudence and moderation in sectional matters who had always shown a marked disdain for the "flaming fiery speeches" and antics of the disunionist Yancey crowd. There is evidence that these qualities would have made Pratt much more palatable to up-country voters in 1860 than in 1855, when the canvass had mainly

23. (Prattville) *Autauga Citizen*, 3 January 1861. Bolling Hall was not, as scholars have asserted, a resident of Chestnut Creek. See Alexander and Duckworth, "Alabama's Black Belt Whigs," 188. Nevertheless, he clearly enjoyed a following there. See Thornton, *Politics and Power*, 138; Leonidas Howard to Bolling Hall, 17 July 1855, Folder 4, Box 4, Bolling Hall Papers.

concerned the issue of state aid. As late as May 1861, Shadrack Mims Jr. mentioned in a letter: "Nearly 400 volunteers have left our county and nearly all of them from the lower part. . . . A great many of the people from Chestnut Creek say they will fight for Lincoln before they will fight for the South."[24]

Despite what many Autaugians may have felt about the matter, the secession convention voted on January 11, 1861, to take Alabama out of the Union. Daniel Pratt took his seat in the legislature on January 16. Thus Pratt ironically reached the summit of his personal political achievement at a time when Alabama had taken a course of action that he believed precipitous and fraught with peril.

The evidence makes clear that in 1861 Pratt opposed secession, both because of a sincere attachment to the Union and a cold calculation that secession might well prove tantamount to southern suicide. In an 1863 letter to the *Montgomery Mail* concerning the problem of wartime profiteering, Pratt suggestively remarked that "we might have pursued a wiser course from the commencement. But as Job says, 'what I greatly feared is upon us.'" Moreover, after Pratt's death, his friends uniformly insisted that he had regarded secession as folly. Writing in 1878, Shadrack Mims declared, "It is generally known that [Mr. Pratt] was opposed to secession, fearing ability to sustain the same." Henry J. Livingston recalled in his eulogy at Pratt's funeral that Pratt had, in both conversation and speeches, "advised moderation" during the 1860 presidential campaign, "asserting that the election of Abraham Lincoln would not be a justifiable cause for secession" and "predicting that in such a course the country would be involved in a gigantic internecine war." In a similar vein, another eulogist, Jesse H. Booth, observed trenchantly that Pratt "did not believe, as some did, that Southern chivalry was superior to any other and [that] the South was going to meet a timid foe." Booth also recalled that Pratt had, "from the early days of Troup and Quitman, . . . called upon all to remember and follow the warning advice of Washington, and the deep and loyal pleadings of Clay and Webster." Booth, a Republican, declared of Pratt that the bloody havoc of the Civil War would "stain not his record in heaven!"[25]

24. (Prattville) *Autauga Citizen*, 3 January 1861; Shadrack Mims Jr. to W. J. Smith, 3 May 1861, Letterbook, ACHC.

25. (Prattville) *Autauga Citizen*, 10 September 1863, reprinted from the *Montgomery Mail*; Tarrant, ed., *Hon. Daniel Pratt*, 57, 111, 156. In his autobiography, Henry Merrell (who, like Pratt, was a northerner manufacturing textiles in the South) recalled that he too

Despite his grave doubts about secession, Pratt strongly supported the Confederate war effort once Alabama had cast her die. To be sure, vocally supporting secession became the safe course after war fever set in during the winter of 1860–1861. One scholar has asserted that Pratt could easily have sat on the sidelines, yet such a course would have assuredly incurred the wrath of a great many Autaugians, not to mention the Alabama government, placing him and his property in grave jeopardy. An example of the heightened emotions—indeed, one could say hysteria—following Lincoln's election can be seen in the violent suppression of alleged "negro conspiracies" in Autaugaville and Prattville precincts over the Christmas holiday. These two precincts were the epicenter of secession in Autauga, giving the immediatist candidate to the secession convention overwhelming majorities. At Prattville, according to the *Autauga Citizen,* some slaves agreed with each other "to join *Lincoln's army* when it should be marched South." As punishment, "many of them were severely whipped." At Autaugaville, the local vigilance committee claimed to have foiled an actual insurrection plot. A white man by the name of Williamson—the alleged ringleader ("he had [the negroes] completely under his control")—was hanged, along with three blacks. Other slaves "were whipped, cropped, and branded." William Howell wrote approvingly of the affair, calling it "a wholesale lesson to the negroes" and "a warning to those white scoundrels who take a delight in tampering with slaves."[26] In such a dangerous environment as this, it is not surprising that a prudent man such as Pratt would fall in line with popular opinion.

Nevertheless, Pratt clearly had strong empathy for the state in which he had lived for nearly thirty years. Merrill Pratt went so far as to pronounce in a letter in May 1861 that "if Uncle Pratt was 10 years younger I believe he would go [fight]." Whether or not Merrill (who was caught up in the excitement) exaggerated, his uncle did send a letter to the *Montgomery Mail* in 1863 in which he urged Alabamians "to think less of making money out of this war, and more of defending our country and our just rights." Pratt had never had any admiration for southern fire-eaters, but by 1860 he utterly loathed abolitionists. And while he thought secession unwise and even unwarranted, he did not believe it illegal.

---

believed secession a fatal error. Likewise, he also voted for the Bell/Everett ticket. Merrell, *Autobiography,* 292.

26. Genovese, *Political Economy of Slavery,* 181, 200; (Prattville) *Autauga Citizen,* 3 January 1861.

Hence he angrily denounced the attempt by the Union to put down secession by force of arms. To Pratt, the South, in defending itself against
northern invasion, was defending its "just rights."[27]

Nor did Pratt think that a Yankee victory would bring about a long-
needed bourgeois revolution. Rather, he believed that northern ascendancy after a bitter, bloody war would mean southerners would lose not
just their slaves, but their other property as well. "Are you willing to live
under a government you can have no control over, and be taxed to the
last dollar to pay for the loss of all that was near and dear to you?" he
asked Alabamians fretfully in his 1863 letter.[28] For Pratt, the survival of
the Confederacy and the advancement of southern industry were far from
mutually exclusive. As a legislator he sought the passage of laws that
would foster industrial development, while as a manufacturer he tried to
do what he could for the Confederate war effort.

Only three weeks after his decisive election, Pratt took his seat in the
Alabama House of Representatives, where he proved an effective, inde-
pendent-minded legislator. Within two days of his enrollment, he introduced two bills, the first "to Encourage and Promote the Manufacturing
Interest in Alabama," and the second "to Prevent Free Negroes from
Being Settled in Suburbs of Cities, etc." After Accounts and Claims committee chairman Percy Walker of Mobile reported adversely on the latter
bill, it was tabled. The fate of Pratt's first proposal is not as clear. After
being referred to Ways and Means, the bill was replaced by a substitute
offered by committee chairman Francis Strother Lyon of Demopolis.
How significantly the substitute bill differed from Pratt's is not apparent.
In any event, the house narrowly passed the substitute, thirty-two to
twenty-seven, Pratt voting with the majority. Opposition to the bill
stemmed mostly from hilly northern Alabama and the wiregrass region
of southern Alabama, areas populated by Jacksonian Democrat yeoman
farmers traditionally skeptical of government aid for internal improvements and manufacturing. Despite passage by the house, the bill did not
ultimately become law.[29]

27. Merrill Pratt to W. W. Montague, 8 May 1861, Letterbook; (Prattville) *Autauga
Citizen,* 10 September 1863, reprinted from the *Montgomery Mail.*

28. (Prattville) *Autauga Citizen,* 10 September 1863, reprinted from the *Montgomery
Mail.*

29. Alabama *House Journal, 1861,* 24, 27, 30, 136, 146–47. Despite the failure of the
manufactures bill, the legislature, spurred by the exigencies of war, passed several measures
during the next session to promote the establishment of war-related industries. These measures included acts To Encourage the Manufacture of Salt, To Encourage the Manufacture

Pratt's first session in the Alabama legislature, then, cannot be viewed as especially fruitful for him. In addition to having his bills fail, Pratt received appointment to only one committee, Patents and Copyrights. However, his two proposals do show that he was attempting to advance Alabama's "manufacturing interest." The first bill obviously sought to provide state aid for war-related industry. The second no doubt was intended to shield Alabama's urban white mechanics from free-black competition, thus encouraging more white men to enter mechanical professions. White workingmen's organizations across the South had loudly urged such a course of action in the 1850s.[30]

Pratt also supported Alabama's railroad companies. He opposed tabling an amendment to a bill that would have required the government to subscribe to $100,000 worth of stock in the Mobile and Great Northern Railroad Company. Similarly, he voted to table a Bill to Regulate and Define the Duties and Liabilities of Railroad Companies, etc. Pratt probably found the bill onerous to the regulated businesses. Most certainly, he supported the Confederate war effort—providing a crucial vote for the Bill to Legalize the Suspension of Specie Payments, for example—but he did not want the manufacturing interest to be harmed as a result of war measures.[31]

Pratt enjoyed greater success and prominence in the fall session of the legislature. He won seats on the important Ways and Means and Banks and Banking Committees and became chairman of the Manufactures Committee. As a legislator, he introduced the Bill to Encourage the Man-

---

of Cotton and Wool Cards, and To Encourage the Manufacture of Firearms and Munitions of War. *Acts of the . . . the General Assembly of the State of Alabama, 1862,* 25–26, 70–1, 75. These measures may well have embodied some of Pratt's original ideas. Significantly, he introduced the bill that became the Salt Act.

30. *House Journal, 1861,* 25; Ira Berlin and Herbert G. Gutman, "Natives and Immigrants, Free Men and Slaves: Urban Working Men in the Antebellum American South," *American Historical Review* 88 (December 1983): 1195–96; Randall M. Miller, "The Enemy Within: Some Effects of Foreign Immigrants on Antebellum Southern Cities," *Southern Studies* 24 (spring 1985): 40; Fred Siegal, "Artisans and Immigrants in the Politics of Late Antebellum Georgia," *Civil War History* 18 (September 1981): 223–24, 228. Pratt's proposed legislation concerning free blacks represented a compromise between the interests of white mechanics and those of slave owners. As Berlin and Gutman have pointed out, "slave-holders generally found it easy to deflect [attacks on slave artisans] and direct them to the most vulnerable element of the black population, the black freeman. Attempts to proscribe free negroes consistently met with greater success than did attempts to limit the use of slave workers." Berlin and Gutman, "Natives and Immigrants," 1195–96.

31. *House Journal, 1861,* 51–52, 123, 144–45.

ufacture of Salt in the State of Alabama. As the chairman of the Manufactures Committee, he favorably reported the Bill to Encourage the Manufacture of Cotton and Wool Cards in the State of Alabama, as well as a bill to incorporate the Wills Valley Coal and Leather Company. All three became law by December.[32]

Both the salt and card bills held significance for Alabamians. Because of the necessity of salt for the preservation of meat and other products, the mineral became, as one historian has observed, "a prime necessity" for the survival of the Confederacy. The northern blockade of the South had cut off the importation of salt from Europe, so southerners found it imperative that they produce their own supply. Pratt's Salt Act authorized the governor to lease "any or all of the Salt Springs or Wells in [Alabama]" for up to ten years. A lessee, who had to post a security bond of $5,000, was required by the terms of his lease to commence manufacturing salt within three months and to continue until the expiration of the lease or the end of the war, at a price fixed at seventy-five cents per bushel, plus transportation costs. Cotton and woolen cards were as much prime necessities as salt, for they were essential to the household manufacture of cloth. The Cotton and Wool Cards Act offered Alabama manufacturers state bounties of up to six to ten cents per pair of cards, depending on the make.[33]

During Pratt's tenure as chairman of the Manufactures Committee, an impressive number of companies were incorporated by legislative acts. In 1861, the legislature incorporated twenty-one companies, including the Wills Valley Coal and Leather Company, the Chemical Manufactory, and the Southern Salt Manufactory. There were fourteen more companies incorporated in 1862, including Pratt's Red Mountain Iron and Coal Company, the Selma Iron Foundry Company, the Bibb County Iron Company, Hale and Murdock's Iron Company of Fayette County, the Chewackla Lime Company, and the Mobile and South Western Railroad Company. The legislature also favorably amended corporate charters, such as that of the Shelby County Iron Manufactory.[34]

32. *House Journal, 1861,* 37–38, 51, 84, 111, 137.

33. Ella Lonn, *Salt as a Factor in the Confederacy* (New York: W. Neale, 1933), 13–18; Malcolm C. McMillan, *The Disintegration of a Confederate State: Three Governors and Alabama's Wartime Home Front, 1861–1865* (Macon, Ga.: Mercer University Press, 1986); 48; *Acts 1862,* 25–26, 70–71.

34. *Acts 1862,* 160–44; *Acts, 1862,* 118–23, 127–28, 133–44; Walter L. Fleming, *Civil War and Reconstruction in Alabama* (New York: Columbia University Press, 1905), 161.

In Pratt's last legislative session, which started in October 1862, he held the same important committee posts as before, including the chairmanship of the Manufactures Committee. Not surprisingly, Pratt unfavorably reported a Bill to Regulate the Price of Factory Thread, etc.[35] Although Pratt likely felt that the Alabama government had a right to set a ceiling on the price of salt produced on land it had leased to private individuals, he evidently did not believe that price controls should be extended to other commodities. A widespread system of price controls, Pratt apparently thought, would undermine entrepreneurial efforts by weakening the ability of prices to allocate resources.

Pratt seems to have had a similar distaste for the Bill to Aid the Confederate Government in Providing Shoes for Alabama Soldiers and to Impress Material for Shoes. He supported an effort to strike the bill's impressment provision, which gave the governor the power to seize shoe-making material from shoe manufacturers for "just compensation." In determining what compensation was just, the governor was to consider the "wants and necessities" of the locale where the impressment was made, the extent the manufacturer contributed to supplying the wants of the community and the government, and the prices he had charged.[36] Pratt probably saw such a provision as a bullet aimed directly at the heart of the private shoe industry. Under its terms, the governor could almost at whim destroy Alabama shoemakers.

In addition to continuing to do what he could to promote manufacturing, Pratt showed a most un-Jacksonian interest in raising the pay of government officials, as well as in levying taxes. When the 1862 session began, a resolution was offered that clergymen be invited to open each day's session with a prayer. Pratt offered an amendment to the resolution that clergymen be paid in proportion to members of the house. The amendment lost and the resolution passed, the majority evidently not feeling inclined to pay for prayers. In November, Pratt introduced a Bill to Increase the Fees of the Probate Judge, Clerk, etc., of Autauga County. It is not clear exactly what happened to this bill after referral to the Judiciary Committee, but it did not become an act. Pratt also introduced a Bill to Authorize the Commissioner's Court of Autauga County to Levy a Special Tax for the Support of Families of Soldiers in the Army. That

35. *House Journal, 1862,* 20–21, 255.
36. *House Journal, 1862,* 46–47, 75, 98–99; *Acts, 1862,* 47–48.

this bill became an act no doubt reflected the greater popularity of giving aid to soldiers' families than to government officials.[37]

After one-and-a-half terms in the Alabama legislature, Pratt decided to retire, even though he enjoyed great popularity in Autauga. When he ran for reelection in 1861, he trounced his opponent, Daniel Wadsworth of Autaugaville, winning 68 percent of the vote. Wadsworth was evidently a classic Jacksonian Democrat planter. When he again declared himself a candidate in the 1863 race for Autauga's seat in the Alabama house, he announced that he favored "short sessions of the Legislature" and lower state and county taxes. "The people are already heavily taxed," he complained, "and the taxes will become more burdensome if the war continues much longer." In addition, Wadsworth's friends pointed out that their man was a "plain and good old farmer." One of his supporters, "Chestnut Creek," declared belligerently "that the people in this section . . . say that the fancy men have had their share of the public offices. We now say, as time changes, let us change our law makers, and give the yeomanry of the county a showing."[38]

With Daniel Pratt, a de facto Autauga Whig had finally captured a seat in the legislature. Without Pratt, Autauga's old Whigs could not hold the seat. The 1863 election pitted the conservative planter-physician T. A. Davis against planter Leonidas Howard, one of the county's most prominent Democrats, and that "plain and good old farmer," Daniel Wadsworth. Davis took only 39 percent of the vote to Howard's 53 percent and Wadsworth's 8 percent.[39]

Pratt had become so popular by 1861 that many Autaugians and

37. *House Journal, 1862,* 22, 26, 150; *Acts,* 47–48.

38. (Prattville) *Autauga Citizen,* 30 April, 8 August 1861, 16 July 1863. Wadsworth was of humble origin, migrating to Alabama from North Carolina as an overseer, but by the Civil War, he was certainly not a poor man. In 1860, his wealth was valued at $82,000. (Prattville) *Autauga Citizen,* 21 December 1876; U.S. Census, Alabama, 1860 Population Schedule, Autauga County.

39. (Prattville) *Autauga Citizen,* 13 August 1863. After Pratt declined to run, a movement to draft Bolling Hall as a consensus candidate started. Howard offered to drop out if his fellow Democrat entered the fray, but Davis refused to do the same. Like Pratt, Hall ultimately decided to sit out the race. (Prattville) *Autauga Citizen,* 7, 14, 28 May, 11 June, 2, 16, 23, 30 July. The Democrats won easily anyway, piling up huge majorities in such traditional Democratic precincts as Chestnut Creek (87 percent to Davis's 7 percent) and Pine Flat (75 percent to Davis's 6 percent). Davis won only Prattville (57 percent to 29 percent), Autaugaville, his home district (81 percent to 14 percent), and Independence (61 percent to 39 percent), and he ran fairly close in Robinson Springs (44 percent to 52 percent).

Montgomerians urged him to run for the Autauga/Montgomery seat in the state senate. John Steele, a prominent Autauga planter from Mulberry precinct, decided to withdraw from the race after learning, he reported, that the "Prattville Dragoons . . . and other soldiers who have patrioti-cally gone forth to fight the battles of the great cause of the South" had declared that Daniel Pratt ("one of our most worthy, industrious and pa-triotic citizens") should carry the mantle. Steele "cheerfully and cor-dially" withdrew his name, hoping "to encourage a spirit of good will among our absent soldiers" and to show his "appreciation of the merit of the honorable gentleman for whom they have expressed a unanimous preference." William Howell, who printed Steele's letter in his paper, agreed that Pratt "would make an excellent Senator," giving "entire sat-isfaction to the voters of [both Autauga and Montgomery] counties."[40]

A letter to the *Citizen,* signed by one "Montgomery," made clear that one of Pratt's most appealing qualities was his reputation for objectivity and nonpartisanship, attributes universally valued during war, if not peace. "At a time like this, the present partyism should be laid aside," declared Montgomery, "and the voice of demagogueism should be hushed." While Montgomery realized that Pratt did not want the office, he urged him, "Cincinnatus like, to lay aside his business and obey the voice of the people." If he did run, he would most assuredly win. "Wher-ever I go I hear men saying he is the man," avowed Montgomery.[41]

Despite such puffing, Pratt's candidacy for the state senate never took sail. Moreover, Pratt declined to run for any office in 1863. Certainly, he may have felt that his new political "career" caused him to neglect his business; but, in addition, health considerations likely played a major role in his decision. Pratt had by this time reached his middle sixties. He was long past "the meridian of life." During the late 1850s, his health began a long decline, ending in his death in 1873. Shadrack Mims re-called that for more than "fifteen years before [Pratt's] death he suffered more than [man?] can tell." Mims was probably referring to chronic at-tacks of neuralgia. In March 1862, Pratt's bookkeeper, Thomas Avery, wrote Pratt's nephew Merrill: "Your Uncle has been confined to the house most of the time since last Saturday with his old complaint Neural-urgy and rheumatism, and is quite lame." Avery hoped that with the war-mer weather, Pratt would be able to leave the house again. By early 1863,

40. (Prattville) *Autauga Citizen,* 6 June 1861.
41. Ibid.

Merrill (encamped at Port Hudson, Louisiana) described his uncle as "old and feeble" in a letter to his wife, Julia. During winter that year, Pratt confirmed his nephew's fears when he became gravely ill. In November, Julia Pratt informed her husband that "Uncle Pratt has been quite sick . . . he is suffering with his old complaint." Only after a week had passed did Pratt become well enough to get out of bed. By January, Julia could report that Pratt had "got nearly well again." Unfortunately, a mere week later Pratt had a relapse. After nearly two weeks, Julia informed Merrill that her father, Samuel Parrish Smith (Pratt's good friend and the family physician), believed Pratt was "out of danger." Nevertheless, Pratt's illness had been extremely serious. At the worst, Smith had been "very much afraid that [Uncle Pratt] would die." Even now, he was confined to bed. Julia had visited him and found him looking "badly but much better than he did a week ago." She explained to Merrill that she had not told him earlier "how sick he was," fearing that if she had done so, Merrill would have felt "anxious about him . . . and it takes my letters so long to go through." Esther Pratt, Julia also admitted, was "not looking very well" either, probably because she had "been up so much with Uncle."[42]

As Julia had expected, Merrill fretted about the state of his uncle's health, writing her in March: "I am feeling great anxiety in regard to Uncle and wish to hear [about him] as often as possible. I do hope he will be more careful. How I wish I could be with him." Fortunately, Julia was able to convey encouraging news: "Uncle Pratt still continues to improve. He was able to attend the meeting of the stock holders of the [cotton] factory Tuesday, yesterday and this morning. He was feeling very tired this evening Aunt Esther said." A few days later, however, Julia noted that while Pratt "was getting along very well," he had lately suffered from "the rheumatism in his hands." Even as late as June 8, Julia reported that while Pratt was improving "all of the time," he still did not walk "a great deal."[43] Indeed, it appears that Pratt never fully recovered his health after the winter of 1863. For the next decade, Pratt would suffer recurrent bouts with "his old complaint." With some frequency, he

42. Mims, untitled ms.; T. B. Avery to Merrill Pratt, 28 March 1862, Folder 32; Merrill Pratt to Julia Pratt, 18 February 1862, Folder 32; Julia Pratt to Merrill Pratt, 30 November 1862, Folder 32; Julia Pratt to Merrill Pratt, 8, 13, 25 January 1864, Folder 35; all in Pratt Papers, ADAH.

43. Merrill Pratt to Julia Pratt, 2 March 1864, Julia Pratt to Merrill Pratt, 3, 18 March, 8 June 1864, Folders 35 and 36, Pratt Papers, ADAH.

was either laid up in bed or taking water cures in upstate Alabama, Arkansas, or Virginia.

Despite his afflictions, Pratt struggled mightily to do all he could for the southern war effort, both as a legislator and a private citizen. Even as his eulogists lauded him for opposing secession, they praised him for supporting the Confederacy. Autaugian Henry J. Livingston, for example, asserted that Pratt never shut his purse to the cause. Livingston had special reason to be grateful for Pratt's munificence, as the industrialist had contributed $17,000 toward mounting Livingston's Eighth Alabama Cavalry Regiment. Others benefited as well. In March 1861, Pratt gave $500 for the support of families of volunteers for the Autauga Rifles and the Prattville Dragoons, promising to turn over ten times more if necessary. In May, Pratt provided dress uniforms for the Prattville Dragoons, a local outfit that was headed for the Confederate encampment at Pensacola. Susan Tarrant recalled the dress uniforms as "made of black broadcloth, trimmed with gold braid. No other company in the state had a uniform so handsome." William Howell lavishly praised Pratt for such largesse, calling him "a noble-hearted, patriotic citizen, whose example deserves to be emulated by others."[44]

Pratt also made a point of performing personal kindnesses for soldiers. A. C. Oxford recalled that he had been traveling from Selma to Montgomery on horseback to join his company when, as he was passing through Prattville, a sudden downpour forced him to take shelter under the eaves of a building. "Mr. Pratt saw me," he reported, "invited me into his hospitable mansion, gave me dinner, fed my horse, then told his good wife to put some garments into my haversack." Oxford claimed that he had "thought of that incident a hundred times" and that he revered "the memory of that noble benefactor of his race."[45]

Demonstrating his support for the Confederacy not merely through outfitting and equipping military units, Pratt also bought war bonds. In June 1861, he responded to a national bond drive by purchasing $14,000 worth of Confederate bonds, $10,000 in his own name and $2,000 each in the names of his wife and daughter. At the same time, Pratt also received an appointment from the Confederate government as a county bond agent.[46]

44. Tarrant, ed., *Hon. Daniel Pratt*, 83, 112; (Prattville) *Autauga Citizen*, 21 March, 2 May 1861.
45. Tarrant, ed., *Hon. Daniel Pratt*, 83.
46. (Prattville) *Autauga Citizen*, 20 June 1861.

Pratt's devotion to the Confederacy had its limits, however. While as a private businessman he cooperated with government authorities by selling at "fair" prices most of his cloth to the Confederacy, he complained at war's end that those same authorities had repeatedly exploited him. Pratt certainly did not possess so fervent a devotion to the Confederacy that he would complacently stand by and watch everything for which he had labored for more than thirty years get swept away in the name of southern independence.

From the commencement of the Civil War, Pratt sold much of his cloth to the state of Alabama. Governor John Gill Shorter expressed great satisfaction with Pratt's prices. In 1862, Shorter requested that General Braxton Bragg transfer some of Pratt's workers from the army to Prattville, noting that Pratt rendered "good service to the Confederacy and the State" and that he charged "extremely low" prices for his osnaburg. In another 1862 letter, this one to Secretary of War G. W. Randolph, Shorter spoke even more highly of Pratt, calling him "a gentleman whose conscientiousness, public-spirit, and liberality are beyond all praise." Of Prattville Manufacturing Company, Shorter declared enthusiastically: "I hazard nothing in the assertion, that even in a war-aspect it is worth a regiment of men to the Confederacy." The governor added that Alabama had "large contracts with the company for the supply of cloth at modest prices."[47]

Pratt needed to maintain a good relationship with Confederate and Alabama authorities to hold together the labor force necessary to run Prattville's manufacturing establishments. With war engulfing Pratt's western sales area, he made far fewer gins, but his cotton and woolen mills had more business than ever before, and he had also started a bobbin, quill, and spool shop, which was run by William Beckwith. The bobbin shop, as it was known, produced items necessary in the spinning of cotton fibers into cloth. Previously, Pratt had relied on northern manufacturers for all his machinery components. Pratt also helped George Smith set up a pike shop and later a rifle shop. The rifle shop was affiliated with the Confederate arsenal at Montgomery. It performed so poorly, however (producing only about one rifle a week, whereas the arsenal produced five or six rifles a day), that George Smith soon closed it and went to work in the Montgomery arsenal. Other men renting shop

47. John Gill Shorter to General Braxton Bragg, [?] May 1862, and John Gill Shorter to G. W. Randolph, 30 July 1862, both in Governor Shorter Papers, ADAH.

space from Pratt had greater success, however. William Penny and Company, which relocated to Prattville from Milton, Florida, in the spring of 1862, operated as a branch of the Confederate States Naval Iron Works of Columbus, Georgia, a manufacturer of massive steam machinery. H. U. Allen and Company, formed by Hassan Allen and his brother William, made myriad items for the Confederacy: knapsacks, enameled cloth, oven spiders and skillets, wooden buttons, and horse brushes.[48]

War threatened to sap the labor supply necessary for these operations. Even as early as May 1861, Shadrack Mims Jr. had written a customer, "Prattville is near deserted as any place you ever saw." Concurrently, Merrill Pratt complained to a business correspondent, "I will assure you that I feel more like going [to war] than I do like writing this letter, but so many of our hands are gone our foreman with the rest that it is impossible for me to get away." Nearly a year later, Frank Smith reported to his brother Ferdinand that "Boss Hale has no one with him now but Mr. Holmes and Kent." In the spring of 1861, twelve likely Pratt workers joined the Prattville Dragoons, an outfit with a total of one hundred men. Of the twelve probable Pratt employees, eight were mechanics and machinists (including Henry DeBardeleben and two of Gardner Hale's sons), three were mill bosses, and one was a mill spinner. Moreover, in September 1861, three other mechanics joined a new unit, the Autauga Guards. The year 1862 saw further labor leakage when Merrill Pratt, most likely in the face of opposition from his uncle, formed Company K, composed of fifty-two men, fifteen of whom probably came from Pratt's employ. Among this group were mostly mechanics, but the unit also included a mill spinner, a mill boss, and wool mill agent A. J. Thompson. In addition, another Pratt mechanic, Ferdinand Smith, volunteered to help in the construction of Mobile Bay defenses.[49]

48. Frank Smith to Ferdinand Smith, 13 April 1862, and Sallie Riggs to Ferdinand Smith, 8, 23 May, 1 June 1862, all in ACHC; Abigail Holt Smith Diary, ACHC; Trial Balance Ledger, 1 March 1864, ACHC; Payrolls of Civil Personnel in Shore Establishments of the Confederate Navy, RG 45, National Archives, Washington, D.C.; Letter from Robert Holcombe, director of the Confederate Naval Museum, Columbus, Georgia; Confederate Government Contracts, Allen Papers, ADAH.

49. Shadrack Mims Jr. To W. F. Smith, 3 May 1861, Merrill Pratt to W. P. Montgomery, 8 May 1861, Letterbook, ACHC; Frank Smith to Ferdinand Smith, 13 April 1862, ACHC; Wilbur F. Mims, *War History of the Prattville Dragoons* (Montgomery, Ala.: by the author, n.d.), 3–4; (Prattville) *Autauga Citizen*, 23 May, 26 September 1861; Daniel P. Smith, *Company K, First Alabama Regiment or Three Years in the Confederate Service* (Prattville, Ala.: n.p., 1885), 15–19, 46–47, app.; Martha Riggs Smith to Ferdinand Smith,

Even more ominously for Pratt's businesses, the passage of the first conscription act in April 1862 made all white males between eighteen and thirty-five subject to military service. The first exemption act, passed a few days later, explicitly gave the secretary of war the authority to exempt superintendents and operatives in cotton and wool factories; and over the summer and fall, Secretary Randolph used his discretionary power to exempt other classifications of industrial workers as well. Given these circumstances, Pratt took steps in the summer of 1862 to secure exemptions for his workers, both those who had remained in Prattville and a few who had already enlisted. Fear of losing his employees had already motivated Pratt to write then governor Andrew Moore the previous summer. Pratt informed Moore that "nearly every man" left in Prattville had joined the Prattville Grays, a reserve unit. If the government called the Grays to active duty, Pratt worriedly informed Moore, "not a work shop . . . would have an overseer or many hands." While Pratt assured the governor that the people of Prattville were "willing to go and battle for our countries rights" and that he himself was "not only willing to go but to give the last dollar I have if necessary for the success of the Confederate States," he nevertheless urged that "should it be necessary to call for more troops would it not be well to leave our company [the Grays] until their actual services are necessary?"[50]

At Pratt's prompting, mill agent William Fay wrote Governor Shorter in 1862, requesting him to seek exemptions and transfers for more than twenty workers, including mechanics, mill bosses, and operatives. Also found among these men were Pratt's son-in-law Henry DeBardeleben and his wife's cousin Thomas Ormsby. Shorter promptly wrote Secretary

6 April 1862, ACHC. On Daniel Pratt's desire "to keep Merrill at home" to attend to business, see Shadrack Mims Jr. to Capt. J. J. Cox, 3 July 1861, Letterbook, ACHC. Three more mechanics joined Company K in January 1863, while another mechanic joined in 1864. Smith, *Company K*, 47–48, app. Thomas Ormsby, James Wainwright, and Shadrack Mims Jr. enlisted in the Prattville Dragoons. Mims, *War History*, 3–4.

50. Albert Burton Moore, *Conscription and Conflict in the Confederacy* (New York: MacMillan, 1924), 13–14, 52–53, 62–63; Daniel Pratt to Andrew Barry Moore, 10 July 1861, Governor Moore Papers, ADAH. Officers in the Prattville Grays included Pratt affiliates and employees Merrill Pratt (fourth lieutenant), Joseph Kent (second sergeant), Shadrack Mims Jr. (third sergeant), Nathan Morris (fourth sergeant), and George Smith (armorer). (Prattville) *Autauga Citizen*, 23 May 1861. Merrill Pratt and Shadrack Mims Jr. later joined active units. The second exemption act of October 1862 explicitly exempted a much broader class of men engaged in manufacturing pursuits. Moore, *Conscription and Conflict*, 67–68.

Randolph and General Bragg, urging these men to make the desired exemptions and transfers. The Alabama governor evidently secured them, for Pratt kept his mills and the bobbin shop going throughout the war. Getting exemptions seems not to have been particularly difficult in 1862. In April, Frank Smith assured his brother Ferdinand in Mobile that "if you were at home you could get hold of some work that would excuse you from going [to fight]." Unfortunately for mechanic Thomas Ormsby, Shorter's transfer came too late. He was killed in a skirmish outside Corinth, Mississippi, a few days before the request arrived. George Hale returned to Prattville with Ormsby's body.[51]

Having limited his labor losses, Pratt continued to successfully manufacture cloth, most of which he sold to the Confederate and Alabama governments. According to his agent, William Fay, Pratt kept "a small reserve" of osnaburg to use as barter for supplies such as iron. Evidence indicates that intrepid civilians could get something for themselves as well. In August 1863, Abigail Holt Smith, one of Pratt's nieces and the wife of George Smith, reported in her diary: "Just after dinner a carriage drove up and two ladies alighted. One of them introduced herself as Mrs. Roundtree whereupon I remembered meeting a person of that name six years ago at the examination in Summerfield [a town in Dallas County and home to a Methodist academy]. They wanted me to go to the Factory with them to get thread, cloth, etc." "Not daring to go" herself, Abigail persuaded her apparently more stouthearted sister Asenath Holt Smith (wife of George's cousin Frank) to accompany her visitors to the mill. They returned empty-handed, however, and the ladies stayed the night at Abigail's house. The next day, Abigail's husband "escorted the ladies to the factory . . . and got some cloth and thread for them."[52]

51. John Gill Shorter to G. W. Randolph, 30 July, 1 August 1862, to General Braxton Bragg, [?] May 1862, to Captain Prattville Dragoons, 19 May, 30 June 1862, all in Governor Shorter Papers; Frank Smith to Ferdinand Smith, 13 April 1862, Martha Smith to Ferdinand Smith, 8, 12 May 1862, and Sallie Riggs to Ferdinand Smith, 8 May 1862, all in ACHC. Once back in Prattville, Henry DeBardeleben and a business partner, northern-born plasterer A. J. Reynolds, began making barrels for the Confederate army. One of the mechanics they employed was Lafayette Ellis. Julia Smith to Merrill Pratt, 13, 19 January 1864, Folder 35, Pratt Papers, ADAH.

52. William W. Fay to A. T. Jones, 27 June 1863, Folder 2, Shelby Iron Works Papers, Hoole Library, University of Alabama, Tuscaloosa; Abigail Holt Smith Diary, ACHC. Jones, the president of Shelby Iron, badly needed clothing for his slave workers and attempted to barter iron for Prattville osnaburg. Fay turned Jones down, however, asserting that his mill had an ample supply of iron.

The incident indicates that Pratt not only kept some of his product aside for barter, but also for sale to civilians. One South Carolina woman recalled the "blessing" of having a cotton factory in the neighborhood to supply "our country and town in thread for our use. A neighbor woman would get ready to make a trip to the factory in a buggy, sending word around to her neighbors that she would carry anything she could for them." All too many locales were not so blessed. Henry Merrell noted in his autobiography that his lone textile mill in western Arkansas could come nowhere close to meeting the demands of a desperate populace, some of whom came from fifty to one hundred miles away in search of cloth and thread. "It well nigh made me down sick," wrote Merrell. "Of course I could relieve many . . . but [I had] not enough to meet the wants of one in ten that came or sent to me. The woods around our village was an encampment of people anxiously waiting their turn."[53]

There is no indication from surviving records that such a scene as the one described by Henry Merrell ever took place in Prattville, which suggests that Pratt's mills, in combination with the Autaugaville mill, were better able to supply the needs of the local population, despite the government's demands. Pratt no doubt would have been glad to have sold more goods to civilians, for he could have commanded a higher price from them if he so chose. In October 1862, the Confederate government made exemptions for mill workers contingent upon the manufacturer's acceptance of a profit ceiling of 75 percent over the costs of production. In 1864, the quartermaster general lowered the profit ceiling to 33.3 percent. The government typically purchased two-thirds of a factory's output.[54]

Pratt may have commanded much higher prices from the government

53. Marilyn Mayer Culpepper, *Trials and Triumphs: Women of the American Civil War* (East Lansing: Michigan State University Press, 1991), 228; Merrell, *Autobiography,* 297. On the severe cloth shortage suffered by southern civilians in the Civil War, see the sources cited above as well as George C. Rable, *Civil Wars: Women and the Crisis of Southern Nationalism* (Urbana: University of Illinois Press, 1989), 92–95; Mary Elizabeth Massey, *Ersatz in the Confederacy* (Columbia: University of South Carolina Press, 1952), 85–91.

54. Charles W. Ramsdell, "The Control of Manufacturing by the Confederate Government," *Mississippi Valley Historical Review* 8 (December 1921): 235–37. Henry Merrell declared emphatically in his autobiography: "It was not for my interest to work for Government at all. Government fixed its own prices. The people by this time had given up the question of price, & would cheerfully have paid me twice what the Government paid. I might have been $50,000, at least, better off had Government let me alone." Merrell, *Autobiography,* 307. Similarly, William Gregg complained bitterly of government profit ceilings in a speech in 1864. Mitchell, *William Gregg,* 234–40. See also Beatty, *Alamance,* 92–93.

during the Civil War than he had on the open market in 1860, but much of this increase reflected the rampant inflation, with its consequent increases in operating costs, replacement costs, and risk, as well as the increases in real costs associated with having to make do with existing equipment, acquiring new equipment, and loss of skilled personnel. In 1860, Pratt had sold osnaburg at ten cents a yard, but by 1863 and 1864, judging from extant records, he sold it to the Confederate government at seventy-two cents a yard and $1.70 a yard, respectively—seven and seventeen times the 1860 figure. If cotton prices are any accurate gauge, Pratt was making about the same profit in 1863 and 1864 as he had in 1860. Between February 1861 and November 1863, cotton prices increased six and one-third times, while between February 1861 and December 1864, they increased seventeen times. These increases nearly mirror those of Pratt's osnaburg. Of course, it is likely that Pratt did make larger profits in 1861 and 1862 before rigid government controls appeared and machinery began to deteriorate. The stockholders of William Gregg's Graniteville factory, for example, realized large profits in 1861 and 1862, but only 7 percent in 1863.[55]

Pratt surely hoped to mix patriotism and profit. He wanted the Confederacy and his business to flourish together. The sentiments expressed in late 1862 by John Lapsley, a former PMC stockholder who became one of the key men in the Shelby Iron Works during the Civil War, probably resembled Pratt's own convictions: "I for one am anxious to avoid the impeachment of wishing to extort on the necessities of government.

55. W. E. Merton Coulter, *The Confederate States of America, 1861–1865* (Baton Rouge: Louisiana State University, 1950), 219–38; Confederate Papers Relating to Citizens and/or Business Firms (CPRCBF), Roll 818, National Archives; John Christopher Schwab, *The Confederate States of America, 1861–1865: A Financial and Industrial History of the South during the Civil War* (New York: C. Scribner's Sons, 1907), 163–85, app. 1; Mitchell, *William Gregg*, 212–19, 225–26. In December 1863, a Columbus, Georgia, company offered to sell osnaburg to Shelby Iron Works for $1.50 a yard. By March 1864 the company's price had increased markedly to $3.50 a yard. Frank E. Vandiver, "The Shelby Iron Company in the Civil War: A Study of Confederate Industry," *Alabama Review* 1 (April 1948): 126–27. These figures indicate that Pratt made considerably less with his government contracts than what he would have made on the open market. For a hostile assessment of southern industrialists' during the war, see Beatty's conclusion in *Alamance*, 105, that "textiles, vital to the Confederacy, were furnished begrudgingly [by private manufacturers] with personal monetary goals clearly taking precedence over national survival." The entire question of alleged wartime profiteering by southern industrialists merits closer study than scholars have so far given it.

We can make enough at reasonably liberal prices, and I would prefer to make less, and do it agreeably." Nevertheless, after 1862 it became progressively more difficult for manufacturers to make profits by "agreeably" contracting with the government. The real problem was not, as several scholars have indicated, government price ceilings, but the South's financial collapse, which made it impossible for the Confederacy adequately to reimburse its suppliers for their goods. Pratt found himself having to accept Confederate and Alabama bonds in payment. By March 1864, his "assets" included nearly $114,000 in Confederate bonds (presumably only $14,000 of which he had purchased on his own accord) and $56,500 in Alabama bonds. This problem became more acute during the rest of the war. In September 1865, Pratt complained to Alabama governor Lewis Parsons that he had delivered "a large amount of [cotton and woolen] goods to the [late Confederate] Government, for which I was compelled to take over [$260,000] in their Bonds & Treasury Notes, which are now on hand and entirely worthless." Sometimes Pratt did not even do so well as to receive bonds. In 1864, the quartermaster general reported that he could not pay for a consignment of PMC goods worth nearly $138,000. According to Shadrack Mims, Pratt "lost more than half a million of dollars" as a result of the war. No wonder Pratt bitterly informed Governor Parsons that supplying goods to the Confederacy "resulted in heavy loss to me."[56]

56. Lester J. Cappon, "Government and Private Industry in the Southern Confederacy," in *Humanistic Studies in Honor of John Calvin Metcalf* (New York: Columbia University Press, 1941), 178–80; Summary of Daniel Pratt's Ledger, 1 March 1864, CECP; Daniel Pratt to Lewis Parsons, 8 September 1865, Governor Parsons Papers, ADAH; CPRCBF, National Archives; Mims, untitled ms. Raimundo Luraghi has characterized the industrial policy of the Confederate government as deliberate "quasi-nationalization" by a heavy-handed planter elite hoping to prevent war industry from destroying their premodern agrarian society. Raimundo Luraghi, "The Civil War and the Modernization of American Society: Social Structure and Industrial Revolution in the Old South before and during the Civil War," *Civil War History* 18 (September 1972): 245. See also Ramsdell, "Control of Manufacturing," 235–37; Emory Thomas, *The Confederate Nation, 1861–1865* (New York: Harper & Row, 1979), 211–13. In actuality, the war initially was a godsend for private southern textile manufacturers, who now had an assured market for their goods. What wrecked this favorable state of affairs was, as one scholar has noted, "the inescapable wear and tear on [mill] equipment and the collapse of Confederate finances." Elizabeth Yates Webb, "Cotton Manufacturing and State Regulation in North Carolina, 1861–1865," *North Carolina Historical Review* 9 (April 1932): 117. See also Mary A. DeCredico, *Patriotism for Profit: Georgia's Urban Entrepreneurs and the Confederate War Effort* (Chapel Hill: University of North Carolina Press, 1990); Beatty, *Alamance*, 79–93.

Despite his loyalty to the Confederate nation, Pratt never hesitated to criticize government economic policies he viewed as harmful. Most significantly, he served as vice-president of the Manufacturers and Direct Trade Association of the Confederate States, an organization that met annually in Georgia and strongly denounced government actions that negatively impacted manufacturers. Though in practice Pratt apparently cooperated more closely with the government than many southern industrialists, his ultimate goal for PMC, once it became clear that defeat was inevitable, hardly can have differed from that of the men running Shelby Iron Works, of whom a Confederate official angrily complained in July 1864: "Their leading idea seems to be, to build up their establishment during the War & have it in good running order after peace is declared."[57]

Pratt held out great hope for another manufacturing concern besides PMC, one that he had helped create in 1862: the Red Mountain Iron and Coal Company, also known as Oxmoor Furnaces. Though Pratt did not dominate Red Mountain as he did PMC, by 1864 he held $25,000 worth of stock in the company. He had long dreamed of tapping the rich mineral region of northern Alabama. With war and the Confederacy's desperate need for coal and iron, he had the impetus he needed. An early historian of Alabama's coal and iron industry characterized "the initial iron making enterprise in Jefferson County" as "practically a war measure."[58]

Red Mountain quickly became a leading southern supplier of coal and pig iron. "Thousands of tons of Red Mountain pig iron were shot away in shot and shell at Charleston and Mobile," a shareholder of the company recalled. Red Mountain would prove one of Pratt's most enduring legacies, serving not only the ephemeral Confederacy, but also helping to

57. Coulter, *Confederate States*, 212, 229; DeCredico, *Patriotism for Profit*, 65; Cappon, "Government and Private Industry in the Confederacy," 182–83. Whether Pratt sold textiles to the Confederacy after 1864 is open to question. Surviving vouchers show that PMC sold to the Confederacy 155,000 yards of cloth (osnaburg and coats and pants) for $190,157 in 1863 and 191,696 yards of cloth (osnaburg, coats and pants, and drilling) for $398,126 in 1864. No records of sales in 1865 have been found, but the records may not have survived the war. Some of the 1863 and 1864 vouchers are likely missing as well, for the amounts of textiles recorded in these vouchers total to only about one-fifth of the amount (874,102 yards) produced by PMC in 1860 (17.8 percent in 1863 and 21.9 percent in 1864).

58. Summary of Daniel Pratt's Ledger, 1 March 1864, CECP; Armes, *Story of Coal and Iron*, 161–64.

build a "new Alabama" after the war. Unfortunately for Pratt in the short term, Federal invaders destroyed the Red Mountain furnaces at Oxmoor in April 1865. They would not be refired until Pratt was on his deathbed eight years later.[59]

Prattville fortunately never received a visit from Federal raiders, but Pratt's cotton factory did not escape the ravages of time. Simply put, the mill machinery fell apart as the conflict raged. As early as September 1863, Pratt complained that "it is next to impossible to build good machinery, and consequently we cannot do good work." Noting that poor equipment turned out an inferior product, Pratt concluded pessimistically that the government would be wiser to import what it needed through smuggling operations than to contract with domestic manufacturers. The next year, Pratt sent his mill agent, William Fay, on a mission to get mill machinery from England through the Union blockade. Fay died from yellow fever in Nassau, Bahamas, in the fall of 1864, his mission unfulfilled.[60] Pratt would not finally obtain new machinery until 1866.

Both Pratt's businesses and his town suffered during the war. In addition to the inevitable combat casualties, Prattville felt a heavy strain in its social fabric. As one scholar has noted, "War considerably abbreviated the normal courtship period and lessened parental influence." In Prattville, as in the rest of the South during the war, impetuous youths married hastily and even eloped, flouting the authority of their elders. Eighteen-year-old Ellen Pratt's elopement with Henry DeBardeleben in 1863 was only one among several troubling incidents. Julia Smith Pratt related one such event in an August 1863 letter to her husband, Merrill: "Henry Hale married one of the factory girls last week. . . . The [Hale] family are very much chagrined." Henry Hale's "factory girl" bride was eighteen-year-old Mary Medlin. In 1860, Mary Medlin lived with her mother and brother in the household of Elisha and Mary Ellis, parents of Lafayette Ellis, and she worked as a spinner in one of the mills.[61] Middle-class Prat-

---

59. Armes, *Story of Coal and Iron,* 164, 201–2; Mims, untitled ms.

60. (Prattville) *Autauga Citizen,* 10 September 1863, reprinted from the *Montgomery Mail;* (Prattville) *Autauga Citizen,* 10 November 1864. If Wilson's Raiders in April 1865 had moved from Selma to Montgomery through Autauga (on the north side of the Alabama River) instead of Lowndes (on the south side), they very likely would have destroyed Pratt's factories.

61. Smith, *Company K,* app.; Rable, *Civil Wars,* 51; Julia Pratt to Merrill Pratt, 4 August 1863, Folder 34, Pratt Papers, ADAH; Ballou, *History and Genealogy of the Ballous,*

tvillians probably found especially shocking the idea that the son of the mill superintendent would run off with a young woman of such humble station in the town. No doubt it was one thing for a mill boy to work his way up to the top as Lafayette Ellis did and quite another for a mill girl to get there through marriage.

An even greater scandal—one involving the crime of bigamy— occurred when Gardner Hale's daughter Susan Frances married a Dr. Custer from Tennessee. "I have some news to tell you that I know will shock you," Julia Pratt breathlessly informed her husband in a November 1862 letter. "Sue Hale's husband has a *wife* and *four children living*. Mr. Hale received a letter last week from someone in Shelbyville, Tenn. telling him all about it." Julia branded Custer "a villain indeed . . . he thought . . . that the Yankees had Tenn. and would probably hold it and there would be no danger of Sue's ever hearing of his wife." Julia concluded her narration of the dark episode with a popular pious maxim: "Marry in haste, and repent at leisure."[62]

Most Prattville women seem to have avoided getting entangled in such wartime predicaments. The ladies of Prattville, however, did break new ground for their sex by becoming members of the town's ladies aid society. This group, historian Malcolm McMillan has noted, was one of "the more active small town societies" in Alabama. Predictably, Daniel Pratt's wife, Esther, served as the society's president. Under her energetic leadership, the Prattville Ladies Aid Society began producing clothing and other articles for the Confederate army. In May 1861, Martha Riggs Smith informed her husband, Ferdinand, "The Society is working again for the Dragoons and some for the Government." That month, the Prattville ladies had 500 pairs of pants slated to go to the Prattville Dragoons, who were stationed at Pensacola, Florida. Later that year, the society agent, Samuel Parrish Smith, reported that the members had furnished the army with an impressive array of items: 1,008 sand bags, 308 pairs of pants, 122 shirts, 110 Zouave caps, 108 haverlucks, 19 haversacks, 9 tents, 98

478; U.S. Census, Alabama, 1860 Population Schedule, Autauga County. See also Drew Gilpin Faust, *Mothers of Invention: Women of the Slaveholding South in the American Civil War* (Chapel Hill: University of North Carolina Press, 1996), 148. On Ellen Pratt's elopement, see chap. 4.

62. Julia Pratt to Merrill Pratt, 23 November 1862, Box 21, McMillan Collection. Susan Frances Hale married educator John Frederick Tarrant in 1864 and edited *Hon. Daniel Pratt* in 1904. On Susan Frances Hale Tarrant, see Owen, *History of Alabama*, 4: 1644–45.

coats, and 78 pairs of socks. In addition to their society work, Prattville ladies made individual contributions to the army. Augusta Pratt Morgan (who was married but had no children) seems to have had especially nimble hands. She made 2 blankets, 1 pair of socks, 1 comforter, 4 shirts, and 4 pairs of drawers. Most Prattville women, from Mrs. Pratt herself (4 blankets and 1 pair of socks) to more humble mill widows and mechanics' wives such as Rachel Houston (2 blankets) and Mrs. Samuel Patillo (2 pairs of socks), made contributions, however. Even Rachel, "servant of Rev. J. A. Spence" contributed a blanket in her own name.[63]

While many southern ladies aid societies fell apart after 1862 as a result of declining morale, supply shortages, financial difficulties, and corruption allegations, Prattville's society remained active at least through 1863. In November of that year, the Reverend T. R. Lynch, a former Methodist minister in Prattville who had transferred to Rockford, the seat of neighboring Coosa County, encountered an officer from the Army of Tennessee who was on detail in Alabama looking for socks for his brigade. Lynch promptly wrote Esther Pratt, informing her that he had recommended that the officer write her in her capacity as president of the Prattville society. Lynch knew that Esther Pratt and her society would come through with some socks, as he had been "a witness to many of the kindnesses which have characterized the actions of the ladies of your devoted Citty and especially you yourself." Lynch assured Mrs. Pratt that he took the officer for "a gentleman" and that his brigade deserved "encouragement." The same day, the officer himself wrote Mrs. Pratt, grandly addressing her as "Mistress President of the Soldiers Aid Society of Prattville" and assuring her that he had "heard much of the Patriotic Zeal with which your Society have labored for the comfort of our Soldiers in the Field." As late as January and March 1864, Julia Smith Pratt received her own letters from two soldiers, who thanked her for shirts she had sewn for a shipment of clothes the society sent Joseph E. Johnston's army in Dalton, Georgia.[64]

63. McMillan, *Alabama Confederate Reader*, 350–52; Martha Smith to Ferdinand Smith, 28 May 1861, ACHC; (Prattville) *Autauga Citizen*, 2 May, 9 October 1861. On Alabama's wartime ladies aid societies, see M. E. Sterkx, *Partners in Rebellion: Alabama Women in the Civil War* (Rutherford, N.J.: Fairleigh Dickinson University Press, 1970), chap. 5. On these groups in the South, see Faust, *Mothers of Invention*, 23–25; Rable, *Civil Wars*, 138–44; Culpepper, *Trials and Triumphs*, 246–48.

64. Rable, *Civil Wars*, 142, 366 n 24; T. R. Lynch to Mrs. Daniel Pratt, 30 November 1863, Thomas Wentworth Davis to Mrs. Daniel Pratt, 30 November 1863, all in Folder

Abigail Holt Smith's diary, which covers a fifteen-month period in 1862 and 1863, reveals that she spent much of her time sewing for relatives and the society. Abigail owned her own sewing machine, which she carried to the society's rooms, sometimes in the company of her sister, Asenath Holt Smith. Even with a sewing machine, she found the work exhausting. In February 1862, she spent three consecutive days working at the sewing rooms, helping to get the clothes for Merrill Pratt's Company K finished. In the evening of the second day, she admitted that she felt "the effects of [sewing all day]." Nevertheless, she reported that the society was "getting on well."[65]

While female organizational activity may have flourished in Prattville during the Civil War, Pratt's factories did not. Indeed, by 1865, these concerns stood close to collapse. And if Pratt's business empire crumbled with the Confederacy, what would become of the town he had founded? Pratt's immediate goal in the aftermath of the Civil War became reviving his nearly comatose businesses. But the indomitable industrialist soon found that Reconstruction impacted everything around him. Once again, he would have to grapple with the rough-and-tumble world of Alabama politics. Although he grew physically weaker every year, the old Yankee proved he was still a good wrestler.

32, Pratt Papers, ADAH; McMillan, *Alabama Confederate Reader*, 350–52. Rable concludes that "relief work provided a slender precedent for postwar reform," but his conclusion does not hold for Prattville. On this point, see chap. 9. Rable, *Civil Wars*, 144.

65. Abigail Holt Smith Diary, ACHC.

9

Rebuilding Prattville: 1865–1873

At the age of sixty-six, suffering from recurrent bouts of neuralgia and rheumatism, Daniel Pratt set out to restore the health of his ailing businesses and his "lovely village." Within a few years, both his gin and textile factories had recovered much of the ground lost during the war, and Prattvillians were again successfully engaging in profitable economic activities and virtuous benevolent endeavors. It would be going too far, however, to claim that Pratt totally succeeded in achieving his economic and social objectives. Most serious in Pratt's estimation, he failed to realize his long-standing dream of securing a railroad that passed through Prattville. Nevertheless, Pratt continued to inject remarkable energy into his multifaceted drive to improve his community, and he accomplished much of what he attempted.

Washing his hands of the shattered Confederacy, Pratt applied for a presidential pardon in August 1865. On August 2, he formally took the oath of allegiance to the United States. By early September, Pratt had still not received his pardon, so he persuaded former U.S. senator and Autauga resident Benjamin Fitzpatrick to write a letter to Lewis Parsons, the man Andrew Johnson had appointed governor of Alabama in June 1865, supporting Pratt's application. "I know Mr. Pratt & his political course well," Fitzpatrick assured Parsons. "You could not recommend a more worthy man [for a pardon] nor one who was more decided in his opposition to secession." Pratt, avowed Fitzpatrick, "is now and ever has been one of the most conservative men in the C[ounty]." Whether the esteemed former senator's words oiled the gears of government is not clear, but Pratt received his pardon on September 29. On October 5, 1865, the *Autauga Citizen* happily reported that Pratt had "just returned from Washington city, thither he went to get his pardon, and [he] procured it without much difficulty." The *Citizen* added hopefully that the trip appeared to have "improved [Pratt's] health, judging from his general appearance."[1]

Restoring Pratt's citizenship proved a much quicker process than reviving his businesses. Gin sales collapsed during the Civil War, and Pratt and Ticknor could not collect payments from ruined planters who had bought gins before the conflict had started. In 1871, Pratt's lawyers asserted that war-related losses to his gin business amounted to nearly $405,000. During the conflict, the lawyers declared, Daniel Pratt and Company "necessarily remained in a state of absolute inactivity."[2]

Pratt could do nothing about lost sales opportunities, but Pratt and Ticknor, the marketing firm headed by his brother-in-law Samuel Ticknor and his nephew Merrill Pratt, could, and did, attempt to compel planters to pay for gins they had purchased. In February 1863, planter debts to Pratt and Ticknor stood at $156,427.36—a crushing amount. That month, Pratt agreed not to "sue, molest or trouble" Samuel Ticknor and Merrill, provided that the two men used "their best endeavors to collect all claims, debts, and sums of money" owed the company. Nearly three years later, in January 1866, Pratt sold the Pratt and Ticknor debt, valued at $160,000, to Samuel Ticknor outright. Ticknor also purchased the planter debt of $150,000 owed to him individually as a partner in Pratt and Ticknor and the Eureka Gin debt of another $51,000. Ticknor was to assume responsibility for any claims the heirs of the now-deceased D. G. Olmsted might make against Pratt over the disposal of the Eureka Gin debt. The amount of the debts purchased by Ticknor from Pratt thus

1. Daniel Pratt Application for Pardon, Amnesty Papers of the Records of the Adjutant General's Office, 1785–1917, RG 94, National Archives; (Prattville) *Autauga Citizen,* 5 October 1865.

2. Brief Filed before the Commissioner of Patents in the Application of Daniel Pratt for Extension of Letters of Patent No. 17806 granted him July 14th 1857 for Improvement in Cotton Gin [1871], 6, Pratt Collection, ACHC.

totaled a staggering $361,000. For this doubtful asset, Ticknor turned over to Pratt seventy-four bales of cotton valued at $15,028.86 and promised "to pay over . . . as collected" $34,971.20. Ticknor was "to make use of all diligence and perseverance in collecting that may be in his power."[3] Essentially, Pratt had let his wife's brother off the financial hook in return for seventy-four bales of cotton. Only when Ticknor actually collected more than $50,000 in debts would he see any personal profit from the deal, but no doubt he was happy to be relieved of a debt of more than a third of a million dollars.

As per agreement, Samuel Ticknor went about collecting payments from delinquent planters. In the summer, he hired attorney Robert H. Bradford of Milliken's Bend, Madison Parish, Louisiana, to present formal "demands of payment" against four estates of planters who had purchased Pratt gins in 1860. Whether Ticknor collected on these estates is unknown, but he did manage to conclude settlements with at least a few customers. In March 1866, J. A. Maxwell of Early County, Georgia, promised to pay "at Col Hafford's office in Blakely" $200 with interest running from January 1, 1862. In at least two cases, Ticknor actually got his hands on some money. In March 1862, Alexander Prudhomme had promised to pay Pratt $245.70, "with interest from date until paid." Six years later, someone (presumably Ticknor) wrote on the note itself: "Received on the written note ninety dollars & eighty one cents the proceeds of one bale of cotton March 13th 1868. $90.81." More than two years later in May 1870, Ticknor settled with Lewis Endt for $164.70. Endt, a Louisiana planter, had purchased a fifty-saw gin fully nine years earlier.[4]

3. Contract between Daniel Pratt and Pratt & Ticknor, 26 February 1863, and Contract between Daniel Pratt and Samuel Ticknor, 23 January 1866, Pratt Collection, ACHC. Merrill Pratt, the first lieutenant of Company K, was present at the surrender of Port Hudson and spent about fourteen months at Johnson's Island in Sandusky Bay, Ohio, a federal prison for Confederate officers. Once Merrill obtained his release in September 1864, his uncle prevailed upon his friend Francis Strother Lyon, a member of Alabama's delegation to the Confederate House of Representatives, to lobby the War Department to get Merrill detailed to help Pratt run his business. Lyon apparently succeeded, for Merrill remained in Prattville for the remainder of the war. C. F. Tuttle to Merrill Pratt, 7 November 1864, and Francis Strother Lyon to Daniel Pratt, 29 November 1864, Folder 36, Pratt Papers, ADAH.
4. Robert H. Bradford to Samuel Ticknor, 10 October 1866; J. A. Maxwell note, 4 March 1866; Receipt for $164.70 from S. F. Ticknor, 5 May 1870; and Alexander Prudhomme note, 13 March 1868, all in Pratt Collection, ACHC; Shadrack Mims Jr. to Lewis Endt, 3 May 1861, Letterbook, ACHC. In November 1862, Samuel Ticknor apparently traveled to Louisiana and Mississippi in an attempt to make collections. Julia Pratt wrote

As late as January and February 1874, months after Pratt's death, Ticknor was still making forays against his debtors. In answer to a "pointed note" from Ticknor, planter S. B. Robertson of Marksville, Avoyelles Parish, Louisiana, insisted that he could not pay for his gin. "While we are thankful that we are not actually starving," Robertson wrote plaintively, "we have absolutely *no money*." Robertson enclosed a draft he held on J. J. Irby and Company for $13 to pay the interest on his note, insisting that this was *"the best I can do."* If Ticknor could not "indulge" Robertson, which he was "almost ashamed to ask" him to do, the planter would "have to *try* to sell the gin . . . though it suits me well & I cannot think of replacing it." Robertson's closing comments could hardly have encouraged Ticknor: "I have plenty of hands this year and still hope to make a crop. As to collecting anything I've just quit trying."[5]

At this late date, Ticknor's problems were, no doubt, enhanced by the devastating panic of 1873. As one of Ticknor's collection agents, Benjamin Thigpen, succinctly put it: "people poorer & poorer & meaner & meaner." Thigpen was based in Paulding, the seat of Jasper County in southeastern Mississippi. He complained that there was "no money scarcely in this county." One of Ticknor's planter debtors, one Jones, had gone bankrupt and was not very agreeable. Thigpen reported: "He is a hard case. He refused to give a new note until I told him I should sue him on the old one and try to get your testimony that he had promised to pay more than $50.00 then I could get a Judgement for whatever I could prove." Jones bowed to this threat, agreeing to give Ticknor's agent a $50 note bearing 10 percent interest from January 1, 1873, and payable on April 1, 1874. Thigpen agreed not to charge Jones interest if he paid the note by the middle of February. Of another debtor, Thigpen was even less comforting: "I have not seen Conner yet. [I] hope I may make an impression on him yet, tho it looks like a bad chance. I can make the money out of Jones at Law but don't think a Judgement on Conner collectible by law. [I] will do the best I can and report at an Early day."[6]

As Samuel Ticknor pursued old debtors, Daniel Pratt beckoned new customers. In 1866, Pratt placed a fresh advertisement for his gins in *De Bow's Review*, proclaiming that his factory was back in operation and

---

her husband, Merrill, that the town had "not heard from Mr. Ticknor since he crossed the Mississippi River." Julia Pratt to Merrill Pratt, 23 November 1862, Box 21, McMillan Collection.

5. S. B. Robertson to Samuel Ticknor, 15 January 1874, Pratt Collection, ACHC.

6. Benjamin Thigpen to Samuel Ticknor, 7 February 1874, Pratt Collection, ACHC.

boasting of his "nearly 40 years' experience in the business." He also noted that he still sold the Eureka model, which he called "the most complete and perfect gin I ever saw." Pratt announced a new, expanded network of sixteen fixed agencies: five firms in Georgia (Augusta, Macon, Atlanta, Eatonton, and Hawkinsville), four in Alabama (Montgomery, Selma, Mobile, and Eufaula), four in Mississippi (Meridian, Columbus, Natchez, and Yazoo City), and one each in Louisiana (New Orleans), Tennessee (Memphis), and Texas (Galveston). This list of gin agencies reveals that Pratt had expanded his market into Georgia. The wartime ruination of Pratt's old friend and business associate Samuel Griswold left Georgia open for Pratt's invasion, and by 1866, he had agents in Atlanta and across the state's plantation belt.[7]

Although the factory was back in operation a year after the end of the Civil War, gin sales did not surpass their 1860 level until 1870. In 1866, Pratt sold about 700 gins. Four years later, he sold 897 gins, nearly 40 more than in 1860. Nevertheless, Pratt had only produced 700 gins. The rest of his sales came from inventory that had piled up in the factory in previous years. With business only just reviving, Pratt employed merely 50 workers (48 men and 2 boys under seventeen years of age), 24 fewer than in 1860. Moreover, wages increased at a much slower rate in the 1860s than in the 1850s. Between 1860 and 1870, wages rose from an average of $12.93 a week to $16.09 a week ($64.38 a month and $772.60 a year), a gain of only 24 percent. By contrast, wages rose 60 percent in the 1850s. Evidently, Pratt responded to hard times by holding down wages.[8]

Probably reflecting this low wage increase, a majority of the gin factory employees in 1870 were African Americans. About two-thirds of Prattville's white mechanics disappeared between 1860 and 1870. Most of the town's northern mechanics left during the secession crisis and

---

7. *De Bow's Review*, 2d ser., 2 (1867): app.; Williams, *Jones County*, 401–2; Griswold, "The Cotton Gin—An Interesting History," 510–11. Federal troops razed Griswoldsville in 1864. Like Pratt (though more successfully), Griswold had manufactured revolvers in his gin factory. Griswold died in September 1867 at the age of seventy-six. Griswold, "The Cotton Gin—An Interesting History," 510–11. Pratt's major competitor after the war, Clemons, Brown and Company of Columbus, Georgia, had twenty-six fixed agencies across the South, but eleven of them were located in Virginia and the Carolinas. *De Bow's Review*, 2d ser., 2 (January 1867): app.

8. Brief Filed before the Commissioner of Patents, 8, 10; Alabama, 2: 12, R. G. Dun & Co. Collection. U.S. Census, Alabama, 1870 Manufactures Schedule, Autauga County.

never returned. Of the Yankees remaining in 1870, moreover, few remained in Pratt's employ. In 1866, Ferdinand Smith, his brother Frank, and his cousin George took over the sash, door, and blind factory under the name F. E. Smith and Company. Ephraim Morgan, the previous owner and a fellow New Hampshirite, retired from the business and purchased a plantation. Enoch Robinson, who also hailed from New Hampshire, resumed his horse mills business but was beset by financial troubles and went bankrupt in 1869. The next year, he and his family migrated to Texas. C. P. Morgan, likely a brother of Ephraim, remained in Prattville but now found employment as a house carpenter. William White of Indiana devoted his time to farming in 1870. One other northern mechanic, Ashby Morgan, the husband of Merrill Pratt's sister Augusta, remained in Prattville after the Civil War started, but he died in 1862. Only two Yankees remained in the gin factory in 1870: superintendent Merrill Pratt and a foundry worker from New York. In addition, one foreign-born worker, an Irishman, worked in the machine shop. The rest of the likely white workers came from Alabama, Georgia, South Carolina, and Tennessee.[9]

Not only was Pratt's white workforce mostly southern, it was also basically new. Probably only five men had worked as Pratt mechanics in 1860. Fourteen other 1860 mechanics persisted in Prattville in 1870, but they did not labor for Pratt. Ten had employment as house carpenters. Two owned their own shops, and two worked for shop owners. Two perished in the war. Why so many Prattville mechanics either left town or Pratt's employ is not clear, but the low wage increase in the 1860s is highly suggestive. White mechanics likely were less willing than blacks to work for the wages Pratt offered after the Civil War.[10]

Pratt in 1870 relied more heavily on black workers in his gin factory than at any time since the 1840s. No doubt in many cases, Pratt's 1870 black gin workers had worked for him as slaves in 1860. Charles At-

9. U.S. Census, Alabama, 1870 Population Schedule, Autauga County; Alabama, 2: 9, 18, 22, R. G. Dun & Co. Collection; Abigail Holt Smith Diary, ACHC.

10. U.S. Census, Alabama, 1860 and 1870 Population Schedules, Autauga County; Smith, *Company K,* app. One of Pratt's new gin employees was twenty-four-year-old William Griswold, a grandson of Samuel. Williams, *Jones County,* 402. One Pratt mechanic of long standing, Samuel Patillo, moved to Montgomery and joined the city police force, which in 1868 paid a salary of $75 a month, or $900 a year, probably surpassing what he would have made under Pratt in 1870. U.S. Census, Alabama, 1870 Population Schedule, Montgomery County; *Montgomery Daily Mail,* 1, 16 December 1868.

wood, a light-skinned, straight-haired mulatto, was purchased as a teen-ager by Daniel Pratt from Samuel Griswold in 1843. It seems a reasonable surmise, given his connection to Griswold and his taking the surname Atwood after the Civil War, that Charles was the offspring of a mulatto slave woman and either Turpin G. or William H. Atwood, Rhode Island mechanics who worked for Griswold in the early 1830s, the time when Charles Atwood was born. Atwood was obviously a highly skilled and successful mechanic. In 1870, he listed his occupation as "gin maker"—a term connoting a feeling of artisanal confidence and pride—and his property value at $1,000, placing him among the four wealthiest of Pratt's known gin workers. Earlier that year, Atwood paid Henry and Ellen DeBardeleben $700 for a house and lot located in the "white section" of Prattville, adjacent to the house and lot of fellow "gin maker" Lafayette Ellis. In 1872, Atwood also subscribed to $100 worth of stock in the proposed Prattville railroad—the only African American in Prattville to do so. The previous year, he had named his fourth son "Pratt."[11]

Two black gin mechanics in 1870 had been with Pratt longer than Atwood. Richard Pratt, a fifty-seven-year-old slave from North Carolina, was probably the slave "Dick," purchased by Daniel Pratt in 1834, a year after Pratt arrived in Alabama. Richard's twenty-one-year-old son, Richard Jr., also made gins in 1870. Richard Pratt Sr. continued to labor in the gin factory as late as 1881. That year, a newspaper correspondent from Montgomery noted that Richard Pratt had "been at work in the factory since it started. He is good for a situation as long as he is able to work, and a pension afterwards." The third likely former Pratt slave mechanic was a fifty-five-year-old mulatto from South Carolina named Henry Robinson. In 1839, Pratt purchased a twenty-five-year-old slave named Henry for the sizable sum of $1,600 from a carpenter named Du-

11. Slave Bill of Sale, CECP; U.S. Census, Mississippi, 1850 and 1860 Population Schedules, Attalla County; U.S. Census, Alabama, 1870 Population Schedule, Autauga County; Deed Book 18, p. 139, Autauga County Courthouse; Map of Prattville, Ala., 1891, Prattville Public Library; Subscription to the Prattville Railroad, CECP. Turpin G. Atwood owned a house and lot in Clinton in 1827. In 1832, Turpin G. Atwood, William H. Atwood, and Daniel Pratt were parties to a legal action in Jones County. Charles Atwood was born ca. 1830 to 1832. Turpin G. Atwood was married in late 1831. *Macon Telegraph*, 5 November 1831; (Milledgeville) *Georgia Journal*, 11 October 1825, 29 October 1827, 25 February 1828, 2 February, 31 May 1832. A photograph of Charles Atwood is in the possession of his grandchild, Mrs. Lillian Atwood Strong of Prattville.

rant Nobles. The slave Henry likely became Henry Robinson after the war.[12]

At least four other black mechanics in addition to Charles Atwood became prominent figures in Prattville's African American community: Frank Dozier, Dudley Green, William Squires, and Anthony Thomas. Dozier, Squires, and Green worked in the gin factory, while Thomas was a foundry worker. In 1887, a Prattville newspaper named Dozier and Squires, along with Charles Atwood, as important and conservative black leaders. The paper also noted much more grudgingly in 1893 that Dudley Green, who had just died, was "a prominent character among the colored population." Green's funeral procession, the paper reported, was one of the largest such events ever seen in Prattville. Anthony Thomas, a forty-three-year-old South Carolinian worth $500 in 1870, proved especially popular with the white press, as he was a vocal Democrat. In 1878, he hosted a political barbecue, at which important white and black Democrats spoke. Prattville's Democratic newspaper commented favorably on Thomas's "well-laden tables" and neat dwelling and grounds and found Thomas himself "an honest, industrious, colored man." When Thomas died in 1882 "under very suspicious circumstances," the same paper angrily asserted he had been poisoned.[13]

Although some of Pratt's black mechanics became men of note in their community, few had achieved any substantial wealth in 1870. Probably only Charles Atwood, the sole black mechanic worth $1,000 or more, owned his own home. Three other black Pratt mechanics were worth $100 or more: Anthony Thomas ($500), Richard Pratt ($200), and Henry Robinson ($100). Nine other men ranged in wealth from $10 to $50, and the remaining fourteen did not provide a listing. Pratt's black workers were, however, only marginally worse off than his white workers. Of his twenty likely white gin mechanics, only three gave wealth listings of more than $1,000: John Williamson ($1,350), Lafayette Ellis ($1,200), and Isaac Ward ($1,100). Three other men had wealth valued at from $100 to $500, while two men had wealth listings of less than $100. Twelve men did not have any wealth listings at all.[14]

12. U.S. Census, Alabama, 1850 and 1880 Population Schedules, Montgomery County, 1870 Population Schedule, Autauga County; *Montgomery Advertiser and Mail,* 12 June 1881.

13. U.S. Census, Alabama, 1870 Population Schedule, Autauga County; *Prattville Progress,* 6 May 1887, 10 March 1893; *Prattville Southern Signal,* 9 August 1878, 16 June 1882.

14. U.S. Census, Alabama, 1870 Population Schedule, Autauga County.

Despite the departure of many of his best mechanics, Pratt still had a highly skilled core of artisans in 1870, namely Charles Atwood, Lafayette Ellis, John Williamson, and Isaac Ward. Ellis, in fact, would go on to invent the important huller cotton gin.[15] These four southern men, three of whom were white and one a mulatto, had stepped into the places once held by such Yankees as the Smith cousins.

Notwithstanding some instability in markets and his labor supply, Daniel Pratt's gin factory was well on its way to recovery by 1870. Indeed, in March 1871, a visiting Dun agent effusively declared of both the gin factory and Prattville Manufacturing Company that "both firms are as good as gold dust . . . as good as ever." By 1870, Pratt had considerably expanded PMC, installing new machinery and more spindles, employing more people, and producing higher quality products. Between 1860 and 1870, the number of spindles in the cotton and wool mills rose from 3,285 (2,700 cotton, 585 wool) to 5,088 (4,608 cotton and 480 wool), an increase of nearly 55 percent. In 1860, the two mills had employed 141 people, while in 1870, they gave work to 167 (159 in the cotton mill and 8 in the woolen mill), an increase of 18.4 percent. With more equipment and workers, production expanded from 874,102 yards in 1860 to 1,324,992 yards in 1870, an increase of more than 450,000 yards, or 51.5 percent. Not only did Pratt's cotton mill produce more, though woolen production had declined, but it also had diversified its output. Now PMC produced not only osnaburg (698,369 yards), but also higher-quality sheeting (361,540 yards) and shirting (159,283 yards). Together, sheeting and shirting accounted for 42.7 percent of the cotton mill's production. Pratt's osnaburg was now priced at only 6 cents a yard, but his sheeting was worth 6.4 cents and his shirting 8.3 cents.[16]

At the end of the war, Gardner Hale traveled to England to buy new mill machinery, both for PMC and for a new cotton factory located at

15. Bennett, *Cotton Ginning Developments,* 32. In 1881, Ellis invented the "split-rib huller cotton gin." In 1889, he invented an "improved double-rib huller cotton gin" that "became a general standard in the United States." Ibid., 32–33. Ellis worked on his 1881 gin for three years, having it ready for show at the great International Cotton Exposition at Atlanta. The gin, which separated "cotton from the hull, depositing the seed in one place and the hull in another," was the "wonder and admiration of all the big planters in the South," according to William Howell. (Prattville) *Autauga Citizen,* 15 December 1881. See also *Prattville Southern Signal,* 30 September 1881.

16. Alabama, 2: 12, R. G. Dun & Co. Collection; U.S. Census, Alabama, 1870 Industrial Schedule, Autauga County.

the newly founded neighboring community of Allenville. The machinery purchased by Hale began arriving in July 1866. Two years later, a Dun agent reported that PMC was "doing very well at present" and was "now making money." The company, he noted, was "well-managed at present by Daniel Pratt, a good financier." The next year, the reports became even better: "This company is doing well, succeeding better than at any time since the war." A few months later in August 1869, the Dun assessment was again encouraging: "Doing well and prosperous."[17]

Pratt gained great personal credit for the revival of PMC. In May 1868, the *Montgomery Daily Mail* reported that earlier in the year, "hundreds upon hundreds of bales of cotton goods were accumulating at [PMC], and . . . the cry was 'no sale.'" Taking matters into his own hands, Pratt traveled "to the Northern cities, introduced samples of his fabrics, spoke of the advantages his factory offered, and selected intelligent commission merchants, with whom he deposited his goods." Within a matter of weeks, the public became aware of "the quality and cheapness of [Pratt's] wares" and bought "his entire accumulated stock." Since then, orders had come in so heavily that Pratt increased the number of his spindles. To assure a large enough volume of water to power his additional spindles, Pratt elevated his dam on Autauga Creek by ten feet.[18]

The *Mail* noted approvingly that Pratt's factory expansion would "give employment to an additional force of [operatives] men, women, and children." This outcome likely had been one of Pratt's goals in the first place. Shadrack Mims claimed that Pratt always kept the welfare of his operatives uppermost in his mind. Mims twice cited one postwar incident as powerful proof of his claim. Having returned as mill agent in January 1865 after the death of William Fay, Mims reported at a meeting of PMC's board of managers in April or May that the mill had seven hundred bales of cotton on hand, but that the machinery had "completely run down." Consequently, the mill could only be run at "a heavy loss to the stockholders." Mims presented the meeting with two alternatives: "either close up or fill up the mill with new and the latest improved machinery." For the "high-toned Christian gentlemen" who composed the board—Daniel Pratt, president; John Whiting; Lewis Whetstone; Samuel Ticknor; and James Hazen, secretary—however, "the interest of the op-

17. Ballou, *History and Genealogy of the Ballous,* 479; Alabama, 2: 15, R. G. Dun & Co. Collection. On Allenville, see below.

18. *Montgomery Daily Mail,* 7 May 1868.

eratives turned the scale." PMC continued to run at a heavy loss until the new machinery arrived and was installed.[19]

Pratt's operatives enjoyed a wage increase of about 28 percent between 1860 and 1870 (from $177.10 to $226.41 a year),which was greater than the increase gin mechanics received. Nevertheless, mill workers made only 29 percent of what mechanics made in 1870, about the same percentage as in 1860. Despite their low salaries, Pratt's operatives were probably thankful simply to have jobs after the Civil War. Governor Robert Patton pointed out in a De Bow's Review article in January 1867 that the Civil War had devastated Alabama white families: "Of young and middle-aged men killed in the war, Alabama lost fully 40,000. About 20,000 were disabled for life, many of whom since died from this cause. At least 20,000 widows and 60,000 orphans are left in the state. Three-fourths of these are today dependent upon government rations for subsistence." Patton calculated that "from this unemployed and impoverished class of women, boys, and girls, there might be employed 20,000 or 25,000 efficient factory operatives."[20] In short, Pratt's mill provided a sort of "workfare" for the people threatened with impoverishment because of the Civil War.

Reflecting the troubled economic times after the conflict, mill families in 1870 had rather low wealth figures compared to Prattville's mill families in 1860. Of seventy-six mill households, only one—that of the new superintendent, Joseph Kent—was worth more than $1,000. Of the twenty-six households besides Kent's that gave wealth listings, two were worth $500 or more, and two were worth under $100. The remaining twenty-two had wealth valued at from $100 to $300. The mean wealth among the mill families with wealth listings (excluding Kent) was only slightly more than $170, less than half the $400 figure for 1860.[21]

Black mill households seem to have had roughly similar economic positions to white mill households. One such family—that of Louisa Jones, a mulatto—was worth $550. Louisa Jones's son, Columbus, worked at PMC, but most of the household's wealth likely came from Louisa's exertions as a free-black washerwoman before the Civil War. Probably more typical of a "successful" black mill household was that of Gabriel Wash-

19. *Prattville Southern Signal,* 23 May 1878; Mims, "Autauga County," 263.

20. U.S. Census, Alabama, 1870 Industrial Schedule, Autauga County; *De Bow's Review,* 2d ser., 4 (1867): 65.

21. The information in this and the next few paragraphs comes primarily from the Population Schedules of the 1850, 1860, and 1870 U.S. censuses for Autauga County.

ington, who likely headed PMC's picker room. Washington was worth $200. His wife, Anna, kept house, while his daughter Eliza attended school.[22]

About one-third of Prattville's mill families persisted between 1860 and 1870, allowing Pratt to build a more efficient corps of workers. A now elderly Thomas Hale still resided in Prattville, living with three of his daughters, more than twenty years after he brought his family to the town. Hale's daughter Eliza, the widow of mechanic Ebenezer Killough, headed the household. Two of her younger sisters, Martha (twenty-six) and Catherine (nineteen), were operatives. Thomas Hale's son William resided in his own household. William Hale worked in the wool mill, while his eleven-year-old son Jesse labored in a cotton mill.

Three other persisting families were those of Nancy Cook, Isabella Jones, and Elnora Killian. Nancy Cook was the widow of John Cook, a mechanic who died in the Civil War. Before the war, Cook's wife and his eldest daughter, Adaline, had worked in a mill. In 1870, Nancy Cook no longer did so, but the children residing with her—Mary (twenty-three), Ellen (seventeen), and Jesse (fourteen)—did. Isabella Jones was the widow of William Jones Jr., who worked as a machinist in Prattville as early as 1850. To support her two little daughters, Ida and Calista, after her husband's demise, Isabella had gone to work in a mill by 1860. In 1870, the forty-year-old widow continued to labor in a mill, as did Ida (seventeen) and Calista (fourteen).

Elnora Killian was already a widow in 1850. By 1860, she had moved to Prattville, where she worked as a weaver, along with her daughters Mary (twenty-four) and Jane (seventeen). In 1870, Elnora, fifty-nine, had retired from factory work, but her unmarried daughter Jane, as well as her widowed daughter Amanda Cox, worked in a mill, and her son Abram found employment as a tinner. Despite having three children working (one as an artisan), Elnora Killian's wealth declined from $250 in 1860 to $100 in 1870. However, her daughter Sarah had made an advantageous marriage to Thomas Fallon, an Irish engine builder worth $750 in 1870.

One persisting family, that of A. J. Weatherly, did well for itself, not so much economically as socially. In 1860, the fifty-eight-year-old Weatherly was a cloth trimmer worth $250. Two of his daughters worked as weavers, and his sons Floyd and William worked as a gin

22. Columbus Jones had become the head of PMC's pickery by 1900. U.S. Census, Alabama, 1900 Population Schedule, Autauga County.

painter and an apprentice tinner, respectively. Weatherly's eldest daughter, Ann, had married Alison Scroggins, a boss in the cotton mill. By 1870, Weatherly had died, leaving his wife, Mary, the head of a household worth only $100. Three of his daughters, Frances (thirty), Mary (twenty-two), and Nancy Tallapoosa (fifteen), worked in a cotton mill. Floyd, who still worked in the gin shop, had his own household. Another son had married Sallie Patillo, a daughter of gin mechanic Samuel Patillo, and moved to Montgomery, where he worked as a harness maker.[23]

Before his death in 1868, Weatherly enjoyed a brief local political career. After Prattvillians voted to incorporate the town in September 1865, Weatherly won one of five spots on the town council. Moreover, his son-in-law, Alison Scroggins, was elected town marshal. A prominent local Democrat in the 1870s, Scroggins eventually became county coroner. Both Scroggins and his mother-in-law received full obituaries from the local paper at their deaths later in the century. Of Scroggins, the newspaper declared that while he had not "possessed much of this world's goods, he was nevertheless rich in kindness of heart and other noble qualities" that made "sordid wealth . . . a mere mockery and a sham." All men who had encountered Scroggins during his "long residence" in Prattville knew him as "a clever, kind, accommodating and gentlemanly man."[24]

After the Civil War, the mills remained almost completely the preserve of white families like the Weatherleys. Of the 211 of 235 identified workers in the Prattville and Allenville mills, only 20 (9.4 percent) were black. Because of the cultural taboo about whites, especially women and girls, working in the company of freed blacks, Pratt, like other southern mill operators, no doubt kept his black workers confined to the worst, most isolated job in his factories: unpacking cotton bales in the pickery (now a separate building). All his black mill workers were males, most aged from twelve to twenty-five.[25]

23. U.S. Census, Alabama, 1870 Population Schedule, Montgomery County.

24. (Prattville) *Autauga Citizen*, 5 October 1865, 20 May 1880; Hazen, *Manual of the Presbyterian Church*, 6; U.S. Census, Alabama, 1880 Population Schedule, Autauga County; *Prattville Southern Signal*, 28 October 1881, 12 March 1886. Scroggins probably got the nomination in part out of sympathy for him generated when he received a serious injury in Pratt's mill in 1876. Scroggins, the night watchman, was starting up the machinery for the day when he "was suddenly seized by the *belting* and seriously crushed." By 1880, Scroggins's only son, twenty-one-year-old Obadiah, had become the new night watchman at the mill. (Prattville) *Autauga Citizen*, 23 November 1876; U.S. Census, Alabama, 1880 Population Schedule, Autauga County.

25. U.S. Census, Alabama, 1870 Population Schedule, Autauga County.

Both the Prattville and the Allenville mills attracted enough new white labor in the 1860s to allow them to avoid turning to African Americans. Not only did about a third of mill families persist between 1860 and 1870, but many new families, frequently headed by widows, appeared. While in 1860 women had headed just over 39 percent of mill households, in 1870 they headed thirty-five of the sixty-eight white mill households in Prattville and Allenville, over 51 percent. Likely many of these families consisted of the indigent Civil War widows and orphans Governor Patton had written about in his *De Bow's* article.[26]

The Mary Sager and Caroline Hall households certainly seem to fit this pattern. In 1860, the two women lived in Autauga County, Sager in Kingston precinct and Hall in Autaugaville. By 1870, their husbands had died, and (the Autaugaville textile factory having failed shortly after the conclusion of the Civil War) they had moved to Prattville, where they put their children to work in the mills. Mary Sager was the wife of J. J. Sager of South Carolina, a farmer worth $500 in 1860. J. J. Sager died around 1865, leaving his wife with eight children. Within a few years, the Sagers moved to Prattville. Mary's eldest son, William, was without occupation, perhaps having suffered a serious wound in the army. The family income was brought in by the three younger children, Eliza (eighteen), Mary (twelve), and Patrick (ten), who all worked in a cotton mill. Despite having three wage earners, the family listed no wealth in 1870.[27]

D. W. Hall worked as a carpenter in Autaugaville. In 1860, Hall, a native Georgian, was worth $200. When he died, probably in the early 1860s, he left his wife, Caroline, with six children. In 1870, Caroline's daughters Ellen and Louisa worked in a cotton mill, while her sons David and Thomas attended school. Her eldest son, Henry, who had married and formed his own household, worked in the wool mill. Like the Sagers, the Halls had no wealth figure listed.[28]

Not all families who came to Prattville in the 1860s, of course, were headed by widows. Like Mary Sager and Caroline Hall, Bolling Anthony, James Buckner, and Sterling Skaggs brought their families to Prattville during that decade. In 1860, Bolling Anthony, a farm laborer from Georgia worth $25, lived in the hilly Mount Olive precinct in northeastern

26. Ibid. On the increase of indigence in Autauga County as a result of the war, see Commissioners' Court Minutes, Book of 1854–1866, 218, Autauga County Courthouse; *Montgomery Daily Mail*, 25 March 1870.

27. U.S. Census, Alabama, 1860 and 1870 Population Schedules, Autauga County.

28. U.S. Census, 1860 and 1870 Population Schedules, Autauga County.

Coosa County, with his wife and eight children. With six daughters and only two sons, Anthony probably felt he had little to lose by moving from the country to Prattville. Moreover, Anthony may have suffered injury in the war, for he is listed in 1870 as "without occupation." Three of his daughters, Nancy (twenty-six), Sarah (twenty-one), and Keziah (eighteen), worked in a cotton mill, as did his son Reuben (fourteen). In addition, his daughter Martha had married longtime mill worker Thaddeus Hoyle, and the couple lived in Anthony's household. The family's wealth was listed as only $10, however.[29]

James Buckner and Sterling Skaggs both migrated from Georgia to eastern Alabama between 1850 and 1860 and thence to Prattville by 1870. James Buckner became a respected, albeit poor, member of the community. He was born near the town of Sparta in Hancock County, Georgia, in 1796. As a youth, he served in the War of 1812. Probably due to his military experience, as well as the "remarkable vigor" he enjoyed "up to a short time before his death" in 1877, Buckner became known around Prattville as "the General." In 1850, he still lived in Hancock County, along with his much younger wife, Frances Barnes, and his six children. By 1860, he had moved near the town of Opelika, located in Russell County in southeast Alabama, where he gave his occupation as machinist. By 1869, he had moved his expanded family—his wife had delivered him eleven children, the first when he was forty-two and the last when he was sixty-six—to Prattville. In 1870, the old "General" was without occupation, but three of his children, Joel (twenty), Susan (sixteen), and Sarah (twelve), worked in the mill. His daughter Adaline had married mill worker Henry Hall, while his daughter America had married Abram Ellis, brother of Lafayette Ellis. Evidently, the General enjoyed his years in Prattville, for William Howell recalled that Buckner "was noted as having a superabundance of wit and good humor," as well as a "pleasant smile" that he wore "through all his worldly journeyings."[30]

Sterling Skaggs also made extensive "worldly journeyings," but his life ended less peacefully than the General's. In 1850, Skaggs lived in Henry County, Georgia, and worked as a farmer. By 1860, he had moved

29. U.S. Census, 1860 Population Schedule, Coosa County, 1870 Population Schedule, Autauga County.

30. (Prattville) *Autauga Citizen,* 18 January 1877; U.S. Census, Georgia, 1850 Population Schedule, Hancock County; U.S. Census, Alabama, 1860 Population Schedule, Russell County, 1870 Population Schedule, Autauga County.

to Tallapoosa County, Alabama, with his expanding family and listed his occupation as house carpenter. Just two years later, Skaggs and his family were living in Prattville, and he again derived his livelihood from farming. Skaggs owned two acres of his own land and also farmed for other Prattvillians. When Ferdinand Smith left for war work in Mobile in 1862, he hired Skaggs to care for his small plot of farmland. Ferdinand's wife, Martha, informed her absent husband in May that Skaggs "is expecting you home soon so he is flying around considerable and is doing very well." Skaggs hoped to borrow the Smith's horse for use on his own land, but Martha was skeptical: "He took [the horse] one day to plow his potatoes and kept him all day and did not give him anything to eat and he plowed for some one [else]." A year later, Martha complained that Skaggs did not give the Smith farm sufficient attention, only coming over "late in the evening" after he had worked on his own acreage.[31]

Skaggs seems to have worked hard—on *his* land, at least—but in 1870 he had not gained any economic ground. That year he was worth the same as in 1860, $100, despite having four of his children, Nancy (twenty-two), Mary (twenty), Jerusha (seventeen), and George (nine) at work in a cotton mill and one son, William (fourteen), laboring on a farm. His eldest son, James, who was married and had a separate household outside town, worked as a laborer on the farm of Henry J. Livingston, a wealthy Prattville attorney. Sterling Skaggs himself gave his occupation as a farmer.[32]

Like Buckner, Skaggs seems to have become a respected figure in the town. By 1876, he had been elected town marshal. Over Christmas of that year, Skaggs, "while discharging his duty as marshal of Prattville," was shot and beaten during an altercation in town with several freedmen. Skaggs lingered for nearly three months before finally succumbing to his injuries. William Howell eulogized Skaggs as "a good, industrious and peaceable citizen" whose death would "be deplored by all who knew him."[33]

---

31. U.S. Census, Georgia, 1850 Population Schedule, Henry County; U.S. Census, Alabama, 1860 Population Schedule, Tallapoosa County; Martha Smith to Ferdinand Smith, 30 March, 19 April, 8 May 1862, 1 June 1863, ACHC.

32. U.S. Census, Alabama, 1870 Population Schedule, Autauga County.

33. (Prattville) *Autauga Citizen,* 11, 15, 22 March 1877. Jim Davis and Jake Sadler received life sentences for Skaggs's murder, while Jerry Lewis and Cato Taylor received sentences of five years for manslaughter. (Prattville) *Autauga Citizen,* 13 May 1877. Cato Taylor was the son of Robert Taylor. In 1870, Robert Taylor worked in the carriage shop

The editor of the *Citizen* never found cause to eulogize Prattville as he had Skaggs. Although some businesses foundered after the Civil War, others quickly took their places, always with Daniel Pratt's encouragement and sometimes his direct aid. Without a doubt, the most important new concern was the Indian Hill Manufacturing Company (commonly known as the Indian Hill textile factory), actually located one mile northwest of Prattville at the nascent village of Allenville. Pratt surely took special pride in the creation of the Indian Hill textile factory, as one of the key men in this enterprise was William Allen, the son of an original PMC incorporator, James Allen. Pratt in fact had sold the site of Allenville to William Allen on December 19, 1861, for $2,000, with the expectation that Allen would start a mill there.[34]

The hard hand of war pushed this project aside, but on August 1, 1866, William Allen conveyed the land he owned on Autauga Creek to the Indian Hill Manufacturing Company in exchange for $20,000 worth of stock. Besides Allen, the company's central figures were Henry Faber, Henry's brother Jacob, and Marcus Munter. Henry Faber and Munter were partners in Munter and Faber, one of the leading mercantile houses in postwar Montgomery, while Jacob Faber ran the new Prattville branch of the business. Henry Faber, who had been born in Bavaria in 1837 and settled in Montgomery in 1858, became a Republican after the Civil War and was elected mayor of Montgomery in 1870. It was Henry Faber who served as president of the Indian Hill Manufacturing Company, while William Allen became agent. Before the Indian Hill textile factory could begin operation, however, a freshet flooded the building and severely damaged the machinery. This setback so strained the financial resources of the company that it had to be sold under a mortgage. Munter and the Faber brothers survived, but William Allen went into bankruptcy in 1868 and fled to his home state, New York, never to return to Alabama, the state where he had lived more than twenty years.[35]

---

and Cato, thirteen, worked in a cotton mill. Jim Davis was probably the same man as James Davis, a gin shop worker worth $25 in 1870. U.S. Census, Alabama, 1870 Population Schedule, Autauga County. After Cato Taylor's release in 1883, he robbed the store of a Prattville merchant but was captured and arrested. *Prattville Southern Signal,* 14 December 1883.

34. Deed between Daniel and Esther Pratt and William C. Allen, 19 December 1861, Allen Papers, ADAH.

35. Alabama, 2: 26, R. G. Dun & Co. Collection; (Montgomery) *Alabama State Journal,* 17 September, 4, 5 October 1871; (Montgomery) *Alabama State Sentinel,* 30 September

The Indian Hill textile factory fell into the hands of Simpson, Moore, and Company and Lehman, Durr, and Company. The former concern manufactured textiles in neighboring Coosa County, while the latter was an important Montgomery firm of cotton brokers that began investing heavily in Alabama industry after the war. With these two successful firms at the helm, the Indian Hill textile factory quickly righted itself. "Prospects good, doing well, regard quite safe and responsible," a Dun agent wrote of the concern in 1869. By 1870, the company was capitalized at $60,000, operated 3,244 spindles, employed 68 persons, and produced 522,032 yards of shirting and sheeting, as well as yarn and thread.[36]

The Indian Hill textile factory admittedly eclipsed the other new manufacturing concerns in the Prattville area, but it was by no means the only one of any significance. In 1870, the most notable manufacturing enterprises after the textile mills and the gin factory were the sash, door, and blind shop, F. E. Smith and Company, and the carriage, buggy, and wagon shop, N. H. Morris and Company. Both businesses were owned by former Pratt mechanics. F. E. Smith and Company consisted of Ferdinand Smith, his brother Frank, and his cousin George. By 1870, the trio was, according to a Dun agent, "prospering and doing very well." That year, the shop was capitalized at $6,000, employed 16 men, and had output valued at $12,000. This successful company was employing a sales agent in Montgomery a year later.[37]

1870; Deed Book 16, pp. 128–29, Autauga County Courthouse; (Prattville) *Autauga Citizen,* 9 August, 13, 29 September 1866; Alabama, 2: 8, 26, R. G. Dun & Co. Collection. In 1882, the Faber brothers gained control of PMC itself, but they held onto the company only until 1886, when a freshet wrecked the building and machinery. *Prattville Progress,* 11 November 1898.

36. *A Centennial: Lehman Brothers, 1850–1950* (New York: Lehman Brothers 1950), 20–22; Alabama, 2: 26, R. G. Dun & Co. Collection; U.S. Census, Alabama, 1870 Industrial Schedule, Autauga County. The Indian Hill textile factory continued to profitably manufacture goods until a fire utterly destroyed the building and machinery in February 1880. (Prattville) *Autauga Citizen,* 12 February 1880.

37. Alabama, 2: 18–9, R. G. Dun & Co. Collection; U.S. Census, Alabama, 1870 Industrial Schedule, Autauga County; *Montgomery Advertiser and Mail,* 7 April 1871 (Prattville) *Autauga Citizen,* 25 January, 8 November 1866. By 1881, the company, now in the hands of George Smith and his younger brother Daniel Pratt Smith, had grown into "the largest and most widely patronized sash, door and blind factory in the State," employing 25 men. *Montgomery Advertiser and Mail,* 12 June 1881.

N. H. Morris and Company also had a Montgomery sales agent, though it was a smaller concern than F. E. Smith and Company. The shop, which was capitalized at $4,000, employed 6 hands and produced carriages, buggies, and wagons worth $13,800, so that it was actually more productive than the highly touted F. E. Smith and Company. N. H. Morris and Company also owned a blacksmith shop, which employed 6 hands and was capitalized at $1,200. The total product value of this shop amounted to nearly $3,000. Two southerners, mechanic Nathan Morris and merchant James M. Smith, owned the company. In 1870, the Dun agent reported that their business was "doing well" and had "good prospects."[38]

To be sure, F. E. Smith and Company and N. H. Morris and Company operated in the shadows of the big textile mills and the gin factory. PMC employed 167 people; the Indian Hill textile factory employed 68; and the gin factory provided work for 50. Together, the three concerns had 285 workers. F. E. Smith and Company and N. H. Morris and Company, together with S. S. Booth and Company (makers of shoes and harnesses) and a sawmill owned by Merrill Pratt, employed only 47 persons. Still, the total number of people working in Prattville factories and shops increased from about 241 in 1860 to 332 in 1870, a significant gain. Prattville remained a place that attracted hardworking, ambitious mechanics.[39]

Other men found opportunity in Prattville after the war. By 1870, the town claimed a dozen merchants (including two druggists), one hotel keeper, eight clerks, two bookkeepers, six physicians, seven attorneys, one dentist, twelve house carpenters, four teamsters, two house painters, one brickmason, one plasterer, and one butcher. Of these, two of the carpenters, three of the teamsters, and both house painters were black. The expansion in the number of attorneys doubtlessly resulted from the re-

38. Alabama, 2: 27, R. G. Dun & Co. Collection; U.S. Census, Alabama, 1870 Industrial Schedule, Autauga County; *Montgomery Daily Advertiser and Mail*, 7 April 1871.

39. One mechanic who failed at this time was tin-shop owner James Wainwright, the husband of one of Pratt's nieces. In 1866, a Dun agent thought his prospects were promising: "W. owes a large amount of money but is industrious and I think that with indulgence and ordinary success [he] will eventually pay all his debts and succeed in life." The agent noted that Wainwright was "carrying on a good tin business and selling a good many goods on commission." Despite these favorable omens, Wainwright had gone into bankruptcy and moved to Mobile by 1868. Alabama, 2: 9, R. G. Dun & Co. Collection.

moval in 1868 of the county seat from Kingston to Prattville, a move long desired by Prattvillians.[40]

In 1870, Prattville had a population of about 1,240, a large increase from 1860, when the figure came to about 943. This expansion resulted, however, from an influx of freedmen into the town—the white population had remained about the same as in 1860. Despite the somewhat misleading nature of Prattville's population increase, it is clear that the town had made a real recovery from its wartime economic disruption. Soon after the war ended, in fact, newspapers began again to point to Prattville as an example for the rest of the South to emulate to recover the prosperity of the antebellum years. In 1868, the *Montgomery Daily Mail,* a Democratic paper, ran a long article titled "Prattville," which asserted: "No one who has visited the little town which [Mr. Pratt] selected as the scene of his labors, and which owes its existence to his enterprise, can fail to be impressed with its importance as a manufacturing point." Another Democratic paper, the *Montgomery Daily Advertiser,* praised "the good order, sound common sense, industrious habits, and high moral characteristics" of the people of Prattville, adding approvingly that "no loafers or beggars can be found in [the town's] limits." The Republican *Huntsville Advocate,* at the conclusion of a piece on Prattville's factories from 1870, enviously declared, "Would that we had such establishments in or near Huntsville, and such Yankees as Daniel Pratt." Another Republican paper, the *Montgomery Daily Journal,* concluded in 1871 that Prattville proved there was "life in the old land yet." Also in 1871, a visiting correspondent from the *New York Journal of Commerce* found Prattville "a very lively little town" with "a thrifty and decidedly New Englandish appearance." The *Mobile Weekly Register* also paid encomiums to Pratt and his "lovely village" in an especially detailed piece from 1870. The *Register*'s correspondent, noting that to visit Prattville without seeing its founder was "like seeing the play of Hamlet, with Hamlet left out," hastened to call on Daniel Pratt, whom he found tall, slim, and "somewhat bent with weight of care and years" and "recent illness," but all the same "attending in person to his vast business with a vitality and energy" that had always characterized him. Pratt's admirer wrote rhapsodically of

40. U.S. Census, Alabama, 1870 Population Schedule, Autauga County. Pratt's longtime bookkeeper Thomas Avery left Prattville after the Civil War. In 1870, his replacement was Edward Wingate of Connecticut. Wingate was related to Pratt's wife by marriage, having wed her cousin and ward, Julia Bill. The town's other bookkeeper was Eustace Robinson, a son of Enoch Robinson who remained in Prattville after the family left for Texas.

"beautiful cottages, with their tasteful grounds, the busy hum of machinery," and "the energetic people" who filled the town. Finally, the correspondent could no longer contain himself and cried, "Would to God, Alabama had more Daniel Pratts!"[41]

While less gushing than the *Register*'s correspondent, Governor Patton also lauded Pratt (whom he twice called "my friend") in his 1867 *De Bow's Review* article. The governor commended his friend for pursuing manufacturing "with zeal and activity for more than a quarter of a century." He also cited "the beautiful village of Prattville" as evidence of what a factory could do for Alabama's benighted war orphans. In Prattville one found good churches and schools that afforded "moral improvement of a certain class of youth which might otherwise grow up in ignorance."[42]

Pratt additionally won notice from his counterparts in the North. In 1868, he received appointment as temporary chairman of the first meeting, held in New York City, of the Cotton Planters and Manufacturers Association—his rival in fame, South Carolina textile manufacturer William Gregg, having died the previous year. Pratt was also made one of the permanent vice-presidents of the association. At the convention, Pratt attempted to persuade northern capitalists to invest in Alabama mills. Some attendees requested him to get them the names and locations of all the textile factories in Alabama, as well as the number of looms and spindles, capital invested, quantity of cotton consumed per annum, the number of yards spun, and the names and post offices of company presidents. When he returned to Alabama, Pratt diligently set to work. Finding he needed help on northern Alabama, he wrote his friend Governor Patton, a fellow mill man from the Tennessee Valley, asking him for information. "Please excuse me for troubling you," Pratt wrote the busy governor, "I feel a good deal interested in this matter."[43]

41. U.S. Census Alabama, 1870 Population Schedule, Autauga County; *Montgomery Daily Mail*, 7 May 1868, 28 May 1870, reprinted from the *Huntsville Advocate*; *Montgomery Daily Advertiser*, 12 April 1869; *Montgomery Daily Journal*, 31 October 1871; *Montgomery Daily Advertiser and Mail*, 29 July 1871, reprinted from the *New York Journal of Commerce*; *Mobile Weekly Register*, 28 May 1870.

42. *De Bow's Review*, 2d ser., 4 (1867): 63, 66. According to one newspaper, Patton's article "attracted much attention, not only in the State; but throughout the country." *Montgomery Daily Advertiser*, 22 March 1868.

43. *Montgomery Daily Mail*, 7 May 1868; Daniel Pratt to Robert Patton, 11 May 1868, Governor Patton Papers, ADAH.

No doubt encouraged by the establishment of the Indian Hill textile factory at Allenville, Pratt tried in his last years to persuade Montgomery investors to get another mill started, but in this effort he failed. In November 1871, "several of [Montgomery's] most enterprising and thoroughgoing business men" met at the rooms of the new board of trade to discuss the need for a textile factory in their city. This group chose a subscription committee, which had as one of its duties the selection of a location for the mill. "It is probable that one or more of our citizens may own land which the committee may set upon," declared the *Journal*. "If so, we trust that such citizen will donate a spot sufficient for all the purposes of a factory." Daniel Pratt, who had started pushing this project in 1869, did not need to be told twice. Three weeks later, the industrialist made the following offer "to the citizens of Montgomery": "I have one of the best water privileges, I think, in the State, on Autauga Creek, below Prattville, with power to turn 20,000 spindles, and all the machinery necessary to make it into cloth, a beautiful and healthy location, which I will give to a Montgomery company if they will improve it."[44]

Unfortunately, Pratt's grand proposal to help Montgomery establish in his vicinity the largest cotton mill in Alabama never was acted upon, leaving the exasperated *Journal* asking in April 1872: "What has become of the factory, a location for which was tendered to our citizens by Daniel Pratt?" The *Journal* complained that while Georgia cities such as Augusta and Columbus had forged ahead into a brave new South, Montgomerians were "most woefully behind as regards manufactures." A year later, shortly before Pratt's death, the *Journal* was still complaining that Montgomery had no mills. "Let us cease to be practical hewers of wood and drawers of water for other sections," urged the Republican *Journal*. "Let us make our own bread, and manufacture our own cotton, and grow rich. Let Montgomery have at least one cotton factory."[45]

Montgomery did exert itself to help get the South and North Alabama Railroad completed, but ironically, this accomplishment did not help

44. (Montgomery) *Alabama State Journal*, 15 November, 8 December 1871; *Montgomery Daily Advertiser*, 27 November 1869. The Democratic *Advertiser and Mail* agreed with the *Journal* that Montgomery needed a cotton mill, declaring in its November 12, 1871 issue: "We hail this movement [to establish a cotton mill at Montgomery] as one of the most auspicious character. It is just what Montgomery needs."

45. (Montgomery) *Alabama State Journal*, 6 April 1872, 1, 2 May 1873. The Democratic *Montgomery Daily Advertiser and Mail* continued to echo the *Journal* on the need for a cotton mill. See the issues of 16 January, 10, 13, 17 February, 3 May 1872.

Prattville, for the simple reason that the railroad bypassed Pratt's "lovely village." The failure to attain the South and North—or even a branch line—likely proved the most galling failure of Pratt's long career. It was also a costly failure, for Prattville did not finally get a railroad until the 1890s, more than twenty years after Pratt's death.

The South and North Alabama Railroad was to run from Montgomery to Decatur, crossing the Alabama and Chattanooga Railroad near Elyton (the future site of Birmingham). Pratt greatly wanted this road built—both because he believed it would unlock northern Alabama's mineral resources and because he hoped to get it routed through Prattville—and he invested both his time and his money in the project. Pratt held a large block of shares in the railroad company from its inception, and by 1868, at least, he sat on the board of directors, along with railroad men Frank Gilmer and Charles Pollard, banker Josiah Morris, and cotton broker Meyer Lehman of Lehman, Durr, and Company.[46]

Montgomery wanted this railroad as much as Pratt did. Yet Jonathan Wiener, in his well-known interpretation of Alabama politics and society in the postwar period, concludes that Montgomery planters, fearing the rise of a great industrial city like Birmingham and indifferent even to developing the mineral region, plotted to reroute the road so that it would become a mere feeder line of the Alabama and Chattanooga. The planters' plan, according to Wiener, was to transport the iron ore mined at Birmingham for manufacture outside the state. Planters, in short, conspired to strangle an infant Birmingham in its mountain crib.[47]

The primary evidence does not sustain Wiener's "planter conspiracy" theory. Montgomery newspapers, Democratic and Republican alike, sang the same tune in regard to industrial development. Editors uniformly advocated building cotton mills, and they were dazzled by northern Alabama's mineral wealth. Nor were they anti-Birmingham. Even the *Montgomery Advertiser,* a Democratic paper that Wiener claims was "consistently a leading spokesman for planter interests," continually ran articles that easily could have been penned by Henry Grady, the great New South spokesman. Concerning Elyton, the town that would soon be absorbed into Birmingham, the *Advertiser* grandly predicted that it would become "a great railroad center" and "the manufacturing emporium of the South." One would have thought that newspapers of this

46. (Montgomery) *Alabama State Journal,* 12 February 1868.
47. Wiener, *Social Origins,* 162–68.

proindustry mentality would have exposed a plot of the sort envisioned by Wiener, but they did not.[48]

Wiener's support comes from one source only: journalist Ethel Armes's *The Story of Coal and Iron in Alabama,* a book published in 1910 under the auspices of the Birmingham Chamber of Commerce. Throughout her book, Armes ceaselessly celebrates her visionary captains of industry and castigates the short-sighted planters who allegedly opposed them. It is a book shaded in black and white, with industrialist heroes on one side and planter villains on the other.[49]

Relying on the South and North's former engineer John Milner, Armes tells us that South and North president John Whiting supported the plot of John C. Stanton, president of the Alabama and Chattanooga Railroad, to make the South and North a mere feeder line to Stanton's road. Stanton, it seems, hoped to ship Alabama iron ore for processing in Chattanooga, where he had extensive business interests. According to Armes, Whiting, a cotton factor, cared nothing about developing northern Alabama industry: "Whiting . . . wanted what was good for cotton." Only his sudden death saved the South and North. Frank Gilmer collected enough proxy votes to win election as president, allowing him to rescue the line from the machinations of Stanton and the cotton men. Although the planters lost this fight, Wiener concludes they had made clear that "in taking over a key railroad, they were not entering the service of the new industrial order, but rather fighting in an effective way against it."[50]

The problem with Wiener's conclusion is that Armes's reconstruction of this episode is extremely suspect. For one thing, her facts are wrong. Whiting died in February 1869. Soon after his death, the stockholders of

48. Ibid., 163; *Montgomery Daily Advertiser,* 26 September 1869. Especially striking is an article from the *Montgomery Mail* (another Democratic paper) demanding that the Alabama legislature appropriate money for a new geological survey of northern Alabama. The *Mail* thought that a "reliable record of these matters should be speedily made, and lodged at the capital for reference, so that capitalists may have data on which they can act, and so that the knowledge may induce capital to flow into the state." *Montgomery Mail,* 13 December 1870.

49. Historian W. David Lewis, noting that "most scholars" have followed Ethel Armes on the subject of the South and North Alabama Railroad and Birmingham, has concluded: "Few topics in Alabama history merit closer reexamination." Lewis, *Sloss Furnaces,* 52. Lewis himself relies largely on Armes, however, as does Wayne Cline, *Alabama Railroads* (Tuscaloosa: University of Alabama Press, 1997), 97–99.

50. Armes, *Story of Coal and Iron,* 216–17; Wiener, *Social Origins,* 166–17.

the South and North—among them Daniel Pratt—unanimously elected as the new president former state governor Robert Patton. Dissatisfied with Patton's performance, a majority of the stockholders replaced him with Frank Gilmer in November. Armes, however, mistakenly states that Gilmer was elected a week after Whiting's death. Nor does she give a hint that Patton served as president of the line for ten months.[51]

Furthermore, Armes's characterization—derived from Milner's recollections—of Whiting as a Montgomery cotton man unconcerned with economic diversification is contradicted by contemporary evidence. First, Whiting belonged not only to the board of directors of the South and North, but also to the board of managers of Pratt's cotton mill. Was he merely a planter "mole" in PMC, or was he someone genuinely interested in Alabama's industrial development? The latter seems a more reasonable conclusion. Wiener assumes that because Whiting was a cotton broker, he must have been "a member of the planter establishment," but this assumption is faulty. After all, cotton brokers were businessmen. The Lehman brothers were Montgomery cotton brokers like Whiting, but that occupation did not prevent *them* from investing heavily in Alabama industry after the war.[52]

Second, John Whiting was held in high esteem by Montgomerians promoting Alabama industrialization. The Republican *Journal* declared emphatically that in losing Whiting, Montgomery had lost her "most gifted son." Most significantly, the *Mail,* a fervently pro-Gilmer Democratic paper, asserted that it had been Whiting (with Milner's help?) who had warded off Stanton's advances against the South and North: "Mr. Whiting . . . secured the last needed legislation by which the whole line from Decatur to Montgomery became a unit, rejected a proposition made by Mr. Stanton and others to build the road (under which Messrs. Stanton & Co. would have built the road out of the money of the company and then owned it) and was about placing the road under contract when his untimely death threw the company into the hands of ex-Gov. Patton."[53]

51. *Montgomery Daily Mail,* 16 February, 28 November 1869; Armes, *Story of Coal and Iron,* 217.

52. *Prattville Southern Signal,* 23 May 1878; Wiener, *Social Origins,* 166. The progressive Whiting also served as a member of the board of managers of the Alabama Bible Society. *Montgomery Daily Mail,* 6 April 1869.

53. (Montgomery) *Alabama State Journal,* 10 February 1869; *Montgomery Daily Mail,* 30 December 1869. Wiener cites the *Journal* for pointing out, "in a brilliantly concise para-

Perhaps Armes confused Whiting with Patton, yet it seems inconceivable that Patton, a man whose economic and political views mirrored Daniel Pratt's, would have suddenly transformed himself into a reactionary planter puppet in 1869. Indeed, Patton was supported as director of the South and North by both the Democratic *Montgomery Advertiser* and the (Montgomery) *Alabama State Journal,* the Republican state organ. Even if the *Advertiser* was in on the supposed planter conspiracy, it is extremely doubtful that the *Journal* would have been so as well. It is true that the hyper-Whiggish *Montgomery Mail* remained hostile to Patton throughout his tenure as director. But the hostility of the *Mail* evidently stemmed from the perception that the ex-governor, as a Tennessee Valley man, would not look after Montgomery's interests. In April, the *Mail* accused Patton of negotiating a contract, rejected by the director, that would have taken the railroad out of the control of Montgomery and the original stockholders and placed it into the hands of a team of building contractors from other cities. The *Mail* angrily dismissed the contract as "a deed of gift . . . to citizens of Nashville, Florence, Decatur, Memphis and Selma." Only the determined opposition of Frank Gilmer, the *Mail* declared, saved the day for Montgomery. Patton's supporters denied the charges the *Mail* made, essentially accusing the paper of attacking Patton because the ex-governor was too moderate on racial issues. Whatever the truth of the matter, nowhere in this debate does anyone charge Patton with trying to undermine the South and North Railroad itself. That the road would run from Montgomery to Decatur seems to have been accepted by all factions as a certain—not to mention desirable—outcome.[54]

Seen in this light, Frank Gilmer's ascendancy to the directorship of the

---

graph," that "the prebourgeois planter class was the obstacle to Alabama's industrial development." Wiener, *Social Origins,* 161. If that is so, the *Journal*'s praise of Whiting is compelling evidence that the Republican paper did not, as Wiener does, view Whiting as "a member of the planter establishment."

54. *Montgomery Daily Mail,* 15, 22 April 1869; (Montgomery) *Alabama State Journal,* 15 April, 8 May 1869; *Montgomery Daily Advertiser,* 28, 30 November, 2 December 1869. In a temperate letter sent by one "Citizen" to the *Advertiser* during the uproar over Patton's ouster in November, the writer insisted that Patton's defenders made a mistake in construing the enthusiasm of Montgomerians for Gilmer as arising from "personal antagonism" to the ex-governor. On the contrary, Patton was "highly appreciated around the Capitol." Yet even a blind man would have to admit that it was only natural for the city to want "a home man" to have charge of a vital concern like the South and North Alabama Railroad. *Montgomery Daily Advertiser,* 1 December 1869.

South and North simply represented the victory of one group of industrial boosters over another. When Montgomery mayor Thomas Glascock, who controlled the city's proxy votes, switched allegiance from Patton to Gilmer, the ex-governor's fate was sealed. Falling with his friend Patton was Daniel Pratt himself, who lost his seat on the board.[55] Ironically, Gilmer's victory, portrayed by Armes and Wiener as the triumph of industrialists over planters, resulted in the removal from the board of the state's most renowned industrialist.

With Montgomerians aspiring to complete the South and North Railroad, not conspiring to undermine it, the line made real progress. Builders finally completed the road in September 1872.[56] In the process, however, the line bypassed Prattville, running about eight miles east of the town. Now that Pratt and his ally Patton were out of the way, Frank Gilmer and the new board apparently decided to complete the long-delayed project as quickly as possible by laying track over the most direct route to Birmingham.

Abandoned by Gilmer and his associates, Pratt attempted to get a branch line built from Prattville to the South and North or another trunk line. In December 1871, the town's most prominent citizens, Democrats and Republicans alike, met at the new county courthouse to discuss the railroad matter. Among the attendees were Democratic attorneys William H. Northington and Henry J. Livingston, Republican planter and former attorney John L. Alexander, Republican merchant Samuel S. Booth, Democratic merchant James M. Smith, Autauga's carpetbagger state senator James Farden, and Democrats Daniel Pratt and Edward Wingate. James Smith chaired the meeting, while Wingate, Pratt's bookkeeper, acted as secretary. Both Daniel Pratt and James Farden made speeches. According to Wingate's minutes, Pratt discussed ("in his usual clear, forcible and practical manner") the various routes proposed for the railroad. Pratt argued ("with great force and plausibility") that the line should run from the South and North through Prattville to some point on the Selma, Marion, and Memphis, a road being built from Selma to Memphis under the leadership of the company's president, Nathan Bedford Forrest. Pratt "demonstrated clearly that when this line was completed it would be the cheapest and most direct route from Memphis to Brunswick [Georgia]." The assembly then chose a five-man correspon-

55. *Montgomery Daily Advertiser*, 28 November 1869.
56. Cline, *Alabama Railroads*, 105.

dence committee "to communicate with the president and directors of the South and North railroad, and write Gen. Forrest, the citizens of Montgomery, and others" about building the Prattville Railroad. Pratt, Farden, Northington, Livingston, and Alexander made up the committee.[57]

The committee reported to a large crowd assembled at the courthouse on December 30. Samuel Parrish Smith chaired the meeting, with William Howell acting as secretary. After preliminary remarks from Daniel Pratt and others (which evidently indicated that the overture to Forrest had failed), William H. Northington offered a resolution that Prattville raise the money for a branch road to the South and North by imposing a direct tax. Northington, Daniel Pratt, Charles Doster, James Hazen, Samuel S. Booth, George Smith, and James Farden, among others, made speeches in favor of the resolution, which the assembly unanimously adopted. Two committees were then appointed: one to petition the legislature to authorize the Prattville town council to levy a special railroad tax and to raise the money necessary to build the branch railroad, and the other to solicit Montgomery's Board of Trade for aid in building the road.[58] Northington, Doster, and George Smith sat on the first committee, while Booth, Farden, and Merrill Pratt sat on the other.

The (Montgomery) *Alabama State Journal* applauded the efforts of its "Autauga friends" and asserted that "Montgomery is deeply interested in the proposed railroad to Prattville." The paper declared that the people of Prattville, who were "progressive, liberal and energetic," would surely succeed in corralling "the iron horse," but it also urged "enterprising and energetic Montgomery" to "lend a helping hand to industrious and manufacturing Prattville." Both locations would benefit from the branch line. "Let us unite the two cities in bonds of iron," urged the *Journal,* "and each will grow and improve as long as the *ties* last." For its part, the Democratic *Advertiser and Mail* wished the project "the greatest possible success."[59]

In February, Senator Farden succeeded in getting a railroad bill passed by the senate, allowing the Prattville town council to impose a direct tax to raise money for the branch line. Confident Prattvillians put forty carts and one hundred hands to work grading the road and made substantial

57. (Prattville) *Autauga Citizen,* 9 March 1871; (Montgomery) *Alabama State Journal,* 12 December 1871.
58. (Montgomery) *Alabama State Journal,* 6 January 1872.
59. Ibid.; *Montgomery Daily Advertiser and Mail,* 10 January 1872.

stock subscriptions to the company. A surviving list shows that the total value of Prattville railroad stock subscriptions in 1872 amounted to $125,400. Of this amount, $50,000 came from the town of Prattville, while another $50,000 came from Daniel Pratt ($10,000) and his heirs Merrill Pratt ($20,000) and Henry DeBardeleben ($20,000). The city of Montgomery subscribed $7,000, and both Moore, Simpson, and Company (of the Indian Hill textile factory) and F. E. Smith and Company subscribed $3,000. The wealthy Republican planter-attorney Charles Doster subscribed $1,500. Both Daniel Pratt and Company and S. S. Booth and Company committed $1,000, as did Edward Wingate, William H. Northington, James Hazen, and A. K. McWilliams. Three prominent Republican politicians, John L. Alexander, W. G. M. Golson, and Daniel Booth, each committed $500, as did physician Samuel Parrish Smith and druggist Joseph Hurd. Nine individuals subscribed $200: Republican officeholders William Boon and James Booth, mechanic Lafayette Ellis, blacksmith John Royals, mill superintendent Joseph Kent, editor William Howell, attorney Gustavus Northington, and longtime resident Llewellyn Spigner. Six individuals subscribed to $100 worth of stock, most notably Charles Atwood. Altogether, twenty-five men (excluding the Pratts and DeBardeleben) had committed a total of $10,400 to the project.[60]

Despite this substantial commitment of financial resources, the project failed. In April, the *Advertiser and Mail* asserted that only $15,000 stood between Prattville and a connection to the South and North Alabama Railroad. In May, however, the *Journal* demanded testily, "What has become of the Prattville railroad?" Two reasons may explain the collapse of the railroad project. First, Montgomery capitalists were likely not as forthcoming as boosters had hoped. A projected railroad from Montgomery southeast to the town of Troy in Pike County competed for investors' attention, and in any event, heavy "pressure upon the money market" in 1872 dampened enthusiasm for all such ventures. Second, and probably more important, Daniel Pratt was engaged at this time in a takeover of the Red Mountain Iron and Coal Company, and he may have found himself short of capital to pursue both projects. Whatever the exact reasons, however, the failure to get the railroad built in 1872 had serious consequences. The panic of 1873 and the long-lasting depression

60. (Montgomery) *Alabama State Journal,* 16 February 1872; Subscription list to the Prattville Rail Road, CECP.

that followed—not to mention Pratt's death in May 1873—further undermined attempts to construct the road in the 1870s. Prattville did not finally win its cherished railroad until 1895.[61]

The Reconstruction years, then, were for Pratt a time of both economic triumphs and failures. He had revived his businesses; another mill had started in the Prattville vicinity; and Prattville itself continued to bustle with busy mechanics and merchants. Yet Pratt had not achieved his goal of twenty years, getting a railroad routed through Prattville, nor had he been able to entice Montgomery capitalists to invest in another mill. Though Pratt was surely disappointed with some of his failures in the economic arena, he likely took some solace in Prattville's rapid return to its antebellum condition as a town of "good morals and good society." In at least one respect, the Civil War actually had fostered middle-class associational activity by prompting Prattville's white women to form the ladies aid society. After the war, ladies continued to gather in groups to promote charitable projects.

History was made in Prattville in May 1866 when some of the town's middle-class women held a public meeting and had the minutes published in the *Citizen.* The subject of their concern, not surprisingly, had to do with the late conflict: the raising of funds for the relief of destitute Autauga County war widows and orphans. The Prattville ladies voted to give a concert tableaux and supper to raise funds, appointing one committee to obtain rooms for the purpose and another to decorate them. Designating the women's goal "a most noble one," William Howell urged Prattvillians to "respond liberally." A week later, at the Methodist Sunday-school room, the Prattville ladies gave two performances, "consisting of music, charades, tableaux, etc." The *Citizen* reported that "a considerable amount [of money] was taken in" and urged the ladies to continue their philanthropic activities. The ladies did just that, holding a concert tableaux at the Methodist Sunday-school room in July 1867 to raise money to enclose the Prattville cemetery with "a neat and durable fence."[62]

Many of the women at the May meeting belonged to the Presbyterian Church. The popular Presbyterian minister James Hazen played at this time the leading role in establishing the Presbyterian Orphans Home at

61. *Montgomery Daily Advertiser and Mail,* 21 April, 15 May, 13 October 1872; (Montgomery) *Alabama State Journal,* 16 May 1872.

62. (Prattville) *Autauga Citizen,* 10, 17 May 1866, 11 July 1867.

Tuskegee, Alabama; and women of his congregation worked hard to raise money for the home through charity suppers, bazaars, and concerts. They also knitted and sewed clothes for the children and personally contributed money when they could.[63]

The home was established in 1868 by the Presbyterian Synod of Alabama. The Reverend Hazen served as chairman of the board of trustees. Admission preference went to the indigent orphans of Confederate soldiers, but other orphaned poor were accepted as well. The goal of the home was not merely to give food and shelter to orphans, but also to provide them with instruction preparing "them for places of service, trade or still higher education, as the case may demand," that they might "become . . . worthy and useful members of society." Hazen and the other trustees, including the much-maligned John Whiting, encouraged ladies aid societies around Alabama to send money or "articles of any kind" for the benefit of children, and the ladies responded to his pleas, sending gifts from such locations as Hayneville, Greenville, Talladega, Wetumpka, Lafayette, Selma, Montgomery, Tuskegee, Marion, and, of course, Prattville. In December 1869, Prattville women sent a package of Christmas presents to the orphans.[64]

One of the more elaborate functions staged by the Prattville ladies for the orphans' home was a benefit concert held at the Methodist Sabbath-school room on June 12, 1868. Among the performers was Sidney Lanier, principal of Prattville Academy in the 1867–1868 term. Lanier played solo flute on two pieces he had written, as well as on Strokoschi's "Magic Bell Fantasie," while Prattville's Quartette Club sang pieces by composers Bellini, Rossini, and Labitzsky. The *Citizen* proclaimed the concert "a complete success."[65]

Not all the associational activity of Prattville women was strictly charitable, however. Ladies also participated in the town's new thespian society, the Prattville Amateurs. This active group performed such works as *Lady of Lyons*, an adaptation of Edward Bulwer-Lytton's novel, and *Ten Nights in a Bar Room,* the extremely popular temperance play. The performances of the Prattville amateurs won considerable local acclaim.

63. Graham, *First Presbyterian Church,* 15–17.

64. *Montgomery Daily Mail,* 16 June 1868, 27 April, 21 December 1869; *Montgomery Advertiser,* 15, 17 May 1868, 18 November 1870.

65. Concert for the Orphans, Prattville, June 12, 1868, Program, Charles D. Lanier Collection, Johns Hopkins University, Baltimore, Md.; *Montgomery Daily Mail,* 29 June 1868, reprinted from the (Prattville) *Autauga Citizen.*

Thomas Hill Watts, a former state governor and attorney general of the Confederacy, and James Holt Clanton, chairman of the Democratic Party, attended the performance of *Lady of Lyons.* A Montgomery newspaper critic who also was present concluded that "there was indeed decided dramatic talent and taste even in the proverbially practical little town of Prattville."[66]

Two Prattville organizations that went into eclipse during the Civil War, the Fire Engine Company and the Bible Society, reemerged after the war ended. In December 1866, the company's members held their first supper since 1860. Oysters, turkey, and roast pig were served, followed by fruit and wine. The attendees, including Daniel Pratt, Shadrack Mims, Samuel Parrish Smith, and a host of Prattville's most prominent men, drank some twenty toasts, Pratt and Mims apparently relaxing their stern standards of sobriety on this occasion (perhaps Mims drank water). William Allen, the toastmaster, tipped his glass to Andrew Johnson, at the moment battling Radical Republicans in Congress, and Henry J. Livingston toasted "Jefferson Davis, who in chains and suffering has become doubly endeared to the South." These political pieties aside, the group got down to the business of lauding their progressive town and its industrious people. Pratt toasted Prattville Manufacturing Company, while Mims drank to the Indian Hill textile factory. William H. Northington, once Autauga's leading Yanceyite, delivered a tribute to southern manufacturing: "The Industrial Resources of the South—Crippled but not destroyed." Also receiving toasts were Prattville's mechanics, merchants, physicians, attorneys, and, naturally, the fire engine—"the great squirt of Prattville."[67]

The Prattville Bible Society did not, of course, sponsor such festivities as the engine company bacchanalia, but, like the engine company, it reactivated in 1866. In January of that year, an agent of the American Bible Society came to Prattville and reorganized the local group, giving it responsibility for distributing Bibles in Autauga and Bibb Counties. Methodist minister A. J. Briggs served as president, Presbyterian minister James Hazen as vice-president, merchant James M. Smith as secretary,

66. *Montgomery Daily Advertiser and Mail,* 14 April 1871.

67. (Prattville) *Autauga Citizen,* 6 December 1866. In 1870, the PMC pickery, a four-story building located next to the cotton mill, caught fire. Although the Fire Engine Company was unable to save the structure, it did prevent the conflagration from spreading. *Montgomery Daily Advertiser,* 23, 29 October 1870.

and physician Samuel Parrish Smith as treasurer. Daniel Pratt, Ferdinand Smith, Shadrack Mims, merchants Samuel S. Booth and A. K. McWilliams, physician Charles Edwards, dentist William Bush, and two other men sat on the board of managers. Upon reorganizing, the society ordered $800 worth of Bibles, which it planned to sell at cost to those who could afford to pay and to give to those who could not. In April, "a fine assortment of Bibles, of all sizes and descriptions" arrived in Prattville.[68]

Prattvillians continued to promote their churches and schools as well. In 1866, citizens attempted to erect a separate male academy building and convert the existing structure into a female academy, but the project collapsed. Citizens had raised $3,000 by July, but this amount was not nearly enough to pay construction costs. Prattville was fortunate, however, that it at least had completed the impressive original structure in 1861 (at a cost of nearly $10,000), before the war halted such projects. Poet Sidney Lanier, who lived in Montgomery after the Civil War and successfully applied for the post of principal of Prattville Academy in 1867, was certainly impressed with the building and its furnishings, describing them in a letter to his fiancée as "the best I have ever seen." Prattville itself he found "a fine manufacturing village."[69]

Once the academy's board of trustees chose Lanier for principal on August 28, he started his job confidently, hiring two assistants, Nick Williams of Meriwether County, Georgia, and Augusta Pratt Morgan, Merrill Pratt's sister. He reported that he found Mrs. Morgan "a fine woman," and he predicted that he would "like her extremely." He contracted to pay her $800 a year to head the primary department. Twenty-one-year-old Nick Williams, who had taken honors at Erskine College, South Carolina, taught French, Italian, and Spanish. Lanier found him "a man of progressive ideas, good-looking, highly compatible, and ready for work." In addition to running the academy, the busy Lanier taught piano

68. Montgomery Daily Advertiser, 11 January, 19 April 1866.

69. *Montgomery Daily Advertiser,* 19 July 1866; Sidney Lanier, *Letters, 1857–1868,* ed. by Charles R. Anderson and Aubrey H. Starke, vol. 7, *The Centennial Edition of the Works of Sidney Lanier* (Baltimore, Md.: John Hopkins University Press, 1945), 308–9. Among the contributors to the school fund were William Fay's widow, Eliza ($100), A. K. McWilliams ($200), William Howell ($100), Merrill Pratt ($100), James Wainwright ($100), Samuel S. Booth ($300), Ferdinand Smith ($50), Frank Smith ($50), and William Root ($50). The trustees themselves subscribed $1,800. (Prattville) *Autauga Citizen,* 19 July 1866.

to "five music-scholars," played organ at the Presbyterian church, and arranged charity concerts and debates for the Prattville Debating Society.[70]

The president of the board (probably Pratt) informed Lanier that he could "expect 150 scholars at an average tuition of 50 Dollars a year," but the estimate proved overly optimistic. Attendance peaked in November at "nearly ninety" boys and girls. Lanier diagnosed the difficulty as "the terrible depression of the country people" and "the recent poor price of cotton." He hoped the spring would be better, but his hope proved a forlorn one. In January 1868, he wrote despondently: "My school is smaller than last year. The people come to me almost with tears in their eyes, and represent their fearful impoverishment which prevents them from sending their children to school." Lanier had only sixty-five students. By March, "about 50 scholars" remained, and he was forced to let Williams go. In April, Lanier complained, Augusta Morgan abruptly decided to quit and visit relatives in the North. Lanier worried that he would not be able to collect enough from his pupils' parents to enable him to meet his indebtedness to her. Pleading ill health, Lanier resigned in May. He owed the academy trustees money but left Prattville on amicable terms with his employers, who recognized the difficult situation into which they had placed him. As his replacement, the trustees hired Lanier's former assistant, Nick Williams, who remained principal of the academy through at least 1870. Apparently, the situation improved, for a *Journal* correspondent claimed in October 1871 that Prattville's schools were "flourishing."[71]

While Prattville schools did not progress in the 1860s as Pratt would have desired, the churches remained strong during the postwar years. In

70. Lanier, *Letters*, 313, 316, 334–35, 339, 343, 345. Lanier, however, found intellectual life in Prattville not up to his standard, writing his fiancée, "I find no soul to whom I can talk our talk. I suspect that, besides Mr. Hazen, thou and I will be alone." Ibid., 338. Perhaps Lanier was disappointed with the local reception to his novel *Tiger Lilies*. Writing his daughter Mary, who was away at a school in Germany, Samuel Parrish Smith commented: "We are to have for principal of our Academy next year a young man by the name of Lanier. . . . He came recommended very highly as a scholar and polished gentleman. He is also an author, having recently published a book of fiction called 'The Tiger Lilly.' I don't fancy the title much. I have not seen it and therefore cannot speak of its merits or demerits." Samuel Parrish Smith to Mary Smith, 30 August 1867, Box 96, McMillan Collection.

71. Lanier, *Letters*, 309, 349, 359, 378, 381, 383–84, 387, 389–90; U.S. Census, Alabama, 1870 Population Schedule, Autauga County; (Montgomery) *Alabama State Journal*, 31 October 1871.

1870, the Prattville Presbyterian church enjoyed a membership of about 87 individuals, an increase from 1860, while the Methodist church probably had more than 200 members. After the war, the Union Sunday School broke apart, but each denomination—Baptist, Methodist, and Presbyterian—began conducting its own school. The Methodists retained Pratt's splendid Sabbath-school room. (On freedmen education and religion, see chapter 10.)[72]

Both mechanics and mill operatives continued to join Prattville's churches in the 1860s, but the two groups seem to have again divided by sex. Young men joining a church, such as William Griswold (one of Samuel Griswold's grandsons), Henry Jones, and John Tunnell, tended to be mechanics, though some mill operatives, such as Henry Hall and William Pullen, did so as well. Most of the mill people who became church members, however, were women. There appear to be more cases after the Civil War where church membership in individual households turned on the question of gender. Sarah Welden, Nancy Skaggs, and Frances Buckner all joined the Methodist church, for example, but their husbands did not. To cite another case, Caroline Hall and her daughters Ellen and Lula all belonged to the Methodist church, but only one of her three sons did. In fact, in only one mill family is it certain that both husband and wife joined a church. In March 1865, A. J. Weatherly and his spouse, Mary, joined the Presbyterian church, Mary by letter and her husband by exam. Although he was about sixty-two when he found religion, Weatherly quickly became a prominent figure in the congregation, serving as one of two deacons from January 7, 1866, until his death on November 30, 1868. Weatherly's sudden commitment to church is striking, but he seems to have been rather exceptional among mill men. The typical mill person belonging to a Prattville church appears to have been a woman, like thirty-six-year-old Frances Gentry, a widow with all six of her children working in the cotton mill, or a girl, like fourteen-year-old mill operative Calista Jones, who followed her mother, Isabella, and sister, Ida, into the Methodist church in 1873. Thus, while Prattville churches did reach a portion of the mill community during Reconstruction, as in the antebellum period, they certainly did not touch everyone, particularly the men.[73]

72. Church Register; Hazen, *Manual of the Presbyterian Church*, 4–8, 10; Stone, *Prattville Baptist Church*, 29.

73. This information is derived from the Methodist Church Register, Hazen's *Manual* (Presbyterian), and the U.S. Census. Baptist records apparently have not survived. Surely many families belonged to the Baptist Church.

Prattville's economic and social institutions admittedly had both ups and downs in the postwar years, but the public reputation of the man who founded the town only climbed during Reconstruction. Both Democrats and Republicans lauded Pratt and his economic vision. In the last years of his life, Pratt became more involved in Alabama politics than ever before. He also launched his final, most ambitious project, the rekindling of Oxmoor furnaces.

10

BUILDING A NEW SOUTH: 1865–1873

After the Civil War, Daniel Pratt, who had warned against secession and urged the South to accelerate its pace of industrialization, seemed, like his biblical namesake, a powerful prophet. He became not only a confidant of Governor Robert Patton—like Pratt, a former Whig and passionate industrial booster—but an increasingly powerful political personage in his own right. Pratt's economic vision and his reputation for personal integrity made him, despite his infirmities, a serious contender for the Democratic gubernatorial nomination in 1870. Although he failed to receive the nomination, no one in the state of Alabama exceeded him in personal prestige during the postwar years. And while his death cut short his effort to propel the economic development of the state during Reconstruction, he lived to see the rekindling of one of the furnaces at Oxmoor and the beginning of the realization of his dream of building a great industrial city in Alabama's mineral belt. The nearly universal esteem in which Alabamians held Pratt at this time challenges the thesis that postwar Alabama was bitterly divided between reactionary planters and progressive industrialists. On the contrary, many Alabamians proved receptive to what former governor Andrew Barry Moore called the "spirit of ongoing change."[1]

Not surprisingly, the *Autauga Citizen* became one of Alabama's most enthusiastic advocates of southern industrialization. No longer did the *Citizen* hesitate to assert the primacy of the factory over the plantation. In a December 1866 editorial, "Manufacturing in Alabama," William Howell declared that the sun had gone down on Alabama agriculture: "The loss of slave labor has paralyzed our agricultural interests. The planter this year has been fortunate if he has not lost the little on which he commenced operations. . . . Another such season of failure and disaster to the farmer will involve with them in irremediable ruin our merchants and tradesmen. . . . The most sanguine among us feel that to depend upon free negro labor for another cotton crop is indeed to lean upon a broken reed." Howell added that planters fortunately had "an escape from the impending evils," namely "the establishment of manufactures of cotton and iron and . . . the development of our mineral resources." Manufactures, Howell noted, "have made sterile New England rich." He insisted they would do the same for Alabama, unless planters persisted "in futile efforts to regain their lost wealth by the cultivation of cotton." In another editorial from the same month, "Southern Manufactures," the *Citizen* challenged the notion that the people of the South "are not adapted to a manufacturing life." Manufacturers had met with success "in Georgia and other points prior to the War." Now, "in an age of revolution," southerners would "look steadily forward," not gaze "back mournfully upon the faded past."[2]

Newspapers in Alabama and across the South echoed Howell's views in the aftermath of the Civil War.[3] To many Alabamians, Daniel Pratt and Prattville revealed to the state the way of the future. Indeed, Pratt became such an important figure by 1870 that both Democrats and Republicans touted him as a possible candidate for governor. Many of Pratt's supporters hoped that a Governor Pratt would lead them into a promised land

1. Dan T. Carter, *When the War Was Over: The Failure of Self-Reconstruction in the South, 1865–1867* (Baton Rouge: Louisiana State University Press, 1985), 146. For Jonathan Wiener's view that an anti-industry planter elite that allegedly controlled Alabama politics in the antebellum period continued to do so into the 1890s, see his *Social Origins*.

2. (Prattville) *Autauga Citizen*, 13, 20 December 1866. See also (Prattville) *Autauga Citizen*, 17 January 1867.

3. See the perceptive analyses in chap. 4 of Carter's *When the War Was Over*, and Shore, *Southern Capitalists*, chaps. 4 to 7.

of renewed economic prosperity, based not on plantation agriculture, but on manufacturing and small farms.

Pratt did not actively seek any office during Reconstruction, with the exception of Prattville intendant, a position he held from 1866 to his death in 1873. When Prattville incorporated in 1865, elections were held for intendant, town council, town clerk, and town marshal. Pratt did not run that year, and merchant James M. Smith was chosen for Prattville's highest office. The following year, Pratt ran against the incumbent, defeating him by a vote of 59 to 5. Three Prattville mechanics, George Smith, Lafayette Ellis, and Nathan Morris, won places on the town council, as did the staunchly Democratic former postmaster, old Benjamin Durden, and the *Citizen*'s editor, William Howell. Pratt won reelection every year until his death in 1873. A surviving list of polled votes from the 1869 election reveals that Pratt received 101 of 104 votes cast. At least twenty-four freedmen voted in the election, including gin mechanics Charles Atwood, Richard Pratt, and William Squires; foundry worker Anthony Thomas; mill worker Gabriel Washington; blacksmith Charles Abbot; and AME minister George Snowden. Other voters included mill men Simon Welden, Thomas Hale, A. J. Simmons, James Fitzgerald, James Buckner, G. W. Golden, Thaddeus Hoyle, Marion Stewart, and Joseph Kent. The names of numerous mechanics also appear on the list.[4]

The greatest concern of Pratt and his council appears to have been maintaining public order. Friction between whites and newly enfranchised blacks threatened to ignite into conflict in the late 1860s. Fearing a freedmen crime wave, the previous council already had erected a brick guardhouse in January 1866. In the summer of 1867, the council passed two ordinances, one prohibiting the carrying of concealed weapons and the other protecting citizens engaged in holding public meetings. The council hoped that both these measures would help forestall violence during the fall election over whether to hold a constitutional convention. Whether the ordinances had any effect is not clear, but the election occurred without incident. Those men participating in the fall election— most whites had abstained—voted overwhelmingly in favor of holding the constitutional convention. Voters also chose an almost completely

4. (Prattville) *Autauga Citizen*, 5 October 1865, 6 September 1866; List of votes polled for the Town of Prattville, 28 September 1869, CECP. In the 1869 election, voters returned George Smith and Lafayette Ellis to the council, while also electing three new members: Samuel Parrish Smith, planter Stephen Pearce, and butcher William Morgan. Merrill Pratt succeeded his uncle as intendant in 1873. Tarrant, ed., *Hon. Daniel Pratt*, 96.

Republican delegation to attend the gathering, held in November and December. The convention produced a constitution enfranchising black males and disenfranchising some whites. Democrats balked at these provisions. The ratification election was set for early February 1868, which made January a tense month. Whites hoped that by boycotting the election they could defeat the constitution, since ratification hinged upon the support of a majority of registered voters.[5]

In Autauga, most blacks favored the constitution, while most whites opposed it. Autauga's most prominent white Republican, Charles Doster, defected to the Democrats over the issue of white disenfranchisement. In December, fifty-one whites and nine blacks formed the Prattville Conservative Club, which had as its aim the defeat of the constitution. Among the whites joining the club were Daniel Pratt, Charles Doster, Samuel Parrish Smith, William H. Northington, George Smith, Enoch Robinson, and Shadrack Mims—a constellation of Prattville's professionals, merchants, and shop owners. Among the much smaller number of blacks joining were foundry worker Anthony Thomas and gin mechanic William Squires.[6]

Pratt joined the Prattville Conservative Club because he fiercely objected to the proposed state constitution, believing that if Alabama fell under the control of newly freed slaves, poor white "scalawags," and northern "carpetbaggers," economic catastrophe would result. In Pratt's view, the prospects for his adopted state after the war looked promising until Radical Republicans overturned Presidential Reconstruction. Robert Patton, an industry booster and former Whig, was the kind of man Pratt had always hoped would become governor, but the Republicans would turn him out of office if they took control.[7]

The depths of Pratt's feelings on this subject are clearly evident in two letters he wrote in 1867. The first he sent to Robert Patton in August.

5. (Prattville) *Autauga Citizen*, 11 January 1866, 13 June, 4 July 1867; Sarah Woolfolk Wiggins, *The Scalawag in Alabama Politics, 1865–1881* (Tuscaloosa: University of Alabama Press, 1977), 18–38. In its zeal to maintain public order, Prattville's town council went so far as to ban slingshots in 1872. *Montgomery Daily Advertiser and Mail*, 13 March 1872.

6. *Montgomery Daily Mail*, 21 November, 15 December 1867; (Prattville) *Autauga Citizen*, 12 December 1867. Alabama Democrats frequently referred to themselves during Reconstruction as Democratic-Conservatives, reflecting the fact that many former Whigs belonged to the party as well.

7. On the governorship of Patton, see Carter, *When the War Was Over*, 45–47, 258–59; Wiggins, *Scalawag*, 13–17.

The ostensible reason for writing it was Sidney Lanier, whom Patton had recommended for the post of principal of Prattville Academy. "Your letter by Mr. Lanier has ben handed me. I am much pleased with the appearance of the young man. I will lay your letter before the Board. I rejoice to see that you feel so great an intrest in our little vilage." That pleasantry aside, Pratt launched into a remarkable five-page tirade against the Radical Republicans, whom he feared would destroy everything for which he had worked for the last thirty-five years.[8]

While Pratt had drawn much encouragement in 1865 and 1866 from President Johnson's lenient policy toward the South, the current ascendancy of the Radicals now plunged him into despair for his state. "I have always contended since I have known Alabama that no state had greater natural advantages and all that was necessary [to exploit them] was capital and enterprise," Pratt explained. Patton, he continued bitterly, was "making strong efforts to induce capital to come into our State," but his efforts were doomed to failure. "No inteligent capitalists are coming to Alabama with capital to invest unless they think there investments secure and how can [they] be secure under a Negro Government?" Pratt could only conclude that the Radical Republican Congress had been "mad" when it imposed black enfranchisement and partial white disenfranchisement on the South. "They ought to be confined to an insane Hospital," Pratt spat.[9]

That Pratt objected so strenuously to black suffrage is not surprising in light of his deeply ingrained conservatism. In his opinion, Alabama already had too many uneducated, unpropertied voters, such as those men of Chestnut Creek who drove pitchforks through his 1855 senatorial campaign. "It is a gloomy thought to me that our Law makers and the inteligance of our state are debared from participating in our publick af-

8. Daniel Pratt to Robert Patton, 2 August 1867, Governor Patton Papers. That Pratt's letter was hastily written in the white heat of anger is suggested by its poor spelling, quite the worst in a Pratt missive since the late 1840s.

9. Ibid. Pratt was not alone in making this argument. See, for example, the letter of an English capitalist quoted in the *Montgomery Daily Mail,* 5 November 1867: "To give the Negroes the rule of the State is to keep out white men, and drive away capital. . . . Europeans will not invest where ignorant Negroes rule, and where their legal rights may be decided by Negro judges and Negro juries." Eric Foner has noted that whatever their exact ideological persuasion, all postwar members of the Democratic-Conservative Party "viewed the overthrow of Republican rule as a prerequisite for pursuing their political and economic goals." Eric Foner, *Reconstruction: America's Unfinished Revolution, 1863–1877* (New York: Harper & Row, 1988), 424.

fairs and that it must be left to Negros and a few ignoramuses," he wrote Patton despondently.[10]

With "the infranchising of the Negro," Pratt thought that southern "distruction" was now "complete." Nothing could be expected from a Republican government but corruption and confiscatory taxes. Pratt preferred that the Republicans "take what I have now than to take everything I make by my hard labor anualy." He had no desire to keep fighting a fight he could not win. "No man feels a deeper interest in the welfare of Alabama than I do. No man would do more than I would (in proportion to my means) to promote that interest," he insisted. Yet now he saw no hope for the future: "I believe our doom is sealed."[11]

In December, Pratt sent an open letter to the state meeting of the Conservative Club at Montgomery. In this letter he repeated many of the same themes found in his August epistle, though his tone was less despondent and more combative, as befitted a public political event. The *Mail* reprinted his letter in its entirety, asserting that it would "carry great weight" with the people. Pratt, the *Mail* noted, was "a Northern man by birth," as well as "a Constitutional Union man." No other Alabamian had "done more to establish Southern manufactures and [to] develop the resources of the State." The town he had founded, Prattville, stood as "a lasting monument to his mechanical skill, indomitable energy, and good citizenship." This was a man, in short, whose views compelled respectful attention.[12]

Pratt addressed much of his missive to the question of political and social equality for freedmen. The industrialist asserted that blacks were not ready to claim either. Concerning social equality, Pratt wrote: "There are different grades of society. A man who works at ditching or plowing and hoeing in the field, or shoveling his jack plane, or working at the anvil, or making shoes, or tailoring, deserves just as much respect in his own sphere as those in high circles in life, but there is, and always will be, different grades who feel more at ease and at home amongst their own associates. Do any of our colored people feel that they, as a class, are on social equality with educated and enlightened citizens?" As for political equality, Pratt lectured his "colored friends" that Alabama "must be a white man's country and be governed by white men." If freedmen ig-

10. Daniel Pratt to Robert Patton, 2 August 1867, Governor Patton Papers.
11. Ibid.
12. *Montgomery Daily Mail*, 21 December 1867.

nored this admonition, their "race" would be "doomed." Whites would allow blacks the "privileges" due them, including the vote, as soon as they "qualified for it," but only if blacks accepted their proper place in Alabama society. "You must bear to their [whites'] counsels and improve yourselves and children by education, and raise yourselves in the community as every person white and black must do if they expect to be respected."[13]

Pratt asserted that northern carpetbaggers only wanted to use freedmen to obtain offices and their spoils. He recalled that during his travels the previous summer, he had fallen in "with a negro man from Philadelphia" who called himself Bishop Campbell. Pratt listened one day as Campbell lectured some freedmen. According to Pratt, Campbell warned the group not to expect better treatment in the North: "They could not labor there as mechanics, as they could not get employment; said he, . . . you must be a shoe-black, barber or hostler." Campbell advised the freedmen to stay close to their "old masters and mistresses," who would be their "best friends," given the chance.[14]

It may be that Pratt genuinely believed that blacks deserved the opportunity, as he put it, to raise themselves "in the community as every person white and black must do if they expect to be respected." His few surviving written records do not betray the extreme racial animus against blacks evinced by many southern whites during Reconstruction. Moreover, Pratt did make some efforts to help blacks raise themselves. Besides keeping many black mechanics in his employ, he provided the freedmen the old wooden Methodist church building to serve as both a church and a school, the school on the first floor and the church on the second. The building and its lot were valued at $1,500. In his 1873 eulogy to Pratt, Charles Doster (one of the church-school's trustees) effusively praised Pratt's gift: "The splendid schoolhouse and church of our colored people—so highly appreciated by them, their pride and their glory—and the lot on which they stand, were a free offering from him to them." Doster believed "that race should honor and revere his memory, because he was their friend, and did for them many acts of charity."[15]

13. Ibid.
14. Ibid.
15. Carter, *When the War Was Over*, chap. 5; U.S. Census, Alabama, 1870 Population Schedule, Autauga County; Mims, untitled ms.; Tarrant, ed., *Hon. Daniel Pratt*, 138. Charles Atwood also served as a trustee of the church school. In August 1867, Samuel Parrish Smith reported to his daughter Mary: "There is considerable excitement among the

If Pratt really believed that all white Alabamians had nothing but goodwill toward freedmen, however, he was uncharacteristically naive. In Prattville itself, the *Citizen,* a paper that followed its master, Charles Doster, in and out of the Republican Party several times, often displayed an uncharitable attitude toward blacks. For example, in February 1867, the *Citizen,* reflecting white bitterness over the imminent passage of the first of the Reconstruction Acts, lashed out at blacks by reprinting an article from the *Tuscaloosa Independent Monitor,* a Democratic paper edited by Ryland Randolph, one of Alabama's most inflammatory newspaper editors and a member of the Ku Klux Klan, in which Randolph called on Tuscaloosans to hire only white mechanics. "We are informed that some men will enquire of a white mechanic, what they would ask for their work, and then go to a negro, and contract with him for lower wages," reported an outraged Randolph. "The consequence of this course will be that all of our best white mechanics will leave us, as many have already done, and we will be left to the botch work of the darkie." Randolph insisted that "a white man cannot live upon what a negro can" and that customers therefore should not ask him to do so.[16] Howell's object in reprinting this article in the *Citizen* obviously could not have been to help blacks raise themselves, yet Pratt ignored such antiblack sentiments (while simultaneously hiring black mechanics at lower wages than many skilled whites apparently would work for). It seems fair to conclude that Pratt's overriding concern with the promotion of Alabama industry blinded him to the evils of slavery and racism. Blacks always remained peripheral to even his expansive economic and social vision.

Although there was obvious tension between Prattville's whites and blacks, apparently only one case of racial violence occurred in the town during Reconstruction. This event took place on January 11, 1868, during the campaign over the ratification of the state constitution. Versions of the event are provided by Hassan Allen, Sidney Lanier, and the Montgomery newspapers (There is a five-year gap in the *Autauga Citizen* between 1868 and 1872.). Allen, the brother of ruined merchant William Allen, wrote a two-page account of the affair the day after it took place.

Negroes about getting up a high school for their children. . . . They are having a meeting every week to make arrangements and to organize a system of education." Samuel Parrish Smith to Mary Smith, 30 August 1867, McMillan Collection. Three years later, the census revealed that more black than white children attended school in 1870.

16. (Prattville) *Autauga Citizen,* 21 February 1867, reprinted from the *Tuscaloosa Independent Monitor.*

Hassan Allen faulted the Republicans, who had held a rally for the constitution and their political ticket, which included state senate candidate James Farden, an Ohio carpetbagger. Allen admitted that heckling had occurred during the Republicans' speeches. Afterward, some freedmen retired to the livery stables of Republican W. G. M. Golson, returning with a whiskey jug from which they freely imbibed. When Charles Doster, who had recently defected to the Democrats, mounted the podium to respond to the Republicans, freedman Gabriel Robinson "commenced making a disturbance." Rebuffing efforts to quiet him, Robinson drew a concealed pistol (violating a town ordinance) and fired it into the air. Councilman George Smith thereupon ordered Robinson to surrender his weapon. Robinson refused, swearing "he would shoot anyone who came near him." Smith, procuring his own pistol, again ordered Robinson to "deliver up his arms," but the angry freedman again refused. At this point, Smith "rushed at [Robinson] & bore him down." According to Allen, "a general melee ensued."[17]

Several people were injured in the brawl, but no one died. Among the whites, Llewellyn Spigner "received a cut from a knife," painter George Simmons was shot in the face, Alph Hall, a visitor from Montgomery, was shot in the shoulder, and another man, probably wool mill operative Matthew Hale, was "shot in the hat." Among blacks, Robinson "was seriously cut & badly beaten about the head," house carpenter Dick Gardner was "wounded in the arm," and "Painter Bill" (probably William Beavers) was "severely cut and shot." Noting that the latter man was "an outspoken conservative," Allen speculated that "some negro wounded him." Prattville whites began gathering all the arms they could lay their hands on and "called out that all well disposed negroes, those that did not want a fight, had better leave the place *at once*." This threat finally "scattered" the freedmen.[18]

A Republican newspaper, the (Montgomery) *Alabama State Sentinel*, edited by Pratt's old supporter John Hardy, placed the blame for the riot squarely on the shoulders of "a parcel of rowdies and rebels" who attempted to disrupt the Republican speaking. Hardy declared ominously that "the rebels" had "commenced their plots of bringing on a war of the

17. Hassan Allen to William C. Allen, 12 January 1868, William C. Allen Papers, Southern Historical Collection.

18. Ibid. Sidney Lanier's account is substantially the same as Hassan Allen's, though with less detail and greater flair. See Lanier, *Letters*, 365. See also *Montgomery Daily Mail*, 12 January 1868; *Montgomery Daily Advertiser*, 14 January 1868.

races." According to Sidney Lanier, however, many in Prattville's white community feared that the *freedmen* wanted to start a racial conflagration. "I begin to entertain serious doubts of the safety of remaining out of the city [Montgomery]," Lanier wrote his father. "There are strong indications of much bad feeling between whites and blacks, especially those engaged in the late row at this place." Lanier had "fears, which are shared by Mr. Pratt and many citizens here, that some indiscretion of the more thoughtless of the whites may plunge us into bloodshed. The whites have no organization at all, and the affair would be a mere butchery." The day before Lanier penned his letter, one hundred Republicans, armed with rifles and shotguns for protection, met for another Prattville rally. Hardy reported that the group had "resolved that the outrage [at the previous meeting] should not be repeated, unless at a risk of a terrible retaliation on the guilty parties." Clearly, the Republicans had succeeded in throwing a scare into their Democratic opponents.[19]

After the unpleasantness of January, the two groups seem to have avoided any more outright violence in the town. Pratt remained staunchly opposed to the Republicans, becoming chairman of Autauga's "Conservative" party. He and other prominent Prattvillians, including Samuel Parrish Smith, Llewellyn Spigner, A. K. McWilliams, Shadrack Mims, Charles Doster, and John L. Alexander, were chosen as delegates to the state Democratic convention held in June 1868. At the state convention, attendees selected Pratt as an alternate delegate to the national Democratic convention. Yet Pratt and the other conservative business leaders in Prattville confined their opposition to Republicans to the political arena. The (Montgomery) *Alabama State Journal* was pleased to note in 1869, for example, that Pratt and several other prominent conservatives had attended a Republican meeting and listened to the speakers "with profound and respectful attention." For their part, Autauga's Republicans also apparently hoped to avoid trouble. Particularly after Charles Doster returned, the party took on a more conservative tone. By the early 1870s, Republicans, including Autauga's carpetbagger state senator, James Farden, worked closely with Democrats to promote such economic projects as the branch railroad. Indeed, by 1874, Shadrack Mims could write complacently: "I do not know of one single instance that has occurred since the war closed that would in the least savour of a

19. (Montgomery) *Alabama State Sentinel,* 13, 22 January 1868; Lanier, *Letters,* 372–73.

disposition on either side of the two political parties to hinder a free vote being polled. . . . Our elections have passed off quietly and satisfactorily to both parties, and this state of things would exist in the whole state if we had such radical white leaders as there are in this county."[20]

Both Democrats and Republicans agreed in 1870 that Pratt would make an excellent governor, and a serious "draft Pratt" movement started among the former group. Pratt had admittedly come into criticism from one Republican paper in 1867. In June of that year, former admirer John Hardy excoriated Pratt in the pages of the paper he edited, the (Montgomery) *Alabama State Sentinel*. Hardy noted angrily that Pratt had circulated an open letter "around rebel newspapers," in which he had expressed indignation that southern white men would become Republicans, allegedly "for the sake of office, popularity, or money-making." An offended Hardy denounced Pratt as a "most violent disunionist" who had "done as much or more for the rebellion of Jeff Davis, than almost any other man in Alabama." When William Howell challenged Hardy, countering that "Mr. Pratt was bitterly opposed to secession," Hardy refused to give ground, forcefully insisting that Pratt "went heartily into the rebellion with the vim characteristic of him and contributed his money and his influence unceasingly to dissolve the Union. His public record as a member of the legislature like his private conduct places him where we stated he was. Few men, too, in the late insurgent States invested as promptly and as liberally in Confederate and State bonds as Mr. Pratt."[21] Hardy's harsh words clearly reflect his astonishment that a fellow progressive Whig from the 1850s was now spurning Republicans and supporting their old nemeses, Democrats. His bruising rhetoric soon put him out of step with even his own party, however.

By 1870, the Republican attitude to Pratt had changed from one of

20. *Montgomery Daily Advertiser*, 6 May, 6 June 1868; (Montgomery) *Alabama State Journal*, 29 July 1869, 12 December 1871, 6, 9 January, 16 February 1872; Shadrack Mims to [?] [1874], Box 37, Special Collections Library, Auburn University. For a perceptive article on the closeness of some Reconstruction Democrats and Republicans on issues "of economic development, the promotion of community progress and even race," see Paul D. Escott, "Clinton Cilley, Yankee War Hero in the Postwar South: A Study in the Compatibility of Regional Values," *North Carolina Historical Review* 68 (October 1991): 404–26. Also see Michael Perman, *The Road to Redemption: Southern Politics, 1869–1879* (Chapel Hill: University of North Carolina Press, 1984).

21. (Montgomery) *Alabama State Sentinel*, 6, 15 July 1867; (Prattville) *Autauga Citizen*, 11 July 1867.

resentment to unstinting admiration. Pratt was, Republicans had come to realize, at one with them on economic matters and at least somewhat more moderate on racial matters than many Democrats. When the Democratic *Montgomery Mail* floated Pratt's name as a possible gubernatorial candidate in April, the Republican organ, the *Montgomery Journal,* responded with great enthusiasm to the idea, while simultaneously getting in some good jabs at the Democratic Party. The *Mail* had asked: "Why would not Daniel Pratt, of Autauga, be a good candidate for Governor of Alabama?" The *Journal* allowed that Pratt "would make not only a good candidate, but an able ruler, as far as the highest qualities of manhood contribute to that end." Nevertheless, the *Journal* saw many objections to Pratt as the candidate of the *Democrats:* "Pratt is a 'damned Yankee,' and orthodox Democrats detest Yankees. He is a 'carpet-bagger,' and carpet-baggers are odious to the Democracy. He is a laborer with his own hands, a mechanic . . . which is, being Democratically interpreted, a 'mudsill,' 'essentially a slave,' something that stinks in the delicate nostrils of the 'chivalry.'" The most "insuperable objection to Mr. Pratt, as a Democratic candidate," involved, according to the *Journal,* "his fine sense and uniform respect for the law." Pratt "would not be sufficiently urgent and earnest in busting up the government." Moreover, he was "too decent to blackguard opponents on account of political differences, too kind to concentrate his ability and energy in a war upon the struggling colored men of the state." The *Journal* ironically concluded: "Altogether, we can't think of a more utterly unfit man for Democratic candidacy."[22]

The *Demopolis Southern Republican* agreed with the *Journal* that Pratt would make a wonderful gubernatorial candidate—for the Republicans. As "a regular New Hampshire Yankee," "a good old Whig of the Henry Clay school," and "a large manufacturer," Pratt would be the perfect man, declared the *Republican.* The paper warned Pratt's Democratic supporters to "call the nominating convention pretty soon," before the Republicans stole him away.[23]

The Democratic *Mail* astutely noted that "the fact that the Radical newspapers have all been at a loss to know where or how to attack [Mr.

22. (Montgomery) *Alabama State Journal,* 7 April 1870.

23. *Montgomery Daily Mail,* 2 April 1870, reprinted from the *Demopolis Southern Republican.* Jonathan Wiener writes that the *Republican* "taunted Pratt for betraying his true class interests," which is a mischaracterization. Rather, the paper taunted the Democrats for not living up to Pratt's standards. Wiener, *Social Origins,* 152.

Pratt's] personal record is the very best evidence that he is peculiarly available as a candidate." Moreover, Pratt joined the quality of availability "with great purity of character, mental rigor and decision, unflinching devotion to political principles, and a long life of deserving and arduous labors." "Daniel Pratt's personal record," the *Mail* concluded, "*is invulnerable.*"[24]

Returning to the subject of Daniel Pratt four days later, the paper argued that Pratt as governor would represent the interests of both industry and "the laboring classes." Pratt, the *Mail* emphasized, stood as "a noble monument to that social pride of the Southern people which delights in honoring merit and industry" and "an imposing rebuke" to Republicans who charged Democrats "with despising labor." The New Hampshire Yankee had come to Alabama "as an humble mechanic, without friends, and with nothing to push him forward, but an inconquerable will and a strong arm"; and he had "built up a flourishing town and furnished occupation to hundreds of families." For these accomplishments, he now "commanded the respect of the whole State."[25]

The *Mail* soon gave an official endorsement of Pratt for governor, along with a long letter on Pratt's life, submitted by one "Montgomery." Asserting that Alabamians had "entered upon a career in which the surplus revenues of our lands must seek investment in factories and mining," the *Mail* asked "who would be better able to guide, direct and encourage the labor interests of Alabama than such a man as DANIEL PRATT?" The *Mail* emphasized that Pratt had been "an old Whig" who had opposed secession, and it noted that while Pratt personally extended "all charity and protection to the negroes" freed as a result of the Civil War, he "ardently opposed . . . all attempts looking towards social equality of the races." Moreover, despite his humble origins as a mechanic, Pratt had an "intelligence . . . recognized by distinguished men of letters." According to the *Mail*, one of the state's best lawyers, a man who had known Pratt for twenty years, had remarked that he had never found fault with Pratt's judgment.[26]

Allowing that Pratt was "an old man," the paper nevertheless insisted that he was "still in the vigor of life," citing as proof Pratt's tireless activ-

24. *Montgomery Daily Mail*, 2 April 1870.
25. Montgomery Daily Mail, 6 April 1870.
26. *Montgomery Daily Mail*, 14 April 1870. The lawyer referred to was likely former governor Thomas Hill Watts.

ity of the last five years. At war's end he had suffered terrible financial losses and faced utter ruin, yet, amid "difficulties which crushed younger men to earth," Pratt had triumphed: "He rose with his mountain of adversities pressing upon his shoulders, shook them off like the moral giant he is, restored order out of chaos, reopened his factories, marched into the assembly of the great cotton lords of New England, took his seat as Chairman of the Manufacturer's Association of America, visited the Northern cities and opened up markets for his goods, returned to set his wheels in motion, gave occupation once again to the town he founded, and offered bread to hundreds of laboring families."[27]

The *Mail* was not, by any means, the only paper to speak highly of Pratt in the election year of 1870. The *Elyton Herald,* edited by Henry Hale, a son of Gardner Hale, declared that no man deserved "the honor of the Gubernatorial chair" more than Pratt. The *Talladega Watchtower* insisted that Pratt was "undoubtedly the choice of a large majority of the intelligent and taxpaying citizens of Talladega county, as the Democratic candidate for Governor." These comments from newspapers located in northern Alabama suggest the popularity of Pratt in a region that stood to benefit enormously from the development of the coal and iron industries. Significantly, many of Talladega's "intelligent and taxpaying citizens" were planters.[28]

Pratt also received favorable mention from the *Montgomery Daily Advertiser,* a paper that Jonathan Wiener classifies as part of the "planter press." To be sure, the *Advertiser* never got behind the idea of a Pratt candidacy with the same gusto as the *Mail.* Nevertheless, the paper bestowed lavish praise on Pratt in the period leading up to the state Democratic convention. In July, the paper called Pratt a "great Alabamian" and extolled "his wonderful energy and influence in the further development of Alabama's resources," while in September, it speculated that "there is no man in Alabama who is more thoroughly esteemed in all the relations of life than the benevolent and energetic Founder of the flourishing village of Prattville."[29]

27. Ibid.

28. *Montgomery Daily Mail,* 19 April 1870; *Montgomery Daily Advertiser,* 21 August 1870.

29. *Montgomery Daily Advertiser,* 30 July, 13 September 1870. That Pratt was popular with the progressive planting interest is indicated by his election as president of the State Agricultural Society in 1868. William Warren Rogers, *The One-Gallused Rebellion: Agrarianism in Alabama, 1865–1896* (Baton Rouge: Louisiana State University Press, 1970), 57–58.

Not surprisingly, the Democratic convention in Autauga County, held on August 6 at Autaugaville, strongly urged the nomination of Daniel Pratt for governor. Pratt, the convention declared, had endeavored all his life "to give dignity to labor" and had contributed greatly to the development of Alabama's "industrial resources" through his "industry, energy, and perseverance." Moreover, Pratt possessed "high social, moral and religious virtues, exemplifying an enlarged public liberality no less than an enlightened Christian beneficence." Therefore, the gathering resolved to instruct the county delegates to the state Democratic convention to "urge [Pratt's] claims to the nomination with an earnestness equal to our estimate of his worth and qualifications."[30]

That September at the Democratic state convention Pratt enjoyed considerable support. Former governor Thomas Hill Watts, a Montgomery attorney and probably the most prominent old Whig in southern Alabama, placed Pratt's name in nomination. On the first ballot, Pratt came in second behind Robert Burns Lindsay, a Douglas Democrat who had come originally from Scotland and practiced law in Tuscumbia, a town in the Tennessee Valley. Pratt received 23 percent of the votes, while Lindsay received 32 percent. Three other men, William C. Oates, William H. Barnes, and George Goldthwaite, received smaller blocks of votes. When the second ballot was taken, however, Pratt dropped to third behind Lindsay and Barnes. At this point, Lindsay clearly had momentum. After the third ballot, the names of Lindsay's opponents were withdrawn, leaving the Scotsman to be declared the convention's unanimous choice for governor.[31]

Pratt's ultimate defeat at the 1870 convention should not be viewed as a planter victory over manufacturers. Lindsay, the only candidate from northern Alabama, enjoyed a decided regional advantage. Moreover, Pratt's age and poor health crippled his chances. For one thing, the elderly Pratt had no heroic war record to parade before the delegates, as did men such as Lindsay or Oates, the famous one-armed hero of Little Round Top. The *Journal* noted sarcastically that the man who nominated Lindsay made a rousing martial speech, "which would have done honor

30. *Montgomery Daily Advertiser,* 10 August 1870. The Autauga delegates to the state convention included many farmers from around the county, as well as Prattvillians Llewellyn Spigner, Samuel Parrish Smith, A. K. McWilliams, Henry DeBardeleben, Merrill Pratt, and Gustavus Northington.

31. (Montgomery) *Alabama State Journal,* 2 September 1870; *Montgomery Daily Mail,* 2 September 1870.

to any member of the Secession Convention of 1861." More seriously, Pratt's obviously bad health must have weighed heavily on delegates' minds. In 1867, Pratt had spent some time at Hot Springs, Arkansas. In July 1870, he traveled to Healing Springs, Virginia, remaining there until mid-September, after the Democratic convention had ended. In late July, the *Advertiser* claimed that Pratt was "rapidly recovering his health" in Virginia, but his absence in early September must have sown doubt in Alabama's political community.[32]

Whether or not Pratt's health had temporarily improved, it soon began inexorably to decline. Already by 1870, Pratt had effectively transferred the management of the gin factory to Merrill Pratt and that of the textile factory to Henry DeBardeleben, though he still kept a hand in things when he could. In April 1872, a correspondent to the *Montgomery Advertiser and Mail* confided that "Mr. Pratt has been confined to his room for a long time from rheumatism, but is again [going] out though quite feeble." Six weeks later, Pratt himself complained in a letter to Shadrack Mims: "I have ben laid up about two weeks not able to attend to business. My hand is so lame now I am hardly able to hold a pen." Pratt admitted he desired to take a cure at Talladega Springs, believing, as he rather pessimistically put it, that "it would be more beneficial to me than anything I am to do." Nevertheless, he did not see how he could leave his "business in the situation it now is."[33]

Despite his failing health, Pratt remained an important figure on the public scene until his death in May 1873. The same Montgomery correspondent who informed readers of Pratt's physical frailty avowed that the industrialist's "mind is as active and vigorous as ever, and he takes great interest in the future of the country." The stockholders of Montgomery's First National Bank evidently agreed, electing Pratt one of their directors in January 1872. The *Journal* congratulated the "flourishing and enterprising" bank for having secured "the services of that well

32. (Montgomery) *Alabama State Journal,* 2 September 1870; (Montgomery) *Alabama State Sentinel,* 6 July 1867; *Montgomery Daily Advertiser,* 15, 30 July, 13 September 1870. In 1871, a correspondent to the *New York Journal of Commerce* on a tour of the South asserted that but for his advanced age and "feeble health," Pratt "would have been nominated and elected Governor on the Democratic ticket last year." *Montgomery Daily Advertiser and Mail,* 29 July 1871.

33. *Montgomery Daily Advertiser and Mail,* 7 April 1871, 21 April 1872; Alabama, 2: 12, R. G. Dun & Co. Collection; Daniel Pratt to Shadrack Mims, 3 June 1872, McMillan Collection.

known gentleman, who has done so much for our State, and has succeeded in infusing his energetic spirit into the good people of Autauga
and elsewhere." The paper rejoiced "to see Daniel Pratt giving our city
attention" and concluded that he would "prove an invaluable acquisition
to the [bank] directors."[34]

Pratt kept abreast of current events until the end of his life. He eagerly
supported Horace Greeley for the presidency in 1872, writing two pro-
Greeley letters to the Democratic *Advertiser and Mail* and chairing an important pro-Greeley meeting in Prattville. In his letters to the *Advertiser
and Mail,* Pratt complained that the Grant administration had spread the
malicious lie that Alabama was "disloyal and infested with 'Ku-Klux.'"
Pratt believed that "no sensible person would invest or move to such a
State" as the one falsely portrayed by the Republicans. If the Grant administration remained in power, Pratt direly predicted that "railroad[s]
and manufacturing will move slowly." If, however, Alabamians elected
the upright Greeley "and an intelligent State ticket and a legislature of
honest men who are above being bought," Pratt insisted that a "favorable change" would take place, "not only in Alabama, but the whole government."[35]

There appears to have been no movement in 1872 to draft Pratt as the
Democratic nominee for governor, though his name was advanced in an
interesting letter to the *Advertiser and Mail,* penned by "Rustic." This
self-styled Rustic apparently was a farmer in eastern Alabama (probably
Lee or Chambers County), for he mentioned having recently attended a
meeting of the East Alabama Agricultural Society at Opelika. Rustic declared that what Alabama's "honest masses" wanted was "*a reduction
of taxes*" and "*the best possible State government with the least possible
expense.*" Rustic urged that the best man to achieve these ends was "Old
Man Honorable" himself, Daniel Pratt. Besides being honest, Pratt also
possessed "pre-eminent financial ability." While Rustic recognized that
there were many well-qualified younger men, he pointed out that they
could be rewarded with Alabama's "highest gift" in the future. Pratt,
moreover, would make a very strong candidate. "Ripe in years and rich
in experience, and having the confidence of everybody, he would roll up

34. *Montgomery Daily Advertiser and Mail,* 21 April 1872; (Montgomery) *Alabama
State Journal,* 23 January 1872. Merchant Marcus Munter and cotton broker John W. Durr
were also elected directors.

35. *Montgomery Daily Advertiser and Mail,* 7 June, 7 August, 30 October 1872.

such a majority . . . as would drive Radicalism back to its cold home," Rustic enthusiastically concluded.[36]

Despite the boosting from Rustic, a Pratt candidacy never got off the ground in 1872. Nevertheless, Pratt continued to publicly air his opinions on pressing political issues. One post–Civil War development that especially vexed him, provoking him to write agitated letters to the *Citizen,* was the movement to limit by law the working hours of factory laborers. Concerning this popular labor movement, Pratt adopted the same crabbed and querulous tone of his letters on carpetbaggers, scalawags, and freedmen. As early as 1866 he criticized proposals that state governments set a working day of ten or eight hours maximum in a *Citizen* article, "A Few Words to Those Who Choose to Read Them." Pratt noted that advocates of the ten- or eight-hour day asserted that a shortened working day gave the laborer "more time to do small jobs for himself," "an opportunity to read and improve his mind," "a chance to spend more time with his family," and "relaxation from labor, therefore strengthening his constitution and giving him better health." With his extra time, the worker might even "study mechanics, make drawings of different sorts of machinery, make improvements [and] get up new inventions, thereby benefiting the world in which he lives." Having set out these hopeful notions (all of them seemingly in accord with his own views on self-improvement), Pratt proceeded to throw a bucket of cold water on them, asserting that "probably not one out of twenty [laborers] improve their leisure hours to benefit themselves or the community in which they live." Pratt proclaimed man "naturally a social being." During leisure time, most workers liked to socialize among themselves, drinking and smoking "a segar or pipe." After supper, they continued loafing: "They feel that another smoke is necessary. They can enjoy it better with their old associates. They meet again, and sometimes spend the evening to a late hour, without improving their minds or benefitting their families. It is not important that they should retire early, as they have a leisure hour in the morning, in which they can make up their lost rest or sleep." Pratt asserted that the truly industrious mechanic would make profitable use of whatever amount of leisure time he had. He offered himself as an example: "I have been a laboring mechanic the past fifty years. . . . I have made it a rule to commence work about sunrise, and quit at sunset, the

36. *Montgomery Daily Advertiser and Mail,* 15 June 1872.

year round. Never light up to work after dark" (Clearly, Pratt took Franklin's "Early to bed, early to rise" maxim to heart.)[37]

In 1873, Pratt found that this irksome national movement had worked its way into his backyard. In March of that year, the Alabama House of Representatives almost unanimously passed a bill regulating "the hours of labor, especially of women and children, in the cotton factories in Alabama, so as to provide that it shall be unlawful to require labor therein, except from seven in the morning till six in the afternoon." This bill, which effectively set the maximum work day for mill workers at about ten hours (if a lunch break was included), was precisely the sort of legislation that Pratt had feared. As the bill made its way into the senate, Pratt wrote a rather frantic letter denouncing the effort to legislate working hours. "Labor must and will regulate itself," he testily lectured. "If interfered with in our State or neighborhood, it will go where it is not . . . labor will follow capital, and capital will go where it receives the greatest encouragement. Any man with two eyes can see that."[38]

Pratt's letter offers tantalizing hints that the ten-hour movement claimed some vocal adherents in Prattville. Pratt complained obliquely of persons in the town who "have not business of their own to attend to, who occupy their time in interfering with the business of others, for the sake, as they think, of making themselves popular with a certain class of persons." He angrily asserted that these designing men "would have the Legislature interfere with private contracts, tamper with a business they know but little about, and to seriously affect the interest of those whom they pretend to benefit."[39]

Before Pratt died, he had the pleasure of seeing the bill brought to a dead stop in the Alabama Senate, although he must have found some of the rhetoric spoken in favor of the bill extremely offensive. Charles Dos-

37. (Prattville) *Autauga Citizen*, 10 May 1866. The eight-hour movement came into great prominence in December 1865 when Congress began hearings on whether it should establish an eight-hour day for federal workers. Pratt likely read articles on this subject in such northern magazines as *North American Review* and the *Nation*. David Montgomery, *Beyond Equality: Labor and the Radical Republicans, 1862–1872* (Urbana: University of Illinois Press, 1967), 233–49. Pratt's argument that the worker would not use his extra time wisely mirrored the declarations made by northern capitalists. "I believe," declared one businessman, "*that too much leisure is a detriment to* [the worker's] *welfare.*" Montgomery, *Beyond Equality*, 235.

38. (Prattville) *Autauga Citizen*, 20 March 1873; (Montgomery) *Alabama State Journal*, 13 March 1873.

39. (Prattville) *Autauga Citizen*, 20 March 1873.

ter, Alabama's Republican state senator, led the opposition to the bill, while Democrat John Mason Martin of Tuscaloosa, a son of a populist Jacksonian governor from the 1840s, acted as its warmest advocate. Martin argued that long work hours destroyed the health of helpless women and children. The senator asked, "Who has ever seen an old person that was an operative in a factory?" He answered that no one had, because "the heated rooms of factories and the incessant cruel toil demanded of the poor creatures . . . consigned them all to early graves." Martin spoke passionately "of the wan, sallow, death-like appearance of operatives generally" and declared that if senators could but see these poor people themselves, they would not dare oppose the bill. Martin also claimed that a reduction in working hours would foster "self-culture and moral and intellectual improvement."[40]

Martin had no kind words for his industrialist opponents. He spoke witheringly of "the huge fortunes built up by manufacturers," which were "made up of the bones of their fellow men . . . cemented with their hearts' blood." Martin could not believe "any creature desired to wring from helpless women and children more than eleven hours of toil per day." If there were such a creature, Martin "hoped never to see him, and prayed that heaven in its mercy would spare the state of such a presence . . . a leprous splotch upon the body politic."[41] With these strident words, Martin challenged the ascendant notion that mill owners were benevolent saviors of humanity. Instead, he shunned them as moral lepers mercilessly exploiting women and children. For the first time, a state political figure had splattered mud on Pratt's lily-white personal reputation.

Charles Doster countered that such legislation would damage Alabama's industrial prospects. After the Civil War, the state lay "impoverished and full of widows and orphans." Its one remaining asset was its "*undeveloped* mineral and manufacturing wealth." Now Martin would

40. (Montgomery) *Alabama State Journal*, 23 April 1873. John Mason Martin, a professor of county jurisprudence at the University of Alabama, had been elected to the state senate in 1871 and reelected in 1872, after which he was chosen as president pro-tem. He was the son of Joshua Lanier Martin, the maverick Jacksonian and former governor who had opposed providing relief to state bank debtors in 1845. The older Martin and other antidebtor Democrats portrayed bank debtors as corrupt aristocrats who deserved no sympathy from the people. Owen, *History of Alabama*, 4: 1165; Thornton, *Politics and Power,* 49–50. Nearly thirty years later, the younger Martin had discovered a new class issue hobbyhorse to ride, though his query about operatives must be seen as either incredibly naive or deliberately disingenuous. Elderly people did not work in mills for the obvious reason that they would not have performed as well as younger people.

41. (Montgomery) *Alabama State Journal*, 23 April 1873.

have the government drive capital out of the state. Doster asserted, moreover, that operatives desired to work in the factories as much as possible. "Their labor is *voluntary, not coerced*. They, or their parents, make their own contracts, and the more work they do, the more money they get."[42]

Doster also addressed Martin's dramatic attacks on textile manufacturers, which he labeled "the heated but honest fancies of a wild imagination." He denied that mill operatives were "overworked victims of manufacturing tyrants, wasted away by disease" and that mill owners were "heartless tyrants and unfeeling shylocks." He challenged such "unjust and untrue" charges with the example of the town he had known for over a quarter century, Prattville. "The venerable Daniel Pratt," he asserted, was "a noble illustration of all the virtues of an elevated humanity." In the town he had founded, mill workers were "a most estimable part of the population," attending churches and Sunday schools and benefiting greatly from "their present association, social friction, contact and relationship." These people, Doster concluded, were "generally intelligent, happy, virtuous, and prosperous," but the bill, if passed, would only succeed in throwing many of them out of work. Doster closed by condemning the bill as a dangerous example of socialism: "This species of legislation is wrong. It is agitating, *agrarian*—incendiary—and disturbs the peaceful relations now existing in our state between capital and labor. It unhappily introduces into our midst the old irrepressible conflict now threatening Northern and European prosperity, and which has been the nefarious implacable enemy of the social compact and the peace and good order of society since the day of Caius and Tiberius Gracchus."[43]

Not only did the senate heed Doster's arguments and turn back the bill regulating the hours of the work day, the legislature also passed a bill, later enacted, to encourage manufacturing and the industrial and mechanical arts in Alabama. The act provided that "all buildings, factories, works and machinery, erected . . . to the value of $100,000" would be exempted from municipal, county, and state taxation for five years. At the same time, the Alabama government revived the state geological survey. Eugene Allen Smith, son of Pratt's friend Samuel Parrish Smith and the professor of geology at the University of Alabama, received the appointment as state geologist. Smith had one of the most respected intellects in the state, having received in 1868 the degrees of M.A. and Ph.D. summa cum laude from Heidelberg University. Pratt deserved some small

42. Ibid.
43. Ibid.

share of credit for Smith's success, as he had written, on the same day in 1865 that Smith took the oath of allegiance, to Alabama governor Lewis Parsons requesting that Smith be granted a certificate of state citizenship, which would allow him to obtain a passport in Washington, D.C., to "go to Germany to finish his education."[44] In the end, then, Pratt must have drawn considerable satisfaction with the results of the spring session of the 1873 legislature.

Pratt addressed Alabama industrial policy in his last-known publication "A Practical View of Alabama," which appeared in the New York magazine the *South* on April 5, 1873. Pratt prescribed for Alabama "good, wholesome laws, such as will foster and encourage enterprise, do away with all surplus offices and economise our State expenses." He also urged the state to "encourage capitalists to invest in manufacturing by not taxing their capital invested in a reasonable length of time." If such "good, wholesome laws" were indeed enacted, Alabama would become "what nature designed her, a thriving, prosperous and desirable State, such as will not only attract the people of other States but also those of Europe."[45]

In his article in the *South,* Pratt devoted a paragraph to Prattville, of which he declared, "There is no better or more desirable place in Alabama for investments in manufacturing." Nevertheless, Pratt spent most of his time discussing his final project, the Red Mountain Iron and Coal Company. After six years of dormancy, this company had rekindled in 1871. Little headway appears to have been made, however, until Pratt acquired controlling interest in the spring of 1872. At a crucial meeting in May, stockholders elected Pratt to the board of directors. At a subsequent meeting, the directors chose Pratt as the company's president and

44. (Montgomery) *Alabama State Journal,* 9 March, 3 April 1873; Lloyd, *Eugene Allen Smith,* 8, 21–22; Daniel Pratt to Lewis E. Parsons, 7 September 1865, Governor Parsons Papers. Smith claimed that "the only shadow of opposition which the bill met was from detestable carpet-baggers, who thought an office with a large salary should be created, and filled by appointment of the radical Governor." Lloyd, *Eugene Allen Smith,* 22.

45. *South,* 5 April 1873. Pratt's plea for laws eliminating surplus offices and economizing on government expenses was, no doubt, in part a response to the concerns of many Democrats that the state had drastically overextended itself in lending aid to railroad companies, a policy that Pratt had eagerly supported. See Perman, *Redemption,* 101–2; Mark W. Summers, *Railroads, Reconstruction, and the Gospel of Prosperity: Aid under the Radical Republicans, 1865–1877* (Princeton, N.J.: Princeton University Press, 1984), 213–36. Pratt also touched on agriculture in his article, urging that "the owners of large tracts of land divide it into small farms and make it an inducement for persons of small means to settle among us."

his son-in-law, Henry DeBardeleben, as superintendent. The *Advertiser and Mail* was elated that Pratt had managed to grasp the reins of power with his increasingly infirm hands: "There is perhaps no man in the South so generally known throughout the whole country as a successful business man as Mr. Pratt. He has never failed in any important undertaking. Cautious, prudent, and with a judgment almost infallible, he never engages in an enterprise without thorough consideration, and when once entered upon, he prosecutes it with the most systematic energy and ceaseless industry." This man of "ceaseless industry," however, was nearly seventy-three and in failing health. He, at least, must have known that he did not have much time remaining to carry out his grandest design.[46]

A few days after his election as president of Red Mountain Iron and Coal, Pratt, only recently recovered from his latest bout with rheumatism, traveled north to purchase machinery for the company. By June, the *Advertiser and Mail* declared that "under the direction of Mr. Dan'l Pratt and Mr. DeBardeleben the Red Mountain Iron Works will soon be in full blast." In a rush of enthusiasm, the paper went on to assert: "The manufacture of iron . . . will, at no distant day, be at once the greatest and most permanently profitable of American, and especially Alabama[n], industries. . . . We think that the building of furnaces and the development of mines offers the safest and most promising investment for capital that can be found."[47]

Despite the *Advertiser and Mail*'s declaration that furnaces would soon be "in full blast," it was not until April 1873 that Pratt was able to announce, in his article in the *South*, that his company had "two hot blast iron furnaces nearly ready to go into operation, which are calculated to make fifty tons of pig iron per day." Noting that the company owned 7,000 acres of land rich in iron ore and coal and located by the South and North Alabama Railroad, Pratt confidently predicted: "Such persons as are desirous to engage in the iron business would do well to examine the location. The vicinity will, no doubt, be the great centre of the iron business." Pratt also urged investors to "look at Birmingham, which is located at the foot of Red Mountain. It is about two years since the town

46. *South*, 5 April 1873; *Montgomery Daily Advertiser and Mail*, 16 May 1872, 15, 20 May 1873. According to Pratt, the capital stock of Red Mountain Iron and Coal Company was $1,000,000, so his takeover of the company must have involved a huge financial commitment that may have incidentally brought about the collapse of the Prattville branch railroad project.

47. *Montgomery Daily Advertiser and Mail*, 25 May, 27 June 1872.

was laid out and now there are, I suppose, between three and four thousand inhabitants." From the height of Red Mountain, Pratt could envision a great new manufacturing city, but he was not destined to reach this industrial promised land.[48]

Soon after his article in the *South* appeared, Pratt fell seriously ill. Although he had been in poor health for years, suffering from neuralgia and rheumatism, his final ailment is not known. On April 24, the *Citizen* reported that Pratt had recovered, but he quickly relapsed and, on May 13, died "after a long, lingering and painful illness." During his last days, he learned that one of the Oxmoor furnaces had gone into blast. Henry De-Bardeleben returned to Prattville with pig iron specimens from the furnace about a week before Pratt died. Yet in Pratt's final days, his thoughts were of religion, not business. According to Shadrack Mims, his last words, spoken to George Smith, who was sitting up with him, were "George, work for the church, work for the church."[49]

Pratt's obituaries in the *Citizen* and the Montgomery papers uniformly treated the man as a fallen hero. The state Republican organ, the *Journal*, called Pratt "one of the best and most useful men that ever lived in the state of Alabama." He left "but few, if any, equals behind him," making his death "a public loss." The *Advertiser and Mail*, the Democratic organ, also gave Pratt a highly adulatory eulogy. "The death of this singularly pure and upright man," the paper pronounced, "will be received with emotions of profound sorrow throughout the entire State." The editors emphasized that Pratt's stunningly successful career in Alabama absolutely refuted "the charge that Northern men are not respected at the South." The death of this Yankee industrialist was "a great public calamity." While the editors gave Pratt's family their deepest sympathies "in this hour of trial and deep gloom," they could not help but extend "to each and every citizen of Alabama a similar recognition of the loss which in this instance we have one and all sustained."[50] Without a doubt, Pratt closed his forty-year career in Alabama as one of the most admired men in the state. If few men matched his level of accomplishment, many men respected him for what he had done and hoped others would daringly follow the path he had blazed.

48. *South,* 5 April 1873.

49. (Prattville) *Autauga Citizen,* 24 April, 8, 15 May 1873; Tarrant, ed., *Hon. Daniel Pratt,* 36; Shadrack Mims to Charles M. Howard, 17 September 1883, Box 37, McMillan Collection; Mims, untitled ms.

50. (Prattville) *Autauga Citizen,* 15 May 1873; *Montgomery Daily Journal,* 14 May 1873; *Montgomery Daily Advertiser and Mail,* 14 May 1873.

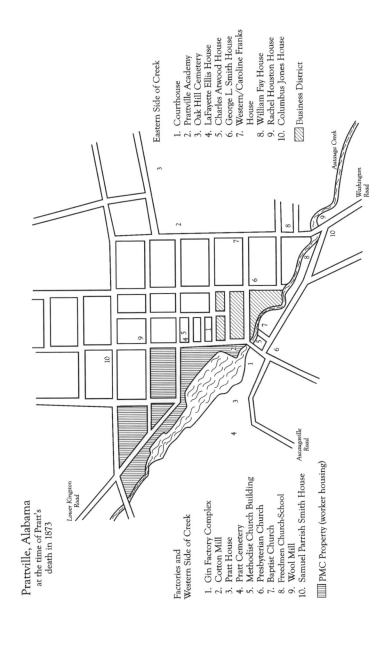

Prattville, Alabama
at the time of Pratt's
death in 1873

Factories and
Western Side of Creek

1. Gin Factory Complex
2. Cotton Mill
3. Pratt House
4. Pratt Cemetery
5. Methodist Church Building
6. Presbyterian Church
7. Baptist Church
8. Freedmen Church-School
9. Wool Mill
10. Samuel Parrish Smith House

▨ PMC Property (worker housing)

Eastern Side of Creek

1. Courthouse
2. Prattville Academy
3. Oak Hill Cemetery
4. LaFayette Ellis House
5. Charles Atwood House
6. George L. Smith House
7. Western/Caroline Franks
    House
8. William Fay House
9. Rachel Houston House
10. Columbus Jones House

▨ Business District

EPILOGUE:
DANIEL PRATT'S LEGACY

Daniel Pratt began disposing of his real property in 1871, deeding most of it to his daughter, Ellen DeBardeleben, and his nephew Merrill. Less than two weeks before his death on May 3, 1873, Pratt signed a deed of trust, under which Samuel Parrish Smith, as trustee for Esther Pratt, was conveyed all Pratt's remaining property, consisting mainly of stock in the First National Bank of Montgomery, the Red Mountain Iron and Coal Company, and Prattville Manufacturing Company. Pratt made clear in the deed that Esther Pratt would have complete power to "manage, control, handle and dispose" of the property "just as she pleases." Samuel Parrish Smith had no other interest in the property than that of a "mere naked trustee." Esther Pratt, who died in February 1875, made her daughter her principal beneficiary.[1]

With Daniel Pratt's wealth to bankroll him, Henry DeBardeleben began purchasing more mineral land in Jefferson County. In June 1875, DeBardeleben became president of the Eureka Company, the successor

1. Deed Book 19, p. 497, Deed Book 21, p. 440, Probate Office, Autauga County Courthouse; Justin Fuller, "Henry DeBardeleben: Industrialist of the New South," *Alabama Review* 42 (January 1986): 5.

296 / THE CONQUEST OF LABOR

corporation to the Red Mountain Iron and Coal Company. In 1878, he and two other capitalists formed the Pratt Coal and Coke Company. Within a few years, DeBardeleben bought out his partners, leaving him sole owner of "the largest and most successful coal and coke company in Alabama." In 1882, he liquidated his interests in Prattville, selling Ellen's shares in Prattville Manufacturing Company to Henry Faber for $61,000 and her half interest in the gin factory to Merrill Pratt. Merrill also purchased Daniel Pratt's mansion from the DeBardelebens. During the 1880s, DeBardeleben started several other important companies, most notably the Bessemer Land and Improvement Company, which developed the industrial city of Bessemer in Jefferson County, and the DeBardeleben Coal and Iron Company. By 1890, DeBardeleben was said to be "the richest man in Alabama," worth from $3 million to $8 million, but he lost most of his fortune in a characteristically risky financial gamble in 1893. The next year, Ellen Pratt DeBardeleben died at the age of forty-nine. When a heart attack felled Henry DeBardeleben in 1910, he was worth $84,000.[2]

Although the methodical Pratt would have frowned on DeBardeleben's restlessness and recklessness, he would have taken great pleasure in seeing his daring son-in-law play one of the major roles in industrializing northern Alabama. Shadrack Mims, who visited DeBardeleben's Pratt Mines at the age of seventy-seven in 1881, expressed sentiments Pratt would have shared when he declared: "It absolutely strikes me with wonder and agreeable surprise how any man could accomplish so much in so short a time. . . . It is nothing more than natural for an old man to feel proud of such an enterprising man reared up and educated in the workshops of Prattville."[3]

While Henry DeBardeleben toyed with one big manufacturing scheme after another, Merrill Pratt remained true to Prattville. Upon buying out Ellen DeBardeleben's interest in the gin factory in 1882, Merrill became sole proprietor of the business, which continued to prosper in the 1880s and 1890s. After a freshet destroyed the cotton mill in 1886, Merrill helped form the Prattville Cotton Mill and Banking Company, which

2. Fuller, "Henry DeBardeleben," 5–16; (Prattville) *Autauga Citizen,* 3 June 1875; *Prattville Southern Signal,* 6 January, 9 June, 20 October 1882; *Prattville Progress,* 24 January 1890, 16 February 1894, reprinted from the *Birmingham Age-Herald.*

3. *Prattville Southern Signal,* 17 June 1881. Mims made no mention of DeBardeleben's use of convict labor at the Pratt Mines. See Allen Johnston Going, *Bourbon Democracy in Alabama, 1874–1890* (Tuscaloosa: University of Alabama Press, 1951), 178.

quickly rebuilt the factory building and filled it with machinery. In 1889, the company added an additional building and more machinery. Original stockholders of the company included Merrill Pratt and his eldest son, Daniel; Lafayette Ellis; Charles Doster; and William T. Northington. The latter man, a son of Daniel Pratt's old enemy William H. Northington, had married Ella Smith, making him a son-in-law of Samuel Parrish Smith and a brother-in-law of Merrill Pratt.[4]

Upon Merrill Pratt's death in 1889, his son Daniel succeeded him as head of the gin factory, and Daniel's uncle-in-law William T. Northington became president of the Prattville Cotton Mill and Banking Company. Lafayette Ellis and Daniel Pratt II served, respectively, as vice-president and secretary-treasurer. In 1898, twenty-five years after the first Daniel Pratt's death, the gin factory made 1,500 gins annually, and the cotton mill produced 18,000 to 22,000 yards of cloth per day. Both mill buildings had 300 looms and 10,000 spindles and were equipped with an electric plant with 430 incandescent lights.[5]

Like his uncle, Merrill Pratt tried but failed in his lifetime to get a railroad routed through Prattville. At one point in the 1890s, the editor of the town's newspaper lamented that "when the good Lord . . . made the earth He never intended that a railroad should pass through the little valley in which Prattville is situated." Despite the editor's momentary loss of faith, a railroad finally found its way to Prattville in 1895. With the completion of the Montgomery and Prattville Railroad, Prattville was linked with the Louisville and Nashville network. Two years later, another branch line connected Prattville with the Mobile and Ohio network.[6]

Additional advances were achieved in Prattville during the last decade of the nineteenth century. Prattville received electric lighting in 1894, the Globe Light and Heat Company of Chicago installing some fifty street lamps in the town. In addition, a telephone exchange was erected in Prat-

4. *Prattville Progress,* 11 November 1898.

5. Ibid. By 1892, Daniel Pratt and Company had shipped 1,000 gins to Russia, including an exhibition gin, black walnut with nickel-plated iron work and a silver-plated inscription, valued at $500. The maker of the gin, a Prattville resident of nearly half a century, William Beckwith, was elected in 1892 to the Parisian Academy of Science's Society of Inventors for his improvements in cotton gins and water wheels. *Prattville Progress,* 8 August 1890, 29 July 1892.

6. *Prattville Progress,* 15 February, 1 November 1895, 8 April 1897, 11 November 1898.

tville in 1897. In 1902, Abigail Holt Smith wrote Sidney Lanier's widow of the great changes: "The village has become quite city like with its two Rail Roads, Electric lights, etc." Prattville's aptly named newspaper, the *Progress* (edited by a son of Charles Doster), embodied the town's go-ahead attitude with its motto: "Push and Perseverance Bring Progress and Power."[7]

Prattvillians remained concerned with moral as well as economic improvement, founding a great range of benevolent societies in the last quarter of the nineteenth century. Many of these groups were women's organizations, such as the Women's Christian Temperance Union, the Women's Missionary Society, and the Merrill Pratt Chapter of the Daughters of the Confederacy. Merrill Pratt's indomitable widow, Julia, headed all three of these groups. The major project of the Women's Missionary Society in the 1880s was "to educate a Chinese girl in the Christian faith, to labor in her own native land in aid of missionary work." The society planned to name the girl Esther Pratt, "in grateful memory of the noble deceased woman [who] bore that name as the beloved wife of the illustrious Daniel Pratt."[8]

Newspapers continued to describe Prattville as Alabama's model factory town. Prattville's own paper made the community sound like a modern-day utopia: "Our society is one harmonious and agreeable family, and we know of no place, so congenial, pleasant and profitable to the factory man as is peaceful, busy and lovely little Prattville." The town's white laboring population enjoyed "neat and comfortable houses . . . with gardens" and benefited from strong sanitary regulations, good physicians and churches, concerned charitable organizations such as the Prattville Benevolent Society and "one of the best public schools in the State, where the poorest boy or girl can attend free of charge, for a full scholastic year." Prattville, the paper insisted, had "no 'strikes,' no complaints of imposition by employer upon employee, no prejudices and unpleasant relations between the classes."[9]

7. *Prattville Progress*, 16 March 1894, 16 July 1897; Mrs. George Smith to Mrs. Lanier, 30 December 1902, Charles D. Lanier Collection. The factory offices at Prattville already had been added to the telephone exchange in 1883. *Prattville Southern Signal*, 14 September 1883.

8. *Prattville Progress*, 17, 24 March 1893, 30 July 1903; *Prattville Southern Signal*, 10 June 1882.

9. *Prattville Southern Signal*, 19 February 1886. Despite the *Signal*'s relentlessly optimistic tone about class relations, a few years later the *Progress* published a melancholy

Relations between the races obviously were another matter entirely. Prattville's African American population did not share in this good life described by the newspapers. Black economic opportunities declined over the last quarter of the nineteenth century, notwithstanding Pratt's assurance that white Alabamians had the best interests of their "colored friends" at heart. When Charles Atwood died around 1890, he left a great void in the black community, one that could not be filled. Atwood's daughter, Alice, spent two years at Clark University in Atlanta in the 1880s, later becoming the assistant to the principal of Prattville's "colored school," but Atwood's sons did not fare so well. In 1894, his three youngest sons, Gilmore, Henry, and Pratt, became involved in a bloody fight with a black barber and his assistant. Henry Atwood lost his left ear in the melee and was convicted later that year of carrying a concealed pistol. Pratt Atwood remained in Prattville all his life, working as a laborer in the cotton gin factory. Charles Atwood's oldest son, Horatio, also stayed in Prattville, holding onto the family house until his death in 1929. Horatio Atwood worked an occasional odd job, but according to one of his nieces spent most of his time at home where "he didn't do nothing."[10]

Mostly blind to the higher aspirations of Alabama's freedmen, Daniel Pratt would have been very pleased with Prattville's position in the quarter century after his death. He would have found the broader economic and political condition of Alabama somewhat troubling, however. After Democrats "redeemed" the state from Republican rule in 1874 by winning both the governorship and the two legislative houses, the state government moved away from Pratt's favored policies of promoting internal improvements through state aid and encouraging industry through special tax breaks. The ambitious railroad aid programs previously supported by both Democrats and Republicans had mired the state in

---

poem by "A Factory Girl," in which the poet wrote enviously of the dead in the cemetery, where "No clanging bells can wake them to life / No rattling looms, no noise, no din." *Prattville Progress*, 11 August 1893. The *Progress* also started a new section of the paper, "Echoes from the Factory," specifically devoted to details on the cotton mill and the operative community. See for example, 2 July 1897.

10. *Prattville Progress*, 12 May 1893, 16 March, 23 November 1894; Oral interview with Lillian Atwood Strong, 16 August 1995; U.S. Census, Alabama, 1910 Population Schedule, Autauga County. A white former neighbor, John Barnes (born in 1910), recalls seeing Horatio Atwood picking fruit off the Atwood pear trees and quarreling with Barnes's parents over whether the Barnes's rosebushes were on his property. He remembers "old Horatio" as a "curiosity." Oral interview with John Barnes, 21 August 1997.

corruption and debt, leading to a powerful reemergence in the Democratic Party of Jacksonian opposition to an activist state government. Austerity became the byword of Alabama's ruling Democratic Party. Still, this retrenchment did not necessarily reflect agrarian animus against industry. As Allen Going, the historian of this so-called "Bourbon" period of Alabama has admitted, "a majority of Democratic leaders and newspapers espoused the cause of industrial progress in Alabama."[11] Most Alabamians wanted more industry in their state. They simply did not want to pay out of their own pockets to attract it.

Throughout the last quarter of the nineteenth century, newspaper correspondents made pilgrimages to Prattville and invoked the name of Daniel Pratt. Perhaps Prattville's greatest moment in the press spotlight occurred in 1882, when the town hosted the Alabama Press Association and Governor Rufus W. Cobb. A reception was held in the Sabbath-school room of the Methodist church building, which thirty years earlier, Pratt had called "probably the best brick building in Alabama." Under a banner emblazoned with the legend "Welcome to the Press of Alabama" hung portraits of Daniel and Esther Pratt. Speeches were made by Charles Doster and the governor, the latter declaiming on how Pratt had not only built up Prattville, but also had left the means by which "much of the mineral wealth of Alabama had been developed." After the speeches, Merrill Pratt conducted the group on a tour of the town's factories. At the cotton mill, "factory girls" handed the press delegation bouquets of flowers, pinned with cards bearing not-so-subtle messages such as "Our compliments with the hope that you, as one of the Pressmen

11. Going, *Bourbon Democracy*, 18–26, 109–46. Also see Perman, *Road to Redemption*; Mark W. Summers, *Railroads, Reconstruction, and the Gospel of Prosperity*; J. Mills Thornton III, "Fiscal Policy and the Failure of Radical Reconstruction in the Lower South," in *Region, Race, and Reconstruction: Essays in Honor of C. Vann Woodward*, ed. by J. Morgan Kousser and James M. McPherson (New York: Oxford University Press, 1982), 349–94; Samuel L. Webb, "A Jacksonian Democrat in Postbellum Alabama: The Ideology and Influence of Journalist Robert McKee, 1869–1896," *Journal of Southern History* 62 (May 1996): 239–74. Ironically, Alabama's austerity policy inflicted great financial hardship on Merrill Pratt. In 1879, the government had repealed, for reasons of expense, the section of the Alabama Code requiring an annual examination of the state treasurer's books. In 1883, State Treasurer Isaac Vincent fled to Mexico after having lost $230,569 in state money through speculating in cotton futures. Vincent had signed a bond for $250,000, but the only surety who had the financial wherewithal to pay after Vincent absconded was Merrill Pratt. The state finally reached a settlement with Daniel Pratt's nephew, whereby he paid Alabama $37,000. Going, *Bourbon Democracy*, 88–89.

of Alabama, will aid us in securing a railroad." After the tour, Prattvillians treated their guests to a bountiful barbecue in the new town park, Magnolia Grove.[12]

When the well-fed press representatives returned home, they promptly printed extremely favorable notices about Prattville in the newspapers they edited, which included southern Alabama papers such as the *Montgomery Advertiser,* the *Opelika Times,* the *Hayneville Examiner,* the *Union Springs Journal,* the *Greenville Advocate,* the *Troy Messenger,* and the *Evergreen News* and northern Alabama newspapers such as the *Decatur Weekly News,* the *Randolph County News,* the *Talladega Mountain Home,* and the *Fort Payne Journal.* The statements expressed by the *Greenville Advocate* make clear that progressive sentiment in Alabama had hardly died with Reconstruction: "What manufacturing can do for a Southern town, Prattville shows so plainly that he who runs may read. Prattville is a standing instance of the blessings which result from diversified industries in our Southern land. To the great fact that the South can, if it will, become preeminently the manufacturing section of the globe, Prattville bears mighty and convincing testimony." For its part, the *Montgomery Advertiser* paid homage to Daniel Pratt, noting: "Prattville shows what one man can do." Nevertheless, the paper urged Alabamians not to sit around waiting for a Daniel Pratt to rescue them from the economic doldrums: "Are the citizens of the hundred and one little cities of Alabama, with natural advantages in their favor, to sit quietly down and grow old crying for Moses to lead them to the land of promise? If Mobile, Selma, Montgomery, Huntsville and other cities of smaller size have no Pratt among their people, cannot their citizens by combining their means, energy and enterprise, do the work of Pratt?"[13]

The great lesson to draw from Daniel Pratt's astonishingly successful career in Alabama is that, contrary to the assertions of a few contemporaries and the claims of some historians, many southerners, before and after the Civil War, did want manufactures. That Daniel Pratt became a cultural hero in Alabama shows that the South was a much more diverse region than scholars often have allowed. From the 1840s to the 1870s, Daniel Pratt preached his industrial gospel to a largely sympathetic audience, and when he died, he left his listeners an inspiring legacy of accomplishment to emulate, if they could.

12. *Prattville Southern Signal,* 12, 19 May 1882. See also *Prattville Southern Signal,* 29 May 1885.
13. *Prattville Southern Signal,* 12, 19 May 1882.

Appendix:
Pratt and Ticknor Genealogy

PRATT

Daniel Pratt (1725–1795)
    Edward Pratt (1765–1829) m. Asenath Flint (1769–1817)
        Asenath Pratt (1793–1826) m. Joseph Chandler
        Dorcas Pratt (1795–1872) m. Joseph Chandler
        Edward Pratt (1797–1838) m. Dorcas Pevey
            Augusta Dorcas Pratt (1825–1906) m. Ashby Morgan (1816–1862)
            Merrill Edward Pratt (1828–1889) m. Julia Smith (1843–1932)
        DANIEL PRATT (1799–1873) m. Esther Ticknor (1803–1875)
            Mary Pratt (1843)
            Ellen Pratt (1844–1893) m. Henry DeBardeleben (1840–1910)
            Maria (1847–1849)
        Abigail Pratt (1804–?) m. Artemas Howard
            Artemas Howard
            Eliza Howard
            Esther Howard
        Eliza Pratt (1808–1889) m. Daniel Holt
            Melissa Holt (1834–1869) m. James Wainwright (1830–1888)
            Abigail Flint Holt (1836–1914) m. George Littlefield Smith (1827–1903)
            Sara Asenath Holt (1838–1908) m. Benjamin Franklin Smith (1827–1873)
            Frances Dorcas Holt (1840–1929) m. B. F. Davis (1821–1881)
            Daniel Edward Holt (1844–1905) m. Mattie Burt (1848–1883)
            Esther Holt (184701929) m. Alonzo Haralson (1825–1899)

TICKNOR

Isaac Ticknor (c.1757–1814) m. Esther [?](c.1757–1827)
    David Ticknor (1781–1814) m. Edith [?](1780–1855)

Esther Ticknor (1803–1875) m. DANIEL PRATT (1799–1873)
John Ticknor (1806–1887) m. Amanda Downer (1809–1890)
    Daniel Pratt Ticknor (1835–1908)
Simon Ticknor (1809–1850) m. Harriet Luce
    Juliet (1842–?)
Samuel Ticknor (1811–1885) m. Esther Porter (1813–1879)
    Mary Ticknor (1838–?) m. Rev. James K. Hazen (1833–1902)
John Ticknor (1788–c. 1833)
Orray Ticknor (1791–1823) m. Harriot Coolidge (1793–1854)
    Lucy Elizabeth Ticknor (1814–?) m. George Washington Dillingham
    James Henry Ticknor (1820–1881)
    Francis Orray Ticknor (1822–1874)
Clarissa Ticknor (1799–1864) m. Ebenezer Ormsby (?–1837)
    William Orray Ormsby (1825–1858) m. Isabella Brock
    Thomas J. Ormsby (1827–1862) m. Hannah Hale
    Theodore Ormsby (1831–?)
    Mary Ormsby (1833–1859) m. George Littlefield Smith (1827–1903)

BIBLIOGRAPHY

PRIMARY SOURCES

Manuscripts

Allen Papers. Alabama Department of Archives and History, Montgomery.

William C. Allen Papers. Southern Historical Collection. University of North Carolina, Chapel Hill.

Autauga County Collection. Autauga County Heritage Center, Prattville.

John C. Calhoun Papers. Clemson University, Clemson, S.C.

Church Register. First Methodist Church of Prattville, Ala.

Continental Eagle Corporation Papers. Prattville, Ala.

R. G. Dun & Co. Collection. Baker Library. Harvard University Graduate School of Business Administration, Cambridge, Mass.

Bolling Hall Papers. Alabama Department of Archives and History, Montgomery.

Charles D. Lanier Collection. Johns Hopkins University, Baltimore, Md.

Lewis Papers. University of Texas Library, Austin.

Malcolm McMillan Collection. Special Collections. Auburn University, Auburn, Ala.

Governor Moore Papers. Alabama Department of Archives and History, Montgomery.

Enoch Parsons Papers. Alabama Department of Archives and History, Montgomery.

Governor Parsons Papers. Alabama Department of Archives and History, Montgomery.

Governor Patton Papers. Alabama Department of Archives and History, Montgomery.

Pratt Papers. Alabama Department of Archives and History, Montgomery.

Shelby Iron Works Papers. Stanley Hoole Library. University of Alabama, Tuscaloosa.

Governor Shorter Papers. Alabama Department of Archives and History, Montgomery.

Charles Tait Papers. Alabama Department of Archives and History, Montgomery.

Government Documents

Alabama. Acts . . . of the General Assembly of the State of Alabama.

Alabama. Commissioner's Court Minutes. Autauga County Courthouse.

Alabama. Deed Books. Autauga County Courthouse.

Alabama. *House Journal.*

Alabama. 1855 Census.

Alabama. 1852 State Property Tax Assessment.

Alabama. Marriage Books. Autauga County Courthouse.

Alabama. Reports and Wills. Autauga County Courthouse.

Alabama. Reports of Cases Argued and Determined in the Supreme Courts of Alabama.

Alabama. *Supreme Court Records.*

Georgia. Annual Returns, Inventories and Appraisements, Sales and Divisions of Estates. Jones County Courthouse. Gray.

Georgia. Deed Books. Jones County Courthouse. Gray.

Georgia. Marriage Books. Jones County Courthouse. Gray.

New Hampshire. Will Books. Hillsborough County Courthouse. Nashua.

United States. Census Returns, Alabama, Arkansas, Georgia, Louisiana, Mississippi, New Hampshire.

United States. Confederate Papers Relating to Citizens and/or Business Firms. Reel 818, National Archives.

United States. Record Group 45. National Archives.

United States. Record Group 94. National Archives.

United States. *Reports of the Commissioner of Patents.*

Newspapers and Magazines

American Cotton Planter. 1853.

American Cotton Planter and Soil of the South. 1857, 1860–1861.

Birmingham News/Age Herald. 1935.

De Bow's Review. 1846–1848, 1851–1852, 1867.

Farmer's Cabinet. 1851.

Fort Smith Herald. 1850.

(Gray) *Jones County News.* 1908.

Macon Telegraph. 1827, 1831.

(Milledgeville) *Georgia Journal.* 1816, 1825–1828, 1832.

Mobile Advertiser. 1850, 1852, 1869.

(Mobile) *Alabama Planter.* 1848.

Mobile Register. 1870.

Montgomery Advertiser. 1866, 1868–1872.

Montgomery Advertiser and Mail. 1871–1873, 1881.

(Montgomery) *Alabama State Journal.* 1850–1853, 1855, 1869–1873, 1886.

Montgomery Flag and Advertiser. 1847–1849.

Montgomery Mail. 1855, 1857, 1859, 1867, 1868–1870.

(Montgomery) *Alabama State Sentinel.* 1867–1868, 1870.

(Prattville) *Autauga Citizen.* 1853–1867, 1871–1882.

Prattville Progress. 1887–1903, 1922.

Prattville Southern Signal. 1872–1886.

Prattville Southern Statesman. 1854–1855, 1857–1860.

Savannah Advertiser. 1819.

(Selma) *Alabama State Sentinel.* 1855, 1857.

The South. 1873.

Tuscaloosa Independent Monitor. 1847.

Tuscumbia North Alabamian. 1848.

Tuskegee Republican. 1857, 1859.

Weekly Vicksburg Whig. 1858.

Wetumpka Daily State Guard. 1849.

Contemporary Articles, Books, and Diaries

Alabama Mortality Schedule 1850, Seventh Census of the United States, Original Returns of the Assistant Marshalls, Third Series; Persons Who Died during the Year ending June 30, 1850. Compiled by Marilyn Davis Hahn. Easley, S.C.: Southern Historical Press, 1983.

Alabama Mortality Schedule 1860, Eighth Census of the United States, Original Returns of the Assistant Marshalls, Third Series; Persons Who Died during the Year ending June 30, 1860. Compiled by Marilyn Davis Barefield. Easley, S.C.: Southern Historical Press, 1987.

Ballou, Adin. *An Elaborate History and Genealogy of the Ballous in America.* Providence, R.I.: E. L. Freeman & Son, 1888.

Blood, Henry Ames. *The History of Temple, N.H.* Boston: G. C. Rand & Avery, 1860.

Brewer, Willis. *Alabama: Her History, Resources, War Record, and Public Men. From 1540 to 1872.* Montgomery, Ala.: Barrett & Brown, 1872.

Crumpton, Washington Bryan. *A Book of Memories, 1842–1920.* Montgomery, Ala.: Baptist Mission Board, 1921.

Descriptive Catalogue of Paintings in the Gallery of Daniel Pratt, Together with a Memoir of George Cooke, Artist. Prattville: n.p., 1853.

Escott, Paul, D., ed. *North Carolina Yeoman: The Diary of Basil Armstrong Thomasson, 1853–1862.* Athens: University of Georgia Press, 1996.

Flint, John and John H. Stone. *A Genealogical Register of the Descendants of Thomas Flint of Salem.* Andover, Mass.: W. F. Draper, 1860.

Gregg, William. *Essays on Domestic Industry, or an Inquiry into the Expediency of Establishing Cotton Manufactures in South Carolina* [1845]. Reprinted in *Cotton Mill, Commercial Features,* by D. A. Tomkins, 207–40. Charlotte, N.C.: by the author, 1899.

Griswold, S[amuel] H[ardeman], "The Cotton Gin—An Interesting History of the Gin and Its Maker." (Gray) *Jones County News,* 2 April 1908. In *History of Jones County, Georgia: 1807–1907,* by Carolyn White Williams. Macon Co., Ga.: J. W. Burke Co., 1957.

Hardy, John. "History of Autauga County." *Alabama Historical Quarterly* 3 (spring 1941): 96–116. Reprinted from (Selma) *Alabama State Sentinel,* 10 August 1867.

———. *Selma: Her Institutions, and Her Men.* Selma, Ala.: Times Book and Job Office, 1879.

Hazen, James K. *Manual of the Presbyterian Church.* Richmond, Va.: Shepperson & Graves, 1878.

Hunnewell, James Melville. *The Ticknor Family in America.* Boston: by the author, 1919.

"Journal of Benjamin Franklin Smith." Typescript. Autauga County Heritage Center. Prattville.

Lanier, Sidney. *Letters, 1857–1868.* Edited by Charles R. Anderson and Aubrey H. Starke. Vol. 7, *The Centennial Edition of the Works of Sidney Lanier.* Baltimore: John Hopkins University Press, 1945.

Livermore, Abiel Abbot and Sewall Putnam. *History of the Town of Wilton, Hillsborough County, New Hampshire, with a Genealogical Register.* Lowell, Mass.: Marden & Rowell, 1888.

Memorial Record of Alabama . . . Together with the Personal Memoirs of Many of Its People. Madison, Wis.: Brant & Fuller, 1893.

Merrell, Henry. *The Autobiography of Henry Merrell: Industrial Missionary to the Old South.* Edited by James L. Skinner III. Athens: University of Georgia Press, 1991.

Mims, Shadrack. "History of Autauga County" [1886]. Reprinted in *Alabama Historical Quarterly* 8 (fall 1946): 241–68.

———. "History of the M.E. Church in Prattville." Typescript. Box 37, McMillan Collection, Auburn University, Auburn, Ala.

―――. "History of Prattville." In *Hon. Daniel Pratt: A Biography, with Eulogies on His Life and Character,* edited by S. F. H. Tarrant. Richmond, Va.: Whittet & Shepperson, 1904.

Mims, Wilbur F. *War History of the Prattville Dragoons.* Montgomery, Ala.: by the author, n.d.

Nobles, Larry W., ed. *The Journals of Ferdinand Ellis Smith.* Prattville, Ala.: by the editor, 1991.

―――, ed. *The Journals of George Littlefield Smith.* Prattville, Ala.: by the editor, 1991.

Olmsted, Frederick Law. *A Journal in the Back Country.* London: S. Low, Son & Co., 1860.

Phelps, Oliver Seymour and Andrew T. Servin. *The Phelps Family of America and Their English Ancestors.* Pittsfield, Mass.: Eagle Publishing, 1899.

Porter, Benjamin F. *Reminiscences of Men and Things in Alabama.* Edited by Sara Walls. Tuscaloosa, Ala.: Portals Press, 1983.

Smith, Daniel P. *Company K, First Alabama Regiment or Three Years in the Confederate Service.* Prattville, Ala.: n.p., 1885.

Smith, Samuel Parrish. "Burts and Colemans" [1885]. *Autauga Ancestry* 5 (May 1995): 21–27.

Tarrant, S. F. H., ed. *Hon. Daniel Pratt: A Biography, with Eulogies on His Life and Character.* Richmond, Va.: Whittet & Shepperson, 1904.

Ticknor, Francis Orray. *The Poems of Francis Orray Ticknor.* Edited by Michelle Cutliff Ticknor. New York: Neale Publishing , 1911.

Tompkins, Daniel Augustus. *Cotton Mill, Commercial Features.* Charlotte, N.C.: by the author, 1899.

West, Anson. *A History of Methodism in Alabama.* Nashville, Tenn.: Publishing House, Methodist Episcopal Church, 1893.

Wiley, Bell Irwin, ed. *"This Infernal War": The Confederate Letters of Edwin H. Fay.* Austin: University of Texas Press, 1958.

SECONDARY SOURCES

Books

Abbot, Frank M. *Genealogies.* Vol. 1, *History of the People of Jones County, Georgia.* Macon, Ga.: National Publishing, 1977.

Abernethy, Thomas P. *The Formative Period in Alabama, 1815–1828.* 1922. Reprint. University: University of Alabama Press, 1965.

Armes, Ethel. *The Story of Coal and Iron in Alabama.* Birmingham, Ala.: University Press, 1910.

Ashworth, John. *Slavery, Capitalism, and Politics in the Antebellum Republic.*

Vol. 1, *Commerce and Compromise, 1820–1850*. New York: Cambridge University Press, 1995.

Ayers, Edward L. *Vengeance and Justice: Crime and Punishment in the Nineteenth-Century American South*. New York: Oxford University Press, 1984.

Barney, William L. *The Secessionist Impulse: Alabama and Mississippi in 1860*. Princeton, N.J.: Princeton University Press, 1974.

Bateman, Fred and Thomas Weiss. *A Deplorable Scarcity: The Failure of Industrialization in the Slave Economy*. Chapel Hill: University of North Carolina Press, 1981.

Beatty, Bess. *Alamance: The Holt Family and Industrialization in a North Carolina County, 1837–1900*. Baton Rouge: Louisiana State University Press, 1999.

Bennett, Charles A. *Saw and Toothed Cotton Ginning Developments*. Dallas: Texas Cotton Growers Association, n.d.

Black, Robert C., III. *The Railroads of the Confederacy*. Chapel Hill: University of North Carolina Press, 1952.

Blumin, Stuart M. *The Emergence of the Middle Class: Social Experience in the American City, 1760–1900*. New York: Cambridge University Press, 1989.

Boal, Louise Taylor Nelson. *The History of the Smith-Riggs Families*. Prattville, Ala.: by the author, 1991.

Bode, Carl. *The American Lyceum: Town Meeting of the Mind*. New York: Oxford University Press, 1956.

Bolton, Charles C. *Poor Whites of the Antebellum South: Tenants and Laborers in Central North Carolina and Northeast Mississippi*. Durham, N.C.: Duke University Press, 1994.

Boney, F. N. *Southerners All*. Macon, Ga.: Mercer University Press, 1984.

Bonner, James C. *Milledgeville: Georgia's Antebellum Capital*. Athens: University of Georgia Press, 1978.

Boylan, Anne M. *Sunday School: The Formation of an American Institution, 1790–1880*. New Haven, Conn.: Yale University Press, 1988.

Brownell, Blaine A. and David R. Goldfield, eds. *The City in Southern History: The Growth of Urban Civilization in the South*. Port Washington, N.Y.: Kennikat Press, 1977.

Bruce, Dickson D., Jr. *Violence and Culture in the Antebellum South*. Austin: University of Texas Press, 1979.

Carter, Dan T. *When the War Was Over: The Failure of Self-Reconstruction in the South, 1865–1867*. Baton Rouge: Louisiana State University Press, 1985.

A Centennial: Lehman Brothers, 1850–1950. New York: Lehman Brothers, 1950.

Cline, Wayne. *Alabama Railroads*. Tuscaloosa: University of Alabama Press, 1997.

Coleman, Peter J. *The Transformation of Rhode Island, 1790–1860*. Providence: Brown University Press, 1963.

Cooke, Eleanor Smith. *The Genealogy of Daniel Pratt*. Prattville, Ala.: by the author, 1990.

Cooper, William J., Jr. *The South and the Politics of Slavery, 1828–1856*. Baton Rouge: Louisiana State University Press, 1978.

———— and Thomas E. Terrell. *The American South: A History*, 2d ed., vol. 1. New York: McGraw-Hill, 1996.

Coulter, W.E. Merton. *The Confederate States of America, 1861–1865*. Baton Rouge: Louisiana State University Press, 1950.

Culpepper, Marilyn Mayer. *Trials and Triumphs: Women of the American Civil War*. East Lansing: Michigan State University Press, 1991.

DeCredico, Mary A. *Patriotism for Profit: Georgia's Urban Entrepreneurs and the Confederate War Effort*. Chapel Hill: University of North Carolina Press, 1990.

Dew, Charles B. *Bond of Iron: Master and Slave at Buffalo Forge*. New York: W. W. Norton, 1994.

Doster, James F. and David C. Weaver. *Tenn-Tom Country: The Upper Tombigbee Valley*. Tuscaloosa: University of Alabama Press, 1987.

Doyle, Don Harrison. *The Social Order of a Frontier Community: Jacksonville, Illinois, 1825–1870*. Urbana: University of Illinois Press, 1978.

Dupre, Daniel S. *Transforming the Cotton Frontier: Madison County, Alabama, 1800–1840*. Baton Rouge: Louisiana State University Press, 1997.

Faust, Drew Gilpin. *James Henry Hammond and the Old South: A Design for Mastery*. Baton Rouge: Louisiana State University Press, 1982.

————. *Mothers of Invention: Women of the Slaveholding South in the American Civil War*. Chapel Hill: University of North Carolina Press, 1996.

————. *A Sacred Circle: The Dilemma of the Intellectual in the Old South, 1840–1860*. Baltimore: Johns Hopkins University Press, 1977.

Fay, Mary Smith. *Edwin Fay of Vermont and Alabama, 1794–1876*. Houston, Tex.: by the author, 1988.

Federal Writers Project. *New Hampshire: A Guide to the Granite State*. Boston: Houghton Mifflin, 1938.

Fleming, Walter L. *Civil War and Reconstruction in Alabama*. New York: Columbia University Press, 1905.

Flynt, Wayne. *Poor but Proud: Alabama's Poor Whites*. Tuscaloosa: University of Alabama Press, 1989.

Foner, Eric. *Reconstruction: America's Unfinished Revolution, 1863–1877*. New York: Harper & Row, 1988.

Ford, Lacy K., Jr. *Origins of Southern Radicalism: The South Carolina Upcountry, 1800–1860*. New York: Oxford University Press, 1988.

Fox-Genovese, Elizabeth. *Within the Plantation Household: Black and White Women of the Old South*. Chapel Hill: University of North Carolina Press, 1988.

Friedman, Milton and Anna Jacobson Schwartz. *A Monetary History of the United States, 1860–1960*. Princeton, N.J.: Princeton University Press, 1963.

Gamble, Robert. *The Alabama Catalog, Historic American Buildings Survey: A Guide to the Early Architecture of the State*. Tuscaloosa: University of Alabama Press, 1987.

Gandrud, Pauline Jones. *Autauga County*. Vol. 75, *Alabama Records*. Easley, S.C.: Southern Historical Press, 1981.

Genovese, Eugene D. *The Political Economy of Slavery: Studies in the Economy and Society of the Slave South*. New York: Pantheon, 1965.

———. *The Slaveholders' Dilemma: Freedom and Progress in Southern Conservative Thought, 1820–1860*. Columbia: University of South Carolina Press, 1992.

Glass, Brent D. *The Textile Industry in North Carolina: A History*. Raleigh: Division of Archives and History, North Carolina Department of Cultural Resources, 1992.

Going, Allen Johnston. *Bourbon Democracy in Alabama, 1874–1890*. Tuscaloosa: University of Alabama Press, 1951.

Goldfield, David R. *Cotton Fields and Skyscrapers: Southern City and Region, 1607–1980*. Baton Rouge: Louisiana State University Press, 1982.

———. *Urban Growth in an Age of Sectionalism: Virginia, 1847–1861*. Baton Rouge: Louisiana State University Press, 1977.

Graham, James M. *A Brief History of the First Presbyterian Church of Prattville, Alabama*. Prattville: by the author, 1935.

Green, Fletcher M. *The Role of the Yankee in the Old South*. Athens: University of Georgia Press, 1972.

Greenberg, Kenneth S. *Masters and Statesmen: The Political Culture of American Slavery*. Baltimore: Johns Hopkins Press, 1985.

Hall, David D. *Worlds of Wonder, Days of Judgment: Popular Religious Belief in Early New England*. Cambridge, Mass.: Harvard University Press, 1990.

Hearden, Patrick J. *Independence and Empire: The New South's Cotton Mill Campaign, 1865–1901*. DeKalb: Northern Illinois University Press, 1982.

Historical Society of Temple, New Hampshire. *A History of Temple, New Hampshire, 1768–1976*. Dublin, N.H.: W. L. Bauhan, 1976.

Hundley, Daniel R. *Social Relations in Our Southern States*. 1860. Reprint. Edited, with an introduction, by William J. Cooper Jr. Baton Rouge: Louisiana State University Press, 1979.

Jackson, Harvey H., III. *Rivers of History: Life on the Coosa, Tallapoosa, Cahaba, and Alabama*. Tuscaloosa: University of Alabama Press, 1995.

Jemison, E. Grace. *Historic Tales of Talladega*. Montgomery, Ala.: Paragon Press, 1959.

Johnson, Guion Griffis. *Ante-bellum North Carolina: A Social History*. Chapel Hill: University of North Carolina Press, 1937.

Jordan, Weymouth T. *Ante-Bellum Alabama: Town and Country.* 1957. Reprint. Tuscaloosa: University of Alabama Press, 1987.

Kasson, John F. *Rudeness and Civility: Manners in Nineteenth-Century Urban America.* New York: Hill & Wang, 1990.

Keyes, Donald D. *George Cooke, 1793–1849.* With additional essays by Linda Crocker Simmons, Estill Curtis Pennington, William Nathaniel Banks. Athens, Ga.: Georgia Museum of Art, 1991.

Kolchin, Peter. *American Slavery, 1619–1877.* New York: Hill & Wang, 1993.

Kruman, Marc W. *Parties and Politics in North Carolina, 1836–1865.* Baton Rouge: Louisiana State University Press, 1983.

Kulik, Gary, Roger Parks, and Theodore Z. Penn, eds. *The New England Mill Village, 1790–1860.* Cambridge: Massachusetts Institute of Technology Press, 1982.

Lander, Ernest McPherson, Jr. *The Textile Industry in Antebellum South Carolina.* Baton Rouge: Louisiana State University Press, 1969.

Laurie, Bruce. *Working People of Philadelphia, 1800–1853.* Philadelphia: Temple University Press, 1980.

Lebsock, Suzanne. *The Free Women of Petersburg: Status and Culture in a Southern Town, 1784–1868.* New York: Norton, 1984.

Lewis, Ronald L. *Coal, Iron, and Slaves: Industrial Slavery in Maryland and Virginia, 1715–1865.* Westport, Conn.: Greenwood Press, 1979.

Lewis, W. David. *Sloss Furnaces and the Rise of the Birmingham District: An Industrial Epic.* Tuscaloosa: University of Alabama Press, 1994.

Linley, John. *Architecture of Middle Georgia: The Oconee Area.* Athens: University of Georgia Press, 1972.

———. *The Georgia Catalog, Historic American Buildings Survey: A Guide to Architecture in the State.* Athens: University of Georgia Press, 1982.

Lonn, Ella. *Salt as a Factor in the Confederacy.* New York: W. Neale, 1933.

Lloyd, Stewart J. *Eugene Allen Smith: Alabama's Great Geologist.* New York: Newcomen Society in North America, 1954.

Luraghi, Raimondo. *The Rise and Fall of the Plantation South.* New York: New Viewpoints, 1978.

Mahé, John A., II, and Rosanne McCaffrey, eds. *Encyclopedia of New Orleans Artists: 1718–1918.* New Orleans: The Historical New Orleans Collection, 1987.

Massey, Mary Elizabeth. *Ersatz in the Confederacy.* Columbia: University of South Carolina Press, 1952.

McMillan, Malcolm C. *Alabama Confederate Reader.* Tuscaloosa: University of Alabama Press, 1963.

———. *The Disintegration of a Confederate State: Three Governors and Alabama's Wartime Home Front, 1861–1865.* Macon, Ga.: Mercer University Press, 1986.

Miller, Perry. *The New England Mind: From Colony to Province.* Cambridge, Mass.: Harvard University Press, 1953.

Miller, Randall M. *The Cotton Mill Movement in Antebellum Alabama.* New York: Arno Press, 1978.

Mitchell, Broadus. *William Gregg: Factory Master of the Old South.* Chapel Hill: University of North Carolina Press, 1928.

Montgomery, David. *Beyond Equality: Labor and the Radical Republicans, 1862–1872.* Urbana: University of Illinois Press, 1981.

Moore, Albert Burton. *Conscription and Conflict in the Confederacy.* New York: MacMillan, 1924.

Moore, Glover. *William Jemison Mims: Soldier and Squire.* Birmingham, Ala.: Birmingham Printing, 1966.

Moore, John Hebron. *Andrew Brown and Cypress Lumbering in the Old Southwest.* Baton Rouge: Louisiana State University Press, 1967.

———. *The Emergence of the Cotton Kingdom in the Old Southwest: Mississippi, 1770–1860.* Baton Rouge: Louisiana State University Press, 1988.

Morgan, Edmund S. *The Puritan Family: Essays on Religion and Domestic Relations in Seventeenth-Century New England.* Boston: Trustees of the Public Library, 1944.

Murphy, Teresa Ann. *Ten Hours' Labor: Religion, Reform, and Gender in Early New England.* Ithaca, N.Y.: Cornell University Press, 1992.

Negri, Paul, ed. *Civil War Poetry: An Anthology.* Mineola, N.Y.: Dover Press, 1997.

Nichols, Frederick Doveton. *The Early Architecture of Georgia.* Chapel Hill: University of North Carolina Press, 1957.

Nobles, Larry W. *Compendium of Old Autauga History.* Prattville, Ala.: by the author, 1997.

Owen, Thomas McAdory. *History of Alabama and Dictionary of Alabama Biography.* 4 Vols. Chicago: S. J. Clarke Publishing, 1921.

Ownby, Ted. *Subduing Satan: Religion, Recreation, and Manhood in the Rural South, 1865–1920.* Chapel Hill: University of North Carolina Press, 1990.

Perman, Michael. *The Road to Redemption: Southern Politics, 1869–1879.* Chapel Hill: University of North Carolina Press, 1984.

Poesch, Jesse J. *The Art of the Old South: Painting, Sculpture, Architecture, and the Products of Craftsmen, 1560–1860.* New York: Harrison House, 1989.

Prude, Jonathan. *The Coming of Industrial Order: Town and Factory Life in Rural Massachusetts, 1810–1860.* New York: Cambridge University Press, 1983.

Quist, John W. *Restless Visionaries: The Social Roots of Antebellum Reform in Alabama and Michigan.* Baton Rouge: Louisiana University Press, 1998.

Rable, George C. *Civil Wars: Women and the Crisis of Southern Nationalism.* Urbana: University of Illinois Press, 1989.

Remington, W. Craig and Thomas J. Kallsen, eds. *Historical Locations by County*. Vol. 1, *Historical Atlas of Alabama*. Tuscaloosa: University of Alabama Press, 1997.

Rogers, William Warren, et al. *Alabama: The History of a Deep South State*. Tuscaloosa: University of Alabama Press, 1994.

———. *The One-Gallused Rebellion: Agrarianism in Alabama, 1865–1896*. Baton Rouge: Louisiana State University Press, 1970.

Russell, James Michael. *Atlanta, 1847–1890: City Building in the Old South and the New*. Baton Rouge: Louisiana State University Press, 1988.

Russel, Robert Royal. *Economic Aspects of Southern Sectionalism, 1840–1861*. Urbana: University of Illinois, 1924.

Schwab, John Christopher. *The Confederate States of America, 1861–1865: A Financial and Industrial History of the South during the Civil War*. New York: C. Scribner's Sons, 1901.

Shore, Laurence. *Southern Capitalists: The Ideological Leadership of an Elite, 1832–1885*. Chapel Hill: University of North Carolina Press, 1986.

Southerland, Henry Deleon, Jr., and Jerry Elijah Brown. *The Federal Road through Georgia, the Creek Nation, and Alabama, 1806–1836*. Tuscaloosa: University of Alabama Press, 1989.

Stampp, Kenneth M. *The Peculiar Institution: Slavery in the Ante-Bellum South*. 1956. Reprint, New York: Vintage Books, 1989.

Starobin, Robert S. *Industrial Slavery in the Old South*. New York: Oxford University Press, 1970.

Startup, Kenneth Moore. *The Root of All Evil: The Protestant Clergy and the Economic Mind of the Old South*. Athens: University of Georgia Press, 1997.

Sterkx, M. E. *Partners in Rebellion: Alabama Women in the Civil War*. Rutherford, N.J.: Fairleigh Dickinson University Press, 1970.

Stone, Karen A. *Prattville Baptist Church: Sharing Our Past with a Vision for the Future, 1838–1988*. Montgomery, Ala.: Brown Printing, 1988.

Student Writers Club of Selma. *Some Old Churches of the Black Belt*. Birmingham, Ala.: Banner Press, 1962.

Summers, Mark W. *Railroads, Reconstruction, and the Gospel of Prosperity: Aid under the Radical Republicans, 1865–1877*. Princeton, N.J.: Princeton University Press, 1984.

Taylor, George Rogers. *The Transportation Revolution, 1815–1860*. Vol. 4, *The Economic History of the United States*. Armonk, N.Y.: M. E. Sharpe, 1989.

Thomas, Emory. *The Confederate Nation, 1861–1865*. New York: Harper & Row, 1979.

Thornton, J. Mills, III. *Politics and Power in a Slave Society: Alabama, 1800–1860*. Baton Rouge: Louisiana State University Press, 1978.

Tolbert, Lisa C. *Constructing Townscapes: Space and Society in Antebellum Tennessee*. Chapel Hill: University of North Carolina Press, 1999.

Turner, Lynn Warren. *The Ninth State: New Hampshire's Formative Years.* Chapel Hill: University of North Carolina Press, 1983.

Varon, Elizabeth R. *We Mean to Be Counted: White Women and Politics in Antebellum Virginia.* Chapel Hill: University of North Carolina Press, 1998.

Wallace, Anthony F. C. *Rockdale: The Growth of an American Village in the Early Industrial Revolution.* New York: Knopf, 1978.

Walters, Ronald G. *American Reformers, 1815–1860.* New York: Hill & Wang, 1997.

Wheeler, Kenneth W. *To Wear a City's Crown: The Beginnings of Urban Growth in Texas, 1836–1865.* Cambridge, Mass.: Harvard University Press, 1968.

Wiener, Jonathan M. *Social Origins of the New South: Alabama, 1860–1885.* Baton Rouge: Louisiana State University Press, 1978.

Wiggins, Sarah Woolfolk. *The Scalawag in Alabama Politics, 1865–1881.* Tuscaloosa: University of Alabama Press, 1977.

Williams, Carolyn White. *History of Jones County, Georgia: 1807–1907.* Macon, Ga.: J. W. Burke, 1957.

Wyatt-Brown, Bertram. *Southern Honor: Ethics and Behavior in the Old South.* New York: Oxford University Press, 1982.

Articles

Alexander, Thomas B. and Peggy J. Duckworth. "Alabama's Black Belt Whigs during Secession: A New Viewpoint." *Alabama Review* 17 (July 1964): 181–97.

Atherton, Lewis. "Mercantile Education in the Ante-Bellum South." *Mississippi Valley Historical Review* 39 (March 1953): 623–40.

Banks, William N. "Temple, New Hampshire." *Antiques* 108 (October 1975): 127–29.

Berlin, Ira, and Herbert G. Gutman. "Natives and Immigrants, Free Men and Slaves: Urban Working Men in the Antebellum American South." *American Historical Review* 88 (December 1983): 1175–1200.

Cappon, Lester J. "Government and Private Industry in the Southern Confederacy." In *Humanistic Studies in Honor of John Calvin Metcalf.* New York: Columbia University Press, 1941, 151–89.

Cheney, Sarah. "Francis Orray Ticknor." *Georgia Historical Quarterly* 22 (June 1938): 138–59.

Dean, Lewis S., "Michael Tuomey and the Pursuit of a Geological Survey of Alabama, 1847–1857." *Alabama Review* 44 (April 1991): 101–11.

DeCredico, Mary A. "War Is Good Business: Georgia's Urban Entrepreneurs and the Confederate War Effort." *Georgia Historical Quarterly* 73 (summer 1989): 230–49.

Dew, Charles B. "Disciplining Ironworkers in the Antebellum South: Coercion, Conciliation, and Accommodation." *American Historical Review* 79 (April 1974): 393–418.

Downey, Tom. "Riparian Rights and Manufacturing in Antebellum South Carolina: William Gregg and the Origins of the 'Industrial Mind.'" *Journal of Southern History* 65 (February 1999): 77–108.

Escott, Paul D. "Clinton Cilley, Yankee War Hero in the Postwar South: A Study in the Compatibility of Regional Values." *North Carolina Historical Review* 68 (October 1991): 404–26.

Evans, Curtis J. "A Gentile in Israel?: Daniel Pratt and Alabama Politics." In *The World of Daniel Pratt: Essays on Industry, Politics, Art, Architecture, Reform, and Town-Building in Alabama*. Montgomery, Ala.: Black Belt Press, 1999, 34–56.

Flynt; Wayne. "Daniel Pratt, Poor Whites, and Evangelical Paternalism on the Alabama Frontier." In *The World of Daniel Pratt*, 57–69.

Fuller, Justin. "Henry DeBardeleben: Industrialist of the New South." *Alabama Review* 42 (January 1986): 3–18.

Griffin, Richard W. "Cotton Manufactures in Alabama to 1865." *Alabama Historical Quarterly* 18 (fall 1956): 289–307.

———. "Poor White Laborers in Southern Cotton Factories, 1789–1865." *South Carolina Historical Magazine* 61 (January 1960): 26–40.

———. "Pro-Industrial Sentiment and Cotton Factories in Arkansas, 1820–1863." *Arkansas Historical Quarterly* 15 (1956): 125–39.

Hole, Donna C. "Daniel Pratt and Barachias Holt: Architects of the Alabama State Capitol?" *Alabama Review* 37 (April 1984): 83–97.

Holmes, William F. "Charivari; Race, Honor, and Post Office Politics in Sharon, Georgia, 1890." *Georgia Historical Quarterly* 80 (winter 1996): 759–84.

Linden, Fabian. "Repercussions of Manufacturing in the Ante-Bellum South." *North Carolina Historical Review* 17 (October 1940): 313–31.

Luraghi, Raimondo. "The Civil War and the Modernization of American Society: Social Structure and Industrial Revolution in the Old South before and during the Civil War." *Civil War History* 18 (September 1972): 230–50.

Miller, Randall M. "Daniel Pratt: A New England Yankee in King Cotton's Court." In *The World of Daniel Pratt*, 11–33.

———. "Daniel Pratt's Industrial Urbanism: The Cotton Mill Town in Antebellum Alabama." *Alabama Historical Quarterly* 34 (spring 1972): 5–35.

———. "The Enemy Within: Some Effects of Foreign Immigrants on Antebellum Southern Cities." *Southern Studies* 24 (spring 1985): 30–53.

———. "The Fabric of Control: Slavery in Antebellum Textile Mills." *Business History Review* 55 (winter 1981): 471–90.

———. "Love of Labor: A Note on Daniel Pratt's Employment Practices." *Alabama Historical Quarterly* 37 (summer 1975): 146–50.

Nobles, Larry W. "Prattville's Petition for Incorporation." *Autauga Ancestry* 1 (May 1991): 2–5.

Quist, John W. "Slaveholding Operatives of the Benevolent Empire: Bible, Tract, and Sunday School Societies in Antebellum Tuscaloosa County, Alabama." *Journal of Southern History* 62 (August 1996): 481–526.

Raley, Richard L. "Daniel Pratt, Architect and Builder in Georgia." *Antiques* 95 (September 1972): 425–32.

Ramsdell, Charles W. "The Control of Manufacturing by the Confederate Government." *Mississippi Valley Historical Review* 8 (December 1921): 231–49.

Rorabaugh, W. J. "The Sons of Temperance in Antebellum Jasper County." *Georgia Historical Quarterly* 64 (fall 1980), 263–79.

Rudolph, Marilou A. "George Cooke and His Paintings." *Georgia Historical Quarterly* 44 (June 1960): 117–53.

Rutman, Darrett B., with Anita H. Rutman. "The Village South." In *Small Worlds, Large Questions: Explorations in Early American Social History, 1600–1850,* edited by Darrett B. Rutman and Anita H. Rutman. Charlottesville: University of Virginia Press, 1994.

Siegal, Fred. "Artisans and Immigrants in the Politics of Late Antebellum Georgia." *Civil War History* 18 (September 1981): 221–30.

Stone, James H. "Economic Conditions in Macon, Georgia, in the 1830s." *Georgia Historical Quarterly* 54 (spring 1970): 209–25.

Terrell, Tom E. "Eager Hands: Labor for Southern Textiles, 1850–1860." *Journal of Economic History* 36 (March 1976): 84–99.

Thompson, Laquita. "Daniel Pratt and George Cooke: Developing a Gallery." In *The World of Daniel Pratt,* 107–19.

———. "Daniel Pratt's Picture Gallery." *Alabama Review* 48 (July 1995): 166–74.

Thornton, J. Mills, III. "Fiscal Policy and the Failure of Radical Reconstruction in the Lower South. In *Region, Race, and Reconstruction: Essays in Honor of C. Vann Woodward,* edited by J. Morgan Kousser and James M. McPherson. New York: Oxford University Press, 1982.

Tyrrell, Ian R. "Drink and Temperance in the Antebellum South: An Overview and Interpretation." *Journal of Southern History* 48 (November 1982): 485–510.

Vandiver, Frank E. "The Shelby Iron Company in the Civil War: A Study of Confederate Industry." *Alabama Review* (January, April, July 1948): 12–26, 111–27, 203–17.

Webb, Elizabeth Yates. "Cotton Manufacturing and State Regulation in North Carolina, 1861–1865." *North Carolina Historical Review* 9 (April 1932): 117–37.

Webb, Samuel L. "A Jacksonian Democrat in Postbellum Alabama: The Ideology and Influence of Journalist Robert McKee, 1869–1896." *Journal of Southern History* 62 (May 1996): 239–74.

Wright, Gavin. "Cheap Labor and Southern Textiles before 1880." *Journal of Economic History* 39 (September 1979): 655–80.

Dissertations, Theses, and Unpublished Papers

Cawthon, William Lamar. "Clinton: County Seat on the Georgia Frontier, 1808–1821." M.A. thesis, University of Georgia, 1984.

Evans, Curtis John. "Daniel Pratt of Prattville: A Northern Industrialist and a Southern Town." Ph.D. diss., Louisiana State University, 1998.

McMillan, Malcolm C. "The Manufacture of Cotton Gins: A Southern Industry, 1793–1860." Typescript (n.d.). McMillan Collection, Auburn University, Auburn, Ala.

Owsley, Frank Lawrence, Jr. "Albert J. Pickett: Typical Pioneer State Historian." Ph.D. diss., University of Alabama, 1955.

Index